Housing Law in Scotland

HOUSING LAW IN SCOTLAND

Peter W. G. Robson, LL.B., Ph.D., Solicitor

Professor of Social Welfare Law,
The Law School,
University of Strathclyde

DUNDEE UNIVERSITY PRESS
2011

Published in Great Britain in 2011 by
Dundee University Press
University of Dundee
Dundee DD1 4HN

www.dundee.ac.uk/dup

ISBN 978-1-84586-111-7

No natural forests were destroyed to make this product;
only farmed timber was used and replanted

British Library Cataloguing-in-Publication data
A catalogue for this book is available on request from the British Library.

Typeset by Waverley Typesetters, Warham, Norfolk
Printed by Bell & Bain Ltd, Glasgow

CONTENTS

Housing Law in Context   vii

Table of Cases   xv

Table of Statutes   xxiii

Table of Statutory Instruments   xlvii

1   Introduction   1
2   Access to Housing and Homelessness   29
3   Residential Tenures   67
4   Housing Standards and Good Repair   107
5   Paying for Housing   149
6   Loss of Housing and Eviction   191
7   Succession   245
8   Regulation of Housing   267
9   Shared Housing and Houses in Multiple Occupation   295
10   Relationship Breakdown, Abuse and Housing   319

Bibliography   343
Index   355

HOUSING LAW IN CONTEXT

This text is primarily an introductory legal text. It aims to provide a brief guide to the most salient aspects of the law as it affects housing in Scotland. It does not cover material related to housing where there are already specialist works and where a distinct niche has been established, such as planning and conveyancing. It seeks to provide a modest amount of historical background to those areas where the development of the law and/or politics sheds some light on the current legal position. This is particularly true in relation to the landlord and tenant relationship, where the multiplicity of tenures and different sets of rights require some explanation. The chapters focus principally on those matters which are justiciable and about which those denied their rights have some kind of opportunity to pursue a remedy. These remedies are principally in the court system, including various tribunals. The text looks back principally to the answers which have been given to issues which have been raised in the conflict between individuals and also between individuals and the State. Definitive answers to specific questions which might arise are notoriously difficult to provide. I am constantly amazed by the difficulties people of good will can get themselves into when dealing with housing. The range and nature of the questions which I have been asked over the years, just as in comparisons between fiction and real life, make me very wary of providing extensive "what if" scenarios and likely answers. To this sense of uncertainty I would also add the changes which I have witnessed in the past 40 years of practice in the area through changes in social attitudes and beliefs about the rights of a whole range of individuals and groups. The difference in the way the majority of citizens now treat non-marital and same-sex relationships, ethnic minority citizens and women has been truly astonishing and hugely welcome. There is, though, much more to housing than the formal legal rules, even allowing for my own limited ability to predict unimagined problems [1] and changes over time.

---

[1] Former US Defense Secretary Donald Rumsfeld was mocked for his suggestion at a press briefing on 12 February 2002 when he opined "There are known knowns. These are things we know that we know. There are known unknowns. That is to say, there

THE LEGAL STRUGGLE

Scottish Housing in 2010 – La Lotta Continua?

The picture in 2010 is one of great activity in a housing landscape that is the product of previous political belief systems. There is new housing legislation dealing with the social rented sector to absorb and more legislation likely in the near future on the private rented regime. Tenure change within Scotland's housing stock showed a shift in owner occupancy from 36 per cent to 67 per cent between 1982 and 2005.[2] Social renting went from over 50 per cent to 25 per cent.[3] Private renting did not undergo any radical change during this period. Scotland has the smallest private rental sector in Western Europe, compared with Germany at 45 per cent, France at just over 20 per cent and such countries as Greece, Belgium, Sweden, Norway, Denmark and Finland at between 10 and 20 per cent.[4]

House building peaked in the early 1970s at over 40,000 houses but has fallen to some 25,000 houses built per year for some time from 1980 to 2005.[5] The aim of the Scottish Government in 2007 was to reach 35,000 per year,[6] with a per capita rate of building "far ahead of that for which the UK Government is aiming in England".[7] Even before the financial crisis of 2008 and the bank collapses triggered by that of Lehman Brothers,[8] it had not escaped the attention of politicians that Scottish housing faced structural problems. The size of deposit required by first-time buyers had risen from 12 per cent in 2000 to 35 per cent in 2006[9] and the earnings-to-property price ratio had shifted considerably across much of Scotland. Greater assistance for first-time buyers[10] has been proposed, with the LIFT scheme discussed in *Firm Foundations* – Low-cost Initiative for First Time Buyers.[11] The aim of this was to broaden the range of products available to assist people to achieve and sustain home ownership, including

---

are things that we now know we don't know. But there are also unknown unknowns. These are things we do not know we don't know." I have considerable sympathy with his intellectual plight, although not his politics in general, and his warmongering in particular.

2 Scottish Government (2007), Chart 1 at 6.
3 *Ibid* at 36 – although Chart 1 at 6 shows it at 30%.
4 *Ibid*, Chart 8 at 27.
5 *Ibid*, Chart 4 at 13.
6 *Ibid*, Chart 4 at 13.
7 *Ibid* at 22.
8 On 15 September 2008, the firm filed for Chapter 11 bankruptcy protection following the massive exodus of most of its clients, drastic losses in its stock, and devaluation of its assets by credit rating agencies. It was the largest bankruptcy in US history.
9 Scottish Government (2007), Chart 7 at 21.
10 Making a neat link from the Small Dwellings Acquisition Act 1899 and its rather similar goals – see Chapter 5.
11 Scottish Government (2007), Chart 4 at 13.

a grant of £2,000.[12] A retreat from the owner occupancy solution can be seen in the policy, at the time of writing, recognising the importance of social housing in the future, with the suggestion that "social housing has a positive future … far from being an anachronism, it is often the affordable and secure alternative to owner occupation".[13] Even private renting has received a boost, albeit with a back-handed compliment that it is suitable for a certain expanding market:

> "We want to see more homeless households being offered the benefits of private rented accommodation, where that is appropriate[14] … it is sensible to explore this option for tenants who may be more suited to private rented accommodation and would benefit from the flexibility and choice provided by the sector."[15]

The most recent overview of the prospects for housing appears in *Housing: Fresh Thinking, New Ideas*, which locates the issues for housing policy in a future troubled by recession.

The Edge of the World of Practice

Rather different concerns and policies are the principal daily work of those administering housing. This process has been professionalised in a way of which Octavia Hill and the Kyrle Society would, I am sure, be proud.[16] Those involved in the day-to-day management of housing in the social rented sector are seldom concerned with the legality of their actions. That is taken for granted and ingrained in the policies and structures of their organisations. Operating housing access policies which do not discriminate on the grounds of ethnicity or disability or sexuality has become a standard part of a properly run housing provider's service, whether in the private or the social sector. As we will see in relation to the role of the Scottish Housing Regulator, the latter has little option but to operate at the highest levels of professionalism or find its organisations subject to "improvement plans" or the imposition of stringent management controls.

At the strategic level, issues such as housing renewal and regeneration are part of the remit of both government and social landlords. From central government too come such issues as the future shape of existing houses and such matters as stock transfer. Putting into effect pro-active policies on homelessness and community care are matters which only tangentially have been part of the world of housing lawyers. They are,

---

12 Scottish Government (2007), Chart 4 at 13.
13 *Ibid* at 40.
14 *Ibid* at 28.
15 *Ibid* at 129.
16 Robson (1979).

however, a crucial part of the education and daily tasks of housing practitioners. In that respect this book does not deal with these matters as being beyond the normal reach of the lawyer's brief. This is an issue of judgement of immediate relevance and I trust that the failure to address such issues as property management techniques and funding social housing will not be seen as too insular. There are excellent publications and institutions, such as the Scottish Chartered Institute of Housing and the Scottish Federation of Housing Associations, which are able to deal with such matters with far greater authority and clarity than a simple legal functionary could muster. By the same token, rural development and the need for access to employment, schools and other services do not feature significantly in the legal perspective. Nor does the value of having balanced or sustainable communities make any kind of appearance in a study of the legal framework for housing.[17] The relationship of health and housing is a rather trickier issue. There are times where the inadequacy of housing provision has health outcomes which are indeed part of the lawyer's remit.[18] There is, though, a difference between this role and the concerns of housing and health professionals to develop policies which operate in a preventative manner. So much so that, for instance, one impressive collection of essays looking at health and housing and highlights the need for housing opportunities for people with health needs.[19] This is of interest to lawyers in the sense that it may provide evidence of practical problems with legislation's limitations or good practice in some kind of judicial review in the future. For the present, though, it remains outwith our remit, although the lines are blurred and shifting.

If there are differences between "legality", "standard practice" and "best practice", then these are frequently hard to distinguish. Housing practitioners and those who run courses, such as the CIH, are concerned to encourage the latter. From a point of view of strict demarcation of tasks, the law limits itself to the question of "legality", conscious that what amounts to legality is, in fact, often what is simply "standard practice". This kind of approach has sometimes informed decision on the obligations of local authorities to their tenants for repairs where refurbishment is planned.[20] Sometimes, as we can see in the discussion of the *Mitchell* case,[21] the legality line is drawn well short of "standard practice". This is one reason why lawyers infuriate ordinary people by making a distinction between what one must do and what one ought to do: the legal and the moral.

---

[17] Murie (1985).
[18] *Morrison* v *Stirling District Council* 1996 Hous LR 6.
[19] Smith, Knill-Jones and McGuckin (eds) (1991).
[20] *McLaughlin* v *Renfrew District Council*, unreported, 4 November 1986.
[21] *Mitchell* v *Glasgow City Council* [2009] 1 AC 874.

MAKING SENSE OF THE REALM OF THEORY

There is also considerable interest in relating the narrow concerns of housing lawyers and housing professionals to the wider world of politics and society. How does housing fit into the broader concerns of urban development and the rise of the city? Some of the theory of those who sought to relate housing to broader social and political theory was concerned with concrete political debates of the time. Thus, the contribution of Friedrich Engels in *The Housing Question* is located in his debate with Proudhon on the nature of property. It is centred on his analysis of how capitalism exploits the waged worker and such secondary effects as the shortage of housing.[22] Interestingly, it notes the difference between surplus value and workers' relationships to the capitalist and the notion of the fair price payable by tenants. These debates can be mined for the consistency of the conflicts between capital and labour, and owner and tenants, and offer insights to inform political struggle rather than assist day-to-day practice.

The shift of emphasis from the political arena to the academy is reflected in the shift of focus to "urban studies". The "production, consumption and exchange of housing" has been described as being "at the core of urban studies".[23] While housing does indeed play a major role in urban studies, it sits alongside other concerns which are less central in the first two aspects of housing Forest and Williams identify. Issues of social segregation and race, which we have touched on below, are relevant principally in relation to housing exchange. While all social and economic matters are, to an extent, inter-dependent, transport and issues of crime have been traditionally rather less central in housing policy concerns. The key trends and developments which shaped housing in the period since the Second World War, as identified by Forrest and Williams, include the transition from private landlordism to individualised home ownership. In this perspective, mass state provision is seen as an "abnormal" intervention.[24] However, the success of home ownership, as is noted below, is by no means assured. It depends on stability and predictability in relation to labour conditions and income. This interdependency between the housing market and the rest of the economy has consequences which have been exposed in the recessions and house price slumps of the early 1990s and from 2008 in the United Kingdom and across the developed world.

Those who wrote about these topics in the 1970s were clearly not used to speaking with simple lawyers. Their language was complex and their concepts not always easy to grasp. David Harvey, in his intriguingly

---

[22] Engels (1872).
[23] Forrest and Williams (2001).
[24] Harloe (1995).

titled *Social Justice and the City*,[25] explores the contribution of grand theory to how the city can be understood. Rent and landlords' goals are discussed in terms of housing as a means of exchange rather than rooted in the concrete experience of specific tenants.[26] Hence, the overarching theoretical formulation he adopts gives us a way of conceptualising the relationship rather than an insight into the struggles of tenants to effect changes in their lives. His insights, like those of Engels, provide us with a link to solutions and struggles of the past, such as 19th-century Paris,[27] or contemporary ones such as Baltimore.[28] Manuel Castells has worked in a similar vein to Harvey, with theory and the city.[29]

The politics of these writers is inspirational in the way it links the grand themes of politics with the complexity of studying urban space. In practical terms, resisting the changes brought about by changes in the Rent Acts or securing decent houses for those displaced by short-sighted urban development[30] seemed to benefit less from an in-depth understanding of notions of the production of space than the issues raised by those like Alinsky[31] and Piven and Cloward[32] in advocating the importance of agency and political engagement.

A newer breed of writers, however, has put this earlier work in the shade. The approach of the contributors to *Law and the City* and the thrust and style of the essays encountered in this text provide a perspective that is frankly surreal.[33] They look at such issues as law's spatiality and the city's legal dreams. Although mocking such work may sound like the worst kind of anti-intellectualism, it does make one yearn for the days when Howard Becker could pose to sociologists the question "Whose Side are We On?"[34] That question remains as relevant today as it did when asked and the answer does not appear clear from the pages of post-modern urban theory.

This, then, is a flavour of the context within which the complex and convoluted regulation of housing in Scotland now operates. If you were designing a system of legal regulation, you probably would not start from here. It is, though, vital to appreciate that the anomalies and weaknesses of the system stem from the struggles of the past and the successes and failures of groups to realise the dream of decent housing for all in a society in which access to jobs, capital and opportunities continues to be

---

[25] Harvey (1973).
[26] *Ibid* at 164.
[27] Harvey (1985).
[28] Harvey (2000).
[29] Castells (1977) and (1978).
[30] Jacobs (1975).
[31] Alinsky (1971).
[32] Piven and Cloward (1971).
[33] Philippopoulos-Mihalopoulos (2007).
[34] Becker (1966).

profoundly unequal and is not likely to get any fairer in the immediate future. However, the point is not to become preoccupied with excessive analysis of how things have reached the state they are in but rather how to change them. Law may from time to time have a role to play in the struggle. Its development and reification certainly provide a valuable key to understanding why the few continue to have so much and the many so little.

TABLE OF CASES

Abrahams *v* Wilson [1971] 2 All ER 1114 218
Albyn Properties *v* Knox 1977 SLT 41..... 122, 159, 161, 178, 181, 182
Ali *v* Birmingham City Council; Moran *v* Manchester City Council
    [2009] 41 HLR 727 HL... 35, 57
Anderson *v* Fife Council, unreported, Sheriff G J Evans, 22 March
    2006... 305
Anglo-Italian Properties Ltd *v* Greater London Rent Assessment
    Panel [1969] 2 All ER 1128 176
Angus Housing Association Ltd *v* Fraser 2004 Hous LR 83........... 217
Armour *v* Anderson 1990 SLT 490 324
— *v* — 1994 SLT 1127 4
Aslan *v* Murphy (No 1) and (No 2) [1990] 1 WLR 766 .... 223, 237
Associated Provincial Picture Houses Ltd *v* Wednesbury Corp
    [1948] 1 KB 223 305

Barrie *v* Glasgow DC 1991 1 SHLR 82... 117
Battlespring *v* Gates (1988) 11 HLR 6 216
Beggs *v* Kilmarnock and Loudon DC 1995 SCLR 435 85
Bell *v* Bell 1983 SLT 224... 328
Boreh *v* Ealing LBC [2009] HLR 22 CA 57
Boyle *v* Verrall [1997] 1 EGLR 25... 198, 200
— *v* Weddell (1870) 11 M 223... 114
Bradley *v* Chorley BC (1985) 17 HLR 305............................. 111, 117
— *v* Motherwell DC 1994 SLT 739 57
Brickfield Properties Ltd *v* Hughes [1988] 1 EGLR 108... 73, 239, 250
British Transport Commission *v* Assessor for Inverness 1952 SC 511.. 82
Brock *v* Wollams [1949] 2 KB 388.. 257, 260
Buchanan *v* Warley 245 US 60 (1917)... 23
Buchmann *v* May [1978] 2 All ER 993.. 201
Burns *v* Monklands DC 1997 Hous LR 34 .... 113, 114
— *v* Secretary of State for Social Services 1985 SC 143.................. 252

Cadogan Estates Ltd *v* McMahon [2001] 1 AC 378 .... 79, 210
Cameron *v* Abbey National Building Society 1999 Hous LR 19 201
— *v* Glasgow DC 1991 1 SHLR 5.. 119
Campbell *v* Aberdeen City Council 2007 Hous LR 26.................. 112
Carega Properties SA (formerly Joram Developments Ltd) *v* Sharratt
  [1979] 1 WLR 928... 260
Cassell *v* Broome [1972] AC 1027.. 4
Caterleisure Ltd *v* Glasgow Prestwick International Airport Ltd
  2005 SLT 1083.. 75
Chapman *v* UK (2001) 10 BHRC 48... 23
Charing Cross and Kelvingrove Housing Association *v* Kraska 1986
  SLT (Sh Ct) 42.. 87, 202
Christian *v* Aberdeen City Council 2005 Hous LR 71 112
City of Edinburgh Council *v* HT 2003 Hous LR 74....................... 219
Clarke *v* Hatten 1987 SCLR 527.. 330
Cobstone Investments Ltd *v* Maxim [1985] QB 150...................... 218
Conway *v* Glasgow City Council 2001 SLT 1472............................ 297
— *v* — (No 2) 1999 SCLR 1058 296
Cooper *v* Fraser 1987 GWD 22-824... 102
Crawley BC *v* Sawyer (1988) 20 HLR 98 222
Crofton Investment Trust Ltd *v* Greater London Rent Assessment
  Committee [1967] 2 QB 955..................................... 175, 178, 179

Davidson *v* Sprengel 1909 SC 566 .... 116, 138
Deans *v* Glasgow Housing Association Ltd 2009 Hous LR 82....... 113,
                                                                                                          114, 211
Denovan *v* Blue Triangle (Glasgow) Housing Association Ltd
  1999 Hous LR 97... 296
Din *v* Wandsworth LBC [1981] 3 All ER 881................................ 270
Donald *v* McKenzie 1949 SLT (Sh Ct) 75....................................... 257
Dover DC *v* Farrar (1980) 2 HLR 32 114
Duke *v* Porter [1986] 2 EGLR 101.. 239, 250
— *v* Wynne [1990] 1 WLR 766... 223
Dyson Holdings Ltd *v* Fox [1976] 1 QB 503.................. 258, 260, 263

Eastleigh BC *v* Betts [1983] 2 AC 613 49
Equal Opportunities Commission *v* Department for Trade and
  Industry [2007] IRLR 327 18

Falkirk DC *v* McLay 1991 SCLR 895 .... 216, 222, 237
Fife Council *v* Buchan 2008 Hous LR 74 .... 216, 218, 220, 221
Fitzpatrick *v* Sterling Housing Association [1999] AC 705, [1999]
  4 All ER 705.................................. 4, 250, 255, 258, 261, 262, 264
Frankenberg *v* Dundee City Council 2005 Hous LR 55 113

Galloway *v* Glasgow City Council 2001 Hous LR 59 .... 112, 119
Gammans *v* Ekins [1950] 2 KB 328 .... 258, 259, 260
Gavin *v* Lindsay 1987 SLT (Sh Ct) 12 .... 77, 81
Ghaidan *v* Godin-Mendoza [2004] 2 AC 557 265
Glasgow City Council *v* Al-Abassi 2001 Hous LR 23 .... 24, 211
Glasgow DC *v* Lockhart 1997 Hous LR 99 219
— *v* McCrone 1991 1 SHLR 45 117
— *v* Murray 1997 Hous LR 105 209
Glasgow Heritable Trust case, unreported, cited in 1977 SLT 44 181
Glasgow Housing Association *v* Hetherington 2009 Hous LR
    28 218
— *v* McNamara 2008 Hous LR 38 220
— *v* Marshall 2006 Hous LR 56 219
GLC *v* LB Tower Hamlets 1989 (1983) 15 HLR 57 114
Glenrothes *v* Graham, unreported, 14 December 1994 212
Golden Casket (Greenock) Ltd *v* BRS (Pickfords) Ltd
    1972 SLT 146 118
Gordon DC *v* Acutt 1991 SLT (Sh Ct) 78 .... 205, 216
Govanhill Housing Association *v* Malley 1996 Hous LR 61 216
— *v* Palmer 1997 Hous LR 133 .... 100, 210
Green *v* Sheffield City Council (1994) 26 HLR 349 210
Gunn *v* Glasgow City Council 1992 SCLR 1018 113
— *v* — 1997 Hous LR 3 211
Guppy's (Bridport) Ltd *v* Sandoe (1975) 30 P & CR 69 181
Guppy's Properties *v* Knott (No 1) [1978] EGD 255 ...... 124, 172, 182
— *v* — (No 2) (1981–82) 1 HLR 30 182
Guy *v* Strathkelvin DC 1997 SCLR 405, 1997 Hous LR 14 112,
                                                                113, 211

Haggerty *v* Glasgow Corp 1964 SLT (Notes) 54 139
Hammersmith and Fulham LBC *v* Clarke (2001) 81 P & CR
    DG 20 222
Hampstead Way Investments Ltd *v* Lewis-Weare [1985]
    1 EGLR 120 .... 73, 250
Harrogate BC *v* Simpson (1984) 17 HLR 205 .... 255, 261, 264
Hart *v* Aberdeen City Council, unreported, Sheriff Cusine,
    23 June 2006 305–306
Hawes *v* Evenden [1953] 2 All ER 737 259
Helby *v* Rafferty [1978] 3 All ER 1016 260
Hodges *v* Blee [1987] 2 EGLR 119 254
Holmes-Moorhouse *v* Richmond upon Thames LBC [2009]
    HLR 34 42
Huber *v* Ross 1912 SC 898 118
Hughes' Tutrix *v* Glasgow DC 1982 SLT 70 139

Islington LBC v Demetriou [2001] CLY 4216 222

John v Donnelly 1999 JC 336.. 123
Johnstone v Finnernan 2003 SCLR 157................................. 215–216
Jones v Trueman (1949) 99 LJ 541 257
— v Whitehill [1950] 2 KB 204.. 257
Joram Developments v Sharratt [1979] 1 WLR 3 256

Karner v Austria (2004) 38 EHRR 24 265
Kelly v Cannock Chase DC [1978] 1 WLR 1................................ 30
— v Monklands DC 1986 SLT 169 51
Kennealy v Dunne [1977] QB 837.. 200, 249
Killen v Dundee City Council 2008 SLT 739 305
Kippen v Oppenheim (1847) 10 D 242.. 137
Kozak v Poland (2010) 51 EHRR 16 265

Langdon v Horton [1951] 1 KB 666... 258
Langstane Housing Association v Morrow 2005 Hous LR 103 219
Learmonth Property Investment Co Ltd v Aitken 1971 SLT 349 .. 159,
                                                                177, 178, 181
Little v Glasgow DC (1991) 1 SHLR 195 .... 111, 117

McAlinden v Bearsden and Milngavie DC 1986 SLT 191.............. 206,
                                                                226, 332
McArdle v City of Glasgow DC 1989 SCLR 19 .... 114, 121, 140
McCabe v Wilson 2006 Hous LR 86.. 77
McCafferty v McCafferty 1986 SLT 650 328
McCarrick v Liverpool Corp [1947] AC 219................................ 139
McCarthy v Glasgow DC 1991 1 SHLR 181 139
McCreight v West Lothian DC 2009 SCLR 359 252
MacDougall v Ho 1985 SCCR 199 123
McEachran v Glasgow DC 1991 1 SHLR 149............................. 117
MacGowan v MacGowan 1986 SLT 122...................................... 326
MacGregor v Dunnett 1949 SC 510... 82
McGuire v Monklands DC 1997 Hous LR 41 .... 113, 114, 119, 211
McHale v Daneham (1979) 249 EG 969 201
Mack v Glasgow City Council 2006 SLT 556 (Extra Div)...... 114, 115
McKay v Livingstone Development Corp 1990 SLT (Lands Tr) 54.... 86
McKimmie's Trs v Armour (1899) 2 F 156 137
McLaughlin v Renfrew DC, unreported, 4 November 1986 x
McLellan v Bracknell Forest [2002] 1 All ER 899.......................... 27
MacMillan v Kyle and Carrick DC, unreported, 7 February 1995
    OH 50
Mason v Skilling 1974 SLT 4.. 161
Mazzaccherini v Argyle and Bute DC 1987 SCLR 475.................... 54

Mearns v Glasgow DC 2001 Hous LR 130 119
Mechan v Watson 1907 SC 25 .... 116, 137
Metropolitan Properties Ltd v Lannon [1968] 1 WLR 815 180
— v Laufer (1975) 29 P & CR 177 180
Midlothian DC v Brown 1991 SLT (Sh Ct) 80 .... 205, 216
— v Drummond 1991 SLT (Sh Ct) 67 .... 205, 216
Milnbank Housing Association v Murdoch 1995 SLT (Sh Ct) 11,
    1994 SCLR 684 .... 74, 76, 227
Minchburn Ltd v Fernandez [1986] 2 EGLR 103, 1986)
    19 HLR 29 .... 205, 207, 216
Mitchell v Ealing LBC [1979] QB 1 QBD 59
— v Glasgow City Council [2009] 1 AC 874 .... x, 24, 26
Moran v Manchester City Council [2009] 41 HLR 727 43
Moray Council v Hamilton 2003 Hous LR 83 92
Morgan v Liverpool Corp [1927] 2 KB 131 139
— v Stirling Council [2006] CSOH 154 46
Morrison v Stirling DC 1996 Hous LR 6 x

Neilson v Scottish Homes 1999 SLT (Sh Ct) 2 112
North v Allan Properties (Edinburgh) Ltd 1987 SLT (Sh Ct) 141 ... 270

O'Connor v Kensington and Chelsea RLBC [2004] 37 HLR 601 ... 48
Osei v Southwark LBC [2007] EWCA Civ 787 48
Osman v United Kingdom (1998) 29 EHRR 245 25

Pepper v Hart [1993] AC 593 76
Perry v Dembowski [1951] 2 All ER 50 259
Pollock v Assessor for Inverness-shire 1923 SC 693 82
Poplar Housing and Regeneration Community Association Ltd v
    Donoghue [2001] EWCA Civ 595 27
Price v Gould [1930] All ER 389 .... 256, 257
Proctor v Cowlairs Co-op Society Ltd 1961 SLT 434 .... 116, 137
Puhlhofer v Hillingdon LBC [1983] AC 484 .... 3, 44, 52, 64

R v Brent LBC, ex p Awua [1996] AC 55 HL 44, 57
— v Camden LBC, ex p Pereira (1999) 31 HLR 317 46
— v Cardiff City Council, ex p Cross (1983) 81 LGR 105 109
— v City of Westminster, ex p Ali and Bibi (1992) 25 HLR 109
    HL 54
— v Hammersmith and Fulham LBC, ex p Lusi (1991) 23 HLR
    260 QBD 48
— v Harrow LBC (1994) 26 HLR 32 QBD 53
— v Hillingdon LBC, ex p Streeting [1980] 3 All ER 413 49
— v Kensington and Chelsea RLBC, ex p Bayani (1990) 24 HLR
    406 51

R v Kensington and Chelsea RLBC, ex p Hammell [1989]
    QB 518 339
— v Lambeth LBC, ex p Carroll (1988) 20 HLR 142 QBD 53
— v Newham LBC, ex p Sacupima [2001] 33 HLR 1 53
— v Portsmouth City Council, ex p Knight (1982) LGR 184 270
— v Preseli DC , ex p Fisher (1984) 17 HLR 147 QBD 40, 54
— v Purbeck DC, ex p Cadney (1985) 17 HLR 534 333
— v Rent Officer of the Nottinghamshire Registration Area,
    ex p Allen (1985) 52 P & CR 41 .... 102, 105
— v Salford City Council, ex p Davenport (1984) 82 LGR 89 212
— v Sheffield City Council, ex p Leek (1993) 26 HLR 669 CA 54
— v Swansea City Council, ex p John (1982) 9 HLR 58 212
— v —, ex p Thomas (1982) 9 HLR 66, (1983) 9 HLR 64 ...... 40, 212
— v Tower Hamlets LBC, ex p Ferdous Begum [1993] QB 447 41
— v Vale of White Horse DC, ex p Smith and Hay (1985)
    17 HLR 160 50
— v Wandsworth LBC, ex p Nimako-Boateng (1984) 11 HLR 95 .. 333
— v Waveney DC, ex p Bowers [1983] 2 QB 238 46
— v Wolverhampton MBC [1997] 29 HLR 931 35
— v Wyre BC, ex p Joyce (1983) 11 HLR 73 QBD 54
R (on the application of Ahmad) v Newham LBC [2009] HLR 31 .. 35
R (on the application of Mei Ling Lin) v Barnet LBC
    [2009] HLR 30 35
Razack v Osman [2001] 9 Ch 426 204
Redspring v Francis [1973] 1 All ER 740 207
Renfrew DC v Gray 1987 SLT (Sh Ct) 70 204
— v Inglis 1991 SLT (Sh Ct) 83 .... 205, 216
Renfrewshire Council v Hainey 2008 Hous LR 43 217
Retail Parks Investments v Royal Bank of Scotland (No 2) 1996
    SLT 669 100
Robinson v Hammersmith and Fulham LBC [2006] EWCA Civ
    1122 52
Rodriguez v Minister of Housing of Gibraltar [2009] OKPC 52 ... 265
Rose v Bouchet 2000 SLT (Sh Ct) 170 23
Ross v Collins [1964] 1 All ER 861 260
Roxburgh DC v Collins 1991 SCLR 575 .... 73, 85, 199, 250
Royal Bank of Scotland v Boyle 1999 Hous LR 42 and 67 201
Russell v Russell, unreported, 18 February 1986 OH 326

S Schneiders & Sons Ltd v Abrahams [1925] 1 KB 301 CA 217
Salter v Lask [1925] 1 KB 584 .... 256, 260
Scottish Heritable Security Co (Ltd) v Granger (1881) 8 R 459 137
Scottish Residential Estates Development Co Ltd v Henderson
    1991 SLT 490 101
Sefton Holdings v Cairns [1988] 1 EGLR 99 .... 256, 260

Shelley v Kraemer 334 US 1 (1948)... 23
Shepherd v Naylor (1948) 98 LJ 603 258
Shipman v Lothian RC 1989 SLT (Lands Tr) 82........................... 90
Siddiqui v Rashid [1980] 1 WLR 1018....................................... 207
Simms v Islington LBC [2009] 20 HLR 343 CA 47, 53
Skilling v Arcari's Executrix 1973 SLT 139........................... 177, 178
Smith v Dundee City Council 2003 Hous LR 55 222
— v Poulter [1947] KB 339 205
— v Smith 1983 SLT 275 328
Smyth v Caledonian Racing (1984) Ltd 1987 GWD 16-612 101
Souter v McAuley 2010 SLT (Sh Ct) 121 324
South Lanarkshire Council v Nugent 2008 Hous LR 92 .... 218, 221
Southwark LBC v Williams [1971] Ch 734.................................. 39
Spath Holme v Greater Manchester & Lancashire RAC [1996]
    28 HLR 107 160
SSHA v Lumsden 1984 SLT (Sh Ct) 71....................................... 212
Stanton v Southwark [1920] 2 KB 642 139
Stevenson v West Lothian DC 1985 SLT (Lands Tr) 9 86
Stevenston v Monklands DC 1987 GWD 15–576........................... 51
Stewart v Higgins [1951] CL Y 2901... 257
Summers v Salford Corp [1943] AC 283 139

Tamroui v Clydesdale Bank plc 1997 SLT (Sh Ct) 20.................... 201
Tandy v Bamford [1929] Estates Gazette Digest 216 257
Thomson v City of Glasgow DC 1986 SLT (Lands Tr) 6................. 85
Tormes Property Co Ltd v Landau [1970] 3 All ER 653............... 171,
                                                                        176, 180
Trs of Kinrara Estate v Campbell 1999 Hous LR 55................ 82, 207

Ugiagbe v Southwark LBC [2009] 35 HLR 600............................ 48
Uratemp Ventures Ltd v Collins 2001 Hous LR 133 85

Valente v Fife Council, unreported, Sheriff G J Evans,
    21 November 2006.. 305
Velosa Barreto v Portugal [1996] EHRLR 211 24
Verity v Fenner 1993 SCLR 223 324

Walker v Strathclyde RC 1990 SLT (Lands Tr) 17 90
Watson v Lucas [1980] All ER 647.. 261
Webster v Brown (1892) 19 R 765 .... 116, 137
West Lothian Council v Reape 2002 Hous LR 58 .... 216, 223, 237
West Lothian DC v Morrison 1987 SLT 361 102
Western Heritable Investment Co v Hunter 2004 SC 765...... 160, 161
— v Husband 1983 SLT 578 (HL) 159
Whitelaw v Fulton (1871) 10 M 27.. 100

William Grant & Son Distillers Ltd v McClymont 2009 SCLR 388,
  2007 Hous LR 76 .... 77, 79, 210
Wilson v Nithsdale DC 1992 SLT 1131 46
— v Wilson, unreported, 10 January 1986 OH 326
Wishaw and District Housing Association v Neary 2004 SC 463 75, 77
Wolfson v Forrester 1910 SC 675 116
X v FRG (1956) 1 YB 201 23

Yemshaw v Hounslow LBC [2010] 23 HLR 399 340
Yewbright Properties Ltd v Stone (1980) 40 P & CR 402 207
Young v Gerard (1843) 6 D 347 247

TABLE OF STATUTES

1449   Leases Act (cc 17–18) 11, 194, 267
1865   Trespass (Scotland) Act (28 & 29 Vict c 56) 39
1868   Artisans and Labourers Dwellings Act (31 & 32 Vict
       c 130) 132
1881   Married Women's Property (Scotland) Act (44 & 45 Vict
       c 21) 319
1890   Housing of the Working Classes Act (53 & 54 Vict
       c 70) 8, 139
1897   Public Health (Scotland) Act (60 & 61 Vict c 38) 5
       ss 46–47 13
1899   Small Dwellings Acquisition Act (62 & 63 Vict c 44) ... viii, 150
1903   Burgh Police (Scotland) Act (3 Edw 7 c 33) 295, 316
1907   Sheriff Courts (Scotland) Act (7 Edw 7 c 51)
       ss 34–38 83
1909   Housing, Town Planning etc Act (9 Edw 7 c 44) 67, 139
1911   House Letting and Rating Act (1 and 2 Geo 5 c 53) 229
1915   Increase of Rent and Mortgage Interest (War Restrictions)
       Act (5 & 6 Geo 5 c 97) 79, 166, 191, 210, 211, 247, 254, 255
       s 1(3) 211, 247
       s 5(2) 255
       s 12(1)(g) 256
       s 43 167
1919   Housing, Town Planning etc Act (9 & 10 Geo 5 c 35) 38
       s 1 38
1920   Increase of Rent and Mortgage Interest (Restrictions) Act
       (10 & 11 Geo 5 c 17) 79, 191, 217, 247, 255
       s 5(b) 211
       s 8 38
       s 12 .... 247, 254
          (1)(g) 247
       Married Women's Property (Scotland) Act (10 & 11 Geo 5
       c 64) 319

1923   Rent and Mortgage Interest (Restrictions) Act (13 & 14
        Geo 5 c 32) 79, 169, 191
1933   Rent and Mortgage Interest Restrictions (Amendment) Act
        (23 & 24 Geo 5 c 32)
        s 1(3) 89
1935   Housing (Scotland) Act (25 & 26 Geo 5 c 41) 316, 317
        s 47(2) 34
1939   Rent and Mortgage Interest Restrictions Act (2 & 3 Geo 6
        c 71) 168, 191
1943   Rent of Furnished Houses Control (Scotland) Act
        (6 & 7 Geo 6 c 44) 75, 168
1944   Disabled Persons (Employment) Act (7 & 8 Geo 6
        c 10) 20
1946   Furnished Houses (Rent Control) Act (9 & 10 Geo 6
        c 34) 168
1947   Town and Country Planning (Scotland) Act (10 & 11
        Geo 6 c 6) 67
1948   National Assistance Act (11 & 12 Geo 6 c 29) 61
        s 21(1)(b) 62
1949   Landlord and Tenant (Rent Control) Act (12, 13 & 14
        Geo 6 c 40) 75
        Tenancy of Shops (Scotland) Act (12, 13 & 14
        Geo 6 c 25) 74, 89
1953   Accommodation Agencies Act (1 & 2 Eliz 2 c 33) 38
1957   Rent Act (5 & 6 Eliz 2 c 25) 79, 153, 169, 170, 172, 191
        Small Dwellings Acquisition Act (Ireland) 150
1958   Tribunals and Inquiries Act (6 & 7 Eliz 2 c 56) 179
1961   Housing Act (9 & 10 Eliz 2 c 65) 140
1962   Housing (Scotland) Act (10 & 11 Eliz 2 c 28) 116, 140
1964   Housing Act (c 56) 281
        Protection from Eviction Act (c 97)
        s 1(3)(a) 227
        (b) 227
        Succession (Scotland) Act (c 41) 245, 341
        s 8 245
        s 9 245
1965   Industrial and Provident Societies Act (c 12) 281
        Race Relations Act (c 73) 14
        s 1 15
        s 5 15
        Rent Act (c 75) 71, 80, 158, 169, 173, 175, 179, 317
        s 30 228
1966   Housing (Scotland) Act (c 49) 116, 297
        s 137 280
        s 138 280

1968 Caravan Sites Act (c 52) 102
    s 3(1)(a)... 105
        (b).. 105
        (c) 105
    s 4... 104
    Race Relations Act (c 71)... 15
    Social Work (Scotland) Act (c 49) 88
    s 27... 88
1970 Conveyancing and Feudal Reform (Scotland) Act (c 35) 192
    s 9(3) 69
    s 24... 192
1971 Rent (Scotland) Act (c 28) 80, 81, 161, 317
    Pt VII.. 81
    Sch 3 230
    Tribunals and Inquiries Act (c 62) 179
1972 Housing Finance Act (c 47).................................. 165, 169, 172
    Housing (Financial Provisions) (Scotland) Act (c 46).......... 165
1973 Prescription and Limitation (Scotland) Act (c 52)
    s 17(2) 115
1974 Housing Act (c 44) 297
    Rent Act (c 51) 80, 81, 213, 230
1975 Mobile Homes Act (c 49) 102, 105
    Sex Discrimination Act (c 65).. 15, 18
    s 76A.. 19
1976 Race Relations Act (c 74)
    s 43(1) 15
    s 71... 18
1977 Housing (Homeless Persons) Act (c 48) 39, 41, 53, 62, 270
    Rent Act (c 42) 153, 251
1978 National Health Service (Scotland) Act (c 29)
    s 108(1) 300
1979 Land Registration (Scotland) Act (c 33)
    ss 20–22 97
1980 Education (Scotland) Act (c 44)
    s 135(1) 87, 202
    Housing Act (c 51) 13, 187
    ss 56–58 77
    Tenants' Rights etc (Scotland) Act (c 52)............ 13, 38, 76, 97,
                                 149, 161, 182, 210,
                                 216, 252, 281, 293,
                                 317, 325, 330, 334
    s 48.. 182
    s 56.. 256
    Sch 2 281
        Pt 1, para 6 331

1981 Matrimonial Homes (Family Protection) (Scotland) Act
      (c 59)............................. 320, 321, 322, 324, 328, 330,
                          331, 332, 333, 334, 336, 339, 340, 341, 342
        s 1(1).. 322
          (7).. 324
          (8).. 324
        s 3(3) 323, 326, 332
        s 4... 328
          (1).. 328
          (2).. 328
          (6).. 328
        s 13... 322
          (1)... 324, 325
          (2).. 324
          (3).. 326
          (4).. 325
          (5).. 325
          (7)(a) 325
             (b)... 325
             (c)... 325
             (d) 325
             (e)... 325
          (9).. 325
          (10)(c).. 325
               (d)(ii) 325
                   (iii)... 325
          (11) 325
        s 14(2) 329
        ss 14–17 322
        s 15(1)(a).. 329
             (b)... 329
        s 18... 323
          (2).. 323
1982 Civic Government (Scotland) Act (c 45) 133, 298
        s 87... 133
      Social Security and Housing Benefits Act (c 24) 208
1983 Mobile Homes Act (c 34) 102
        s 1.. 102
          (2) 103
          (6) 103
        s 2(3) 103
        s 3.. 104
        s 5.. 104
          (1) 102
        Sch 1 103

1983 Mobile Homes Act (c 34) (*cont*)
    Sch 1 (*cont*)
      Pt II 103, 104
        para 1 103
        para 2 103
        para 3 103
        para 4 .... 103, 104
        para 5 .... 103, 104
        para 6 .... 103, 104
        para 8(1B) 104
            (1C) 104
            (1D) 104
            (1F) 104
        para 9 104
1984 Rent (Scotland) Act (c 58) 71, 73, 74, 80, 82, 153,
                       158, 165, 195, 196, 206,
                  207, 209, 210, 211, 212, 223,
                  226, 241, 251, 268, 269
      Pt VII 75, 81, 83, 97
      s 1(a) 12
        (b) 12
        (c) 12
        (d) 12
        (e) 12
      s 2 12
        (1)(c) 80
          (d) 80
          (e) 80
      s 3(1)(a) 73
      s 3A 251
      s 9 76
        (1) 77, 79
      s 22(1) 226
        (2)(a) 226
          (b) 226
        (2A) 228
        (3)(a) 226
          (b) 226
      s 23(1) 226
      s 37 270
      s 48 .... 158, 164
      s 79 97
      s 112 83
      s 113 97
      Sch 1A 261

1984 Rent (Scotland) Act (c 58) (*cont*)
      Sch 1A (*cont*)
         para 2(1).. 251
         para 3 251
            (b)... 251
      Sch 2.. 79, 196, 232
         Pt III 255
         case 2... 211, 212, 255
         case 3... 210
         case 6... 317
         case 7(a).. 82
         case 20... 223
1985 Family Law (Scotland) Act (c 37).................................... 320
      s 9(1)... 320
      s 14.. 321
      s 34.. 320
      Housing Act (c 68) 39, 281, 291
      s 69(1).. 64
      Law Reform (Miscellaneous Provisions) (Scotland) Act
      (c 73)... 89
      s 13(5) 328
      s 60(6) 328
1986 Company Directors Disqualification Act (c 46)
      s 7(1)... 275
      Housing and Planning Act (c 63) 64, 98
      s 14.. 64
      Housing (Scotland) Act (c 65) 97
1987 Abolition of Domestic Rates (Scotland) Act (c 47) 149
      Housing (Scotland) Act (c 26)..................... 31, 39, 64, 76, 87,
                                   89, 118, 120, 132, 193,
                                   216, 274, 293 334,
                                   335, 336, 339
         Pt II 41, 88
         Pt IV 108, 131, 132
         Pt V.. 108, 131
         Pt VI 108, 131, 132
         Pt VII.................. 34, 44, 71, 108, 243, 296, 317
         Pt VIII 297
         s 2(1)(a)(i) 34
              (ii) 34
           (9) 87
         s 3... 59
         s 8... 32
         s 19(1)(a)... 31
            (b)... 31

1987   Housing (Scotland) Act (c 26) (*cont*)
   s 19(1)(c).. 31
          (d).. 31
          (e).. 31
          (2)(a)... 32
          (b).. 32
          (c).. 32
          (d).. 32
          (e).. 32
   s 20.. 35
          (1)(a)(iii).. 35
               (iv)... 35
          (b).. 35
          (2)(a)(i)... 33
               (ii)... 33
               (iii).. 33
               (iv)... 33
               (v).. 33
               (vi)... 33
               (vii).. 33
               (viii)... 33
          (aa)(i).. 34
               (ii)... 34
               (iii).. 34
               (iv)... 34
               (v).. 34
               (vi)... 34
          (b)(i)... 34
   s 21(1).. 37
          (2)... 37
   s 24.. 42, 64
          (2)... 42
          (2B)... 43, 44
          (3)(a).. 43
          (b)... 43, 339
          (bb).. 43, 339
          (c)... 43
          (d)... 44
          (e)... 44
          (4)... 41
   s 25.. 45
          (1)(c)... 46, 47
   s 26(1).. 47
          (3)... 48
          (4)... 47

1987 Housing (Scotland) Act (c 26) (*cont*)
  s 27 48
   (1)(a) 49
    (b) 50
    (c) 50
    (d) 50
  s 28(1) 51, 55
   (2)(a) 51, 56
    (b) 51, 56
  s 29 .... 40, 44, 52
   (1) 55
  s 31 40
   (2) 56
   (3) 56
    (a) 56
    (b) 56
   (5)(c) 88
  s 32(3) 56
  s 33 58
   (1) 49, 58
   (2) 58
    (c) 49, 339
   (3) 34, 49, 336
  s 35A 55
   (2)(a) 55
    (b) 55
    (c) 55
    (d) 55
   (3) 55
   (4) 55
  s 35B 55
   (1) 55
   (3) 55
   (5) 55
  s 36 59
  s 37 51
  s 53 96
  s 61(2)(c) 97
   (4)(c) 98
    (ca) 98
    (e) 98
  s 61A(3) 98
    (a) 98
   (7) 98
  s 61B(1) 98

1987 Housing (Scotland) Act (c 26) (*cont*)
    s 61B(2)(b) 98
        (8) 99
    s 62 98
    s 83 .... 42, 272
        (1) 272
        (2) 272
        (3) 272
    s 85 132
    s 86 34
        (1) 131
    s 108(2)(b) 132
    ss 108–112 68
    s 114 132
        (1) 132
    s 115 132
        (a) 132
    s 135 237
    ss 135–137 34
    s 136 237
    s 137 237
    s 139 237
    s 152 297
    s 178 274
    ss 178–185 297
    s 183 274
    s 216 99
    s 300(1)(b) 302
    Sch 2 98
    Sch 3, para 16 331
    Sch 10, para 3 .... 110, 116, 117
        para 5(1) 120
1988 Housing (Scotland) Act (c 43) 71, 72, 73, 74, 75,
                           76, 78, 80, 81, 85, 139,
                           155, 157, 158, 159, 165,
                           196, 198, 199, 202, 203,
                           205, 214, 216, 228, 242,
                           248, 251, 256, 261, 268,
                           270, 281, 296
    s 12 239
        (1)(a) 73
        (b) 73
    s 18 .... 201, 204
        (4) 210, 219, 249
        (6) 197

1988   Housing (Scotland) Act (c 43) (*cont*)
    s 19.. 204, 232
        (5) 196
    s 20.. 204, 205
        (3) 206
        (4) 206
        (5) 206
    s 25.. 154, 157
        (1) 155
        (2)(a) 155
            (b)... 155
            (c)... 155
    s 30.. 96
        (1) 270
        (2) 271
        (3) 270
        (4) 97
    s 31(1) 203, 248, 249, 250
            (a)... 249
            (b)... 249
            (c)... 249
        (3) 203
        (4) 249
    s 32(1)(a).. 77
            (b)... 78
        (2)(a)... 78
            (b)... 78
            (c)... 78
            (d)... 78
    s 33.. 188
        (1) 215
            (a)... 215
            (b)... 215
            (c)... 215
            (d)... 215
        (2) 215
    s 34.. 271
        (3)(a)... 153
            (b)... 153, 154
    s 36(2).. 228
    s 37(1).. 228
    s 38.. 228
    s 43(2).. 98
        (3) 98
    s 44.. 75

1988   Housing (Scotland) Act (c 43) (*cont*)

s 44(2).. 81
s 46.. 251, 261
s 72.. 139
Sch 2, para 1.. 74
    para 3 74
    para 5 74
    para 6 74
    para 7 75
    para 8 74
    para 9 75
    para 10.. 75
    para 11.. 76
    para 12.. 76
    para 13.. 76
Sch 4 .... 74, 76
    para 7 201
    para 11.. 76
Sch 5 .... 81, 195, 196, 197, 232, 251
    Pt I.. 214, 249
    Pt II.. 204, 205, 214, 249
    Pt III 207
    ground 1.. 197, 200, 214, 249
        (a) 198
        (b).. 199
    ground 2.. 197, 200
    ground 3.. 197, 201
    ground 4.. 197, 201
    ground 5.. 202
    ground 6.. 202
    ground 7.. 203
    ground 8.. 203
    ground 9.. 206
    ground 10.. 207
        (d) 208
    ground 11.. 208
    ground 12.. 209
    ground 13.. 209
    ground 14.. 210
    ground 15.. 211
    ground 16.. 213
    ground 17.. 213, 214
Sch 6 251
    para 2(2).. 261
Sch 8, para 9.. 139

1988   Housing Act (c 50) 158, 198
       s 19A... 198
1990   Environmental Protection Act (c 43)............................... 130
       s 79... 130
      Law Reform (Miscellaneous Provisions) (Scotland) Act (c 40)
       s 21... 64
      National Health Service and Community Care Act
      (c 19)... 86, 214
       Sch 8, para 20... 86
1991   Agricultural Holdings (Scotland) Act (c 55)............. 74, 89, 97
1992   Further and Higher Education (Scotland) Act (c 37)
       s 56(2)... 87
      Local Government Finance Act (c 14) 69
1993   Crofters (Scotland) Act (c 44)
       ss 12–19 97
1994   Local Government etc (Scotland) Act (c 39)
       s 157(7) 76
1995   Children (Scotland) Act (c 36)..................................... 301
       s 26(1)(a).. 301
      Criminal Law (Consolidation) (Scotland) Act (c 39)
       s 52... 123
      Criminal Procedure (Scotland) Act (c 46)
       s 234A(2) 341
       s 234AA.. 95
      Disability Discrimination Act (c 50)......................... 16, 18, 20
       s 1(1)... 20
       s 8... 22
       s 19... 21
       s 21... 22
       s 25... 22
       s 49A.. 18
       Sch 1, para 2.. 20
          para 4 21
          para 5 21
          para 6 21
1996   Housing Act (c 52) 35, 41, 46
       s 96.. 153, 198
       s 101... 204
1997   Protection from Harassment Act (c 40) 336, 341
       s 8.. 34, 234
       ss 8–11 322
       s 9(1).. 342
1998   Crime and Disorder Act (c 37) 92
      Human Rights Act (c 42) 23, 24, 27
       s 3... 24

1998 Human Rights Act (c 42) (*cont*)
      s 4.. 24
      s 7.. 24
      Scotland Act (c 46) 19, 283
      Sch 5, Pt II, para L2.. 19
1999 Disability Rights Commission Act (c 17) 20
2000 Abolition of Feudal Tenure etc (Scotland) Act (asp 5) 267
      Race Relations (Amendment) Act (c 34) 18
2001 Housing (Scotland) Act (asp 10)................... 35, 39, 55, 63, 71,
                                               86, 88, 98, 109, 114, 195,
                                               197, 211, 213, 216, 217,
                                               219, 241, 250, 252, 268,
                                         282, 286, 288, 290, 297, 334
      Pt 1 41
      Pt 3 282
      s 1.. 64
      s 3(3).. 57
        (4) 57
      s 4.. 55
      s 5.. 36
        (1) 40, 58
        (2) 58
        (3) 40, 58
        (4) 58
        (6) 58
      s 7(1).. 297
      s 9.. 31
      s 10.. 31
      s 11.. 84
        (1)(c).. 84
      s 14.. 220
      s 15.. 220
      s 16(2)(a)(ii) 219
        (c).. 224, 331, 334
        (3) 213, 220, 221
      s 22(1) 252
        (2) 252
        (3) 252
        (4) 252
        (5) 252
        (8) 252
        (10) 253
      s 27(1) 109
      s 32.. 296, 317
      s 34(1) 90

2001   Housing (Scotland) Act (asp 10) (*cont*)
   s 34(1)(a) 90
           (b) 90
           (c) 91
        (7) 94
   s 35 94
        (5)(d) 225
        (6) 95
   s 36 225
        (2) 225
        (3) 225
        (5)(a) 225
           (b) 225
           (c) 225
   s 37 .... 95, 224, 225
        (1) 95
        (2)(a) 95
           (b) 95
        (3) 95
        (4) 95
   s 41 286
        (1)(a)(i) 286
              (ii) 286
   s 42 97
   s 44 .... 98, 99
   s 57(1) 283
   s 61 283
   s 63 288
   s 69 286
   s 71 288
        (1)(a) 288
           (b) 288
   s 75 288
   s 80 283
   s 83(3) 88
   s 84 282
   s 88(1) 114
        (3) 114
   s 102 34
   s 108 .... 42, 250, 265
   Sch 1, para 2(a) 86
                  (b) 87
                  (c) 87
        para 4(b) 87
        para 5 88

2001 Housing (Scotland) Act (asp 10) (*cont*)
Sch 1, para 6.. 88
(c).. 89
para 8(a) 89
(b).. 89
para 9 89
para 10... 90
Sch 2 .... 87, 232
Pt 1, para 15 .... 329, 331, 334
ground 1.. 217
ground 2.. 217, 221
ground 3.. 221
ground 4.. 222
ground 5.. 222
ground 6.. 100, 222
ground 8.. 211
ground 9.. 223
ground 11... 223
ground 12... 223
ground 13... 223
ground 14... 224
(b) 224
ground 15 .... 224, 325
(b) 224
Sch 3 252
para 2 253
(1)(a)(i) 252
(ii) 253
(b) 253
(2) 253
(3) 253
para 3 253
para 4 253
paras 6–9 253
para 9 253
para 10... 252
para 11(1)... 252
(3)(a)... 252
Sch 4 .... 96, 107, 109
Sch 6 691
para 1 92
para 2 92
para 3 93
para 4 93
para 5 93

2001   Housing (Scotland) Act (asp 10) (*cont*)
            Sch 6, para 6.. 93
                para 7 94
            Sch 7, Pt 2, para 5 288
            Sch 7, Pt 2, para 6 288
                Pt 4, para 16 288
                    para 17... 288
            Sch 8 288
            Sch 10, para 14.. 76
        Mortgage Rights (Scotland) Act (asp 11) 69, 192
            s 2.. 69, 192
            (2) 69, 192
        Protection from Abuse (Scotland) Act (asp 14) 336, 339,
                                                                                  341, 342
            s 1.. 322
            s 7.. 46, 339, 341, 342
        Regulation of Care (Scotland) Act (asp 8) 301
        Transport (Scotland) Act (asp 2)....................................... 305
2002   Homelessness Act (c 7).. 41
2003   Agricultural Holdings (Scotland) Act (asp 11) 74, 97, 116
        Building (Scotland) Act (asp 8)................................... 68, 69
        Criminal Justice (Scotland) Act (asp 7)
            s 49.. 342
        Homelessness etc (Scotland) Act (asp 10)................ 39, 41, 45,
                                                                    48, 63, 64, 65, 204
            s 2.. 64
            s 3(2)(a).. 45
            s 4.. 48
            s 5.. 57
            s 11.. 65
            s 12... 204, 209, 217, 233
        Land Reform (Scotland) Act (asp 2)
            Pt 3 97
        Title Conditions (Scotland) Act (asp 9)............................... 68
2004   Antisocial Behaviour etc (Scotland) Act (asp 8)..... 95, 271–275
            Pt 7 278
            Pt 8 .... 13, 271
            s 3A... 275
            s 4.. 95
            s 4A... 275
            s 68.. 278
            s 69.. 278
            s 71.. 279
            s 72.. 279
            s 73.. 279

2004 Antisocial Behaviour etc (Scotland) Act (asp 8) (*cont*)
    s 74.. 279, 302
    s 74(3) 280
    s 79 280
    s 82 272
    s 83(1)(a) 274
          (b) 272
          (c) 274
       (6)(b) 274
          (c) 274
       (7) 274
    s 84(3) 275
       (6) 273
    s 85 .... 274, 275, 302
       (2) 275
       (4) 276
    s 87A 275
    s 88A 274
    s 89 276
    s 90 276
    s 91 276
    s 92 276
    s 92A 275
    s 93 .... 276, 277
    s 94 277
    s 100 197
    Sch 3 280
  Civil Partnership Act (c 33) 320
    s 101(7) 320
    Sch 1, para 3 323
    Sch 28, Pt 1 245
  Tenements (Scotland) Act (asp 11) 68, 133
2005 Disability Discrimination Act (c 13)
    s 18 21
2006 Equality Act (c 3) 16, 18
    Pt 1 16
    Pt 2 16
    s 3 16
    s 8 16
    s 10 17
    s 11 17
    s 12 17
    s 13 17
    s 14 17
    s 17 17

2006 Equality Act (c 3) *(cont)*
  s 19 17
  s 20 17
  s 21 17
  s 22 17
  s 23 17
  s 25 17
  s 26 17
  s 27 17
  s 28 17
  s 30 17
  s 31 18
  s 32 18
  Sch 2 17
Family Law (Scotland) Act (asp 2) 320, 322, 324
  s 5 324
  s 29 246
    (4) 246
  s 34 323
Housing (Scotland) Act (asp 1) 13, 102, 109, 110,
                                     116, 120, 131, 158,
                             274, 277, 295, 298, 318
  Pt 1 .... 108, 124, 125
  Pt 2 107
  Pt 6 102
  s 1(b) 132
  s 11 .... 132, 134
  s 12(1)(a) 116, 121
    (b) 121
    (c) 116, 121
    (d) 116, 121
    (e) 116
  s 13 .... 116, 125
    (1) 110
    (a) 116, 126
    (b) 126, 127
    (c) 126, 127
    (d) 127
  s 14 96
    (1) 116
    (b) 128
    (2) 117
  s 16 .... 118, 120
  s 17 120
  s 18 120

2006 Housing (Scotland) Act (asp 1) (*cont*)
    s 22(5) 120
    s 24(2) 128
    s 26(4) 129
    s 27 129
       (2) 111
       (3) 111
    s 42(1) 133
       (2)(b) 133
    ss 42–51 68
    s 52(2) 99
       (5) 99
       (9) 99
    ss 52–54 99
    s 71(1)(b) 99
       (2) 99
    s 73(1)(a) 99
       (2) 99
       (4) 99
    s 88A 272
    s 124(1) 299
       (2) 299
    s 125 299
       (1) 300
       (2) 300
       (3) 300
       (4)(a) 300
         (b) 300
         (c) 300
         (d) 300
    s 126 301
       (1)(a) 301
         (b)(i) 301
           (ii) 301
           (iii) 301
           (iv) 301
         (c) 301
         (d) 301
         (e) 302
         (f) 302
         (g) 302
       (2) 301
    s 127(1) 301
       (2) 301
    s 128(2) 300

2006   Housing (Scotland) Act (asp 1) (*cont*)
    s 128(2)(b).. 301
          (c) 301
          (d).. 301
          (e) 301
    s 129.. 302
          (1) 302
          (2) 302
          (3) 302
    s 129A.. 299
    s 130.. 302
          (1)(b).. 302
          (2)(c).. 302
          (3) 302
    s 131.. 303
          (1) 303
          (2) 303
    s 132.. 304
    s 133.. 304
          (1) 304
          (2) 304
            (a).. 304
          (4) 304
          (5) 304
    s 134.. 304
          (1) 304
    s 135.. 306
          (1) 306
          (2) 306
    s 136(1) 304
          (2) 304
    s 138.. 306
          (3) 306
          (4) 306
          (5) 306
          (7) 306
    s 139.. 306
          (1) 306
            (a).. 306
            (b).. 306
            (c) 307
          (2) 307
          (3) 307
            (c) 307
          (4) 307

2006 Housing (Scotland) Act (asp 1) (*cont*)
s 139(5) 307
s 140 307
  (1) 307
  (3) 307
s 141 307
s 142 307
  (1) 307
  (2) 307
  (3) 307
  (4) 307
  (5) 307
  (6) 307
  (7) 308
  (8) 307
s 143 308
s 144 312
  (1) 312
    (b) 312
  (2) 312
  (3) 312
  (4)(a)(i) 312
       (ii) 312
    (b) 312
  (6) 312
s 145 312
  (1) 312
  (2) 312
s 146 312
  (1) 313
  (2) 313
  (4) 313
  (5) 313
  (6) 313
  (7) 313
s 147(1) 313
  (2) 313
s 151 313
s 154 313
  (1) 313
  (2)(a) 313
    (b) 313
    (c) 313
s 154(3) 313
  (4)(a) 314

2006 Housing (Scotland) Act (asp 1) (*cont*)
s 154(4)(b)... 314
(5) 314
(6) 314
s 155(1)(a).. 314
(b) 314
s 155(3) 314
s 156(1) 314
s 157(2) 314
s 158... 308
(11) 308
s 159... 314
(1) 304, 314
(2) 314
(4) 304, 314
(5) 314
(6) 314
(a)... 305
(b) 305
(c)... 305
(8) 314
(9) 305, 315
(10) 305, 315
s 160(1) 298
(2) 298
(3) 298
(4) 298
s 161(1) 299
(2) 299
(3) 299
s 163... 315
s 164(1) 303
s 165(1) 308
ss 166–171 102
s 167... 102, 103
s 168(b) 103
(3) 104
s 169... 103
(3) 104
s 175... 275, 302
s 176... 272, 274
s 180... 197
Sch 2 .... 120, 121, 124
Sch 2, para 1... 121
para 2 121

2006 Housing (Scotland) Act (asp 1) (*cont*)

Sch 2, para 2(3) 122

para 2(4) 122

para 3 122

para 4 123

para 5 .... 123, 147

para 6 123

para 7(3)(b) 129

para 8 120

Sch 4, para 1(a) 110

(b) 110

para 2(a) 110

(b) 110

para 3(a) 111

(b) 111

para 4 111

para 5(1) 110

para 6 110

para 7(1) 302

(2) 302

Sch 5 311

2007 Bankruptcy and Diligence etc (Scotland) Act (asp 3) 297

Pt 4 191

s 217 297

Welfare Reform Act (c 5) 269

Pt 2 165

2008 Housing and Regeneration Act (c 17) 291

2010 Criminal Justice and Licensing (Scotland) Act (asp 13) 342

s 38 342

s 39 342

Equality Act (c 15) 19, 22

Home Owner and Debtor Protection (Scotland) Act

(asp 6) 69, 192, 201

s 1 69

ss 1–6 192

s 2 69

s 3 69

s 4 70

s 5 .... 70, 201

s 6 70

Housing (Scotland) Act (asp 17) 99, 284, 286, 289,
291, 295, 298

Pt 14 99

s 1 284

s 7 284

2010   Housing (Scotland) Act (asp 17) (*cont*)
     s 8.. 284
     s 13.. 284
     s 30(1) 285
        (2) 285
     s 31 284
     s 32 284
        (1)... 285
        (2)... 285
     s 34 284
     s 55 289
        (1)(a) 289
          (b)... 289
          (c) 289
        (2) 289
        (5) 289
     s 56.. 290
        (2)(c) 290
        (3) 290
     s 57 290
     s 58 290
     s 61 290
     s 62 290
     s 65 290

TABLE OF STATUTORY INSTRUMENTS

1959   Further Education (Scotland) Regulations
           reg 8 202
1985   Protected Tenancies and Part VII Contracts (Rateable Value
           Limits) (Scotland) Order (SI 1985/314) 80
1988   Assured Tenancies (Exceptions) (Scotland) Regulations
           (SI 1988/2068).. 202
           Assured Tenancies (Scotland) Regulations (SI 1988/2109).... 78
           Assured Tenancies (Tenancies at Low Rent) (Scotland)
           Regulations (SI 1988/2085) 74
           Furniture and Furnishings (Fire) Safety Regulations
           (SI 1988/1324).. 97
           Landlord's Repairing Obligations (Specified Rent)
           (Scotland) (No 2) Order (SI 1988/2155) 139
1989   Furniture and Furnishings (Fire) Safety Regulations
           (SI 1989/2358).. 97
1993   Prior Rights of Surviving Spouse (Scotland) Order
           (SI 1999/2690).. 341
           Furniture and Furnishings (Fire) Safety Regulations
           (SI 1993/207)... 97
1994   Electrical Equipment (Safety) Regulations (SI 1994/3260)... 97
           Secure Tenants (Right to Repair) (Scotland) Regulations
           (SI 1994/1046).. 111
1996   Disability Discrimination (Meaning of Disability)
           Regulations (SI 1996/1455) 21
1998   Gas Safety (Installation and Use) Regulations
           (SI 1998/2451).. 97
1999   Prior Rights of Surviving Spouse (Scotland) Order
           (SI 1999/445)... 341
           Unfair Terms in Consumer Contracts Regulations
           (SI 1999/2083).. 97

2000   Civic Government (Scotland) Act 1982 (Licensing
       of Houses in Multiple Occupation) Order
       (SSI 2000/177).. 297, 298
2001   Housing (Scotland) Act 2001 (Commencement No 2,
       Transitional Provisions, Savings and Variation) Order
       (SSI 2001/397).. 282
       Unfair Terms in Consumer Contracts Regulations
       (SI 2001/1186)... 97
2002   Civic Government (Scotland) Act 1982 (Licensing
       of Houses in Multiple Occupation) Amendment Order
       (SSI 2002/161).. 298
       Housing (Scotland) Act 2001 (Housing Support Services)
       Regulations (SSI 2002/444)................................. 94
       Scottish Secure Tenancies (Exceptions) Regulations
       (SSI 2002/314)
          reg 11 87
       Scottish Secure Tenants (Right to Repair) Regulations
       (SSI 2002/316).. 111
          reg 12(2)... 112
       Short Scottish Secure Tenancies (Notices) Regulations
       (SSI 2002/315).. 91
2003   Civic Government (Scotland) Act 1982 (Licensing
       of Houses in Multiple Occupation) Amendment Order
       (SSI 2003/463).. 298
       Employment Equality (Age) Regulations (SI 2003/1031) 16
       Employment Equality (Religion or Belief) Regulations
       (SI 2003/1660)... 16
       Employment Equality (Sexual Orientation) Regulations
       (SI 2003/1661)... 16
2004   Homeless Persons (Unsuitable Accommodation) (Scotland)
       Order (SSI 2004/489)................................. 44, 57, 64, 93
          para 3(c)... 57
2005   Employment Equality (Sex Discrimination) Regulations
       (SI 2005/2467).. 18
       Private Landlord Registration (Information and Fees)
       (Scotland) Regulations (SSI 2005/558)................... 273
2006   Civic Government (Scotland) Act 1982 (Licensing of Skin
       Piercing and Tattooing) Order (SSI 2006/43)..................... 298
       Private Landlord Registration (Information and Fees)
       (Scotland) Amendment Regulations (SSI 2006/28)............ 273
2007   Equality Act (Sexual Orientation) Regulations
       (SI 2007/1263)... 16
       Housing (Scotland) Act 2006 (Commencement No 5,
       Savings and Transitional Provisions) Order
       (SSI 2007/270).. 102

2007 Private Rented Housing Panel (Applications and
      Determinations) (Scotland) Regulations
      (SSI 2007/173).. 120, 141
          reg 3(1).. 141
              (2)... 141
          reg 4(1).. 141
              (2)... 141
          reg 5(1).. 141
              (2)... 141
              (3)... 141
              (4)... 141
              (5)... 141
              (6)... 141
          reg 6(a)... 142
              (b)... 142
              (c)... 142
              (d)... 142
          reg 7 142
          reg 8 142
          reg 9 142
          reg 10 143
          reg 11 143
          reg 12 143
          reg 14 143
              (1)... 143
              (3)... 143
              (6)... 144
          reg 15(1).. 143
              (2)... 144
          reg 16 144
          reg 17 142
          reg 18(1).. 144
              (2)... 144
              (3)... 144
              (4)... 144
          reg 19(1).. 144
              (2)... 144
              (3)... 145
          reg 20(1).. 144
              (2)... 144
          reg 21(1).. 145
              (2)... 145
              (3)... 145
          reg 22(1)–(3) 145
              (4)... 145

2007   Private Rented Housing Panel Regulations (*cont*)
            reg 22(5)..   145
                    (6)..   145
            reg 23(1)..   146
                    (2)..   146
                    (3)..   146
                    (4)..   146
                    (5)..   146
                    (6)..   146
                    (7)..   146
                    (8)..   146
            reg 24   146
            reg 25   146
            reg 26(1)..   146
                    (2)..   125, 146
                    (3)..   146
            reg 27   147
2008   Private Landlord Registration (Information and Fees)
            (Scotland) Amendment Regulations (SSI 2008/403)...........   273
2009   Civic Government (Scotland) Act 1982 (Licensing of
            Booking Offices) Order (SSI 2009/145)   298

1 INTRODUCTION

THE CONTEXT OF HOUSING LAW DEVELOPMENTS

Throughout the 20th century, housing in Britain[1] altered both in its nature and in its volume. Some 90 per cent of housing provision was from the commercial private rented sector in 1910.[2] Rental housing itself changed from being run almost solely by private landlords for profit in the early 20th century to being largely operated by not-for-profit bodies at the end of the period. In terms of its dominance, rental housing provided as a commercial enterprise declined from over 90 per cent of provision[3] to under 10 per cent[4] between 1910 and 2010. During the same period there was a rise of municipal and later social housing provided by the community on the basis of need, from less than 5 per cent to over 60 per cent and then fell to around 30 per cent.[5]

When looking at how this has developed it is crucial to bear in mind two quite distinct notions. On the one hand, these changes can be seen in the context of broad shifts in political and social developments. The extension in the rights of working people and control over aspects of their daily lives is part of the narrative. These changes, including the development of security of tenure rights for tenants and community-owned housing provision, were argued for and fought for through actions within and without the political sphere.[6] By the same token we have the role of finance capital with the emergence of accessible mortgages whose impact has been to lock the middle and working classes into the profit-based system of production. This is achieved through these former

---

[1] The broad pattern of events is similar in England, Wales and Scotland in this area of law and policy during the 20th century. I have sought to indicate where differences lie at the appropriate junctures in the text.
[2] Scottish Government (2009d).
[3] Royal Commission on the Housing of the Industrial Population of Scotland, Urban and Rural (1917).
[4] Scottish Government (2009d) at 14: the numbers were as low as 5.1% in 1999 and have revived under the impact of new landlords buying properties to rent to benefit principally from capital growth – see para 2.18.
[5] Scottish Government (2007) at 36.
[6] Melling (1980) and (1983).

renters having a direct stake in the continuity of the economic set-up and the "carrot" of a rise in personal wealth via rising property values.[7] The inbuilt instability of this process has been exposed during the various crises of capitalism in the past century and the negative equity problems and homelessness problems resulting.[8]

On the other hand, we need to focus on the specific and the local to make sense of exactly what has taken place. What has occurred in Great Britain is not part of an inevitable universal process. Many problems have been universal and there have been very similar responses to the challenges to private profit as the core of housing provision.[9] Not all developed countries have experienced the alterations in the level and nature of rented social and owner-occupied housing in the same way. Some, such as Germany, Sweden and Switzerland, have high levels of private renting.[10] Within Britain, as well as the recent extension of owner occupation, we have also seen community-owned rented housing rise in Scotland to over 50 per cent of the stock by the start of the 1980s.[11] The different political configuration of England resulted in lower levels of municipal housing being constructed during the same period.[12] The decline and rise of different parts of the sector relate to specific political developments. The problems for mobility of labour are, of course, not best addressed through either home ownership or municipal renting with lifetime security.[13] The post-war political scene, nonetheless, has included times when there has been a high degree of political consensus on the desirability of housing irrespective of tenure.[14] The role and nature of social renting have been subject to shifts in perception and presentation.[15] Finally, the notion of owner occupation as both spiritually "rewarding" and "natural"[16] remains questionable. Owner occupancy as a feature of Scotland's housing stock, with its growth from 36 per cent to 67 per cent between 1982 and 2005,[17] has come under pressure in times of recession.[18]

---

[7]   Goldthorpe *et al* (1969).

[8]   Gentle, Dorling and Comford (1994).

[9]   See Brown (1970) for parallel problems and responses in Europe.

[10] (2007), Chart 8 at 27; Harloe (1985).

[11] Scottish Development Department (1980); Begg (1996): "Scottish Housebuilding 1919–1993" at 217.

[12] Merrett (1979), Tables 2.2, 2.4, 9.3 and 9.4.

[13] Burnett (1986) at 199.

[14] Duclaud-Williams (1978) at 20–22.

[15] Scottish Government (2010): contrast with the suggestions of David Cameron in August 2010 suggesting the end of security of tenure for tenants in the social rented sector – *Guardian* (9 August 2010).

[16] DoE (1971).

[17] Scottish Government (2007), Chart 1 at 6.

[18] See Chapter 6 below.

Within these broad shifts, the courts have also played an interesting role in the development of specific rights. Accordingly, the precise way that the conflicting interests of tenants and landlords have played out over the past century have been determined to a significant degree by the judiciary. How it has interpreted and given meaning to such phrases as "suitable alternative accommodation", "member of the family" and "fair rent" has been crucial in how extensive or limited tenants' and landlords' rights have been. For reasons suggested elsewhere,[19] these meanings have been left largely to the judges as to what weight would be accorded to tenants' and landlords' interests and what "rights" would be recognised. While this dichotomy between broad policy and precise interpretation is a given in a complex democratic system, the degree of autonomy afforded to the unelected and unaccountable judiciary in shaping social policy is an issue which has at various times exercised political and social commentators.[20] It is also one on which judges themselves have expressed different opinions.[21]

Both aspects of this history are noted here. This text seeks to make links between the developments in the broad economic and political level with the decisions in the courts and to recognise the relative contributions of these sectors. It should be noted that the ways in which politicians have regarded the pronouncements of the judiciary has not been entirely constant throughout. Politicians have been pragmatic in the ways in which they have at different times been content to allow judges to produce the "meaning" of housing statutes[22] while at other times they have been happy to employ a rather different strategy.[23] The extent of the doubts about perceived judicial "politics" has varied with the issues of the day and the level of judicial "activism".[24]

The admission by judges that they were involved in making social and political choices in their work has been a relatively recent one. Even in the 1970s, judges in the House of Lords were clinging to the fiction of common law and statute having an inherent meaning which the courts

---

[19] Robson (1981) at 45.
[20] Griffith (1977); Robson (1979); Bell (1981); Robson and Watchman (eds) (1981).
[21] Denning (1979) and (1980).
[22] The 2nd edition of the Code of Guidance in relation to the Housing (Homeless Persons) Act 1977, for instance, blandly accepted the narrow and restrictive interpretations of the courts in extending the meaning of "intentionality". It was as though the decisions which went against the wording of the 1st edition produced the only reading of s 17 – see Watchman and Robson (1983) at 83–87.
[23] The rejection of the limited approach to the meaning of "accommodation" adopted by the House of Lords in *Puhlhofer* v *Hillingdon LBC* [1983] AC 484 is an instance of such an intervention – spurred on by a coalition of interest groups led by Shelter.
[24] Robson (1979) and (2000).

were merely declaring.[25] Contrast this with the seizing of the moment for
law reform encountered in *Fitzpatrick* and the shift in language, if not
actual activity, has been major.[26]

The purpose of this survey of developments in housing rights over the
past century is to seek to shed further light on these discussions. In other
work I have argued that crude class analyses of the judiciary fail to provide
a satisfactory account of those areas of law where the class element is
hard to identify.[27] They do not satisfactorily deal with divergences among
judges. Nonetheless I feel that there are broad trends within judicial
work which cannot be attributed to the throw of the dice or to some
kind of disinterested professionalism. I have suggested that, in the past,
the notion of "differential politicisation" helps to shed light on trends in
judicial policy. This seemed to provide the key to how, during the latter
part of the 19th century, trade union interests fared badly in the courts[28]
while tenants' rights waxed and waned.[29] More recently, it seems to me,
some groups have been perceived as deserving and "above politics" while
the political implications of favouring other groups have been identified
as deserving of consideration above those of others.[30] So it has been that
homeless people have fared quite badly and disabled litigants relatively
well in the 20th century.[31] Nothing that has happened in the current
century has led me to have serious doubts about these conclusions.[32]

The Law Commission, in its excellent account of the formal developments in housing regulation in England and Wales through the 19th
and 20th centuries, smooths out the conflict and describes the process
of change rather as one of universal enlightenment.[33] This is rather akin
to what Gunningham described as "social imperialism".[34] It manages to
remove the agency of progressive forces and the efforts of its opponents
in presenting a picture from the vantage point of the 21st century. The
sense in which it is possible to characterise the pre-1914 situation as
normal and peaceful and the Rent Acts as an interruption to that state of
peaceful normality is, the evidence suggests, misleading. If one looks at

---

[25] Viscount Dilhorne, for instance, in *Cassell* v *Broome* [1972] AC 1027 stated at
1107 that "the judicial functions of this House ... do not include bowing to the
wind of change. We have to declare what the law is not what it should be".
[26] *Fitzpatrick* v *Sterling Housing Association* [1999] AC 705. See also *Armour* v
Anderson 1994 SLT 1127 on what the function of the courts is in relation to
statutory intention.
[27] Robson (1979) and (2000).
[28] Paterson (1974).
[29] Robson (1979).
[30] Robson (2000).
[31] *Ibid* at 428.
[32] See Chapter 2 below and Chapter 4 below.
[33] Law Commission (2002).
[34] Gunningham (1974).

the evidence of landlord–tenant relations in both Scotland and England it is more helpful to see this as a state of permanent conflict. There were victories for landlords south of the Border in obtaining the right to eject[35] and for tenants in Scotland in obtaining the right to shorter tenancies.[36] The conflicts have continued and the language has altered. Alternatives to the concept of the market rent had been secured in the sometimes violent struggles of rural activists in Ireland and Scotland in the 19th century and, less iconically, in England.[37] The National Land League of Great Britain had taken up the slogan of the Irish Tenant League from the 1850s of the "Three Fs" – a *fair rent*, to be decided by an impartial tribunal; *fixity of tenure*, subject to payment of this fair rent; and *freedom* for the tenant to sell his interest in his holding. The success of rural tenants, in replacing the market system with a process whereby rents were, indeed, fixed by an independent body and security of tenure was a right, was seized by groups working for the extension of the rights of the working classes in general. Fred Knee and the National Housing Council were concerned to replace the market rent with the "fair rent". David Englander's work shows the context of these struggles in the 19th century.[38]

In the second half of the 19th century, in a rather more prosaic way, the new professionals working for the emergent local authorities were struggling to effect some kind of effective regulation on the urban and rural squalor they encountered. In theory, with their extensive powers to affect people's lives, they are the kind of 19th-century professionals about whom Foucault wrote so tellingly.[39] The practical limitations of resources they experienced might lead one to doubt the exact amount of power they exercised Thus, in Scotland, William Kelso's description of his time in Paisley provides us with a glimpse into the reality of the operation of the Public Health (Scotland) Act 1897. He describes the limitations on the resources available to administer legislation which we still recognise today as providing a viable framework for dealing with environmental health issues. What is missing, though, is the fact that this work for a town of 60,000 people was being undertaken by a young Kelso and two colleagues. The disease context was quite different. Kelso swithered about taking the post of Assistant Sanitary Inspector, noting that his predecessor had died of typhus. Under-resourced and with the ever-present possibility of attack by those defending the lucrative human middens that were a feature of 19th-century Scottish cities, it is instructive to note the context in which this early regulation operated.[40]

---

[35] Englander (1983) at 18.
[36] Damer in Melling (1983), Ch 2.
[37] Hunter (2010); Drudy (1982; Newby (2007); Law Commission (2002) at 2.11.
[38] Englander (1983).
[39] Foucault (2001).
[40] Kelso (1922) at 45.

The publication and meetings of Scottish Sanitary Inspectors indicate this disjunction between worthy motives and the constraints of law. The power to close buildings that were insanitary were in place. How people could obtain further accommodation when ejected from such properties was less evident and resulted in complaints from the Inspectorate about the position in which they found themselves.[41] The same kind of conflict is encountered in the operation of the overcrowding controls that were introduced in Glasgow and Greenock.[42] What was described by the inspectors whose task was to control overcrowding was grim, even making allowances for the changes brought by affluence.[43] There was also the nascent nature of much regulation. We have towns such as Perth employing a lone Sanitary Inspector at £7 per annum and Arbroath with a similar employee receiving £5 annually, although as little as £1 annually was reported.[44]

The struggle against bad housing took many forms and involved different interests. Some involved challenges to the very structures of the capitalist state. There were those organising rent strikes against rent rises and evictions.[45] Tenants and their representatives were also working within the system to effect modest improvements such as the shorter tenancy to enable those out of work or in straitened circumstances to be able to move to more modest accommodation.[46] The introduction and operation of controls over housing conditions operated in parallel to this work. Radical alternatives were also being pursued. The rise of the organised working class with trade unions and political parties provided a locus for the emergence of alternatives to privately rented slums or the workhouse. Some were a direct result of the struggles; others the product of a different perception of the poor as deserving more than the most meagre shelter in exchange for work that the workhouse represented.

The alternatives, then, came in a number of forms: philanthropy; philanthropic commercial investment; and community-owned housing. All three major alternatives to traditional private landlords started to make their appearance in the middle of the 19th century. The philanthropist with whom people in the 21st century are likely to be familiar, because of the longevity of the buildings and their appearance in iconic films,[47] is Joseph Peabody and his London tenements. They were, however, disorganised

---

[41] Fyfe (1902) at 351.

[42] Robson (1979) at 336ff.

[43] Butt (1971) at 68ff.

[44] Robson (1979) has further detailed references for 19th-century developments (221–260).

[45] Petrie (2008) at 34ff; Englander (1983) at 152ff and 182ff; Melling (1983) *passim*.

[46] Guthrie Committee (1907).

[47] Peabody Buildings appear in Ken Loach's *Poor Cow* (1967) as well as in the TV play *Cathy Come Home* (1966).

and dependent on what any particular local philanthropist might provide. In Scotland they included such fine dwellings as Dorward House in Montrose: a stunning example aimed at those whose alternative would have been the workhouse or poorhouse.[48] Providing a slight twist on this provision were the 5 per cent philanthropists. The most charismatic of these was Ms Octavia Hill who undertook intensive management of her tenants to "prove" to doubters that the poor were not all feckless and most could be taught home economics. She and her fellows took the view that it would be more viable to persuade those with money and an inclination towards doing good to combine the two things and help provide housing for the poor and still make a decent profit. In Scotland this kind of work was carried out by groups with broader aesthetic as well as social reform aims, such as the Kyrle Society and the various social unions.[49]

Housing owned by the community has a long history entwined with slum clearance and, initially, making money. Some of the early properties erected by the authorities in Glasgow, for instance, were aimed at the better off.[50] Municipal housing was, however, generally, provided by councils to meet housing need. The provision was patchy in Britain and a pamphlet from Fred Knee's Workmen's National Housing Council recorded on its back all the municipal housing provided at that time in Britain. It could be fitted onto the back of an A5 booklet.[51] The Royal Commission on Housing provided a detailed breakdown of local authority housing across Scotland. There were 11 schemes across Scotland, ranging from 10 houses in Bo'ness to 2,199 houses provided in Glasgow. Nationally, there were some 3,484 municipal properties for a population in these towns and cities of 346,387.[52] Where there was a political will, the programmes were impressive.[53] Municipal housing was a major issue between 1908 and 1915 in Glasgow as an alternative

---

[48] It currently operates as a care home. There had been in earlier centuries alms houses but these encapsulated the dependency culture against which radical politics was struggling. The most attractive are those in Beaune, France.

[49] Robson (1979) at 241ff.

[50] Oscar Slater, for instance, took a lease of 18 months on a property built by the council at 69 St George's Road, Glasgow, in November 1908 – a month before the murder of Miss Marion Gilchrist which led to him spending 19 years in Peterhead Prison. His conviction was quashed in 1928 (Roughead (1929)).

[51] Workmen's National Housing Council (1902).

[52] Royal Commission (1917) at 387, para 179.

[53] In Battersea the record of the vestry/council between 1894 and 1909, when it lost control for 3 years was impressive. A 48-hour working week had been introduced following a conference considering the results of a joint trade union and vestry survey into wage rates in the area, published in 1895. Through its Direct Labour Department it had built library extensions, slipper baths and a public laundry, swimming baths, a sterilised milk depot, electric light station, the Latchmere estate and the Town Hall dwellings of 18 houses, providing 351 tenement dwellings (Creighton (2005)).

to private rented provision.[54] The voluntary nature of the powers under the Housing of the Working Classes Act 1890 meant that the nature and extent were, however, a matter for local political struggle.[55] In places such as Barrhead, near Paisley, specific local interests shaped the kind of housing produced.[56] In the private rented sector itself, untrammelled by regulation before 1915, there had been property volatility in the pre-1914 market with a knock-on effect on those renting, so that there were times when the supply of housing at most levels was abundant.[57] The underlying picture was, however, one of chronic undersupply of accommodation to those with least money.[58]

The picture that emerges is not a simple one. Lawyers looking back have tended to follow the path of legislative change of particular statutes, trace the development of specific tenures or show how an issue has been treated over the years. The chapters following look at individual features of housing and seek to provide a picture of the legal position we are in at the time of writing and what the major factors were in deciding how this situation came about. On the one hand we have some tenants fighting battles in the courts and on the streets in places such as Clydebank, defending their hard-won rights. In other places the political effort was put into developing decent housing at an affordable rent for those in need, through municipal development. Others sought to improve their housing through taking out mortgages and buying properties to avoid being in thrall to any landlord, private or municipal. Which solution was successful depended on the local politics. For instance, it was not until late into the 1930s that a town such as St Andrews built any municipal housing, while Glasgow had started such enterprises in the middle of the 19th century. Some initiatives, too, were national, as in the development of the Scottish Special Housing Association with its strategic role for the development of Scottish industry and meeting the need to provide "work projects" for the unemployed.[59] The consensus of those who have examined developments in Scottish politics in the era prior to direct state involvement from 1915 emphasises that housing was a site for struggle between those with entrenched property interests and those who had started to organise to better their own working and living conditions in a systematic and sustained way.[60] The results were, like the opposing interests, complicated and confusing for anyone looking at the legal structures that resulted

[54] Robson (1979) at 281ff.
[55] *Ibid* at 343ff.
[56] Barrhead Community Council (c 1985).
[57] Butt (1971) at 85.
[58] Royal Commission Report (1917).
[59] Begg (1987).
[60] Rodger (1989) at 42–43, summarising the findings of a range of historians on 19th-century Scotland from Southgate to Melling – see n 79 at 53 for details.

with the 20th-century Rent Acts and Housing Acts. The fact that these were the product of disagreement about fundamental goals rather than some grand scheme of consensual social engineering helps to explain why litigation and political conflict and, to a lesser extent, litigation, are endemic features in the development of Scottish housing.

THE BACKGROUND TO HOUSING LAW

The concept of contract is often taken as the starting point for doctrinal legal education. Property rights derive neatly from contract. There is, though, more to property than the initial contract. There are the restraints on the property owner. Despite the notion that planning, building control, health and safety and the like are all modern phenomena to constrain hitherto untrammelled independent property owners, the legal regulation of property ownership rights is contiguous with its existence as a legal concept in Scotland. There have always been restraints imposed by feudal superiors, limitations on building through the Dean of Guild Court and rights of neighbours to object to nuisances.[61] What has occurred as society has expanded with industrialisation is that these limitations have become more visible. The rights of tenants have also emerged as an issue of some marginal significance. These limitations on the rights of owners of heritable property have traditionally been dealt with as part of property law and conveyancing in Scots legal education. It has been regarded as one of the core areas of private law – it deals with relations between private individuals and bodies as opposed to those between citizen and the state. Given the role of the state in relation to planning, building and enforcement of standards, this is not a particularly helpful taxonomy.

Looking at housing law as a distinct entity from property law is a very recent phenomenon in Scotland. There are, at the time of writing, only two "stand alone" courses in Scottish universities of this title.[62] The items covered in this book have traditionally been ignored or dealt with very perfunctorily as part of property law. For the most part the former has been the approach. Insofar as housing does make an appearance, it does so as part of property law where the focus has been on the buying and selling of heritable property, ie land and housing. The elaborate rules and procedures involved in this process and the rights of buyers and sellers have been accorded significant time in the Scottish law curriculum. The principal focus has been on the rights of owners. Landlord and tenant law has, in property law courses, received some attention insofar as it deal with limited, fixed-term rights of property. Often, it has been overlooked. Housing law has fared even less well. It does not fit well into

---

[61] Gordon (1999, 2nd edn); Reid and Gretton (2008).
[62] University of Strathclyde and Caledonian University, Glasgow.

any conceptual approach to law which seeks to start with legal principles. Nor does it fit into a customer-driven curriculum where what is taught is what is likely to be encountered in practice. Tenants of local authority housing and homeless people have not been the clients towards whom traditional legal firms have targeted their efforts.

Housing law has no clear conceptual core. It is a mixture of private contract with public standards overlaid on these, along with direct and indirect regulation. It breaches the public law/private law divide, centring on issues that involve citizens and other citizens and the state. Some aspects of it centre on what is in the contract between individuals and organisations. Here, it consists of those rules and regulations deemed necessary to buttress various rights and interests beyond what might be found in the contract. It also deals with state-centred duties and obligations as far as they affect citizens. This mixed heritage is reflected in the various textbooks which have come under the title of *Housing Law*. It was dealt with by Whyte and Gordon as being focused on the rights of municipal tenants as affected by the Housing Acts in the inter-war period.[63] Cochrane centred his text on the sources of the powers of those operating in local government.[64] Himsworth, for his part in his work on housing law, initially limited himself in his first three editions between 1982 and 1989 to public sector housing law in Scotland.[65] The starting point was the local authority and what powers and duties it had in relation to housing. In the 1994 edition he expanded the coverage to include a chapter on tenancies in the private sector.[66] As far as landlord and tenant law is concerned, Rankine[67] and McAllister[68] cover the whole field from agricultural and commercial tenancies through to residential tenancies. The coverage of residential tenancies[69] in which the author has been involved is self-evident. It has that focus for reasons of professional and personal interest. It has been the area on which I have written articles and been asked to provide opinions and, as it has continued to become more complex and extensive, it has precluded effective wider coverage for commercial reasons. This text focuses on the experience of owners and tenants. It starts with how housing is allocated and how homelessness is addressed. It then looks at the principal forms residential occupancy takes. It goes on to examine the principal issues people confront in their housing – securing decent living conditions; how

---

63 Whyte and Gordon (1938).
64 Cochrane (1976).
65 Himsworth (1982); (1986); (1989).
66 Himsworth (1994).
67 Rankine (1887); (1893) and (1916).
68 McAllister (1989); (1995); (2002).
69 Robson (1994); Robson and Halliday (1998); and Robson, Halliday and Vennard (2011).

the commodity is paid for; loss of accommodation; and succession to the family home. It then looks at the newer forms of regulation of housing and housing providers, finishing with a more detailed examination of the problems faced by two groups who have traditionally had limited political and social bargaining power: those in shared accommodation and those experiencing relationship breakdown and/or abuse. I have already sought to locate this study in the context of other broader work on the nature of property and the struggle ahead in the preliminary pages of this book.

THE DEVELOPMENT OF THE LEGAL REGULATION OF HOUSING

Government has long had an interest in the impact of contracts on citizens. The concern to interfere with simple contractual arrangements is not limited to recent conflicts. It dates back to the securing of the most fundamental rights of tenants in Scots law, enshrined in the Leases Act 1449. This provided security of tenure to tenants during the term of their leases. It was no longer possible for purchasers of properties to decline to take on their sitting tenants and evict them. Although this was introduced principally to protect agricultural tenancies, it applied equally to tenants of residential properties – or "urban tenements" as they were confusingly termed.[70] As noted above, the idea that landlord and tenant relations were smooth and harmonious during the period prior to 20th- century intervention is misleading. The struggles over the right to eject and the right to shorter tenancies are testament to this. The structure of rights and the landlord–tenant relationship were not significantly altered during this period and the contract was central. The most fundamental rupture of the significance of the contract occurred in the early days of the First World War. Universal exploitation by landlords of their market position around the whole of Europe led to various measures in many countries to control rents and prevent eviction at the contract term.[71]

The British response, with the introduction of rent control and restrictions on repossession of tenancies, effectively stifled industrial discontent which had threatened the war effort.[72] Pressure from tenants' actions along with threats to the shipbuilding and armaments industries during the early days of the Great War produced a remarkable response from the coalition Government. It suspended market forces for the duration of the War in the dominant private rented sector. The impact

---

[70] Rankine (1916) at 241.
[71] Brown (1970).
[72] Melling (1983).

of the decision to introduce rent controls in 1915 had an impact out of all proportion to what those debating the issues could have imagined. Although this has been characterised as "legislation to protect the poor",[73] it is fairer to say that it was simply a knee-jerk reaction to a clear and present threat.[74] Luxury properties were not covered but in Scotland the vast majority of dwelling-houses fell below the £40 rateable value cap. It seems equally valid to suggest that it was legislation to protect the long-term interests of property owners. This, combined with the chronic lack of supply of working-class housing and investment by the private capital in this sector, led to the commitment to require local authorities to engage seriously in housing provision.[75]

The complex pragmatic politics of the years between 1915 and the start of the 21st century mean that anyone seeking to get to grips with housing law must grapple with at least 10 distinct kinds of residential tenancy. Prior to 1915, tenants who rented properties had their rights determined largely by the terms of their contracts, with the exception of the 1449 security for the term of the contract irrespective of a change of landlord. The plan to return to the pre-1915 contractual regime never materialised for the vast majority of tenancies which fell within the rateable value limits market.

The recommencement of controls on rent levels and the provision of security of tenure beyond the contractual term introduced in 1965 applied to all tenancies below a certain rateable value. In effect, all non-luxury properties were covered by the optional provision of the Rent Act 1965. A tenancy was covered by this legislation provided that it met specific requirements. These were designed to ensure that the protection to these "regulated" tenancies applied to those properties where there was a possibility of exploitation and the market provided no real protection. The legislation excluded a range of tenancies where there was either no perceived need for protection or where another regime of protection was in operation. Section 2 of the Rent (Scotland) Act 1984 specifies a range of such tenancies covering lets where there is a low rent;[76] where the tenancy is let at a rent which includes payments in respect of board or attendance;[77] student tenancies from a specified institution;[78] holiday lets;[79] and ones where there is land other than the site of the dwelling-house.[80]

---

[73] Law Commission (2002) at 2.12.
[74] Petrie (2008).
[75] Royal Commission (1917) at 347, para 2237.
[76] Rent (Scotland) Act 1984 (RSA 1984), s 1(a) – specifically where either no rent is payable or the rent payable is less than two-thirds of the rateable value.
[77] *Ibid*, s 1(b).
[78] *Ibid*, s 1(c).
[79] *Ibid*, s 1(d).
[80] *Ibid*, s 1(e).

In seeking to provide an accurate picture of the developments in protections for tenants it must be recognised that no coherent plan of action existed. Problems of public health are intertwined with conflicts over rents and evictions and alternatives to the private profit basis for the provision of housing. The responses to these included providing powers to deal with insanitary houses, including demolition.[81] There were also attempts, as we have noted, to provide housing both from philanthropic trusts as well as from more commercial organisations.[82] The power to build municipal housing was made available and in the inter-war period led to the provision of over 50 per cent of the Scottish housing stock. In this inter-war period the emphasis of politicians was on slum clearance and the provision of new housing.[83] There was little obvious concern with what form of tenure this housing took. There was a commitment across the political spectrum to solve the "housing problem" through mass housing provision.[84]

As we see in subsequent chapters here, the approach of governments to housing policy has been "light touch" throughout the 20th century. While private sector landlords' rights have been constrained at various times in terms of the rents they can charge and the circumstances when they can regain possession of the properties, Governments in Britain have been slow to introduce any kind of regulation as to who should be able to enter this area of activity. Harold Wilson recognised the potential for serious exploitation where supply of a necessity was outweighed by demand when he declared back in 1964 that "renting housing is not a proper field for private profit".[85] It was not, however, until the end of March 2006 that this kind of concern for those likely to be exploited in the landlord–tenant relationship bore fruit in the requirement for private-sector landlords in Scotland to meet a minimum standard of fitness of character and to be registered.[86]

In the arena of social renting, too, central government was content until very recently to assume that social landlords would act responsibly towards their tenants, and provided them with no specific protection against repossession, rent increases or unfit housing conditions: that altered with the Tenants' Rights etc (Scotland) Act 1980.[87]

By the same token, providers of housing for owner occupancy have been left outwith regulation until very recently. It is only with the introduction of Housing Information Packs in the Housing (Scotland) Act 2006 that

[81] Public Health (Scotland) Act 1897, ss 46–47.
[82] Robson (1979); Law Commission (2002) discusses parallel developments in England at 2.53.
[83] Simon (1933).
[84] Dunleavy (1981) at 34; Duclaud-Williams (1978) at 20–22.
[85] Speech to Leeds Labour Party, 9 February 1964.
[86] Antisocial Behaviour etc (Scotland) Act 2004, Pt 8; see Chapter 8 below.
[87] Equivalent protections were provided in the Housing Act 1980 for England and Wales.

we finally find a form of protection to property buyers that seeks to go beyond what the market is able to secure.

What we had in terms of protections for those living in residential accommodation has been a patchwork of protections against some forms of market exploitation alongside powers for local authorities to intervene both to provide housing and to ensure that reasonable standards were available in housing. The bulk of the subsequent text here looks at these matters in a little more detail and shows those areas where the protection against the limitations of the market is afforded. Before that, though, it is worth outlining some interesting new developments which have added to the richness as well as complexity of work in this area.

DEVELOPMENTS IN THE LAW OF HOUSING

Housing law as it developed in the 20th century was concerned mainly with those statutory interventions which supplant market solutions to the distribution and operation of the market in rental and, to a lesser extent, owner-occupied housing. There have been developments, however, in other areas of social policy that impinge on the occupancy of accommodation. These sets of rights have been significantly concerned with exclusion from the world of work and social life but also have an important impact on the housing that is available to individuals. In a world of increasing specialisation they tend to be passed over to experts working in these specialised fields and in an introductory work this coverage is, perforce, restricted. It is important, though, to remember that they are an important part of the controls that may assist individuals to obtain decent housing at a price they can afford in a location they desire – which has to be the underlying purpose of any self-respecting housing lawyer.

Discrimination

The framework of the regulation of housing which this book is principally addressing developed in an era when legal protection against discrimination on the grounds of race, ethnicity, nationality, gender, sexuality and religious belief was either non-existent or focused on workplace issues. It is, however, part of the framework within which housing problems emerge. The obligation not to discriminate includes within it the provision of housing. "To let" signs with the qualifications "No coloureds; No Irish" are recorded in London in the 1950s.[88] Most racial discrimination was subtler but widespread.[89]

---

[88] Special Report, *The Colour Bar* (BBC, 1954): excerpts appear in the *People's Century* series (BBC, 1998).
[89] MacEwan (1991).

The Race Relations Act 1965 is principally remembered as being the first attempt to put an end to discrimination in "places of public resort" such as hotels, restaurants, cinemas and places of public entertainment.[90] There was, though, also a provision covering assignations of leases or sub-leases. Landlords were prohibited from withholding their consent on the grounds of colour, race or ethnic or national origin; and agreements which sought to prohibit the disposal of tenancies on these racial grounds was also included.[91] The coverage of the race discrimination legislation was expanded significantly by the Race Relations Act 1968. This covered the provision of goods and services, employment, trade union and trade association membership, housing and advertising. It relied on two approaches. First, individual complaints that an individual had been discriminated against on the grounds of race, colour, nationality, national or ethnic origin could be raised. Discrimination could be direct, as where a person stated that certain nationalities were barred from housing on the grounds of their racial origin or colour. The Milner Holland Report on Housing, admittedly looking at the situation in Greater London, had found that only 11 per cent of lettings of private accommodation were advertised without a "colour bar".[92] The notion of indirect discrimination is rather more complex. This involves the provision of a standard or criterion which applies to, in effect, exclude one particular group. An example would be a requirement to work every Friday or Sunday, which would affect members of some religious groups disproportionately. Indirect discrimination is rather harder to envisage in the process of selling or renting accommodation.

In addition to individuals pursuing claims for acts of discrimination they have may have suffered, there was provision for a body to work for the elimination of racial discrimination and work for the promotion of equality of opportunity.[93] This included the power to conduct formal investigations where it had reasonable grounds to believe that acts of discrimination had taken place on a systemic basis. Coming some years after the original race discrimination legislation but with the same double set of remedies, the Sex Discrimination Act 1975 was introduced to cover discrimination on the ground of sex. Again, individual complaints were to be addressed by employment tribunals and the Equal Opportunities Commission was charged with the duty of eliminating sex discrimination and had similar powers to conduct formal investigations into systemic sexual discrimination.[94] The Community Relations Council's functions

---

[90] Race Relations Act 1965, s 1.
[91] *Ibid*, s 5.
[92] Milner Holland (1965) at 188.
[93] Race Relations Act 1976 (RRA 1976), s 43(1).
[94] Sex Discrimination Act 1975 (SDA 1975).

and those of the Equal Opportunities Commission were subsumed by the Equality and Human Rights Commission in 2007.[95] Subsequently, the scope of discrimination legislation was extended to cover disability in 1995[96] and more recently sexual preference,[97] religious beliefs[98] and age.[99]

There are two aspects, as indicated, to the equality legislation. First, there is the availability of remedies for individuals which they can pursue either themselves or with support from the Equality and Human Rights Commission (EHRC). The EHRC was established by the Equality Act 2006 in October 2007 and replaced the pre-existing separate Commissions.[100] It has a general duty to encourage and support development of a society in which people's ability to achieve their potential is not limited by prejudice or discrimination; there is respect for and protection of each individual's human rights; there is respect for the dignity and worth of each individual; each individual has an equal opportunity to participate in society; and there is mutual respect between groups based on understanding and valuing of diversity and on shared respect for equality and human rights.[101]

The EHRC also has specific equality and diversity duties to promote understanding of the importance of equality and diversity; encourage good practice in relation to equality and diversity; promote equality of opportunity; promote awareness and understanding of rights under the equality enactments; enforce the equality enactments; work towards the elimination of unlawful discrimination; and work towards the elimination of unlawful harassment. It should be noted too that, in the promotion of equality of opportunity between disabled persons and others, the Commission may promote favourable treatment of disabled persons.[102]

There are specific group relations duties: to promote understanding of the importance of good relations between members of different groups and between members of groups and others; to encourage good practice in relation to relations between members of different groups and between members of groups and others; to work towards the elimination of prejudice against,

---

95   Equality Act 2006 (EA 2006), Pt 1.
96   Disability Discrimination Act 1995 (DDA 1995) – covered below as a separate issue.
97   Employment Equality (Sexual Orientation) Regulations 2003 (SI 2003/1661) (employment); Equality Act (Sexual Orientation) Regulations 2007 (SI 2007/1263) (goods, services, education, public authorities).
98   Employment Equality (Religion or Belief) Regulations 2003 (SI 2003/1660) (employment); Equality Act 2006, Pt 2 (goods, services, education, public authorities).
99   Employment Equality (Age) Regulations 2006 (SI 2006/1031) (employment).
100 Equal Opportunities Commission (EOC–SDA); Commission for Racial Equality (CRE–RRA) and Disability Rights Commission (DRC–DDA).
101 EA 2006, s 3.
102 Ibid, s 8.

hatred of and hostility towards members of groups; and to work towards enabling members of groups to participate in society.[103] The monitoring duties cover the effectiveness of equality and human rights law and progress towards the aims of its general duties.[104]

The Commission's powers to meet these duties include the power to publish ideas and information; undertake research; carry out education and training; give advice or guidance; give assistance;[105] issue grants;[106] monitor crime affecting particular groups; make arrangements for social, sporting and other activities for particular groups;[107] and issue Codes of Practice.[108] In terms of investigations, the Commission may conduct an investigation into whether or not a person has committed an unlawful act, but only if it suspects that the person concerned may have done so.[109] In a formal investigation, terms of reference must be drawn up; notice must be given to those investigated; if a named person is to be investigated he must be informed of the Commission's belief that an unlawful act may have been committed and the proposal to investigate and must be offered an opportunity to make oral or written representations; any revisals must be dealt with in the same manner. In the light of findings the Commission may make recommendations; report; either publish the report or make it available for inspection.[110] If, in the course of a formal investigation, the Commission is satisfied that someone has committed an unlawful act, an unlawful act, notice may be issued which requires the person to prepare an action plan to avoid the unlawful action, and recommends action. There is a right of appeal.[111] Alternatively, the Commission may enter into an agreement by which the person undertakes not to commit the unlawful act or not to take certain action, and this may involve drawing up an action plan.[112]

The Commission has extensive powers to enforce individual duties. It may take legal action to enforce certain sections of the Acts by publishing discriminatory advertisements; instructing discrimination and putting on pressure to discriminate;[113] providing conciliation services;[114] giving legal assistance;[115] or instituting or intervening in legal proceedings, including judicial review, in connection with its functions.[116] An example of a

---

[103] EA 2006, s 10.
[104] *Ibid*, ss 11 and 12.
[105] *Ibid*, s 13.
[106] *Ibid*, s 17.
[107] *Ibid*, s 19.
[108] *Ibid*, s 14.
[109] *Ibid*, s 20.
[110] *Ibid*, Sch 2.
[111] *Ibid*, ss 21 and 22.
[112] *Ibid*, s 23.
[113] *Ibid*, ss 25 and 26.
[114] *Ibid*, s 27.
[115] *Ibid*, s 28.
[116] *Ibid*, s 30.

judicial review instituted by one of the previous Commissions concerned *inter alia* whether the legislation on harassment and sexual harassment failed to implement Equal Treatment Directive 2002/73/EC by how the Employment Equality (Sex Discrimination) Regulations 2005 were drafted.[117] It was argued, successfully, that the use of the words "on the ground of" in the Regulations imported the concept of causation, requiring an investigation of the reason complained of, rather than following the Directive. This had defined "harassment" by association with sex. Thus, for instance, there could be conduct which created an offensive working environment, such as where there was denigratory conduct of a man related to sex which would not have been covered by the 2005 Regulations.

The EHRC is also responsible for ensuring compliance with the public equality duties. This may be done by issuing a compliance notice to an authority which has failed to comply with its duty, requiring it to advise the Commission of what steps it has taken to comply with the duty. If the authority fails to provide the necessary information, the Commission may apply to the sheriff court which may make an order in the terms applied for. There are no additional compliance/enforcement powers.[118]

Placing a requirement on public authorities to promote equality and end discrimination was introduced progressively. First, the Race Relations (Amendment) Act 2000, passed as a response to the MacPherson Report, amended the Race Relations Act so as to place a duty on specified public authorities to have due regard to the need to eliminate discrimination which was unlawful under the Race Relations Act and to promote equality of opportunity and good relations between persons of different racial groups.[119]

Secondly, a similar requirement was introduced in December 2006, under the Disability Discrimination Act, to place a duty on specified public authorities to have due regard to the need to eliminate discrimination which is unlawful under the Disability Discrimination Act; to eliminate harassment of disabled persons related to their disabilities; to promote equality of opportunity between disabled persons and others; to take steps to take account of disabled persons' disabilities, even where that involves treating disabled persons more favourably than others; to promote positive attitudes towards disabled persons; and to encourage participation by disabled persons in public life.[120]

Thirdly, the Equality Act 2006 introduced a similar duty into the Sex Discrimination Act in April 2007 to place a duty on specified

---

[117] *Equal Opportunities Commission* v *Department for Trade and Industry* [2007] IRLR 327.
[118] EA 2006, ss 31 and 32.
[119] RRA 1976, s 71.
[120] DDA 1995, s 49A.

public authorities to have due regard to the need to eliminate unlawful discrimination and harassment and to promote equality of opportunity between men and women.[121] There are additional duties on certain public bodies to promote equality through race/disability/gender equality schemes.[122]

The concept of "mainstreaming" refers to the incorporation of anti-discrimination practice into decision and policy making in general. In relation to specific grounds sometimes the term "audit" is used, as in "gender audit" or "disability audit". While the power to legislate on equal opportunities and discrimination is reserved to the Westminster Parliament,[123] the Scotland Act 1998 makes an exception in relation to encouraging and observing equal opportunities requirements itself, and in relation to imposing duties on office holders in the Scottish Administration and certain public bodies regarding non-reserved matters to observe equal opportunities requirements. This in turn covers the prevention, elimination or regulation of discrimination in carrying out their responsibilities "on grounds of sex or marital status, on racial grounds, or on grounds of disability, age, sexual orientation, language or social origin, or of other personal attributes, including beliefs or opinions, such as religious beliefs or political opinions".[124] This obligation does not permit equality legislation but requires this duty to be incorporated into the functions of the Parliament and the Government. The Equal Opportunities Committee is a mandatory committee of the Scottish Parliament and has responsibility for overseeing this duty. The current Equality Act 2010 continues these protections, albeit with a different structure.[125]

Disability

Accommodation for citizens with disabilities has been provided in a number of very different ways over the years. The policy of identifying those with certain disabilities and providing them with separate living and working accommodation emerged in the late 19th century and the early 20th century.[126] The provision of Institutions for the blind, deaf, mentally challenged and mentally ill stemmed from worthy motives. This recognition that society's workplaces and living spaces were constructed with no concern for those with no physical or mental issues was exacerbated

---

[121] SDA 1975, s 76A.
[122] http://www.hmso.gov.uk/legislation/scotland/ssi2002/20020062.htm(race); http://www.opsi.gov.uk/legislation/scotland/ssi2005/20050565.htm (disability); http://www.opsi.gov.uk/legislation/scotland/ssi2007/20070032. htm (gender).
[123] Scotland Act 1998, Sch 5, Pt II, para L2.
[124] Ibid.
[125] Equality Act 2010.
[126] Bolderson (1991).

in the period after the Great War. The response to the large numbers of men damaged in that conflict was the construction of hospitals and homes on the lines of institutions such as the Erskine Homes. It was in the tradition of the Victorian specialised institutions.[127] As a result of this separation the interests of individuals with disabilities were absent from policies in relation to the provision of and access to housing, its standards and loss of housing rights. It is only since 1944 initially and most recently 1995 that there has existed legislation designed to provide protection from discrimination to individuals with special needs. Initially the Disabled Persons (Employment) Act 1944 provided a limited degree of positive discrimination in the workplace, with its requirement that larger employers set aside 3 per cent of their posts for individuals drawn from a list of disabled applicants.[128]

This "quota" approach was replaced by the discrimination policy found in the much-criticised Disability Discrimination Act 1995 which echoed the individual focus of the earlier two discrimination statutes. It initially lacked a body to ensure that the legislation was operated satisfactorily. This defect was remedied in 1999 with the introduction of the Disability Rights Commission.[129]

The Disability Discrimination Act 1995 proceeded to adopt the medical model approach to discrimination. It started from the assumption that there are those in society who have an impairment which the law may be able to assist by outlawing discrimination and requiring adjustments to be made in the workplace and in the provision of services to negative the impact of the impairment. Hence there must be "a physical or mental impairment which has a substantial and long-term adverse effect on a person's ability to carry out normal day-to-day activities".[130] This impairment covers physical and mental impairments and must have long-term effects, ie it must have lasted at least 12 months or be likely to last at least 12 months or be likely to last for the rest of the life of the person affected.[131] It covered impairments to *normal day-to-day activities* – mobility; manual dexterity; physical co-ordination; continence; the

---

[127] The Royal Blind School was founded in 1793 and remains a specialist day and boarding school located in Edinburgh. Donaldson's School was founded in Edinburgh in 1851 as Donaldson's Hospital by Sir James Donaldson (1751–1830). The original benefaction allowed for special bursaries for poor children. Not all were deaf, although applications on behalf of deaf children were encouraged. From 1938, pupils were exclusively deaf. Founded in 1916, Erskine Hospital has provided nursing and medical care for former members of our armed forces through two World Wars and the more recent conflicts and peace-keeping initiatives of the 20th and 21st centuries.

[128] Disabled Persons (Employment) Act 1944.

[129] Disability Rights Commission Act 1999.

[130] DDA 1995, s 1(1).

[131] *Ibid*, Sch 1, para 2.

ability to lift, carry or otherwise move everyday objects; speech, hearing or eyesight; memory or ability to concentrate, learn or understand or perception of the risk of physical danger.[132] There must be *substantial adverse effects*, meaning that the long-term impact is more than a minor or trivial effect.[133] The effect of medical treatment is ignored so that an impairment which would be likely to have a substantial adverse effect on the ability of the person concerned to carry out normal day-to-day activities, but for the fact that measures are being taken to treat or correct it, is to be treated as having that effect.[134] Progressive conditions are included. Where a person has a progressive condition and as a result he has an impairment which has an effect on his ability to carry out normal day-to-day activities but that effect is not a substantial adverse effect, he is taken as having an impairment if the condition is likely to result in his having such an impairment. Cancer, multiple sclerosis, muscular dystrophy and HIV are specified as examples of progressive conditions covered by this extension of the law.[135]

Looking specifically at the provision of goods, facilities and services, the Act lays down that it is unlawful for a provider of services to discriminate against a disabled person by refusing to provide, or deliberately not providing, to the disabled person any service which he provides, or is prepared to provide, to members of the public. In addition, it amounts to discrimination if there is failure to comply with any duty imposed on the provider to make adjustments or if the standard of service which he provides to the disabled person or the manner in which he provides it to him makes it impossible or unreasonably difficult to make use of the service.[136] Examples of the services would include access to and use of any place which members of the public are permitted to enter; and access to and use of information services. In addition, the provision of accommodation in a hotel, boarding house or other similar establishment is covered.

Where a provider of services has a practice, policy or procedure which makes it impossible or unreasonably difficult for disabled persons to make use of a service which he provides, or is prepared to provide, to other members of the public, it is his duty to take such steps as it is reasonable, in all the circumstances of the case, for him to have to take in order to change that practice, policy or procedure so that it has no longer has that effect. For instance, where a physical feature makes it impossible or unreasonably difficult for disabled persons to make use of such a service,

---

[132] DDA 1995, Sch 1, para 4.
[133] *Ibid*, Sch 1, para 5; Disability Discrimination (Meaning of Disability) Regulations 1996 (SI 1996/1455).
[134] DDA 1995, Sch 1, para 6.
[135] Disability Discrimination Act 2005, s 18.
[136] DDA 1995, s 19.

it is the duty of the provider of that service to take appropriate action. This involves taking such steps as is reasonable, in all the circumstances, for him to have to take in order to remove the feature; alter it so that it no longer has that effect; provide a reasonable means of avoiding the feature; or provide a reasonable alternative method of making the service in question available to disabled persons.[137]

Again, the legislation provided for individual complaints through the sheriff court about discrimination in relation to the provision of services such as housing.[138] There have been a number of instances where actions have been raised. In one case a landlord refused to provide bed and breakfast accommodation during the Edinburgh Festival for a blind person who then sought damages. The reason put forward by the landlord was that work was being undertaken on the steps leading up to the property and he did not consider that it would be safe for Mr Rose to access the property at that time.[139] The claim was in this instance unsuccessful on the ground that the sheriff was satisfied that the owner's view was objectively reasonable. He noted that the relevant Code of Practice advised in situations like these: "When in doubt, ask the disabled person" (para 1.7 of the Code). Mr Rose had not allowed this enquiry by slamming the phone down on Mr Bouchet.[140]

Human rights

INTRODUCTION

Housing has long been recognised as a human right. It forms part of the United Nations Declaration of Human Rights which states that:[141]

> "(1) Everyone has the right to a standard of living adequate for the health and well-being of himself and of his family, including food, clothing, housing and medical care and necessary social services, and the right to security in the event of unemployment, sickness, disability, widowhood, old age or other lack of livelihood in circumstances beyond his control."

It also occurs in the Constitutions of a number of states, in some guise or another. For instance, in the 1978 Spanish Constitution it is stated at s 47 that "All Spaniards have the right to enjoy decent and adequate housing". The Portuguese Constitution is slightly more detailed. Article 65 states: "Everyone shall possess the right for themselves and their family

---

[137] DDA 1995, s 21. The law is now found in the Equality Act 2010.
[138] *Ibid*, s 25; in relation to employment discrimination these are heard by an employment tribunal – s 8 (as amended).
[139] *Rose* v *Bouchet* 2000 SLT (Sh Ct) 170.
[140] *Ibid* at 176.
[141] UN Universal Declaration of Human Rights, Art 25(1) – at http://www.un.org/en/documents/udhr.

to have an adequately sized dwelling that provides them, with hygienic and comfortable conditions and preserves personal and family privacy." In the United States, the Fourteenth Amendment to the Constitution guaranteeing to citizens "the equal protection of the laws" has been used to provide a means by which to combat racism in housing. In *Buchanan* v *Warley*, the Supreme Court, applying the Fourteenth Amendment for the first time in a housing discrimination case, struck down a city ordinance *requiring* neighbourhood racial segregation in housing.[142] Subsequently, in *Shelley* v *Kraemer*, the court outlawed judicial enforcement of racially restrictive covenants in housing.[143]

EUROPEAN CONVENTION ON HUMAN RIGHTS AND THE HUMAN RIGHTS ACT 1998

There is not, however, in Britain a strong culture of seeking remedies through the courts. As has been suggested, tenants and others with housing problems over the past century have opted for direct political channels. Although the European Convention on Human Rights was accessible with the individual right of petition since 1966,[144] it was with its incorporation into our law through the Human Rights Act 1998 that it became a much more visible and viable route for enforcement. It is less concerned with social and economic rights, however, than civil and political rights.

Articles 8 and 6 of the European Convention on Human Rights were the principal sources of litigation in relation to housing prior to the enactment of the Human Rights Act 1998. Article 8 provides that:

"(1) Everyone has the right to respect for his private and family life, his home and correspondence.

(2) There shall be no interference by a public authority with the exercise of this right except such as in accordance with the law and is necessary in a democratic society in the interests of national security, public safety or the economic well-being of the country, for the protection of health or morals, or for the protection of the rights and freedoms of others."

"Respect for the home" did not automatically establish a right to a home,[145] although, in a later case, there was considerable support for the view that refusal of the authorities to take steps in assisting in housing problems could raise an issue under this article.[146] The European

---

[142] 245 US 60 (1917).
[143] 334 US 1 (1948).
[144] Reed and Murdoch (2008) at 1.11–1.13.
[145] *X* v *FRG* (1956) 1 YB 201 – failure of West German Government to provide East German refugee with a home.
[146] *Chapman* v *UK* (2001) 10 BHRC 48.

Court of Human Rights determined in a Portuguese application concerning the requirement that a lease could be terminated only if the landlord required to live in the property themselves: "effective protection of respect for private and family life cannot require the existence in national law of legal protection enabling each family to have a home for themselves".[147]

Article 6 covers the rule of law and provides a right to a "fair and public hearing": "In the determination of his civil rights and obligations or of any criminal charge against him everyone is entitled to a fair and public hearing within a reasonable time by an independent and impartial tribunal established by law."

The Human Rights Act 1998 came into force in October 2000. UK legislation must be interpreted in accordance with Convention rights.[148] It is also provided that the Convention shall have direct or "vertical" effect[149] and provides a remedy in local courts rather than requiring to take a case to the Court of Human Rights in Strasbourg.

The issue of human rights violation has been raised in Scotland on a number of occasions in relation to housing matters. In *Glasgow City Council* v *Al-Abassi* the local authority sought to evict a tenant for anti-social behaviour.[150] The tenant had noisy and violent children who spat and urinated in the common close. She also used a barbecue to heat her house and threw her rubbish out of the window. She had flooded her downstairs neighbours' properties on several occasions. She lived on the top floor of a tenement flat in Woodlands Road, Glasgow. It was argued that the eviction breached the tenant's right to a family life found in Art 8 of the Human Rights Act 1998. The sheriff noted that there was a balance to be struck between the rights of Ms Al-Abassi and the interests of other people. Sheriff Cathcart noted that Ms Al-Abassi had a right to respect for her private and family life, home and correspondence but was satisfied that interference with these rights through eviction was justified under Art 8(2).[151]

It was also suggested that a breach of the right to life in terms of Art 2 had occurred where a landlord commenced eviction proceedings against one of its tenant's neighbours, with tragic consequences.[152] James Drummond was moved by his landlords, Glasgow District Council, in May 1985, after anti-social activities including attacking his neighbours with a tyre lever. Things did not improve at the new address with new neighbours. The police arrested him and imprisoned him on several

---

147 *Velosa Barreto* v *Portugal* [1996] EHRLR 211.
148 Human Rights Act 1998 (HRA 1998), ss 3 and 4.
149 *Ibid*, s 7.
150 *Glasgow City Council* v *Al-Abassi* 2001 Hous LR 23.
151 *Ibid* at 33.
152 *Mitchell* v *Glasgow City Council* [2009] 1 AC 874.

occasions for abusive behaviour. He threatened to kill his neighbour, James Mitchell. He had also attacked his neighbour, battering his door, breaking his windows and again threatening to kill him. Finally, in March 1995, the local authority warned Drummond that it would seek to recover possession of the house if his conduct persisted. He repeated the death threats to his neighbour at least once a month. The police continued to call and arrest him. After a further charge of breach of the peace in January 2001 the local authority served a notice of proceedings for recovery of possession. Following further incidents, it arranged a meeting on 31 July 2001 at which it explained that it was commencing repossession proceedings against Drummond. It did not tell Mr Mitchell about this meeting. Some time later in the afternoon of the day of the meeting, Drummond attacked Mr Mitchell with an iron bar, resulting in Mr Mitchell's death. In the court action taken by Mr Mitchell's widow and daughter against the District Council, the principal issue was whether the local authority was vicariously liable at common law for the actions of its tenant, Drummond. In addition it was suggested that there had been a breach of Mr Mitchell's right to life. Neither claim was successful. The House of Lords explained that everyone's right to life should be protected by law and that appropriate steps must be taken by public authorities to safeguard the lives of those within their jurisdiction. The House adopted the "real and immediate" test elaborated in *Osman*.[153] While this might sometimes imply an obligation to take preventive operational measures, this had to be looked at in the context of modern society

> "bearing in mind the difficulties involved in policing modern societies, the unpredictability of human conduct and the operational choices which must be made in terms of priorities and resources, such an obligation must be interpreted in a way that does not impose an impossible or disproportionate burden on the authorities".[154]

More specifically:

> "It must be established to the [court's] satisfaction that the authorities knew or ought to have known at the time of the existence of a real and immediate risk to the life of an identified individual or individuals from the criminal acts of a third party and that they have failed to take measures within the scope of their powers which, judged reasonably, might have been expected to avoid that risk."[155]

The House explained the relevant questions which the representatives of Mr Mitchell had to deal with in their claim that the landlord local authority

---

[153] *Osman* v *United Kingdom* (1998) 29 EHRR 245.
[154] *Ibid* at para 116.
[155] *Ibid*.

knew or ought to have known that there was a real and immediate risk to
Mr Mitchell's life on the day he was killed:

> "The pursuers assert that 'the defenders knew or ought to have that there
> was a real and immediate risk'. But the defenders can only know something
> through the mind of one or more of their officials. The pursuers do not say
> who these officials were or by whom this knowledge was demonstrated."[156]

Looking, then, to the question that the local authority landlord "ought
to have known", this was rejected on a simple pragmatic basis of
probability:

> "These events must, of course, be viewed in their whole context. The long
> history of Drummond's behaviour must be taken into account as well
> as what took place at the meeting on 31 July 2001. Two facts stand out
> from this history. The first is that Drummond had threatened to kill the
> deceased on countless occasions during the past six and a half years. But
> he had never actually used violence against him, apart from the incident in
> December 1994 when he damaged his door and broke his windows. The
> second is that, while Drummond lost his temper at the meeting and was
> abusive, he is not said to have uttered any threats against the deceased or
> to have been armed with any kind of weapon. In short he did not say or do
> anything to alert the defenders to a risk that he would attack the deceased
> when he got home, let alone that he would inflict injuries from which he
> might die."[157]

There does not appear to have been a weighing-up of what standard
good practice is in such circumstances. As indicated elsewhere in this
text,[158] when serving such sensitive orders as interim exclusion orders, it
is standard practice to advise the victim that there may be consequences
where the recipient has been violent in the past. Given the relative rarity
of possession proceedings leading to actual eviction, and the history in this
instance, the District Council appears to have been treated remarkably
generously by their Lordships.

Some interesting case law from English courts is also worth noting
since it covers issues which are pertinent in Scotland. The right to
respect for a person's home under Art 8 did not prevent eviction using
the accelerated procedure available for the English equivalent of short
assured tenancies:[159] the shorthold assured tenancy. Eviction was accepted
as having an impact on family life but the procedure for bringing an end to
the tenancy was regarded as proportionate and a matter where Parliament
had legislated:

---

[156] *Mitchell* v *Glasgow City Council* [2009] 1 AC 874 at 891.
[157] *Ibid.*
[158] See Chapter 10 below.
[159] See Chapter 3 below.

"This is an area where ... the courts must treat the decisions of Parliament as to what is in the public interest with particular deference ... the correctness of this decision is more appropriate for Parliament than the courts and the HRA does not require the courts to disregard the decisions of Parliament in relation to situations of this sort when deciding whether there has been a breach of the Convention."[160]

The same kind of speedy eviction process in the social rented sector was also treated as not breaching the Convention since there were the interests of other tenants and neighbours to consider when there were problems of rent arrears and anti-social behaviour.[161]

OVERVIEW

Scots law that deals with the necessary commodity of housing, then, has altered in many ways in the past century. The regulation of the contracts of individuals to buy and rent housing has varied. As we have noted, in addition to the more familiar constraints of the Rent Acts and Housing Acts, there is also now regulation of the behaviour of citizens to protect their fellows from some forms of discrimination and abuse of recognised human rights. While the picture is still scarred by homelessness, poor-quality housing and various forms of abuse, the majority resident in Scotland in 2010 have greater protection than their forebears enjoyed in 1910. The remaining chapters seek to explain the extent and nature

---

[160] *Poplar Housing and Regeneration Community Association Ltd* v *Donoghue* [2001] EWCA Civ 595 at para 69.
[161] *McLellan* v *Bracknell Forest* [2002] 1 All ER 899.

2   ACCESS TO HOUSING AND HOMELESSNESS

BACKGROUND

The shift to urban locations of rural workers in the 18th century was marked. Hitherto, town growth had been modest. Glasgow's population rose from 30,000 in 1770 to some 77,000 in 1800.[1] Between 1851 and 1911 the population increased from 329,096 to 784,496.[2] The speed of the expansion led to pressures on accommodation which meant that by the turn of the 20th century the level of overcrowding in Scotland was 45.1 per cent as compared with England's 9.1 per cent.[3]

The response to the needs of incoming single workers included the provision of commercial and municipal lodging houses. Glasgow City Council built six Model Lodging Houses for men and one for women by 1900.[4] The private rented sector used references from factors. These were obtainable from the previous landlord's agent or factor.[5] Access to the better kind of housing was, thus, controlled through the requirement for tenants of potential landlords to produce "factors' lines". These were recommendations as to the past conduct of the tenant in terms of rent payment and treatment of the property. Without these, Sim records, obtaining housing was almost impossible.

Various Victorian philanthropists in Britain sought to produce local solutions to the problems they observed in their areas through erection and management of housing, such as Joseph Peabody and Octavia Hill. Their contribution throughout Britain was limited in terms of volume but showed that money could be made in the rental sector through effective management.[6] In Scotland there was a similar pattern of private sector intervention.[7]

---

[1] Dr Irene Maver, University of Glasgow, at http://www.theglasgowstory.com/story. php?id=TGSCA [last visited 19 May 2010].
[2] Butt (1973).
[3] Rodger (1989) at 27–29; for more recent developments, see Paice (2008).
[4] Laidlaw (1955).
[5] Sim (1995).
[6] Hill (1998).
[7] See Robson (1979) on the Glasgow Kyrle Society, Edinburgh and Dundee Social Unions at 24ff.

The call for municipal intervention was made within the nascent Labour movement during the 19th century, although housing was not an issue which dominated local branch activity.[8] In Glasgow, the drive for provision of housing was rather more successful. Through town councillors such as John Wheatley, some progress was made and can still be seen in the city in the 21st century in the High Street, in the Saltmarket and at Charing Cross.[9]

MODERN DEVELOPMENTS

There are two principal statutory developments which have affected the access individuals have to housing. These are rights of access and homelessness provisions.

Access

There were no restrictions on who a private landlord might select as a tenant. Decisions, as noted, might be taken on economic grounds or might reflect prejudices. The influential Milner Holland Report as late as 1965 noted that a "colour bar" was operated by many private landlords.[10]

Prior to 1980 there was no specific legal framework for tenants of social landlords. The courts indicated prior to the introduction of this 1980 legislation that local authorities had no limitations imposed on their right to repossess properties rented out to tenants. In 1978 in *Kelly* v *Cannock Chase District Council* the Court of Appeal noted that if an authority wished to evict someone who had paid her rent regularly and been a good tenant there was no legal impediment to this.[11]

This unregulated situation has been altered by two forms of statutory intervention. In the first place, as was noted in the previous chapter, there are now restrictions on discrimination on the grounds of race, colour, nationality, ethnic or national origin, sex, sexual preference, religious belief and age. In simple terms this means that landlords, whether in the private sector or the social rented sector, do not have full freedom of choice. They may not refuse to allocate on the grounds covered by the discrimination legislation. Establishing that there has been discrimination may be a rather harder issue to overcome and, as recently as April 2010, it seemed that there was encouragement from within the Conservative Party for bed and breakfast owners who wished to discriminate against same-sex couples.[12]

---

8   Robson (1979) at 268ff.
9   *Ibid* at 281ff.
10   Milner Holland Report (1965) at 188ff.
11   [1978] 1 WLR 1 at 10 per Lawton LJ.
12   Chris Grayling, Shadow Home Secretary, sympathised with constituents who refused to accept the booking of a same-sex couple in their boarding house. In the ensuing media storm he denied he was in favour of allowing discrimination against same-sex

There are also restrictions on how social rented housing may be allocated. Following acceptance of the recommendations of the 1980 SHAC Report, "Allocation and Transfer of Council Housing",[13] there have been limitations on how social landlords operate their waiting lists and their transfer policies. The Housing (Scotland) Act 1987, as amended in 2001 and 2003, currently regulates the restrictions on social landlords in determining whom they select as tenants. This operates in three ways.

1. ACCESSING SOCIAL HOUSING

(i) Admission to a housing list

There are common rules governing access to housing belonging to local authorities as well as registered social landlords (RSLs).[14] The matters proscribed reflect some of the practices encountered by authorities in operating their housing lists prior to 1980, with policies excluding the well off and those with any savings, former owner occupiers and young people. In addition, there was the practice of counting debts of the tenant as those of the rest of the family. These policies were not malicious but rather local versions of what were perceived to be allocating according to need. In admitting people to their housing lists social landlords – local authorities and RSLs – now must take no account of

(a) the age of the applicant, provided that he or she has attained 16 years of age;[15] or

(b) the income of the applicant or his family;[16] or

(c) whether any applicant was previously an owner occupier or owned moveable property and whatever the value of such property was;[17] or

(d) any outstanding debt attributable to the tenancy of the house, such as rent arrears or other debt not owed by the tenant;[18] or

(e) whether the applicant was living in the same house as his spouse or partner.[19]

---

couples but indicated "However, this is a difficult area and on Wednesday I made comments which reflected my view that we must be sensitive to the genuinely held principles of faith groups in this country" (April 2010). In the Con–Lib coalition Government formed in May 2010, Grayling became only a Junior Minister – bizarrely, with responsibility for employment.

13 Scottish Development Department (1980).
14 RSLs were added by the Housing (Scotland) Act 2001 (HSA 2001), ss 9 and 10.
15 HSA 1987, s 19(1)(a).
16 *Ibid*, s 19(1)(b).
17 *Ibid*, s 19(1)(c).
18 *Ibid*, s 19(1)(d).
19 *Ibid*, s 19(1)(e).

(ii) Residence rules

One way in which local authorities and housing associations in the past used to give an advantage to those born in their areas was to have rules of residential qualification prior to being admitted to the housing list. The periods were quite extensive and effectively precluded many would-be applicants. The need for a period of residence to qualify for entry onto the waiting list is still permitted but there are now restrictions on this practice. Admission to the common housing registers which must be kept[20] shall take no account of residence in the area for those who have:

(a) employment in the area of the local authority;[21] or

(b) an offer of employment in the area of the local authority;[22] or

(c) a wish to move to into the area of the local authority to seek employment;[23] or

(d) a wish, having reached the age of 60, to move into the area to be near a younger relative;[24] or

(e) special social or medical reasons for needing to be housed in the area.[25]

It should be borne in mind that what we are talking about here is simply *admission* to the waiting list. There is no guarantee that once a person is on the waiting list they will be allocated a property. This depends on the mechanism which the local authority operates to determine priority.

2. TENANT SELECTION FROM THE HOUSING LIST

There are three limitations on how the local authority may select from those on its waiting list.

(i) General discrimination rules

As indicated, there are now limitations on the allocation of goods or services on the grounds of race, colour, nationality, ethnic or national origin, sex, sexual preference, religious belief and age.[26]

(ii) Restrictions on allocation

In the allocation of social rented housing social landlords – local authorities and RSLs – must take no account of certain factors. These reinforce the

---

[20] HSA 1987, s 8 – when required to do so.
[21] *Ibid*, s 19(2)(a).
[22] *Ibid*, s 19(2)(b).
[23] *Ibid*, s 19(2)(c).
[24] *Ibid*, s 19(2)(d).
[25] *Ibid*, s 19(2)(e).
[26] See Chapter 1 above at p 14.

issues covered under admission to the waiting list. An authority may not allow people onto the waiting list who are, for example, non-residents, and then penalise them at the allocation stage. Nor can a past bad payment record be used as a blanket excuse for refusal to allocate. Social landlords may not penalise applicants for debts paid off, or not owed by them or under the value of 1 month's rent. Age is irrelevant except where the allocation of sheltered housing is concerned. The allocation policies which are operated must take no account of:

(i)   the length of time for which an applicant has resided in the authority's area;[27] or

(ii) any outstanding debt attributable to the tenancy of the house, such as rent arrears or other debt not owed by the tenant;[28] or

(iii) any outstanding debt attributable to the applicant's tenancy of the house, such as rent arrears or other debt which is no longer outstanding;[29] or

(iv) any arrears of rent or other debt which are no more than 1 month's liability;[30] or

(v)   any outstanding debt of the applicant (or any other person who it is proposed will reside in the property) which is not attributable to the tenancy of the house;[31] or

(vi) the age of the applicant, provided that he has attained 16 years of age, unless the allocation relates to houses designed for or substantially adapted for occupation by persons of a particular age group;[32] or

(vii) the income of the applicant and his family;[33]

(viii) whether, or to what value, any applicant or member of the family was previously a property owner or owned moveable property.[34]

In addition, prior to treating an applicant as eligible for the allocation of housing, there is a limitation on the requirements which can be lawfully imposed. This is to counter past policies where local authorities imposed a "back door" residence requirement. Allocation from the housing waiting list shall take no account of residence in the area if an applicant:

---

[27] HSA 1987, s 20(2)(a)(i).
[28] *Ibid*, s 20(2)(a)(ii).
[29] *Ibid*, s 20(2)(a)(iii).
[30] *Ibid*, s 20(2)(a)(iv).
[31] *Ibid*, s 20(2)(a)(v).
[32] *Ibid*, s 20(2)(a)(vi).
[33] *Ibid*, s 20(2)(a)(vii).
[34] *Ibid*, s 20(2)(a)(viii).

(a) is employed or has been offered employment in the area;[35] or

(b) wishes to move to into the area to seek employment;[36] or

(c) wishes to move into the area to be near a relative or carer;[37] or

(d) has special social or medical reasons for requiring to be housed in the area;[38] or

(e) is subject to harassing conduct[39] and wishes to move to the area;[40] or

(f) runs the risk of domestic violence[41] and wishes to move into the area.[42]

Finally, some social landlords, in the past, required an applicant for accommodation following an alleged relationship breakdown to "prove" the fact of the breakdown by showing that they had formally ended the relationship through obtaining a divorce or separation. Neither this nor the practice of requiring an applicant to leave the matrimonial home before there can be allocation is now lawful. It is now not permitted to require that:

(i) an application must have remained in force for a minimum period;[43] or

(ii) a divorce or judicial separation be obtained;[44] or

(iii) the applicant no longer be living with, or in the same house as, some other person.[45]

(iii) Reasonable preference

Having made clear what kinds of allocation practices authorities may not indulge in, there is a requirement on local authorities to favour certain groups in the allocation process. There has been, since its introduction in 1935,[46] a requirement that a "reasonable preference" be given to people:

(i) occupying houses below the tolerable standard;[47] or

(ii) occupying overcrowded houses;[48] or

---

[35] HSA 1987, s 20(2)(aa)(i).

[36] *Ibid*, s 20(2)(aa)(ii).

[37] *Ibid*, s 20(2)(aa)(iii).

[38] *Ibid*, s 20(2)(aa)(iv).

[39] In terms of s 8 of the Protection from Harassment Act 1997.

[40] HSA 1987, s 20(2)(aa)(v).

[41] In terms of *ibid*, s 33(3) – see below at p 49.

[42] *Ibid*, s 20(2)(aa)(vi).

[43] *Ibid*, s 20(2)(b)(i).

[44] *Ibid*.

[45] *Ibid*.

[46] Introduced by the Housing (Scotland) Act 1935, s 47(2).

[47] HSA 1987, ss 2(1)(a)(i) and 86, and amended by HSA 2001, s 102.

[48] HSA 1987, s 20(1)(a)(ii) and Pt VII (ss 135–137).

(iii) having large families;[49]
(iv) living under unsatisfactory housing conditions;[50]
(v) to whom is owed a duty under the homeless persons legislation.[51]

This duty to give "reasonable preference" has been described by a leading commentator as "extremely vague" and unlikely to lead to a successful judicial review application.[52] There have been attempts, using the equivalent legislation in England: the Housing Act 1996. Specifically in relation to the reasonable preference to be given to homeless people and those in houses below the tolerable standard and with large families and so on outlined above,[53] the Court of Appeal has talked about this giving such applicants "a reasonable head start".[54] It has been pointed out that a person could have a reasonable preference but never in fact be allocated accommodation.[55] The courts have determined that if there is an allocation scheme, then it does not require to afford priority between those classes of persons to whom a reasonable preference must be given. If, however, it does afford priority then this will only be unlawful if the basis on which it affords priority can be faulted is irrationality.[56] Thus the House of Lords took the view that providing higher priority for one group of homeless people than another was not, on the face of it, lawful.[57] Birmingham had been putting those who were homeless because it was not reasonable for them to continue to occupy their current accommodation in a different priority group from those who were housed by it in temporary accommodation. The House of Lords indicated that such a scheme, which conferred priority on applicants who had been provided with temporary accommodation over applicants who were left temporarily in their existing homes, was unlawful.[58]

The SEDD guidance to the 2001 Act provides the following explanation for "reasonable preference":

"Reasonable preference" refers to the priority given to applicants for housing. It means that local authorities and RSLs should give due weight to the factors listed above, but it does not restrict authorities to taking only such factors into account. Landlords could add other factors of their own. ... However, an authority or RSL should not allow its own secondary

---

[49] HSA 1987, s 20(1)(a)(iii).
[50] *Ibid*, s 20(1)(a)(iv).
[51] *Ibid*, s 20(1)(b).
[52] Watchman (1991) at 35.
[53] HSA 1987, s 20 at nn 47–51 above.
[54] *R v Wolverhampton MBC* [1997] 29 HLR 931 at 938 per Judge LJ.
[55] *R (on the application of Mei Ling Lin) v Barnet LBC* [2007] HLR 30.
[56] *R (on the application of Ahmad) v Newham LBC* [2009] HLR 31.
[57] *Ali v Birmingham City Council* [2009] 41 HLR 727 at 750 per Baroness Hale.
[58] *Ibid* at 750.

criteria to dominate its allocation scheme at the expense of factors in the statutory list."[59]

In addition to the "reasonable preference" category looked at in the courts in England, the Allocation Policy Advisory Group has discussed its status in the context of prioritising individual housing need, with a view to clarifying uncertainty in this area.[60] The Scottish Government research identified a number of issues in relation to "reasonable preference". There were difficulties with the interpretation of the phrase, with no clear definition and differing interpretations causing confusion among landlords at a local level. Questions were raised about the relevance of the specification of "reasonable preference" categories, given the demand for social rented housing. Also, tensions were reported by landlords in responding to their obligations in relation to homelessness and to other "reasonable preference" categories as well as between meeting "reasonable preference" obligations, particularly in relation to homelessness, and giving appropriate access to other applicants.[61]

Specifically, there were questions as to how RSLs could meet reasonable preference responsibilities in relation to applicants on their own housing lists while responding to s 5 referrals from local authorities in their areas.[62] This was particularly relevant for landlords operating in areas of stock transfer, where reliance on local RSLs to meet homelessness obligations was greater. Also, it was not clear in what circumstances an applicant, not in a reasonable preference category, could be given priority in the allocation of a property. The issue of the level of priority which should be given to "cumulative need" was also raised. Where an applicant had needs from more than one category, did, for example, an applicant who was overcrowded and living in Below Tolerable Standard (BTS) housing have a higher priority than an applicant who was overcrowded? Social landlords also reported difficulties with interpreting "reasonable preference" categories, in particular the meaning of "large families" and "unsatisfactory housing conditions" of which there is currently no actual legal definition.

The Scottish Government Research recommended that guidance should set out the scope of local decision making in relation to allocation, particularly in relation to prioritising individual housing need and good practice examples on systems and processes, such as quotas, where a balance is achieved between housing homeless households, those in reasonable preference groups and those outwith the reasonable preference categories.

---

[59] SEDD Circular 1/2002, "Housing Lists and Allocations".
[60] Allocations Policy Advisory Group, 27 March 2009, Meeting – Paper 1 (Report of 9 September 2009).
[61] "Tensions Between Allocations Policy and Practice" (TBAPP) (2007) at 32.
[62] Housing (Scotland) Act 2001, s 5 – see below at p 58.

In the meantime, of course, as is noted above, the requirement for local authorities and RSLs to meet Scottish Housing Regulator Performance Standards impacts upon practice.[63] Under the Performance Standards social landlords are expected to meet and be inspected against the following standards in relation to "reasonable preference":

"AS1.2 Lettings – We let houses in a way that gives reasonable preference to those in greatest housing need; makes best use of available stock; maximises choice; and helps to sustain communities."

In addition, self-assessment questions for AS1.2 ask about the landlord's definition of housing need, giving priority and equality of access. For example:

"I.   Do our allocation policies, procedures and practices comply fully with legislative requirements?
II.   Does our definition of housing need fully accommodate statutory definitions?
III. Is our definition of housing need supported by a robust analysis of the needs of a full range of our service users?
IV.   Do we give priority to applicants in housing need?
V.   Do our allocation policies and practices positively contribute to the prevention, and resolution, of homelessness?
VI.   Does our policy accommodate mobility issues for tenants with changing support needs?
VII. Do we ensure equality of access for all applicants to our full range of housing stock?"

Guidance can be expected in due course which meets the aim of providing advice on assessing the relative priority of the applicants, cumulative need and the approaches, including quotas, in order to support landlords to appropriately balance the needs of homeless households, other reasonable preference groups and other groups in housing need.

3. PUBLICATION OF RULES

There is also a requirement of transparency in relation to the publication of any rules a social landlord has covering admission to the waiting list, priority of allocation of houses, transfer of tenants to those of another housing body and exchange of houses.[64]

The development of access to housing rules and policies

It is most helpful to look at the different sectors, since the development of access rules have been so different. In the dominant private rented sector,

---

[63]   See Chapter 8 below.
[64]   HSA 1987, s 21(1) and (2).

prior to the introduction of the Rent Acts in 1915 there were no restrictions on how landlords determined who their next tenants would be.

The shortage of housing meant that landlords were in a position to charge a premium for anyone taking over when a tenancy fell vacant, with demand for vacant housing meaning that "key money" would be charged. This was proscribed in the early Rent Acts.[65]

An alternative mechanism for benefiting from the combination of high demand exceeding supply and restrictions on what rents could be charged through the Rent Acts was to charge potential tenants for finding the accommodation. The abuse of this practice was countered by the Accommodation Agencies Act 1953. This little-known piece of legislation sought to prevent the payment of indirect "key money" which would have undermined the Rent Acts, although it does not make any appearance in any reported case law.

As far as municipal housing was concerned, the Housing, Town Planning etc Act 1919 required local authorities to assess the need for "houses for the working classes" in their areas and to prepare a scheme to meet the identified needs.[66]

The Government originally provided a central subsidy for general needs housing, that is to say with no restrictions on who was eligible for tenancies of this municipal housing stock. From 1934 onwards, however, subsidies were only available for slum clearance housing. This restriction on municipal housing being provided only "for the working classes" was removed in 1950.

Concern was expressed, however, in the 1950s and 1960s about the way in which local authorities favoured relatives of those already in social rented housing and discouraged allocation to incomers.[67] The consultative document "Scottish Housing" from 1977 recommended the ending of the practice of imposing residential and other qualifications for admission to the waiting list.[68] The Report of the Scottish Housing Advisory Committee in 1980[69] noted that the vast majority of local authorities continued to operate restrictions on access to their waiting lists. The restrictions were based on residential qualifications, age, banning owner occupiers, income limitations and debt. It was with this background, then, that the changes found in the Tenants' Rights etc (Scotland) Act 1980 were introduced which remain with us some 30 years later, as we have noted earlier in this chapter.

---

[65] Increase of Rent and Mortgage Interest (Restrictions) Act 1920, s 8 – restriction on premiums.

[66] Housing, Town Planning etc Act 1919, s 1.

[67] "Choosing Council Tenants" (1957) SHAC (HMSO); "Allocating Council Houses" (1967) SHAC (HMSO).

[68] Cmnd 6852 (HMSO, Edinburgh), para 9.27.

[69] "Allocation and Transfer of Council Houses" (HMSO, 1980), paras 4.1–4.13.

Homelessness

BACKGROUND

In the immediate post-war period one of the responses to the lack of housing was for people to solve the problem of homelessness by squatting in empty property.[70] The courts in Scotland were never called on to test whether or not squatting by those without accommodation could be justified through the claim of necessity. This issue never came to the fore during the squatting movement's activities during the 1960s and 1970s. This may have been because of the existence of the Trespass (Scotland) Act 1865, although it was not a factor affecting the movement in Edinburgh in the late 1960s when actions were being taken to occupy empty British Rail property in Leith.[71] The squatting movement in England did not enjoy any success when it sought to use the "necessity" argument on behalf of homeless applicants. Lord Denning rejected the defence of necessity put forward by a family that was evicted from an empty council house where the family members would be homeless if they were not allowed to squat.[72] Britain went on to lead the world in formal enforceable rights for homeless people not simply to shelter but to be provided with housing. Since devolution, Scotland has developed significantly, expanding the rights of homeless people, and the formal rights seem to be in advance of those in any other system.[73]

The basic structure of the current law was set out in the Housing (Homeless Persons) Act 1977. This statute provided rights for homeless people throughout Great Britain. The legislative framework for England and Wales was subsequently located in the Housing Act 1985 and for Scotland in the Housing (Scotland) Act 1987. The Scottish legislation has been amended by the Housing (Scotland) Act 2001 and the Homelessness etc (Scotland) Act 2003. Guidance on the legislation and appropriate policies and practice advice is contained in Codes of Guidance. The original legislation was implemented in November 1977 in England and Wales and on 1 April 1978 in Scotland. The difference between these dates was to allow for a separate Scottish Code of Guidance to be produced.[74] This was duly published and the most recent Code of Guidance is dated May 2005. The fact that the legislation was originally common to both the Scottish and the English/Welsh jurisdictions and the continued strong resemblance between the tests in the respective legislation means that much of the case law which can be used as guide is drawn from cases

---

[70] Wolmar and Wates (1980).
[71] Author's case notes from Edinburgh Squatting Movement meetings of 1968 and 1969.
[72] *Southwark LBC* v *Williams* [1971] Ch 734.
[73] Yanetta and Edwards (1996) at 178.
[74] Gibson (1979).

heard principally in the courts in England. Wales now has its own "Code of Guidance for Local Authorities on Allocation of Accommodation and Homelessness" (2006) distinct from the "Homelessness Code of Guidance for Local Authorities" (2006) operating in England.[75]

The relatively recent notion of housing rights for homeless people is, of course, related to the issue of access to housing discussed above. While the homelessness legislation lays duties on local authorities and other social landlords to respond to the plight of homeless people, it does this in a slightly oblique way. The statutory obligation is quite specific for those to whom it applies. The local authority must ensure that "accommodation becomes available"[76] or, in the case of those still in a property, "remains available".[77] This includes making property available from the local authority housing stock. When the legislation on which the current regime is based was enacted in 1977, the level of local authority property holdings in Scotland was some 60 per cent. In areas such as Airdrie, Coatbridge and Motherwell the local authority holding was at 80 per cent.[78] Glasgow had at that time some 200,000 units. The assumption was and the practice too was that local authorities would operate their duties using their own stock. Some local authorities, off the record, claimed that they did not operate the intentionality provisions of the legislation because they had so many voids in low-demand estates that they could afford to make offers irrespective of the niceties of the legislation. This assumption of there always being available stock is not accurate. Local authorities in England have shed much of their housing and the trend has been continued in Scotland until very recently. The sale of local authority under the right to buy legislation, allied to the push for smaller managements units, has led to the large-scale de-municipalisation of housing in Scotland.[79]

This former stock is now either privately owned and is unlikely to be available for rent or is owned and run by RSLs. There is now a provision enabling local authorities who have obligations to homeless applicants to request an RSL which holds houses in its area to provide accommodation for a person.[80] A corresponding obligation rests on the RSL to comply with such a request within a reasonable period.[81]

---

[75] The number of reported cases from Wales has been limited albeit striking – *R* v *Preseli DC, ex p Fisher* (1984) 17 HLR 147 (councillors ignoring the advice of their housing department to pursue an anti-traveller policy); *R* v *Swansea City Council, ex p Thomas* (1983) 9 HLR 64 (man deemed responsible for actions of his family while he was in prison).

[76] HSA 1987, s 31.

[77] *Ibid*, s 29.

[78] Rodger (1989); SDD (1980).

[79] Goodlad (2001).

[80] HSA 2001, s 5(1).

[81] *Ibid*, s 5(3) – see below at p 58.

MODERN LEGAL RIGHTS AND OBLIGATIONS

The original British legislation, the Housing (Homeless Persons) Act 1977, is no longer in force and the current Scottish legislative framework is in the Housing (Scotland) Act 1987, Pt II, as amended by Pt I of the Housing (Scotland) Act 2001 and the Homelessness etc (Scotland) Act 2003.[82] The legislation places obligations on local authorities to deal with applications from homeless applicants who are given specific rights. The local authorities must make enquiries and have a duty to provide interim accommodation pending a final decision. They must also seek to prevent homelessness as well as providing advice and assistance. Any applicant must have the capacity to apply as homeless. Any vulnerable person (including those with mental incapacity) and those reasonably expected to live with them have priority need status and should benefit from the provisions of the legislation. The law allows that they or their co-habitants can make the application. There is, however, no statutory duty owed to children or disabled persons who have the capacity neither to make an application themselves, or to authorise an agent to make an application on their behalf.[83]

The original concept of the legislation limited the obligations to a definite set of people. Some of these hurdles are common-sense ones while others are rationing devices to ensure that only certain kinds of applicants qualify. Applicants have to meet criteria in relation four issues:

    (i) homelessness;
    (ii) priority need;
    (iii) intentionality;
    (iv) local connection.

(i) Homelessness

Both those who are homeless and those who are threatened with homelessness are covered. The latter is defined as covering those likely to become homeless within 2 months.[84] The homelessness definitions cover those who are roofless as well as those who have some form of accommodation but where there are severe limitations. The legislation encompasses both situations, defining a person as being homeless when

> "He or she has no accommodation in the United Kingdom or elsewhere[85] which he or she (together with any person who usually resides with the

---

[82] The equivalent legislative provisions for England and Wales are the Housing Act 1996 and the Homelessness Act 2002.

[83] *R* v *Tower Hamlets LBC, ex p Ferdous Begum* [1993] QB 447.

[84] HSA 1987, s 24(4) – originally the period was 1 month.

[85] Originally the reference was to "no accommodation in Scotland or England or Wales".

applicant as a family member, or in circumstances which the local authority considers it is reasonable for that person to reside with the applicant) is entitled or permitted to occupy."[86]

Family

Membership of the family is defined by s 83 of HSA 1987 to include:

(i) a spouse of that person or those living together as husband or wife or the same-sex equivalent;[87]
(ii) parents and grandparents;
(iii) children, step-children or grandchildren;
(iv) brothers and sisters;
(v) uncles and aunts;
(vi) nephews and nieces.

Relationships by marriage are treated as if by blood, so that a parent-in-law is to be treated as a parent. Half-blood relationships are also treated as if they were of the whole blood, so that two men with a shared mother are regarded as members of each other's family. Local authorities are urged to be aware of the complex family structures that exist in practice with step-families, foster relationships and other established relationships.[88]

Reasonable for a person to reside

In addition to family members the legislation provides that a person is homeless if there is no accommodation for the applicant and "any other person who resides with him … in circumstances which the local authority consider it reasonable for that person to reside with him".[89] "Households split up for no reason than that they have nowhere to live should be treated as one household."[90] People who might reasonably be expected to so reside with the applicant would include dependent foster children, carers or other companions.[91]

Whether or not a child might reasonably be expected to reside with an applicant is a matter for the local authority to decide, taking into account any residence or contact orders made by the courts.[92] It seems clear, however, that the local authority's decision should not be dictated by any decision made by a court dealing with family law questions.[93]

---

[86] HSA 1987, s 24.
[87] Introduced by HSA 2001, s 108.
[88] Code of Guidance (2005), para 5.5.
[89] HSA 1987, s 24(2).
[90] COG 2005, para 5.8.
[91] *Ibid.*
[92] COG 2005, para 5.9.
[93] *Holmes-Moorhouse* v *Richmond upon Thames LBC* [2009] HLR 34.

Reasonable to continue to occupy

Even where a person has accommodation it might be unreasonable to expect them to continue to occupy that accommodation. The Code notes that, for instance, caravans and mobile homes may not be suitable for someone with "physical impairments".[94] The local authority, in deciding what is reasonable, must have regard to the general circumstances prevailing in the area[95] but the Code suggests that the "unreasonable accommodation" test would cover accommodation below the tolerable standard, bed and breakfast accommodation, hostel[96] or other accommodation, or where there is external violence, including racial or other harassment.[97] In a case in 2009 the House of Lords confirmed the position, established as far back as 1982, that a woman who left her home because of domestic (or other) violence remained homeless even if she found temporary respite in a women's refuge.[98] They did, however, limit this to "in most cases" and suggested, in a chilling *obiter* statement, that whether a room in a women's refuge could amount to "accommodation" for the purposes of the legislation was a decision for another day.[99]

Other homeless categories

(a) A person is also homeless if they have accommodation but they cannot secure entry to it.[100] Typically, this arises where they have been evicted unlawfully and the landlord changes the locks.

(b) In addition, where an attempt to continue to live in the accommodation would be likely to be met with violence or threats of violence from someone else living in it, or from someone who previously lived with the applicant, whether in that accommodation or elsewhere.[101]

(c) Also, where a person has mobile home caravan, houseboat or other moveable structure but has no place to put it, moor it and live in it.[102]

---

[94] COG 2005, para 5.11.
[95] HSA 1987, s 24(2B).
[96] *Pace* G Brown (September 29 2009) where the then Prime Minister, in a speech to the 2009 Labour Party Conference, suggested that hostel accommodation would be provided henceforth for single mothers: http://news.bbc.co.uk/1/hi/uk_politics/8283198.stm. The pronouncement did not bear fruit.
[97] COG 2005, para 5.13.
[98] *Moran* v *Manchester City Council* [2009] 41 HLR at 727.
[99] *Ibid* at 748.
[100] HSA 1987, s 24(3)(a).
[101] *Ibid*, s 24(3)(b) and (bb).
[102] *Ibid*, s 24(3)(c).

(d) Where accommodation is both statutorily overcrowded and possibly a danger to health.[103]

(e) Finally, where the accommodation is not permanent accommodation, in circumstances where, immediately before the commencement of the occupation of it, a local authority had a duty under the Act and has provided temporary accommodation.[104]

When is it not reasonable for an applicant to continue to occupy a house?

The Code of Guidance notes that in terms of s 24(2B) a local authority may have regard to the general circumstances prevailing in relation to housing in the local authority's area, in determining whether it is reasonable for a person to continue to occupy accommodation.[105] Different tests of "reasonableness" should not be applied to different categories of applicant, for example applications from private tenants should be dealt with on the same basis as those from tenants of local authorities or RSLs. The Code provides some examples of how the "unreasonable to occupy" test might be applied:

"The applicant is living in bed and breakfast accommodation, which is not overcrowded within the meaning of Part VII of the 1987 Act. Bed and breakfast accommodation should be used only as a last resort in the absence of other options, particularly for households with vulnerable people. In fulfilment of their duties under section 29 of the 1987 Act, local authorities cannot place households with children and pregnant women into unsuitable accommodation unless exceptional circumstances apply, where both unsuitable accommodation and exceptional circumstances are defined in the relevant legislation (the Homeless Persons (Unsuitable Accommodation) (Scotland) Order 2004).

The applicant is living in a hostel or other accommodation such as a women's refuge, which is not intended to provide long-stay accommodation. Often there will be a fixed limit to the time a person can stay. The same general point applies to caravans and mobile homes without a permanent or long-term site.

There is external violence, including racial or other harassment. Local authorities should respond sympathetically to applications from people who are in fear of external violence. The absence of previous violence does not prove that these fears are unjustified."[106]

---

[103] HSA 1987, s 24(3)(d) – response to House of Lords in *Puhlhofer* – see Robson and Poustie (1996) at 133ff.

[104] HSA 1987, s 24(3)(e) – response to House of Lords in *R v Brent LBC, ex p Awua* [1996] AC 55 HL.

[105] COG 2005, para 5.12.

[106] *Ibid*, para 5.13.

(ii) Priority need[107]

This is a category in transition. Originally in the 1977 legislation, and in the current 1987 version of the local authority obligations, there is a list of those who are considered in priority need and to whom a duty lies. Those outwith this list, such as single healthy adults, have traditionally been entitled only to advice and assistance, rather than to have accommodation secured for them. The Homelessness Task Force, in its Final Report, recommended that this distinction be eliminated. The Homelessness etc (Scotland) Act 2003 set a target date of 2012.[108]

At present, the following groups have a statutory priority need for housing (subject to their satisfying the other tests described in this chapter – homelessness; intentionality; and local connection).

(a) *Pregnant* woman or a person with whom a pregnant woman resides or might reasonably be expected to reside.

(b) Where a person is *vulnerable* as a result of:
old age;
mental illness;
personality disorder;
learning disability;
physical disability;
chronic ill health;
having suffered a miscarriage or undergone an abortion;
having been discharged from a hospital, a prison or any part of
    the regular armed forces of the Crown; or
other special reason.

(c) Victim of an emergency such as fire flood or any other disaster.

(d) Person aged 16 or 17.

(e) Person aged 18–20 who, by reason of the circumstances in which they are living, runs the risk of sexual or financial exploitation or involvement in the serious misuse of alcohol.

(f) Person who runs the *risk of domestic abuse*, which includes violence, harassment, threatening conduct, and any other conduct giving rise to, or likely to give rise to, physical or mental injury, fear, alarm or distress.[109]

(g) A person who runs the risk, by reason of that person's religion, sexual orientation, race, colour or ethnic or national origin, of violence or is, likely to be, the victim of a course of conduct amounting to *harassment*.[110] "Conduct" includes speech and presence in a

---

107 HSA 1987, s 25.
108 HSA 2003, s 3(2)(a).
109 HSA 1987, s 25 (as amended).
110 *Ibid.*

specified place or area.[111] "Harassment" includes causing a person alarm or distress and a "course of conduct" must involve conduct on at least two occasions.[112]

The Code also points out that the legislation does not require that the children should be living with the applicant at the time of the applicant's request for assistance. They might, for instance, be living temporarily with other relatives because of the applicant's homelessness, or the applicant might be seeking a residence order and waiting for a legal decision, and such children would usually "reasonably be expected" to live with the applicant. The starting assumption should be, it is suggested, that it is reasonable that an applicant's children should live with the applicant; and the practice of splitting families because of their homelessness is not acceptable, even for short periods.[113]

Vulnerability

The Court of Appeal, in the early days of the legislation, suggested a definition of vulnerability:

> "A person is considered vulnerable when they are less able to fend for themselves so that they may suffer in a situation where another homeless person would be able to cope without suffering."[114]

Assessing whether or not an applicant is vulnerable involves, then, a comparison between a person who can cope and one who cannot cope. The Scottish courts have recognised that being made homeless in itself produces a degree of vulnerability but have accepted this notion of the person who has more of a problem than others:

> "It can plausibly be said that everyone is to some extent vulnerable when made homeless ... in assessing vulnerability for the purposes of section 25(1)(c), a comparative assessment requires to be carried out ... The comparison is between the applicant and the 'assumed average or normal or run-of-the-mill homeless person'."[115]

In a case involving a woman with a history of drug abuse, for instance, Lord Glennie confirmed that the person with whom an allegedly vulnerable applicant was to be assessed was another homeless person.[116] The fact that the applicant's key worker, a community nurse, was concerned about the

---

[111] Protection from Abuse (Scotland) Act 2001, s 7.
[112] *Ibid.*
[113] COG 2005, para 6.6.
[114] *R v Waveney DC, ex p Bowers* [1983] 2 QB 238; repeated in the context of the later Housing Act 1996 in *R v Camden LBC, ex p Pereira* (1999) 31 HLR 317, substituting the words "harmful effects" for "suffering".
[115] *Wilson v Nithsdale DC* 1992 SLT 1131 at 1133.
[116] *Morgan v Stirling Council* [2006] CSOH 154 per Lord Glennie.

impact on her client of homelessness did not automatically mean that a decision not to find Ms Morgan vulnerable was flawed:

> "The inability to cope, and the injury or detriment likely to be suffered, may take different forms and manifest themselves in different ways. All the circumstances must be taken into account. But before the petitioner can be said to fall within the definition of 'vulnerable' for the purpose of section 25(1)(c), it must appear that her ability to fend for herself while homeless is more likely to result in injury or detriment to her than would be the case with an ordinary homeless person."[117]

It is, then, not enough simply to be homeless. Something more is required but what will be accepted varies. Interpreting similar provisions in England, the Court of Appeal has also upheld a determination that an applicant with a long history of drug abuse and poor health could lawfully be deemed not vulnerable.[118]

(iii) Intentionality

Where the homeless person is broadly responsible for their own plight they will be treated as having become homeless intentionally. The basic test is: "If he deliberately does or fail to do anything in consequence of which he ceases to occupy accommodation which is available for his occupation and which it would have been reasonable for him to continue to occupy."[119] There are three requirements:

(a) Deliberate actions or failure to act

The applicant must have deliberately done or failed to do something the likely result of which was that he will be compelled to leave accommodation. Wilful non-payment of rent or mortgage would be such a failure. Loss of property as result of real financial difficulties would not be. This section would not cover someone who had *not* acquiesced in the actions or failures of a partner nor someone who knew of the actions or omissions and took reasonable steps to prevent them.

(b) Reasonable to continue to occupy

It must have been reasonable for the applicant to occupy the accommodation. The local authority may look to the general circumstances prevailing in relation to its area in looking to this test. In simple terms, in an area where conditions are generally poor, applicants will have to put up with conditions which are poorer than those living in better areas.[120]

---

[117] *Morgan v Stirling Council* [2006] CSOH 154 at para 4.
[118] *Simms v Islington LBC* [2009] 20 HLR 343.
[119] HSA 1987, s 26(1).
[120] *Ibid*, s 26(4).

(c) Aware of all relevant facts

The applicant must have been aware of all the relevant facts before taking or failing to take deliberate actions. An act or omission in good faith on the part of a person unaware of any relevant is not to be regarded as deliberate.[121] A distinction must be drawn between honest blundering or carelessness and dishonesty.[122] An applicant cannot be said to have acted in good faith where he has shut his eyes to the obvious.[123] Examples have included someone giving up accommodation without requiring her landlord to obtain a possession order because she did not realise she had the right to stay until that date.[124]

The intentionality test should not be applied for all time nor should there be a fixed period of disqualification from full assistance.[125] Subsequent applications should be considered on their merits and if there is reason to believe that there has been a change of circumstances, there may well be grounds to merit a review.[126] The fact that another person might have come to a different conclusion is not enough to overturn a finding of intentionality. In one case the Court of Appeal decided that a local authority was entitled to come to its conclusion that it was reasonable for a Mr Osei and his family to continue to occupy his Spanish flat at least until he had secured other arrangements for them in London. They had security of tenure in Spain for at least 6 months. This decision was not set aside as a conclusion that no reasonable housing authority in the position of Southwark could have reached in all the circumstances of this case.[127]

The Homelessness etc (Scotland) Act 2003 makes changes in relation to intentionality. In place of an obligation to look into the issue, local authorities are given the option.[128] In terms of the obligation to provide accommodation, this is strengthened. These changes had not been brought into effect at the time of writing.[129]

(iv) Local connection[130]

In addition to their previous obligations, local authorities have the option of deciding to investigate whether an applicant has a local connection with their area. Relevant information in assessing this will include

---

[121]   HSA 1987, s 26(3).
[122]   *R* v *Hammersmith and Fulham LBC, ex p Lusi* (1991) 23 HLR 260 QBD – going into a business venture which failed.
[123]   *O'Connor* v *Kensington and Chelsea RLBC* [2004] 37 HLR 601.
[124]   *Ugiagbe* v *Southwark LBC* [2009] 35 HLR 600.
[125]   COG 2005, para 7.24.
[126]   *Ibid*, para 7.25.
[127]   *Osei* v *Southwark LBC* [2007] EWCA Civ 787.
[128]   HSA 2003, s 4.
[129]   As at 1 August 2010.
[130]   HSA 1987, s 27.

details of previous addresses, such as tenancies held or houses owned, as well as employment history and family connections. If they investigate and the applicant is found to be homeless and in priority need and not intentionally homeless, and are considered to have a local connection elsewhere, the applicant may be referred to that other authority.[131] Where there is no connection with another local authority in Great Britain, then the obligation rests with the authority to which the applicant has applied.[132] There may be no referral to another local authority if the applicant or any person reasonably expected to reside with him runs the risk of violence in that other local authority's district.[133] The risk of violence may be from someone with whom the applicant might reasonably expect to reside, such as a spouse or person with whom they formerly resided.[134]

Local connection can be established in one of four ways but it should be noted that the House of Lords has indicated that local connection is not simply a matter of meeting one of the statutory tests but a question of being "established" as "real" rather than technical: "[E]stablished by a period of residence; or a period of employment; or by family associations which endured in the area or by the other special circumstances which spell out a connection in real terms."[135]

(a) Normal past voluntary residence[136]

In order to qualify there must have been residence which was voluntary. It needs to have lasted for at least 6 months during the past 12 months[137] or not less than 3 years during the previous 5 years.[138] It does not include service in the armed forces or detention in prison or a mental health institution, although there may be other previous connections which might be relevant.[139] In considering whether an applicant is usually resident in the area, the local authority is not to take account of time spent in a hospital or prison, a rehabilitation centre, or a holiday or seasonal let.

The provision of accommodation for asylum seekers does not establish a local connection. Refugees and those with leave to remain do not require local connection.

---

[131]   HSA 1987, s 33(1).
[132]   *R v Hillingdon LBC, ex p Streeting* [1980] 3 All ER 413.
[133]   HSA 1987, s 33(2)(c).
[134]   *Ibid*, s 33(3).
[135]   *Eastleigh BC v Betts* [1983] 2 AC 613.
[136]   HSA 1987, s 27(1)(a).
[137]   COG 2005, para 8.12.
[138]   *Ibid*.
[139]   *Ibid*, para 8.13.

(b) Employment [140]

Serving in the regular armed forces does not count as employment. Local authorities are urged to take account of the rise of fixed-term contracts and part-time working when considering employment. Temporary employment for a substantial period should be considered, as well as part-time work. Brief breaks in employment should be ignored. Where a person works in more than one centre, regard should be had to the location of their principal place of work, or main base for travelling workers. [141]

(c) Family associations [142]

This arises where an applicant or other member of the household has family members in the area for at least 5 years. There should be no consideration of local connection where reasons such as past abuse make this inappropriate. Applicants should not be referred elsewhere on family grounds if they object. [143] The closeness of the relationship is a matter for judgement and has been held to include situations where a young woman was thrown out by her parents from their home in the Tyne and Wear area and returned to Ayr where her grandparents, sister and uncles and aunts were living and where she had been brought up. Lord Clyde accepted that these factors demonstrated real and enduring links with Ayr through the residence of relatives over a considerable period of time. [144]

(d) Special circumstances [145]

These would include the need for continuing provision of education or health treatment. In addition, it could include being brought up or having lived for a considerable time in the area previously. Local authorities are urged to consider applications from former members of the armed forces sympathetically where they have no real connection with another area, [146] although in the past service claims have not always been treated so sympathetically. [147] There is nothing to prevent authorities from making arrangements with other authorities to take responsibility for applicants, provided that this accords with the wishes of the applicants. [148]

---

[140]   HSA 1987, s 27(1)(b).
[141]   COG 2005, para 8.19.
[142]   HSA 1987, s 27(1)(c).
[143]   COG 2005, para 8.15.
[144]   *MacMillan* v *Kyle and Carrick DC*, 7 February 1995 (OH).
[145]   HSA 1987, s 27(1)(d).
[146]   COG 2005, para 8.16.
[147]   *R* v *Vale of White Horse DC, ex p Smith and Hay* (1985) 17 HLR 160.
[148]   COG 2005, para 8.17.

CODE OF GUIDANCE

This was first published in 1978 and there has always been a separate Code for Scotland from that of England and Wales. There have been a number of revisions over the years and the version at the time of writing was published in 2005. This is designed to ensure a fair and consistent approach and promote good practice among local authorities. It does not have statutory force but local authorities are required to "have regard in the exercise of their functions to such guidance as may from time to time be given".[149] Failure to have regard to the Code can provide grounds to challenge the legality of an authority's decision in the court, as where a local authority failed to make its own investigations into whether it was likely that a 16-year-old young woman would be vulnerable to sexual or other exploitation. It simply took at face value the police assurance that she would be safe, rather than follow the Code of Guidance which suggested otherwise.[150]

ENQUIRIES

Local authorities are required to carry out such enquiries as are "necessary to satisfy themselves as to whether (the applicant) is homeless or threatened with homelessness".[151] If satisfied on this first issue then they are required to make further enquiries as are necessary to satisfy themselves as to whether the applicant has a priority need;[152] whether the homeless situation is intentional;[153] and, if the authority thinks fit, whether there is a local connection.[154] The applicant challenging a decision on the ground that the enquiries have not been adequate has a difficult task, according to the case law:

> "The duty to make inquiries is to make such inquires as are necessary to satisfy the authority ... It follows that as it is the authority which have to be satisfied the scope and scale of the inquiries is, primarily at least, a matter for them ... The court should not intervene merely because it considers that further inquiries would have been sensible or desirable. It should intervene only if no reasonable housing authority could have been satisfied on the basis of the inquiries made."[155]

---

[149] HSA 1987, s 37.
[150] *Kelly* v *Monklands DC* 1986 SLT 169; but see also *Stevenston* v *Monklands DC* 1987 GWD 15–576, where the Code was noted but not followed and the decision was held to be lawful.
[151] HSA 1987, s 28(1).
[152] *Ibid*, s 28(2)(a).
[153] *Ibid*, s 28(2)(b).
[154] *Ibid*.
[155] *R* v *Kensington and Chelsea RLBC, ex p Bayani* (1990) 24 HLR 406.

During the period of making enquiries, pending any decision, there is an interim duty on the local authority to provide accommodation for any homeless applicant in apparent priority need who it has reason to believe is homeless.[156]

POSTPONING A DECISION

It is unlawful for an authority to postpone making a decision, even for a short period, on the basis that by postponing that decision the child will have reached the age of 18 before the decision is taken. Although reconciliation and mediation are to be encouraged, particularly in the case of 16- and 17-year-old children who have been excluded from the family home, it is wrong for an authority to persuade a family into mediation and then use the time that the mediation would take to deprive the child of a right that it would have had without mediation. The mediation process is wholly independent of the enquiries process and the authority has no power to defer making enquiries on the ground that there is a pending mediation.[157]

REVIEWS AND APPEALS

One of the perceived weaknesses of Stephen Ross's original statute was the absence of any simple local mechanism to challenge a decision at local level. There are a number of ways in which a decision can be re-examined.

Judicial review

Challenge is available by way of the Edinburgh-based process of judicial review in the Court of Session. With a cost for the simplest of hearings in the region of £10,000,[158] this was a mechanism which left much to be desired. The contrast with the availability of the county court in England and Wales since 1996 should be noted. In order to mount a successful judicial review challenge the applicant must show that the decision was unlawful through a range of criteria. The courts have stressed that each case must be seen on its merits and have sought to discourage reliance on previous cases as precedents.[159] The case law is extensive and for the most part stems from England, so that care needs to be taken as the legislation

---

[156] HSA 1987, s 29.
[157] *Robinson* v *Hammersmith and Fulham LBC* [2006] EWCA Civ 1122.
[158] I am grateful to Mike Bruce of Weslo, Bathgate, West Lothian for this information derived from Weslo's challenge to the lawfulness of non-registration as an RSL of Weslo by Communities Scotland. This issue was subsequently resolved to the mutual satisfaction of all parties and Weslo became an RSL in 2007.
[159] *Puhlhofer* v *Hillingdon LBC* [1986] AC 484 per Lord Brightman at 518; the extent and nature of the subsequent reports suggest that this is a pious hope rather than a reality.

has diverged significantly over the past 25 years since the common statute, the Housing (Homeless Persons) Act 1977, first ceased to be operative in England.

(i) Real exercise of discretion

There must be a real exercise of discretion and the local authority can fall down where it simply applies a blanket policy irrespective of the specific circumstances (ie fetters its own discretion) or delegates the decision to someone else.

Fettering its discretion (ie following a predetermined policy too rigidly)   While every decision must be dealt with on its merits, this does not prevent local authorities from having guidelines to aid smooth and efficient administration. For instance, one authority had a policy of never accepting applications from those with local connections elsewhere. It was not lawful to decide in advance that all cases where there was a legitimate connection elsewhere should always be referred elsewhere.[160] A local authority decided to provide temporary accommodation for homeless applicants outside its area in assorted seaside towns, pending a final decision on their cases. This general policy was unlawful, since the authority had failed to consider properly the individual circumstances of the individuals involved. Many were on benefits and had, for example, children being educated within the borough. The effect of the policy was to make any return to the borough impossible.[161]

(b) Delegation of decision making   A local authority must not simply rubber-stamp decisions taken on its behalf by others. This has occurred in the case of decisions about whether or not individuals were vulnerable where the local authority simply accepted the advice of its medical experts without making any enquiries itself.[162] The courts in England have not been particularly robust in upholding this principle.[163]

(ii) Relevant matters only considered

The decision is contrary to law if it fails to consider relevant matters or considers matters which are not relevant. The first requirement is to comply with the statutory requirements. Hence, a decision by a local authority in which it determined that an applicant should be deemed

---

[160] *R v Harrow LBC* (1994) 26 HLR 32 QBD.

[161] *R v Newham LBC, ex p Sacupima* [2001] 33 HLR 1.

[162] *R v Lambeth LBC, ex p Carroll* (1988) 20 HLR 142 QBD.

[163] *Simms v Islington LBC* [2009] 20 HLR 343 CA, where authority's medical assessor had neither examined the patient nor consulted the applicant's GP and had not had sight of the GP's second report.

intentionally homeless because of their nomadic lifestyle, rather than by applying the statutory test, was deemed unlawful as it took account of irrelevant factors.[164] By the same token, one must take account of certain matters. A relevant factor is the Code of Guidance to which the local authority must have regard but can depart from if it is satisfied that there are good grounds to do so. Hence, one council took account of, but chose not to follow, the advice that where an applicant became homeless as a result of losing their employment they should not usually be treated as having become intentionally homeless.[165]

(iii) Decision so unreasonable that no reasonable council could reach it

This is sometimes termed the "perverse" decision or the decision that is plainly unreasonable. It is not a question of there being an alternative reasonable decision which could have been reached but that the local authority's decision borders on the bizarre. An example would be where a local authority rejected the claim that an applicant's son was vulnerable through epilepsy. Its basis was a report from a doctor who knew little about the son or the condition. Failing to seek further clarification or obtain independent evidence meant that there was an absence of adequate evidence on which to base the decision.[166]

(iv) Duty to act fairly

Authorities must give applicants the opportunity to have their case properly heard. The enquiries must be adequate to allow a proper lawful decision to be reached. It is not enough, though, to establish that further enquiries would have been sensible or desirable if the enquiries are enough to allow a proper decision to be made.[167] The failure to provide an opportunity to comment on the results of enquiries has in the past allowed a successful challenge.[168]

(v) Duty to give adequate reasons

There is also the possibility of what sometimes turns out to be a Pyrrhic victory, when the local authority fails to provide an adequate set of reasons. This may simply result in the applicant being furnished with a properly written set of reasons or it may disclose an underlying weakness in the local authority's decision-making process. That is to say that the failure to give adequate reasons may reflect the fact that there are no good reasons or it may be that the writing-up process has been carried out ineffectively.

---

[164] R v Preseli DC, ex p Fisher (1984) 17 HLR 147 QBD.
[165] Mazzaccherini v Argyle and Bute DC 1987 SCLR 475.
[166] R v Sheffield City Council, ex p Leek (1993) 26 HLR 669 CA.
[167] R v City of Westminster, ex p Ali and Bibi (1992) 25 HLR 109 HL.
[168] R v Wyre BC, ex p Joyce (1983) 11 HLR 73 QBD.

Statutory internal review by the local authority

A statutory right to have its decision reviewed by the local authority was added in the Housing (Scotland) Act 2001. This provides that local authorities must notify an applicant in writing of the right of review and the relevant time limits.[169] Reviews must be carried out by a person senior to the person who made the decision being reviewed and who had no involvement in the making of that decision.[170] The applicant must be informed in writing[171] of the reasons in the event of the review confirming the original decision.[172] The issues for review cover substantive issues of entitlement,[173] referrals to other housing authorities[174] and decisions about accommodation.[175] The applicant has 21 days to make a request for review from the date of the notification of the decision to be reviewed.[176] There is no review of the initial review.[177]

Scottish Public Services Ombudsman

This mechanism proved surprisingly effective in changing local authority practices since it was used originally in the guise of the Local Commissioner for Local Administration in the 1970s. Although the Ombudsman had no powers of enforcement, the finding of maladministration was one which led 95 per cent of councils to comply with orders in the first 20 years of operation of the homeless persons legislation.[178]

THE LOCAL AUTHORITY'S DUTIES IN PRACTICE

It is helpful in practical terms to look at the local authority's duties as a series of questions.

Is the applicant homeless?[179]

If the applicant is homeless then the local authority must secure that accommodation is made available to him pending any further enquiries about priority need and intentionality.[180] If the applicant is not

---

[169] HSA 2001, s 4 (inserting new ss 35A and 35B into HSA 1987).
[170] HSA 1987, s 35B(1).
[171] *Ibid*, s 35B(5).
[172] *Ibid*, s 35B(3).
[173] *Ibid*, s 35A(2)(a).
[174] *Ibid*, s 35A(2)(b) and (c).
[175] *Ibid*, s 35A(2)(d).
[176] *Ibid*, s 35A(3) – although the authority may allow a longer period.
[177] *Ibid*, s 35A(4).
[178] Robson and Poustie (1996) at 344.
[179] HSA 1987, s 28(1).
[180] *Ibid*, s 29(1).

homeless then no further duties exist beyond the possible provision of temporary accommodation while carrying out enquiries. If the applicant is threatened with homelessness within 2 months the local authority has to provide advice and assistance to try to prevent homelessness occurring.[181]

Is the person in priority need? [182]

If the applicant is homeless but *not* in priority need then the local authority should ensure the provision of temporary accommodation and give advice and assistance to enable the applicant to secure accommodation.[183]

Is the applicant intentionally homeless? [184]

If an applicant is homeless, in priority need but intentionally homeless then the local authority must secure temporary accommodation for such period as will give that person a reasonable opportunity of obtaining accommodation.[185] It must also provide appropriate advice and assistance to help in the attempts to secure accommodation.[186]

Does the applicant have a local connection? [187]

If the applicant is homeless, in priority need, is not intentionally homeless and has a local connection then the local authority has to secure permanent accommodation.[188] If the person does not have a local connection then the council can refer him back to the area he came from to be housed permanently.

INTERIM OR TEMPORARY ACCOMMODATION

There is a duty to secure that accommodation becomes available for applicants during the period of assessing their claim.[189] One of the problems identified right from the start of the operation of the legislation has been the standard of accommodation which was secured for homeless applicants. There are now statutory regulations which specify what kinds of temporary accommodation are unsuitable for households with children and pregnant women. In order to be suitable, accommodation must:

---

181 HSA 1987, s 32(3).
182 *Ibid*, s 28(2)(a).
183 COG 2005, para 9.5.
184 HSA 1987, s 28(2)(b).
185 *Ibid*, s 31(3)(a).
186 *Ibid*, s 31(3)(b).
187 *Ibid*, s 28(2)(b).
188 *Ibid*, s 31(2).
189 *Ibid*, s 31(3).

(a) be within the local authority area;

(b) have exclusive use of a toilet and personal washing facilities;

(c) have use of a living room;

(d) have adequate bedrooms for the household's exclusive use;

(e) have adequate cooking facilities for the household which is usable 24 hours a day;

(f) be suitable for children.[190]

Certain properties are exempted from these provisions, including Women's Aid refuges, or where the applicant has been offered "unsuitable" accommodation but expressly chooses to go into such accommodation.[191]

The duty to secure permanent accommodation

Accommodation must be reasonable for the applicant to occupy,[192] subject to any alterations and adaptations which are proposed.[193] It must meet any "special needs" of the applicant or members of his household.[194] The local authority must have regard to the best interests of the applicant's dependent children.[195] It must be "permanent accommodation", which includes a Scottish secure tenancy and an assured tenancy. It does not include a short assured tenancy.[196] This deals with the restricted interpretation of "accommodation" in the Scottish courts in *Bradley*,[197] as well as the controversial House of Lords' *Awua* decision in 1996 which had suggested that securing accommodation did not mean securing permanent accommodation.[198] The accommodation offered can include a short Scottish secure tenancy where the applicant has had an order for repossession made against him in the last 3 years or if someone in the household is subject to an anti-social behaviour order.[199] A decision from the House of Lords in 2009 suggests that the inappropriate approach in *Awua* might be set for a revival. In deciding a case about an applicant, Ms Moran, who had become homeless from a refuge,[200] the court opened the question of whether accommodation in

---

190 Homeless Persons (Unsuitable Accommodation) (Scotland) Order 2004 (SSI 2004/489).

191 *Ibid*, para 3(c).

192 HSA 2001, s 3(4).

193 *Boreh* v *Ealing LBC* [2009] HLR 22 CA.

194 HSA 2001, s 3(4).

195 *Ibid*, s 3(4).

196 *Ibid*, s 3(3).

197 *Bradley* v *Motherwell DC* 1994 SLT 739.

198 *R* v *Brent LBC, ex p Awua* [1996] AC 55 HL.

199 Homelessness etc (Scotland) Act 2003, s 5.

200 *Ali* v *Birmingham City Council*; *Moran* v *Manchester City Council* [2009] 41 HLR 727 HL.

a refuge was "accommodation" for the purposes of deciding whether an applicant was homeless.[201]

The Code addresses the issue of the impact of homeless applicants on the letting policies of local authorities. It suggests that where a local authority is using its own stock to provide temporary or interim accommodation, it should ensure that this allows a balance to be struck with duties to provide permanent accommodation to other applicants. A regular turnover of council properties used for temporary accommodation should be considered, to avoid particular dwellings being identified and possibly stigmatised as "homeless accommodation", while allowing a cost-effective lifespan for individual properties. Local authorities are also urged to consider engaging the local communities in which these properties are located in order to counter any negative stereotyping of homeless people.[202]

REFERRALS TO OTHER LOCAL AUTHORITIES

There is provision for such referrals where there is a local connection with the other authority.[203] This can occur where the referring local authority is satisfied that an applicant is not intentionally homeless and in priority need[204] but is of the opinion that there is no local connection with its area but there is with the area of the receiving authority.[205]

REFERRALS TO RSLS

Permanent accommodation

RSLs have a duty to comply with a request from a local authority to house a household which it has assessed as being in priority need and unintentionally homeless,[206] unless the RSL has a good reason not to do so.[207] In making its decision the local authority must have to regard to the availability of appropriate accommodation in its area.[208] The RSL must provide a Scottish secure tenancy or a short Scottish secure tenancy where the prospective tenant either is subject to an existing ASBO or has had one in the previous 3 years.[209] The RSL must comply with any such reasonable request for assistance.[210]

---

[201] *Ali* v *Birmingham City Council* [2009] 41 HLR 727 at 748 per Baroness Hale.
[202] COG 2005, para 9.54.
[203] HSA 1987, s 33.
[204] *Ibid*, s 33(1).
[205] *Ibid*, s 33(2).
[206] HSA 2001, s 5(1).
[207] *Ibid*, s 5(3).
[208] *Ibid*, s 5(2).
[209] *Ibid*, s 5(4).
[210] *Ibid*, s 5(6).

Where a request is made to an RSL to house a homeless applicant it is expected that the RSL should comply by providing accommodation within 6 weeks, unless it offers a good reason for not doing so. If there is a failure to comply with a request and the local authority disagrees with the reason, where both parties cannot reach an agreement then they have to appoint an arbiter and abide by their decision.[211]

The local authority has to provide the applicant with a written notification of its decision and the reasons why it made that decision.[212] The target is 28 days.[213] There are also elaborate rules in operation in relation to the protection of the property of homeless applicants.[214]

THE CONTEXT OF OPERATING THE HOMELESSNESS LEGISLATION

The numbers of those applying as homeless have gradually built up during the past three decades. For the first 5 years the numbers fluctuated around the 15,000 mark. In the 1980s the figures rose from 20,000 in 1984 to 24,741 in 1988–89. In the 1990s the figures reached over 45,000 and in the first decade of the 21st century the rise continued by some 14 per cent.[215] The figures for the first decade of the new millennium were consistent:

2002–03	51,999;
2003–04	56,523;
2004–05	57,454;
2005–06	59,970;
2006–07	59,096;
2007–08	57,169;
2008–09	57,304.[216]

The images of the typical homeless applicant may be that of the family with children, as we saw in *Cathy Come Home*[217] but the modern reality is rather different. In the latest available year (2008–09) the pattern of the 57,304 applications showed a rather different picture. There were 35,000 applications made by single people (61 per cent), of whom 23,000 were men and 12,000 were women. Some 34 per cent of applications were from households with children, most of whom were single-parent

[211] Scottish Government Guidance on s 5 referrals in Code, para 9.66 – available at http://www.scotland.gov.uk/Publications/2002/09/15483/11189.
[212] HSA 1987, s 3.
[213] COG 2005, para 11.16.
[214] HSA 1987, s 36 – the author is aware of only one case on this issue: *Mitchell* v *Ealing LBC* [1979] QB 1 QBD.
[215] "Statistical Bulletin Operation of the Homeless Persons Legislation in Scotland: national and local authority analyses 2006–07" (Scottish Government, 2007).
[216] Scottish Government (2009b).
[217] *Cathy Come Home* (BBC, 1966).

households – 24 per cent of all applications.[218] The figures were the same in the previous year, when there were some 5 per cent of applications from couples with children and a further 5 per cent from couples without children. Prior to applying, 47 per cent of applicants had been living with friends or relatives and a further 35 per cent had been living in their own accommodation which they either rented or owned.[219] The main reason given for becoming homeless was relationship breakdown – 28 per cent cited a dispute within the household and 26 per cent were asked to leave. Rent arrears or mortgage default accounted for around 6 per cent of all homelessness applications in both 2007–08 and 2008–09.[220]

Part of the context in which the legislation operates is the public attitude to homelessness. A large-scale national survey in 2006 found that 48 per cent of people agree that "most homeless people have just been unlucky in their lives", with 28 per cent disagreeing and 22 per cent neither agreeing nor disagreeing.[221] This apparent recognition of the structural nature of homelessness must, however, be seen in the context of the fact that some 45 per cent of those surveyed agreed with the more "critical" statement that "most homeless people could find somewhere to live if they really tried".[222] A further 35 per cent of the sample agreed that "many people say they are homeless just to try and get a house from the council", with less disagreeing – 29 per cent.[223] The Report noted, however, that the issue was highly complex:

> "These findings suggest that people's general attitudes towards homelessness and homeless people are complex. It is not possible to simply amalgamate 'sympathetic' views on one measure with 'sympathetic' views on another to provide an overall measure of attitudes to homeless people. Rather, people's degree of sympathy may vary in relation to their differing beliefs about how people become homeless in the first place (and the role which 'luck' played in this), their beliefs about whether homeless people could help themselves out of their situation and their beliefs about whether all people who present as homeless are 'genuinely' homeless or not."[224]

A number of issues were highlighted in the Report's conclusions. Women were generally more "sympathetic" towards homeless people than men – for example, 53 per cent of women, compared with 42 per cent of men, agree that "most homeless people have just been unlucky in their lives". Attitudes also varied by age, with older people most likely (aged 65 and

---

[218] Scottish Government (2009b), para 3.1.
[219] *Ibid*, para 3.4.
[220] *Ibid*, para 3.5.
[221] Scottish Social Attitudes Survey 2006: Public Attitudes to Homelessness, para 3.3.
[222] *Ibid*, para 3.4.
[223] *Ibid*.
[224] *Ibid*, para 3.7.

above) to agree that "many people say they are homeless just to try to get a house from the council" (49 per cent, compared with 27 per cent of those aged 25–34). *Both* older (65+) and younger (18–24) people are more likely than the middle-aged to agree that "most homeless people could find somewhere to live if they really tried". Education was also strongly associated with holding less "judgemental" attitudes towards the motives and behaviour of homeless people. For example, just 33 per cent of those qualified to higher education level or above agree that "most homeless people could find somewhere to live if they really tried" compared with 58 per cent of those with no qualifications. However, those with no qualifications are in fact *more* likely to agree that "homeless people have just been unlucky in their lives" (61 per cent, compared with 41 per cent of those with degrees). One possible explanation for this apparent inconsistency was that some disagreed with this statement because they believed homelessness has broader socio–economic causes – for example, structural factors such as a lack of affordable housing and/ or there being inadequate care provided by society for vulnerable people – and was therefore not just a question of luck.

There was little difference in attitudes towards homeless people by tenure, after other factors such as age, income and education were controlled for. Perhaps surprisingly, "low-level" awareness or contact with the "visibly" homeless did not appear to have much impact on attitudes towards homeless people. Personal experience of homelessness appeared to be associated with having more definite views in either direction on whether people say they are homeless just to try to get a house from the council. The extent to which someone's underlying beliefs and values were more libertarian or authoritarian was strongly related to attitudes to homelessness. Respondents at the more authoritarian end were much more likely than libertarians to express attitudes that could be described as "unsympathetic" or more "judgemental". For example, 51 per cent of "authoritarian" respondents agreed that many "say they are homeless just to try and get a house from the council", compared with just 18 per cent of more libertarian respondents.[225]

THE DEVELOPMENT OF POST-WAR HOMELESSNESS POLICIES

During the days of the workhouse there was always a theoretical housing solution for anyone who lost their accommodation. Since the removal of the less than welcome "safety net" of the Poor Law with the introduction of the Beveridge cradle-to-grave welfare provisions in the 1940s, local social work departments had taken on the role of meeting the needs of homeless families. The National Assistance Act 1948 required that local authority welfare departments provide "[T]emporary

---

[225] Scottish Social Attitudes Survey 2006, para 3.27.

accommodation for persons who are in urgent need thereof, being need arising in circumstances which could reasonably have been foreseen or in such circumstances as the authority may in any case determine".[226] This provided only temporary shelter for women and their children for a strictly limited period of time. Its use of old workhouses and other unsuitable accommodation was exposed in the drama *Cathy Come Home* in November 1966. Government commitments to provide enforceable housing rights for homeless families finally bore fruit in the Private Member's Bill of Isle of Wight MP Stephen Ross which led to the Housing (Homeless Persons) Act 1977. It covered homeless people in England, Wales and Scotland and remained the basis for the current system, as noted above.

The image conjured up in the public mind by a mention of the word "homeless" or "homelessness" is of rough sleepers. Attempts to confront this aspect of the problem of homelessness commenced in England in 1990 with the launch of the Rough Sleepers Initiative.[227] It was established in Scotland in 1997 with the aim of eliminating the "need to sleep rough" in Scotland by the end of 2003. Although rough sleeping has persisted as the face of homelessness, in terms of those applying for assistance to the local authority the number has never been higher than 10 per cent and is now significantly lower.[228] As a policy issue the 2005 Evaluation of the Rough Sleepers Initiative noted the problems stemming from the diverse nature and size of the problem:

"In practice, rough sleeping only exists at sufficient concentrations in some areas of the country to allow the development of specialist services aimed particularly at people sleeping rough. Outside Glasgow, Edinburgh and some other cities such as Dundee, the numbers reported, both from the fieldwork conducted for this evaluation and from the GHN statistical monitoring and GSR monitoring, are often very low. The development of a suite of specific rough sleeper services in these areas of the country is, realistically, not practical. However, the needs of people sleeping rough can be effectively met through ensuring that other homelessness services can, where possible and practical, adapt to their needs. As the distinction

---

[226] National Assistance Act 1948, s 21(1)(b).
[227] Fitzpatrick (2004).
[228] Average number of applications per month where a household member reported sleeping rough the night before applying for assistance by local authority:

2002–03	443	10%
2003–04	443	9%
2004–05	347	7%
2005–06	326	6%
2006–07	323	7%
2008–09	255	5%

Scottish Government (2009b).

between "types" of homeless household across the country begins to come to an end, this kind of generic homelessness service should become more commonplace. There is a need to ensure that such services can address the needs of people sleeping rough in areas where they are less common."[229]

When the Scottish Executive took over responsibility for homelessness from the Scottish Office in 1999 one of its first actions was to establish the Homelessness Task Force "to review the causes and nature of homelessness in Scotland; to examine current practice in dealing with homelessness; and to make recommendations on how homelessness in Scotland can best be prevented and, where it does occur, tackled effectively".[230] There were a number of themes which the Task Force emphasised.[231] It stressed that everybody is entitled to some form of accommodation and that its recommendations were to apply to all homeless people – single people and families. It noted that one aspect which was crucial was that implementation should be matched by resources. Housing supply was seen as crucial as well as there being a recognition of the importance of informal and formal support. Changes in practice were seen as being of equal importance with changing the legislation. In terms of its analysis of homelessness as a structural issue it emphasised the need to address the acute shortage of affordable housing in Scotland as part of effectively tackling homelessness. Issues of quality as well as quantity were also raised, along with the need to use local housing strategies to assess need. The need for affordable entry-level housing for young people was recognised, along with the value of rent guarantee and deposit schemes.

Action to prevent homelessness was the thinking behind recommending the introduction of homelessness strategies which became a key feature of the Homelessness etc (Scotland) Act 2003. Other less central issues also covered local authorities and RSLs reviewing their eviction, arrears and anti-social behaviour policies as well as illegal eviction and the kind of advice for those leaving care or institutions.

DEVELOPMENTS IN THE LAW OF HOMELESSNESS

One of the most interesting first pieces of legislation to emerge from the devolved Scottish Parliament was the Housing (Scotland) Act 2001 which drew on the work of the Task Force. It introduced the need for authorities to develop homelessness strategies and advice and information strategies. Temporary accommodation was to be provided for all those found to be homeless and enhanced advice and assistance offered. The increased role of the voluntary sector was recognised in the introduction

[229] Scottish Government (2005), para 6.55.
[230] Scottish Executive (2002b) at 1.
[231] Fitzpatrick at 190–192.

of a formal role for RSLs with referrals to them. One anomaly from the divergence of Scottish and English legislation was the addressing of the question of satisfactory criteria for permanent accommodation. Following the quixotic decision of the House of Lords in *Puhlhofer* amendments had been introduced following pressure from SHELTER and other campaign groups via the Housing and Planning Act 1986[232] and the Housing (Scotland) Act 1987.[233]

KEY PRINCIPLES OF HOMELESS STRATEGIES[234]

A "homelessness strategy" is required to demonstrate a clear understanding of the extent and nature of homelessness and the risks of homelessness in an area and should set out how the local authority and identified partners will work to prevent and alleviate homelessness. Homelessness strategies should establish a shared understanding and commitment between partners of the issues, the priorities and the way forward and provide an agreed framework within which aims and objectives are set and options identified. This must cover appraisal and monitoring of progress, evaluation of the impact and allocation of resources and finance. It must be developed consistently with other appropriate thematic and service plans, for example, local housing strategies. It should ensure that equal opportunities policies are implemented at each stage of the process and ensure that the needs of children are considered during the formulation and implementation of policies to prevent and alleviate homelessness as well as recognising the essential contribution to service development provided by consultation with homeless people.

As indicated above, the Homelessness Task Force's Final Report's recommendations led to a range of changes in the Homelessness etc (Scotland) Act 2003, including the extension of priority need, ability for local authorities to not apply the local connection provisions and changes in relation to intentionally homeless households. The inadequacies of the kinds of properties offered as interim accommodation have been addressed in the new standards for temporary accommodation.[235] The final developments to bring the legislation closer to Stephen Ross's original proposal is the plan to abolish the priority need category by 2012.[236] The emphasis in the future continues to be on prevention. With

---

[232] Section 14, amending s 69(1) of the Housing Act 1985 for England – accommodation to be "suitable", having regard to slum clearance, overcrowding and houses in multiple occupation.

[233] Law Reform (Miscellaneous Provisions) (Scotland) Act 1990, s 21, amending HSA 1987, s 24 – accommodation to be neither "overcrowded" nor "a danger to health".

[234] HSA 2001, s 1.

[235] Homeless Persons (Unsuitable Accommodation) (Scotland) Order 2004 (SSI 2004/ 489).

[236] Homelessness etc (Scotland) Act 2003, s 2.

the implementation of the Homelessness etc (Scotland) Act 2003 a number of other valuable goals are achieved. This includes notification of actions for repossession,[237] the suspension of local connection and the shift from the issue of intentionality being a duty on local authorities to it being a power.

---

[237] Homelessness etc (Scotland) Act 2003, s 11.

3 RESIDENTIAL TENURES

In the drive to solve the housing crisis during the 1950s there was a barrage of promises from politicians seeking election to Westminster as to how many houses would be built by the competing political parties. The number of new houses promised varied from 300,000 to 500,000[1] and numbers achieved were in excess of 300,000 annually under both Conservative and Labour administrations.[2] What united the debate, however, was the fact that the tenure of the missing houses was not an issue. Until 1969 all political parties were agreed on the desire to provide new houses.[3] The tenures did not matter. There were three principal forms of housing then, as now, which dominated. These are owner occupancy; private renting; and social renting. As we have noted above,[4] each of these forms of tenure has enjoyed a dominant role in Scottish housing in the 20th century and each continues to house significant numbers of citizens. From a legal perspective, each of the tenures involves a degree of regulation.[5] The involvement of the national and the local state in the process of regulation was largely absent from housing at the start of the last century. Things have changed significantly, as we have noted and will see.

OWNER OCCUPANCY

The citizen who owned land in 1910 could erect a property on that land to his taste and style. The new Town Planning Act 1909 was about to introduce an element of organisation to development but freedom to construct according to one's whims and fancies remained a feature of property ownership until the introduction of development control in the Town and Country Planning (Scotland) Act 1947.[6] The modern owner occupier continues to be limited in what changes he can make to his property both externally and internally. He must seek permission of the

---

[1] Dunleavy (1981) at 35.
[2] Duclaud-Williams (1978) 177 at Table IX.1.
[3] Dunleavy (1981) at 2.
[4] See Chapter 1 above.
[5] See Chapter 8 below.
[6] 10 & 11 Geo 6 c 6.

local planning authority for developments, changes of use, extensions and most construction work. There is a range of issues where no permission is required, such as gates, fences and satellite dishes.[7] In terms of internal changes, these must comply with the Building Regulations and a building warrant must be sought from the local authority.[8] The feudal system, which lasted until 2000, traditionally required owners to comply with a range of conditions as to use imposed by feudal superiors. These covered both the use to which dwellings might be put as well as the materials to be used in effecting repairs. These conditions and their current form as post-feudal "land obligations "are extensively covered in the standard authorities on land law.[9] The popularity of tenement dwellings in Scotland also means that a set of mutual obligations exists to deal with such matters as support between owners of flats.[10] Those developing the rules of Scotland's legal system never had a problem in conceptualising how it is possible for someone to own a flat between other flats and above flats without the need to resort to tenancies and ground rents which make owning a flat in England a rather more complex affair.[11] Even the question of common repairs has been dealt with reasonably effectively over the years, through mutually enforceable title conditions in the property deeds. The Title Conditions (Scotland) Act 2003 made provision for majority decisions where the title deeds were silent, simplifying the process of communal maintenance and repairs.[12] The Tenements (Scotland) Act 2004 introduced the Tenement Management Scheme as the default management scheme for all tenements in Scotland.[13] These have been complemented by the introduction of maintenance orders and maintenance plans, giving the local authority power to deal with houses which have not been or are unlikely to be maintained to a reasonable standard.[14] A recalcitrant owner can also be required to carry out repairs when the properties of others are affected.[15] Owners and owner occupiers are equally subject to the rules about anti-social behaviour (which are dealt with elsewhere).[16] It is clear from the statistics of ASBOs that home ownership is no guarantee against anti-social behaviour.[17]

These matters apart, the only obligations which the owner occupier requires to meet are the demands to pay for services such as education,

---

[7]   McAllister and McMaster (1999), Ch 5; Young and Rowan-Robinson (1985), Ch 7.
[8]   Building (Scotland) Act 2003.
[9]   Gordon (2nd edn, 1999); Reid and Gretton (2008).
[10] Gordon and Wortley (2009), vol 1, Ch 15.
[11] Lu Xu (2007).
[12] See Chapter 4 below.
[13] Section 4.
[14] Housing (Scotland) Act 2006, ss 42–51: see Chapter 4 below.
[15] Repair notice service in terms of Housing (Scotland) Act 1987, ss 108–112.
[16] See Chapter 8 below.
[17] Scottish Government (2007), para 2.42.

policing, water and social services. These have been levied, in the past, in the form of rates based on the size and potential rental value of the property. There was also a short-lived experiment – the community charge – to shift to a charge on occupiers of property. Their current form, the council tax, returns to a property-based payment to meet the costs of local services.[18] In addition to these non-voluntary payments, the only other costs for someone living in a detached property which is not in a dangerous condition[19] would be those involved in buying the property or meeting any loans taken out using the property as security. Such debts differ from other loans which are guaranteed personally. Loans, generally termed "mortgages", which are secured over heritable property have traditionally been regarded as safe investments for the lender since the property can be sold to meet the outstanding debt. The reform of the law in 1970 limited the way in which a person could secure a right over an interest in land, in security of a debt to the use of the "standard security".[20] If, however, the occupier fell into arrears with the loan, the creditor had extensive rights to repossess the property to meet the debt, having served the appropriate notices. Repossession actions were seldom defended.[21] The Mortgage Rights (Scotland) Act 2001 was introduced to enable the courts to suspend certain rights of mortgage lenders where the borrower was in default and to provide greater protection for tenants of borrowers in default. It provides powers for the sheriff court to suspend the enforcement process and apply its discretion. The circumstances where the court may apply its discretion are where the applicant might be able to repay the debt or arrears or fulfil the obligation in the standard security within a reasonable time so as to keep their home or to give the applicant and others staying in the property time to find alternative accommodation.[22] Whether or not they exercise this discretion depends on the nature of and reasons for the default, the ability of the applicant to fulfil within a reasonable time the obligations of the standard security, and any action taken by the creditor to help in this respect and the ability to secure reasonable alternative accommodation.[23] The Home Owner and Debtor Protection (Scotland) Act 2010 provides further protection for owner occupiers. All repossession cases relating to residential property must be heard in court.[24] There are requirements which creditors must undertake before applying to repossess, including taking reasonable steps

---

[18] Local Government Finance Act 1992.
[19] Building (Scotland) Act 2003, dealing with dangerous buildings.
[20] Conveyancing and Feudal Reform (Scotland) Act 1970, s 9(3).
[21] Higgins (2002) at 40.
[22] Mortgage Rights (Scotland) Act 2001 (MRSA 2001), s 2.
[23] *Ibid*, s 2(2).
[24] Home Owner and Debtor Protection (Scotland) Act 2010 (HODPSA 2010), ss 1, 2 and 3.

to avoid repossession taking place.[25] In addition, there is a right to seek to have the repossession decree recalled,[26] as well as protection for residents other than the debtor.[27]

From the point of view of a housing lawyer, then, the principal problems of the owner occupier tend to resolve themselves into those of eviction by the lender;[28] debt; and anti-social behaviour. Those who have no loan secured over their property, who are up to date with their council tax and who are quietly going about their lives are unlikely to seek advice in a housing advice centre except about their neighbours' behaviour.

RESIDENTIAL TENANCIES

By their very nature, tenancies have the potential to produce problems throughout their existence. There is, in addition to the duties of citizenship, which we have noted in relation to owner occupiers, of paying for community charges and respecting the environment through social behaviour, potential conflict with the landlord. The essence of a tenancy means that one party, the tenant, has temporary use of the property of another, the landlord, in exchange for a sum of money paid by way of rent.[29] This means that even were tenants to quietly go about their lives, issues will arise in terms of rent, landlord regulation, repairs, succession and relationship breakdown in which the legal rights of the tenant are largely outwith their own control. This intrinsically more complex area of landlord/tenant relations has been made even more complex because of social and political developments over the past century. These mean that what would have been a difficult area is one containing rules and regulations which are often counter-intuitive and require explanation. Despite the admirable efforts of the Scottish Parliament in its first decade of devolved powers in relation to housing, it is unlikely that the large number of variations in tenancy types discussed below will ever resolve into a single straightforward "Scottish tenancy". Uniformity in this sphere is, of course, desired for the sake of demystifying the legal process so that tenants and landlords are not confronted by what appears to an almost Kafkaesque process in determining which piece of legislation applies to their arrangements and what the implications of signing certain agreements as opposed to others are. Landlords in the social rented sector have an interest in providing extensive rights to their tenants in terms of security of tenure, succession and repairs. Modern private-sector investors in renting property are likely to want

---

[25] HODPSA 2010, s 4.
[26] *Ibid*, s 6.
[27] *Ibid*, s 5.
[28] See Chapter 6 below.
[29] Rankine (1916) at 1.

to retain greater flexibility over their property and the kinds of tenancy arrangements which suit one sector are unlikely to find favour with the other. Given that a shift to a simple "Scottish residential tenancy" is unlikely in the very near future, we seek here to explain the modern residential tenancy in its principal forms.[30]

In 1910, when a tenant of residential entered into an agreement to rent property he either signed a tenancy agreement or exchanged missives of let. Some standard styles were used, with varying degrees of complexity[31] but the terms and the tenancy were covered by almost no restrictions. The rent and term of the lease were a matter for the parties to agree. There was no difference between the lease from a private landlord or from one of the expanding number of local authorities who were building accommodation to house their local inhabitants. A residential lease was a residential lease. There was, in effect, at this time a "Scottish tenancy". The implications of the lease were the same no matter who was the landlord and who was the tenant. One hundred years later, it is possible to conceive of a standard four-storey tenement from a century before being rented out to eight different tenants covered by eight separate tenancy regimes.[32] This section of this chapter seeks to unravel this complex picture and provide a basic guide to the range of different leasing arrangements now possible.

The introduction of controls against exploitation over rents and the rights of landlords to evict at the term of the tenancy commenced, as we have seen, in 1915.[33] This form of protection against the rigours of the market has been maintained into the 21st century. There are currently in existence two types of private tenancy regime which attempt to provide protection against market forces. The first is encountered in the tenancy regime from Richard Crossman's 1965 Rent Act and is currently covered by a successor statute, the Rent (Scotland) Act 1984. This contains two kinds of tenancy which have rental and eviction protection: the protected tenancy and the Pt VII contract. In seeking to return to a much more market-based system the Conservative Government introduced another two types of private tenancy in the Housing (Scotland) Act 1988 for tenancies commencing on or after 2 January 1989: the assured tenancy and the short assured tenancy. There is, since 1980, protection against eviction at the tenancy term in a further two kinds of tenancy in the

---

[30] Some special local forms of tenure – the kindly tenants of Lochmaben; tenancies-at-will and building leases – which are not temporary grants of use have not been included and these are discussed in Gordon and Wortley (2009) at 18.

[31] *Encyclopaedia of Styles* (1937) at 102–107.

[32] For the sake of retaining a modicum of simplicity, the various agreements found in the 1970s to avoid the impact of the Rent Acts are not included in this overview – see Robson and Halliday (1998) at 2.55–2.62.

[33] See Chapter 1 above and the Law Commission Background Consultative Paper No 162 (2002) (http://www.lawcom.gov.uk/docs/cp162.pdf).

social rented sector. These are now found in the Housing (Scotland) Act 2001: the Scottish secure tenancy and the short Scottish secure tenancy. There are in addition standard occupancy tenancies which are not covered by this legislation and the complicated situation of tenancies provided to employees and their rights being dependent on their contract of employment. All in all, it would be possible to encounter in this standard tenement block, in place of the single tenancy of 1910, at least eight different possible tenancy arrangements in 2010 which on the face of it are the same – the tenant pays rent to a landlord for the exclusive use of a property as their only or principal dwelling-house. The rights and obligations of the tenants and landlords, though, are markedly different in relation to rent, succession and security of tenure rights. We will now look at these in greater detail. Rather than focus on them chronologically, however, we will look at them in terms of the crucial private sector/social rented distinction. We will focus in rather more detail on the dominant assured and Scottish secure tenancies since these are the most likely to be encountered in practice:

(1) private-sector tenancies;
    (a) assured tenancies;
    (b) short assured tenancies;
    (c) protected tenancies;
    (d) Part VII tenancies;
    (e) tied tenancies;
    (f) contractual tenancies;

(2) social rented tenancies;
    (g) Scottish secure tenancies;
    (h) short Scottish secure tenancies.

(1) Private-sector tenancies

(A) ASSURED TENANCIES

(i) Introduction

The assured tenancy is the "default" private sector tenancy which will arise where a private individual or company gives over the temporary use of dwelling-house property to another person in exchange for rent. The Housing (Scotland) Act 1988 lays down the requirements for a tenancy to be covered by the assured tenancy regime. The modern private rented sector tenancy comes in two versions. In essence, it encapsulates the return of the rental tenancy regime to being governed by market forces. As we have noted above, legislation was introduced in 1915 to protect tenants from exploitation in terms of rent levels and the possibility of eviction for any attempt to avoid the impact of rent controls. Politically, the repeal of these protections has been fraught with difficulty in the face of the continued high levels of homelessness and undersupply of housing, at prices people can afford, in places where they wish to live. The assured tenancy looks like a continuation of the protection dating back to 1915 and found in the 1965 protected tenancy. It provides security of tenure to tenants beyond the term of their tenancy. The landlord must obtain a repossession order from the local sheriff court if he wishes to regain possession against a tenant who wishes to remain in the property. The grounds of possession, though, as we note elsewhere,[34] are more wide ranging than was the case with the previous private-sector regime, the protected tenancy.

(ii) Requirements for an assured tenancy

These come into existence where a tenancy is entered into on or after 2 January 1989 in the private sector, provided that certain criteria are met. If any of the criteria is not met then the tenancy will fall into another of the categories of tenancy. As indicated, the protections afforded by the assured tenancy regime apply only where people are at risk of exploitation. Hence the legislation requires that the tenant, or at least one of the joint tenants, be an individual.[35] This means that if there is a lease or sub-lease from a private landlord or company to a body such as a charity or a housing association then such an arrangement is not covered by the Housing (Scotland) Act 1988 and cannot be an assured tenancy. It would simply be a contractual tenancy governed by whatever terms are found in that particular contract. Whatever rights the sub-tenant has, they cannot exceed those of the landlord, so that a sub-tenant in such a situation would not be entitled to security of tenure beyond the date of the landlord's tenancy term.

The tenant, or at least one of the joint tenants, must occupy the house as his only or principal home.[36] The wording of the 1988 legislation specifically requires the property to be the only or principal home rather than the rather looser wording of the Rent (Scotland) Act 1984 which merely required a person "to retain possession" in order to benefit from the protections of the legislation.[37] This means that the phenomenon of the tenant with protection in two different places, which was possible under the earlier statute, will not be encountered. Under the regulated tenancy regime it was possible, in certain circumstances, to be occupying two different properties.[38] There can, however, be only one principal residence.[39]

---

[34] See Chapter 6 below.
[35] Housing (Scotland) Act 1988 (HSA 1988), s 12(1)(a).
[36] Ibid, s 12(1)(b).
[37] Rent Scotland Act 1984 (RSA 1984), s 3(1)(a).
[38] Brickfield Properties v Hughes [1988] 1 EGLR 108 – although difficult in practice to assert; Hampstead Way Investments Ltd v Lewis-Weare [1985] 1 EGLR 120.
[39] Roxburgh DC v Collins 1991 SCLR 575.

(iii) Tenancies which cannot be assured tenancies

Schedule 4 to the Act specifies a range of tenancies which cannot be assured tenancies. These cover pre-1988 Act tenancies.[40] Where a landlord seeks to replace an older tenancy arrangement with what appears to be a new tenancy, this does not seem to work by inference from attempts to do this in the social rented sector.[41] The rationale was to prevent landlords reducing the rights of tenants protected under the Rent (Scotland) Act 1984 by simply providing a new tenancy agreement under the Housing (Scotland) Act 1988. Tenants under the latter tenancies enjoy less rights in relation to rent, succession and security of tenure.

Tenancies where either no rent or a low specified sum is payable are also excluded[42] since at such rent levels the question of exploitation is not an issue.[43] There are also tenancies where other kinds of protection exist, and these are excluded. These include tenancies of shops;[44] agricultural land;[45] and agricultural holdings.[46] There are also exclusions of tenancies where protection is deemed inappropriate, such as licensed premises. These premises were not originally excluded from the Rent Acts. This is a pragmatic recognition of the link between the public house and the resident publicans, although this can lead to injustice where there is a conflict between owners and the resident staff.[47] Also not covered by the assured tenancy protection are holiday lettings, where the purpose is to confer on the tenant the "right to occupy the house for a holiday".[48] These are excluded because the intention here is that the occupancy is of a short-term vacation nature rather than the property becoming the "home" of the person on holiday. The issue can become complicated where the occupant is on a "working holiday" and the term of the tenancy exceeds what one might expect for a mere holiday. This was an issue prior to the introduction of the Housing (Scotland) Act 1988 and the short assured tenancy with its lack of security of tenure. Here, the matter was complicated by the mixture of "genuine" working holidays

---

[40] HSA 1988, Sch 2, para 1.

[41] *Milnbank Housing Association* v *Murdoch* 1995 SLT (Sh Ct) 11.

[42] HSA 1988, Sch 2, para 1.

[43] The level at the time of writing was still the same as when the assured tenancy protection was introduced in 1989 – £6 per week (Assured Tenancies (Tenancies at Low Rent) (Scotland) Regulations 1988 (SI 1988/2085)).

[44] HSA 1988, Sch 2, para 3; Tenancy of Shops (Scotland) Act 1949 – see McAllister, Ch 13.

[45] HSA 1988, Sch 2, para 5 – agricultural land exceeding 2 acres – usually covered by the Agricultural Holdings (Scotland) Act 1991.

[46] HSA 1988, Sch 2, para 6; Agricultural Holdings (Scotland) Acts 1991 and 2003.

[47] See Jack and Vera Duckworth's attempt to stage a sit-in after losing their posts at the Rover's Return in *Coronation Street* – just one of many social issues raised in the programme's long run since 1961 (episode 4531, original air date 25 December 1998). See also below at p 89.

[48] HSA 1988, Sch 2, para 8.

and the desire of landlords to avoid the Rent Acts and purport that their tenants were on holiday and hence not covered by the Rent Acts. Where, however, the working holiday is genuine, care would still need to be taken even with the availability of the short assured tenancy and its lack of security of tenure for the tenant. It might well be that the person on the working holiday wishes to stay for a shorter period – longer than a normal holiday: say 3 or 4 months. Since a short assured tenancy must run for a minimum of 6 months, that would seem on the face of it to be ruled out.[49] One mutually satisfactory solution, however, for landlord and tenant in this situation would be to grant a short assured tenancy of 6 months, guaranteeing the tenant the *right* to stay for 6 months but offering break periods at whatever time suits him, whether that be 3 months or 4 months. This achieves the goals of the legislation of guaranteeing the statutory security for 6 months while giving the tenant the flexibility he seeks. Breaks in favour of tenants have been have been discussed and approved in a slightly different context.[50] A break in favour of the landlord would be rejected as it defeats the protective purpose of having a minimum duration for the tenancy.[51]

In addition, where there are resident landlords there can be no assured tenancy.[52] The definition of when a landlord is a resident landlord is far from straightforward. It applies where the landlord and tenant share more than mere access to the building in question. What is required is that the landlord occupies property A and when renting out property B, there being no ordinary means of access to or from property B other than through property A. Previously, such tenants had protection originally under the furnished tenants' protection introduced by the Rent of Furnished Houses Control (Scotland) Act 1943.[53] This was amended to come within the ambit of Pt VII of the Rent (Scotland) Act 1984 and creation of Pt VII contracts ceased under the Housing (Scotland) Act 1988.[54]

Also excluded are tenancies where the landlord is assumed not to be, by nature, a potential exploiter of their tenants. Into this category comes the Crown[55] and approved educational institutions letting to students.[56] It is also not possible to create an assured tenancy where the

---

[49] See below at p 76 for SAT rules.

[50] *Wishaw and District Housing Association* v *Neary* 2004 SC 463.

[51] See *Caterleisure Ltd* v *Glasgow Prestwick International Airport Ltd* 2005 SLT 1083 for a commercial equivalent which would not be adopted for residential tenancies.

[52] HSA 1988, Sch 2, para 9.

[53] Subsequently in the Landlord and Tenant (Rent Control) Act 1949.

[54] HSA 1988, s 44.

[55] *Ibid*, Sch 2, para 10 – although not property managed by the Crown Estate Commissioners.

[56] *Ibid*, Sch 2 para 7.

landlord is a local authority,[57] a water or sewerage authority[58] or a housing association.[59] The Schedule also specifically excludes those who have transient status, as where a tenancy is granted expressly on a temporary basis as part of the homelessness obligations of a local authority or where the tenants are asylum seekers or their dependants.[60] Tenants of shared ownership schemes, who enjoy protection through their rights as owners, are specifically excluded under the Schedule.[61]

Also excluded from being assured tenancies are what the 1988 terms "transitional cases". These cover protected tenancies, housing association tenancies and secure tenancies.[62] A Glasgow housing association in 1992 provided a couple with a document headed "assured tenancy" in place of their previous "housing association tenancy" when granting them a transfer to a larger property on medical grounds. Understandably, the housing association was seeking to rationalise its stock into the required "assured tenancy" demanded by the Housing (Scotland) Act 1988. The tenancy which the Murdochs had previously had was a secure tenancy in terms of the Housing (Scotland) Act 1987 and, as a housing association tenancy, was covered by the fair rent provisions – the housing association sought a declaration that the tenancy was still within the jurisdiction of the Rent Officer. Such tenancies could not be assured tenancies in terms of Sch 4. Sheriff Jardine accepted the argument that the intention of Parliament was clearly not to allow such avoidance of the implications of this restriction. He was urged to apply the rule in *Pepper* v *Hart*,[63] allowing *Hansard* to be used where there was ambiguity in meaning, but declined to do so, being satisfied that this was in line with the avoidance case law.[64]

(B) SHORT ASSURED TENANCIES

The politically adept move found in the Housing (Scotland) Act 1988 was the introduction of a special lesser version of the assured tenancy, called the "short assured tenancy". This notion of a "reduced rights" tenancy had been introduced in 1980 with the concept of the "short tenancy". This was a tenancy which provided no security of tenure beyond the term of the tenancy.[65] For a landlord to take advantage of this ability to repossess

---

[57] HSA 1988, Sch 2, para 11 – the exception covers regional, island or district councils; development corporations; co-operative housing associations and urban development corporations.

[58] *Ibid*, Sch 4 – amended by Local Government etc (Scotland) Act 1994, s 157(7).

[59] *Ibid*, Sch 4, para 11 (as inserted by Housing (Scotland) Act 2001, Sch 10, para 14).

[60] *Ibid*.

[61] *Ibid*, Sch 2, para 12.

[62] *Ibid*, Sch 2, para 13.

[63] [1993] AC 593.

[64] *Milnbank Housing Association* v *Murdoch* 1994 SCLR 684 at 687.

[65] The tenancy also had a minimum term of 1 year and maximum of 5 years – introduced by the Tenants' Rights etc (Scotland) Act 1980 and subsequently covered by the Rent (Scotland) Act 1984, s 9.

the property automatically rather than for an approved reason, a fair rent had to be registered. The "short tenancy" was not a success at attracting investors and has been almost wholly expunged from history.[66] There was no equivalent in Scotland of the 1980 English "shorthold assured tenancy" with its combination of unrestricted rents and commercial tenancy security of tenure.[67]

The short assured tenancy (SAT) adopts the same kind of approach. It offers the landlord an automatic repossession provided that two conditions are met, in addition to the conditions of an assured tenancy noted above (individual's only or principal home; rent level; not one of the excluded categories).

(i) 6 months minimum term

The first requirement is that the tenancy is for a term of not less than 6 months.[68] The 6-month period is calculated to include the whole of the first day of the lease, so that a lease, for instance, commencing on 7 April of one year and terminating on 6 October of the same year meets the 6-month minimum requirement.[69] This means, somewhat paradoxically, that anyone seeking to rent out for, say, 3 months would not be able to use a simple short assured tenancy. In order to be in a position to guarantee the return of the property he might seek to use one of the techniques developed to avoid the pre-1988 Rent Acts, such as a company lets or non-exclusive occupancy agreements.[70] The problem with most of these, however, is that they do not all replicate the arm's-length relationship which many landlords are seeking. For instance, the bed and breakfast alternative does actually require that something by way of services be provided for the tenant.[71]

If, however, it is the tenant who is keen to rent for a short rental period then, of course, as suggested above, there is a mutually satisfactory non-exploitative solution. There is nothing, in the view of the author, to prevent a lease with a minimum term of 6 months but giving the tenant an option to break the lease at 3 months. As long as there is no attempt to provide the landlord with a right to break before 6 months, the goal of the legislation is secured, namely to provide a minimum of 6 months' security to the tenant.[72]

---

[66] See *William Grant & Son Distillers Ltd* v *McClymont* 2007 Hous LR 76 for a discussion of irritating a tenancy for the tenant's bankruptcy, here in relation to a short tenancy in terms of s 9(1) of the Rent (Scotland) Act 1984. These were so rare that they do not feature further in this introduction to the law.

[67] Housing Act 1980, ss 56–58.

[68] HSA 1988, s 32(1)(a).

[69] *McCabe* v *Wilson* 2006 Hous LR 86.

[70] See Robson and Halliday (1998) at 42–46.

[71] *Gavin* v *Lindsay* 1987 SLT (Sh Ct) 12.

[72] *Wishaw and District Housing Association* v *Neary* 2004 SC 463.

(ii) Service of warning notice – the AT5

The whole point of the short assured tenancy was to encourage landlords to enter the rental market. It was assumed that one of the reasons that landlords either did not enter the market or sought to avoid the impact of the Rent Acts was to provide them with flexibility in their property transactions. Providing a tenancy which gives an automatic repossession guarantee to the landlord requires a "health warning" for prospective tenants about the limited nature of their rights. This comes in the form of a requirement laid on landlords to serve a notice on a tenant.[73] This notice must be served before the creation of the tenancy in question,[74] on the prospective tenant,[75] in the prescribed form.[76] This states that the tenancy being offered is to be a short assured tenancy.[77] The current form, the AT5,[78] draws the prospective tenant's attention to the facts, *inter alia*, that the "LANDLORD OF A SHORT ASSURED TENANCY HAS SPECIAL RIGHTS TO REPOSSESS THE HOUSE",[79] as well as that "A TENANT OF A SHORT ASSURED TENANCY HAS A SPECIAL RIGHT TO APPLY TO A RENT ASSESSMENT COMMITTEE FOR A RENT DETERMINATION FOR THE TENANCY". What the AT5 does not say is that, in place of the balance found in the 1980 short tenancy between lack of security on the one hand and rent control on the other, the SAT protections on rent levels are illusory and of minimal practical benefit to the vast majority of tenants.[80]

It should be noted that if neither of these requirements is fulfilled then the default position where the term is too short or there is no AT5 or a late AT5 is an assured tenancy. The safest course is for the service of the AT5 notice and the signing of the lease to take place on different days. Typically, in practice, landlords and their agents include a condition in the lease which narrates that prior to the signing of the lease, the landlord had served an AT5 notice on the tenant. Given the data from the survey of the private rental sector indicating that the vast majority of landlords have small portfolios of tenancies of only a handful of properties, this should not be too troublesome.[81] Solicitors, though, have reported that they are sometimes approached by their clients and asked to "do the paperwork" for a tenancy where the tenant has already taken possession and some in the early days of the operation of the 1988 Act did talk

---

73 HSA 1988, s 32(1)(b).
74 Section 32(2)(b).
75 Section 32(2)(c).
76 Section 32(2)(a).
77 Section 32(2)(d).
78 Assured Tenancies (Scotland) Regulations 1988 (SI 1988/2109).
79 See Chapter 6 below.
80 See Chapter 5 below .
81 Scottish Government (2009) at Table 2.1, 15.

about sending these to the tenant after a period. Seeking to serve an AT5 in these circumstances requires this period of possession to be treated as a "free trial" period on the lines of that found in *To Buy or Not to Buy*.[82] Whether or not the court would accept that this was in line with the purposive approach to the Rent Acts in *Cadogan Estates*[83] is a far from clear.

(C) PROTECTED TENANCIES

As noted above, the original Rent Acts were a crude response to exploitation which was harming munitions production in the Great War. They froze rents and provided security of tenure.[84] The Rent Act 1957 abolished these controls and returned renting property to market forces. This meant, of course, no rent control. Nor was there, thenceforth, any security of tenure beyond the terms of the tenancy. The Labour Party pledged in the 1964 election campaign to repeal this Act with its links to the notorious slum landlord Peter Rachman. What Richard Crossman produced to meet this commitment was quite sophisticated. It re-introduced security of tenure as well as providing a mechanism for tenants to have a "fair rent" registered. There continued to be a significant number of "repossession cases" but for the standard tenant paying rent and acting responsibly there was a strong chance of remaining in his home.[85] The system remains in place since the assured tenancy regime was introduced for only new tenancies entered into on or after 2 January 1989. The problems which had been experienced in the 1920s following the Rent Act 1923[86] and much more recently in the 1960s and the operation of "creeping decontrol" led the Conservative Party to avoid this particular political pitfall. Rather than incur the opprobrium of being seen to take away rights from the visibly vulnerable, they were left alone. There were no obvious losers since the assured tenancy regime looked superficially the same. One learned

---

[82] The daytime TV BBC property programme where couples are shown three homes by experts and are allowed to live in one for a trial period before deciding whether or not to put in a bid. It commenced in 2003 and was still accepting applications for new property buyers in July 2010.

[83] *Cadogan Estates* v *McMahon* [2001] 1 AC 378, where the bankruptcy of the tenant allowed a successful repossession by the landlord. Sheriff Principal Kearney was, however, not impressed with the clarity of this authority: *William Grant & Son Distillers Ltd* v *McClymont* 2007 Hous LR 7. He took the view that, by inserting an irritancy clause in the purported short tenancy, the landlords took the lease outwith the definition of short tenancy in s 9(1) of the Rent (Scotland) Act 1984.

[84] Increase of Rent and Mortgage Interest (War Restrictions) Act 1915, as repealed and re-enacted in the Increase of Rent and Mortgage Interest (Restrictions) Act 1920.

[85] For details of repossession cases under the Rent (Scotland) Act 1984, Sch 2, see Robson and Halliday (2nd edn, 1998) at 131.

[86] Constable Committee (1925); Damer (1982) .

commentator, indeed, was unfairly taken to task for pointing out that the "assured tenancy Emperor" had no clothes. It was suggested by his critics that things would be tougher on landlords since, in effect, they had fewer grounds of possession under the new 1988 legislation rather than under the Crossman legislation. As is clear when one compares the grounds, those available under the 1988 Act may be fewer in number but they are more extensive in their coverage.[87]

This means that it is still possible – and will remain so for many years to come – to encounter a tenancy which was started as late as the mid-1980s and is covered not by the Housing (Scotland) Act 1988 but by the successor to Richard Crossman's Rent Act 1965, the Rent (Scotland) Act 1984.[88] The requirements for a tenancy to be covered by the old protected system are based on the principle of protection from exploitation. Hence they do not cover all properties. They did not cover houses where the rateable value exceeded £200 on the designated "appropriate day" of 23 March 1965 when the legislation was introduced on 1 April 1965. The "appropriate day" was 1 April 1978 for houses which first appeared on the valuation roll after that date. The relevant figure was raised to £600 to reflect the impact of inflation and subsequently raised to £1,600 for houses appearing on the valuation roll on or after 1 April 1985.[89] Also excluded from the old 1984 Act tenancy protection are houses where either no rent was payable or the rent payable was less than two-thirds of the rateable value on the relevant "appropriate day", the rationale again being that at such low levels of rent there was no market exploitation taking place.

There was no coverage of tenancies from "trusted" landlords such as specified educational institutions,[90] or inappropriate tenancies such as holiday lets[91] or properties let with land.[92] Where a tenancy was let *bona fide* at a rent which included payments in respect of board or attendance, that tenancy was also excluded from coverage. This exclusion went on to become one of the simplest and easiest exclusions to exploit by landlords seeking to avoid the Rent Acts with minimal effort through the provision of a box of breakfast goods supplied weekly or a central dining area to which tenants required to travel. While many of these practices were of doubtful effect, they often had the required impact of making tenants

---

[87] See Chapter 6 below.
[88] The 1965 Act was originally repealed and re-enacted by the Rent (Scotland) Act 1971, altered by the Rent Act 1974 (which abolished the special status of furnished tenancies) and finally re-enacted in the Rent (Scotland) Act 1984.
[89] Protected Tenancies and Part VII Contracts (Rateable Value Limits) (Scotland) Order 1985 (SI 1985/314).
[90] Section 2(1)(c).
[91] Section 2(1)(d).
[92] Section 2(1)(e).

think they had no recourse to the Rent Officer to fix a fair rent or any protection against a request to leave.[93]

(D) PART VII TENANCIES

Where one person granted to another person the right to occupy a dwelling-house in exchange for rent which included payment for the use of furniture or services this was known as a Pt VII contract.[94] The Rent Act 1974 provided that there was no longer to be a distinction between tenants solely on the basis of whether furniture had been provided. Furnished tenants were to enjoy the same rights as unfurnished. What was left, however, were those provided with services as well as accommodation.

These contracts, then, are only available where the contract was entered into by the end of 1988. Unlike protected tenancies, however, they are extraordinarily unlikely to be encountered. Section 44(2) of the Housing (Scotland) Act 1988 provided that existing Pt VII contracts ceased to operate once there had been a variation in the rent of the premises. It is possible that someone might have continued paying 1988 rent for over 20 years but the author is unaware of any reports of anyone ever in such a position. The successor body to the Rent Assessment Committee, the Private Rented Housing Panel, records no activity in this area.

(E) TIED TENANCIES

The position of those who have rights to occupy under their contracts of employment is anomalous. Where there is a service occupancy or tied tenancy then the common law allows the tenancy to co-exist with the employment only for as long as the employment exists. Where the tenancy is expressly stated to be dependent on the employee being in that employment, the landlord will have the contractual right to seek repossession of his property at the end of the employment contract. That much is reasonably clear. In such situations the landlord has the right to repossess the property. The rights which exist where the landlord does not repossess at the end of the employment contact have not been the subject of extensive discussion. The Housing (Scotland) Act 1988 seems to recognise that such situations exist. Schedule 5 provides a discretionary ground of possession where a house is let to the tenant "as a consequence of his employment by the landlord ... and the tenant has ceased to be in that employment". This suggests that for post-1989 tenancies the rights which

---

[93] *Gavin* v *Lindsay* 1987 SLT (Sh Ct) 12.
[94] This was the Part covering furnished tenancies in the Rent Act 1971. Furnished premises were given equal rights with unfurnished properties under the Rent Act 1974 and the "rump" of the coverage is located in Pt VII of the Rent (Scotland) Act 1984.

effeir to the ex-employee are normal assured tenancy rights. There is no requirement for the landlord to have another employee wishing to occupy the premises. This contrasts with the equivalent ground of possession found in the Rent (Scotland) Act 1984 which allows repossession where the property is "reasonably required by the landlord for occupation as a residence for some person engaged in his whole-time employment" and the current tenant was in the employment of the landlord and the property was let as a consequence of that employment and he has ceased to be in that employment.[95] This again points up the need to be absolutely clear when a tenancy commenced to determine what set of rules are applicable. The kind of scenario where this arises was encountered in a case involving rural accommodation near Aviemore in the late 1990s. In *Trs of Kinrara Estate v Campbell*[96] a 3-year lease from 1993 was granted to a tenant who was told there was no reason to suppose it would not be renewed indefinitely. It was continued by tacit relocation until 1998, when notice to quit was served on the tenant. The Estate offered alternative accommodation in a property which the tenant had occupied previously. He was not keen to take this as the property was not suitable for visits from his elderly parents or his blind and disabled brother. The Estate, on the other hand, wanted the property for occupation by its long-serving, retired former head keeper whom they had no legal obligation to re-house. He and his wife had "set their hearts" on the property. The matter was settled as a matter of "reasonableness", weighing the competing claims of the parties in the existing tenant's favour.

Problems arise in situations where the employment and the occupancy of the landlord's property are less obviously linked. The question here becomes whether or not a "tied" tenancy is implied. The test applied in the past has been whether the employment is "necessary" for the performance of that person's employment. So, where a tenancy is offered with a job it may be no more than a perk or encouragement to take the job rather than a requirement of that job that an employee be on hand to carry out their duties more effectively. Hence, an estate worker or caretaker can more efficiently do their jobs in the tied accommodation. It matters where they live. Where there is no such link then a tied house will not be inferred from the mere fact of their being an employee,[97] although the principle has not always been consistently applied.[98] Using the terms of a lease and including notice to quit provisions would tend to support the notion that what is being offered a lease rather than a service occupancy.[99]

---

[95] RSA 1984, Sch 2, case 7(a).
[96] 1999 Hous LR 55.
[97] *MacGregor* v *Dunnett* 1949 SC 510.
[98] *Pollock* v *Assessor for Inverness-shire* 1923 SC 693.
[99] *British Transport Commission* v *Assessor for Inverness* 1952 SC 511.

The precise relationship between the tenancy rights of occupiers and the rights of employers in terms of the employment contract, then, is less than pellucid. This conflict appears to have produced little by way of modern litigation. In the author's experience over the years, employees who have tenancies from their employees have assumed that their rights to occupy cease once their employment ceases and have not challenged any subsequent requests for them to move out, even where they appeared to have a colourable tenancy through payment of rent and the passage of time.

(F) CONTRACTUAL TENANCIES

In our fictional eight-flat close we have so far seen that, in theory at least, if various private landlords owned six of the flats, it would be possible for there to be an assured tenant, a short assured tenant, a protected tenant, a Pt VII tenant and a tied tenancy.[100] If, however, the tenancy does not meet the various statutory criteria then there will simply be a contractual tenancy. In such circumstances, there are, however, still statutory rules which apply, providing a degree of protection to such contractual tenants. All occupiers of residential property are protected against illegal eviction and harassment.[101] Those who have contractual tenancies are also entitled to a statutory minimum period of notice to quit. The length of that period varies depending on the length of lease. Where the lease is for more than 4 months the period of notice is 40 days, while it is one-third of the duration of the let for leases of less than 4 months.[102] There is a statutory minimum notice period of 4 weeks.[103]

(2) Social rented tenancies

There is less variation in the social rented sector in the kinds of tenancy which can be encountered. The standard tenancy is the Scottish secure tenancy and the scope for landlords in the social rented sector opting for another form of tenure is limited. In the past few years, in order to provide a wider range of choice to potential tenants, there has been some use by social landlords of market rent tenancies. In order to do this, however, it is necessary for them to set up free-standing subsidiary organisations which rent the properties. These separate organisations themselves use the short assured tenancy for such tenants and are, for these purposes, private landlords.[104]

---

[100] The possibility of a resident landlord is dealt with elsewhere – see p 226.
[101] See Chapter 6 below.
[102] Sheriff Courts (Scotland) Act 1907, ss 34–38.
[103] RSA 1984, s 112.
[104] Weslo Annual Report (2009).

(G) SCOTTISH SECURE TENANCIES

The goal of the single social tenancy appears in s 11 of the Housing (Scotland) Act 2001. This finally unites the different kinds of tenancy encountered in local authority housing and housing associations in a single form. There are a number of requirements which, if satisfied, mean that the tenancy is a Scottish secure tenancy. These are four in total.

(i) Tenant an individual

The whole purpose of providing protection against eviction and rights of succession is that individuals and their families may benefit. Just as the protection of the Rent Acts was aimed at preventing exploitation of housing scarcity, social rented housing has been aimed at meeting local housing need. This is usually done by providing tenancies for individuals rather than any intermediary bodies such as companies or voluntary associations. There are, however, situations where, for instance, accommodation is being provided to vulnerable individuals who have support needs. In such instances the tenants might well be unlikely to sustain a tenancy themselves and the support organisation would have a simple contractual tenancy with the social landlord.[105]

(ii) House is the tenant's only or principal home

Again, the traditional function and purpose of social housing were to meet housing need and provide accommodation at rents which are affordable. It could be inferred that this focus on need meant that landlords would wish to house those in greatest need. They were in the business of allocating scarce resources and would not want to provide accommodation for someone who wished to have a second home. The issue, though, of tenants moving in with ageing relatives to meet their care needs has caused some practical problems for those concerned to lose their rights to their original properties. That is now addressed, to an extent, with the succession rights to secure tenancies being extended to carers.[106] Whether or not a property is the tenant's only or principal home has been examined in the context principally of succession rights to tenancies[107] and in relation to repossession proceedings,[108] dealt with below. At this stage, suffice it to say that the phrase which encapsulates whether or not a property is a person's "only or principal home" is whether or not "the person concerned has

---

[105] Weslo Housing Management, like other registered social landlords, for instance, has standard lease arrangements with various providers of support for those with mental health difficulties. In these instances a Scottish secure tenancy cannot be granted to the support organisation since they are not an individual as required by s 11(1)(c) of the Housing (Scotland) Act 2001.

[106] See Chapter 7 below.

[107] *Ibid.*

[108] See Chapter 6 below.

such real tangible and substantial connection with the house in question that it, rather than any other place of residence, can properly be described as having been his only or principal home".[109] It is implied, of course, that there be residence by the tenant, although temporary absences were permitted.[110] When there is no physical signs that the person was still in occupation or any intention to return then there will be consequences in terms of succession and repossession rights.[111]

(iii) House let as a separate dwelling

Although this requirement features extensively in the private sector, it is rather less of an issue in social renting. The main area where there have been disputes is that of hostel-type accommodation. The specific question which was raised was whether or not the room a hostel dweller occupied counted as a "separate dwelling" for the purposes of exercising the right to buy. The Lands Tribunal was asked whether occupying a bedroom with no facilities other than bed and sink amounted to a let of a separate dwelling. It concluded that it did not. The issue has centred on the major living activities of cooking, sleeping and eating. Where living activities are carried out in accommodation which is not part of the individual's purported let but which is shared with others, then there is no separate let.[112] The lack of cooking facilities was an issue discussed by the House of Lords in a private-sector case involving a man living in a residential "hotel" in Kensington, London. The issue here concerned not the right to buy but whether the owners could evict Mr Collins. The House of Lords determined that what was crucial was not primarily the physical features or facilities of the accommodation but the manner in which it was used by the tenant.[113] Thus, a bedsit with no cooking facilities, into which a tenant brings all his meals and/or eats out, can be a separate dwelling.[114]

(iv) Landlord one of a recognised category of secure landlords

The Scottish secure tenancy now brings together a range of bodies which are not run for profit and, in order to utilise the legislation, landlords must be local authorities, registered social landlords, a water authority or a sewerage authority. This removed the anomalous situation in which housing associations had found themselves from 1989 onwards and the introduction of assured tenancies under the Housing (Scotland) Act 1988. Between 1989 and 2001 new housing association tenants were entitled to

---

[109] *Roxburgh DC* v *Collins* 1991 SCLR 575 at 578 D–E.
[110] *Beggs* v *Kilmarnock and Loudon DC* 1995 SCLR 435.
[111] See Chapters 6 and 7 below.
[112] *Thomson* v *City of Glasgow DC* 1986 SLT (Lands Tr) 6.
[113] *Uratemp Ventures Ltd* v *Collins* 2001 Hous LR 133 and the editors' notes at 142–143.
[114] *Ibid* at 136.

assured tenancies and they were regarded as part of the independent rent sector. That was rectified by the Housing (Scotland) Act 2001.

In addition, the legislation lays down a list of tenancies which cannot be Scottish secure tenancies.[115] Again, like the tenancies in the private sector which cannot be assured tenancies, these are largely excluded due to it being inappropriate for the tenants to enjoy the rights conferred on secure tenants.

(a) Premises occupied under a contract of employment

This exemption makes clear that this applies where the occupancy of the property is required for the "better performance of the tenant's duties". There is extensive case law on this issue from the "right to buy" legislation. As in all matters, each case is treated on its merits and there is no standard formula. Much of the debate stemmed from the fact that when the contracts of employment were drawn up the framers did not have in mind the implications of the contracts in terms of loss of community housing resources. Sometimes issues have been relatively straightforward, as where a groundsman occupied a farmhouse surrounded by nursery grounds which were his responsibility.[116] This contrasts, though, with a swimming pool manager whose house was close by the pool and who had been contacted by the police to deal with emergencies on a number of occasions.[117] In the first case the Lands Tribunal determined that the property was occupied for the better performance of the groundsman's duties, whereas in the latter the pool manager could, like other pool managers, have lived a distance away from the pool. It was just fortunate that he lived across the road when there were security call-outs.

(b) Police and fire service accommodation

In the original 1980 legislation giving rights to public-sector tenants against arbitrary eviction as well as the right to buy, accommodation owned by these services was included. The public interest in having guaranteed accommodation for these vital services seems clear, although it does contrast with the provisions of the National Health Service and Community Care Act 1990 whereby accommodation for doctors and nurses was no longer excluded from being an assured tenancy.[118] In the case of the police exclusion this applies only where the police officer occupies the house without paying rent or council tax.[119] The exclusion for members of the fire brigade applies where there is a condition in their contract of employment which requires them to live in close proximity

---

[115] HSA 2001, Sch 1.
[116] *McKay* v *Livingstone Development Corp* 1990 SLT (Lands Tr) 54.
[117] *Stevenson* v *West Lothian DC* 1985 SLT (Lands Tr) 9.
[118] National Health Service and Community Care Act 1990, Sch 8, para 20.
[119] HSA 2001, Sch 1, para 2(a).

to a particular fire station.[120] There is also a broader exclusion where the house is let expressly on a temporary basis pending it being required for the purposes of either the police force or the fire brigade.[121]

(c) Lettings to students

Lettings are excluded where a student is pursuing or intends to pursue a course of study provided by a specified institution and the landlord is that institution or another specified institution.[122] The institutions specified cover any central institution within the meaning of s 135(1) of the Education (Scotland) Act 1980; any institution within the higher education sector within the meaning of s 56(2) of the Further and Higher Education (Scotland) Act 1992; and any institution which provides further education.[123] The lack of need for security of tenure beyond the term of one's course and the assumed responsibility of these institutions towards those whom they are educating mean that these public institutions are not covered by the Scottish secure tenancy regime.

(d) Temporary accommodation during the carrying out of work

This exemption was introduced to cover the practical problem posed by a tenant who is decanted during work to their own property and who finds that the temporary property is for some reason more congenial. One challenge by a housing association tenant in the 1980s to being asked to move back into a reduced-size version of their original flat led to this limitation on when a tenancy can become a secure tenancy.[124] It applies where the tenant has the right to return to the property after the work is completed. This may be by agreement or by order of the sheriff under s 16(6).[125] In the interim there is provision for the landlord to provide a short Scottish secure tenancy for the decant property.[126]

(e) Accommodation for homeless persons

Within the various obligations towards those who apply for assistance in terms of the homeless persons provisions of the Housing (Scotland) Act 1987 there is an obligation to secure that accommodation becomes available for applicants while enquiries are being made.[127] If the house is being let to the tenant expressly on a temporary basis for a term of less

---

120 HSA 2001, Sch 1, para 2(b).
121 *Ibid*, Sch 1, para 2(c).
122 Scottish Secure Tenancies (Exceptions) Regulations 2002 (SSI 2002/314), reg 11.
123 *Ibid*.
124 *Charing Cross and Kelvingrove Housing Association* v *Kraska* 1986 SLT (Sh Ct) 42.
125 HSA 2001, Sch 1, para 4(b), covering ground 10; HSA 2001, Sch2 – see below at Chapter 6.
126 See below at p 93.
127 HSA 1987, s 29 and see also Chapter 2 above.

than 6 months under the provisions of Pt II of the Housing (Scotland) Act 1987 then such a tenancy cannot be a secure tenancy.[128] There is provision for the social landlord to make a short Scottish secure tenancy available in such circumstances.[129]

(f) Accommodation for offenders

Obligations are also imposed on local authorities in terms of the Social Work (Scotland) Act 1968 to assist people on probation or released from prison.[130] Where, in exercising this duty, the local authority grants a tenancy of less than 6 months, then such a tenancy is excluded from being a secure tenancy.[131]

(g) Shared ownership agreements

Tenants who are beneficiaries of a shared ownership scheme in relation to the premises are not covered by the secure tenancy regime.[132] A shared ownership agreement exists where a proportion of a house is sold and the remaining proportion of the house is leased to a person.[133] This is a theoretical transaction in that the share sold is *pro indiviso*. This means that it is a notional rather than a physical proportion of the house which is sold. The purchaser then has the right to purchase the rest of the property in instalments. This is somewhat akin to the informal arrangements whereby small tenement properties used to be sold up until the 1960s, prior to the registration of title regime, when the title deeds only were treated as evidence of ownership. The purchaser received the title deeds only when the final instalment was paid. It led to some problems where sellers denied that they had sold the property and claimed that the payments were in fact rent. This kind of issue is avoided in that shared ownership schemes recognised by the 2001 Act involve an agreement whereby the rights in the house are conveyed to trustees to hold on behalf of the purchasers. The shared ownership purchaser becomes entitled to exclusive occupancy of the house but can sell only through the trustees.[134]

(h) Agricultural and business premises

Just as these kinds of property may not be covered by the assured tenancy private sector, so they are also excluded from the social rented sector. Where a local authority or registered social landlord owns and rents out property which is used for a shop or office for business, trade or

---

[128] HSA 2001, Sch 1, para 5.
[129] HSA 1987, s 31(5)(c); see below at p 93.
[130] Social Work (Scotland) Act 1968, s 27.
[131] HSA 2001, Sch 1, para 6.
[132] *Ibid*, Sch 1, para 5.
[133] *Ibid*, s 83(3).
[134] *Ibid*.

professional purposes then such a lease will not be a secure tenancy[135] and will be covered by either the Tenancy of Shops (Scotland) Act 1949[136] or by the very limited protections available under the Law Reform (Miscellaneous Provisions) (Scotland) Act 1985 in relation to late rent payments in commercial leases.[137]

Also excluded are houses let with agricultural land exceeding 2 acres in extent[138] and premises licensed for the sale of excisable liquor.[139] As we noted above, there are other protections available for those occupying agricultural land,[140] and licensed premises were covered by the Rent Acts until 1933 because the view was taken by the Onslow and Marley Committees that an "undesirable tenant" could imperil the alcohol licence.[141]

(i) Houses part of within the curtilage of other non-housing buildings

Where there is a tenancy which is part of a property owned by the social landlord and which is held mainly for non-housing purposes and mainly consists of accommodation other than housing accommodation, then such a tenancy cannot be a secure tenancy.[142] So, for instance, a school house which is actually an integral part of the school premises would not be a secure tenancy. That is reasonably straightforward and arises from the complexity of seeking to run an educational establishment with the complications of another person's rights of access and property use rendering safety and security problematic. The issue of "curtilage", while it has the same rationale, has been rather more difficult to define. It has been discussed extensively in relation to the right to buy, particularly in relation to the sale of surplus schools. Excluded from the right to buy are properties which are part of, or in the "curtilage" of, non-housing premises under the Housing (Scotland) Act 1987. The Lands Tribunal, noting that "curtilage" was not a term of art in Scots law, has suggested that it broadly means land adjoining a building necessary for the comfortable enjoyment of that building. This was stated in a case involving the sale of school house with lean-to shed. The shed was part of the house and access was possible only through the playground and a servitude right of

---

[135] HSA 2001, Sch 1, para 8(b).
[136] McAllister (2002), Ch 13.
[137] *Ibid* at 5.18–5.39.
[138] HSA 2001, Sch 1, para 8(a).
[139] *Ibid*, para 8(c).
[140] Agricultural Holdings (Scotland) Act 1991.
[141] The Onslow Committee in 1923 at 13 and the Marley Committee in 1931 at para 106 recommended their removal from Rent Act coverage for this reason. This recommendation was duly enacted and licensed premises have remained outwith the Rent Acts from the enactment of the Rent and Mortgage Interest Restrictions (Amendment) Act 1933, s 1(3).
[142] HSA 2001, Sch 1, para 9.

access would have had to be created.[143] The area involved in "curtilage", however, has been treated as quite modest.[144]

(j) Accommodation in property not owned by the landlord

There can be no secure tenancies where the local authority or registered social landlords are themselves leasing the property unless the terms of the lease permit the letting of a house under a secure tenancy.[145] This might, for instance, occur where there was a sub-lease from another landlord in the social rented sector and the existence of tenants on secure tenancies in the property would, in fact, be in line with the over-landlord's day-to-day policies. Although, in principle, landlords cannot give greater rights than they themselves possess, this provision is inserted for the avoidance of doubt.

(h) Short Scottish secure tenancies

There is also provision for a shorter tenancy which gives much greater flexibility to the local authority in eviction situations. In keeping with the nature of the landlord's goal of meeting housing need in the social rented sector, however, this lesser form of tenancy can be created and operated only in limited circumstances and if it meets certain criteria.[146] Its relationship to the Scottish secure tenancy bears a strong resemblance to that of the short assured tenancy to the assured tenancy. There are, however, some crucial differences. Unlike the private sector, it is not the most common form of tenancy used but one resorted to in special situations only.

A tenancy of a house is a short Scottish secure tenancy if:

(i) It satisfies the criteria for being a Scottish secure tenancy[147]

As is noted above, this covers a house being let as a separate dwelling by a social landlord to an individual as his only or principal home, provided that the property is not excluded by statute from being a Scottish secure tenancy.[148]

(ii) It is for a term of not less than 6 months[149]

No upper time limit is specified. However, the goal behind this kind of tenancy is to provide an opportunity for tenant whose behaviour has in the past been problematic to show that they can sustain a tenancy responsibly. Since, as we shall see, there is also provision for a default

---

[143] *Walker* v *Strathclyde RC* 1990 SLT (Lands Tr) 17.
[144] *Shipman* v *Lothian RC* 1989 SLT (Lands Tr) 82.
[145] HSA 2001, Sch 1, para 10.
[146] *Ibid*, s 34(1).
[147] *Ibid*, s 34(1)(a).
[148] See above at p 84.
[149] HSA 2001, s 34(1)(b).

conversion into a Scottish secure tenancy, extensive use of such "trial" or "test" tenancies would surely be subject to censorious comment from the Scottish Housing Regulator.[150]

(iii) Before its creation the landlord serves on the tenant a notice in prescribed form[151]

There are regulations which specify what information must be provided to the prospective tenant.[152] These regulations require that it must be stated that the tenancy is a short Scottish secure tenancy, what the terms of the tenancy is and why it is a short Scottish secure tenancy. Like the private sector AT5 notice, the social rented form employs the upper case extensively and with diminishing effect.[153] The crucial information in Note 3 informs the "PROSPECTIVE TENANT" that:

> "A LANDLORD OF A SHORT SCOTTISH SECURE TENANCY HAS SPECIAL RIGHTS TO REPOSSESS THE HOUSE. IF THE LANDLORD TERMINATES THE TENANCY BY ISSUING A VALID NOTICE IN TERMS OF SECTION 36 OF THE ACT AND GIVES THE TENANT AT LEAST 2 MONTHS NOTICE (OR A LONGER PERIOD IF THE TENANCY AGREEMENT PROVIDES) OF HIS INTENTION TO REPOSSESS THE HOUSE THE COURT MUST GRANT THE LANDLORD AN ORDER ALLOWING HIM TO EVICT THE TENANT IF HE APPLIES FOR ONE AT THE END OF THE TENANCY PERIOD SET OUT IN THE TENANCY AGREEMENT."

After another page of shouting the details under which short Scottish secure tenancies may be offered, Note 5 advises the "PROSPECTIVE TENANT" that "IF YOU DO NOT AGREE THAT THE TENANCY OFFERED BY THIS NOTICE SHOULD BE A SHORT SCOTTISH SECURE TENANCY YOU HAVE A RIGHT OF APPEAL TO THE COURTS UNDER SECTION 38 OF THE ACT".

The requirement to explain why the tenant has a short Scottish secure tenancy is at the heart of this limited rights tenancy. The essence of the short Scottish secure tenancy is that the landlord can regain the property without having to satisfy the sheriff as to reasonableness. In order to put itself in that position, however, of providing to one of their tenants lesser rights than is standard, the social landlord must have a reason for granting such limited security of tenure. Here, the social rented sector differs from the private sector where landlords who choose to offer short assured tenancies have freedom to offer the lesser rights, without requiring to have any justification. In order to grant a Scottish short secure tenancy the landlord must, then, have grounds for granting such a tenancy. The grounds are specified in Sch 6:

---

[150] See Chapter 8 below.
[151] HSA 2001, s 34(1)(c).
[152] Short Scottish Secure Tenancies (Notices) Regulations 2002 (SSI 2002/315).
[153] See Notes 1, 2, 3, 4, 5 and 6 which employ this "shouting" text technique reminiscent of spam e-mails.

(1) Previous anti-social behaviour[154]

Where, within the 3 years preceding service of the notice, a person has been subject to a repossession order on the grounds of anti-social behaviour, nuisance, annoyance or immoral or illegal behaviour. This covers orders granted in Scotland, Northern Ireland, England and Wales and repossessions both in the private and the social rented sectors.

(2) Anti-social behaviour[155]

In addition to situations where prospective tenants have been subject to repossession on anti-social and nuisance grounds, ASBOs themselves are a ground for making a short Scottish secure tenancy. These may affect either the prospective tenant or a person who it is proposed will reside with them. A wide range of activities have been made the subject of ASBOs in terms of the Crime and Disorder Act 1998.[156] These have ranged from repetitive playing of two songs by buskers, James Ryan and Andrew Stevens;[157] to a 60-year-old man dressing up as a schoolgirl.[158] One would expect only housing-related ASBOs to be used in relation to this ground. These have included people being banned from answering the door in their underwear[159] and from playing loud music[160] to noisy sex sessions which disturbed neighbours.[161]

---

154 HSA 2001, Sch 6, para 1.
155 *Ibid*, Sch 6, para 2.
156 *Moray Council* v *Hamilton* 2003 Hous LR 83.
157 The songs in question were *Faith* by George Michael and *Wonderwall* by Oasis – the buskers played these in Moseley, Birmingham, at all hours of the day and night (http://www.birminghammail.net/news/top-stories/2009/08/19/asbo-for-buskers-who-could-only-play-one-george-michael-and-one-oasis-track-97319-24484187/): Ryan played guitar and Stevens the dustbin lid.
158 The ASBO on 60-year-old Northampton resident Peter Trigger stopped him from wearing skirts or showing bare legs on school days between 08.30 and 10.00 and 14.45 and 16.00 – see http://www.bbc.co.uk/news/uk-10790872, where a disturbing image of him in his outfit appears.
159 *Daily Record*, 4 March 2005 – pp 1, 4 and 5 – I'm banned from going to the door in my undies – http//www.thefreelibrary.com/I'M+BANNED+FROM+GOING+TO+THE+DOOR+IN+MY+UNDIES%3b+EXCLUSIVE+Sheriff..-a0129680403 – although this would be subject to the "Cherie Booth half-asleep defence" from the notorious 2 May 1997 "nightie" incident: http://news.bbc.co.uk/1/hi/uk_politics/4685802.stm – includes a picture (last accessed 1 July 2010).
160 Britney Spears' *Toxic* was played for several hours by 55-year-old grandmother Bridget Marr of Crieff. This formed part of the behaviour that led to her and her family being evicted in October 2006: http://www.dailyrecord.co.uk/news/2006/01/10/asbo-hell-family-are-kicked-out-of-home-86908-16566139/. She died in Perth 2 years later, having been rehoused there in Muirton: http://findarticles.com/p/articles/mi_qn4161/is_20080406/ai_n25142865/.
161 Newcastle Crown Court, 29 June 2010 dealt with breach of an ASBO – Caroline Cartwright, 49, was made the subject of the anti-social-behaviour order, banning her from making loud noises during frequent love-making sessions with her husband, Steve, on 17 April 2009. She attended Newcastle Crown Court on 30 June 2010 and

(3) Temporary letting to person seeking accommodation[162]

As we have noted, there is an obligation not to exclude from the housing waiting list on the ground of lack of residence people moving into the area to take up employment.[163] In order to make such moves a reality, social landlords may provide short Scottish secure tenancies expressly to enable a person to take up employment in their area and to seek accommodation.

(4) Temporary letting pending development[164]

This provision allowing short Scottish secure tenancies for "decants" corresponds to the exclusion of decants from the tenancies which can be Scottish secure tenancies. It enables tenants of social landlords to enjoy a tenancy while the property is being developed. It provides a solution to the problem of the tenant who prefers where they are staying temporarily by allowing the landlord to protect against a refusal to move back.

(5) Accommodation for homeless persons[165]

While we have noted that accommodation provided expressly on a temporary basis for homeless persons may not be a Scottish secure tenancy, it is open to local authorities to offer a short Scottish secure tenancy of not less than 6 months. This will be one of the range of options which local authorities will use to secure that applicants are not left homeless. Such temporary accommodation must meet the standards laid down in the Homeless Persons (Unsuitable Accommodation) (Scotland) Order 2004 as regards both physical proximity and safety standards.[166] The other solutions which the Code of Guidance mentions include bed and breakfast, hostels, lodgings, private-sector leasing and mobile homes.[167] The Guidance, though, makes clear that some accommodation such as mobile homes are generally not satisfactory and should only be provided in limited circumstances.[168]

(6) Accommodation for person requiring housing support services[169]

Where a person requires, or is in receipt of, housing support services, then this is one of grounds for a local authority providing a short Scottish

---

admitted breaching the ASBO on two occasions – the first for having excessively noisy sex with her husband on 14 March 2010 and the second for playing loud music the following day – *Northern Echo*, 30 June 2010, p 2.

[162] HSA 2001, Sch 6, para 3.
[163] See Chapter 2 above.
[164] HSA 2001, Sch 6, para 4.
[165] *Ibid*, Sch 6, para 5.
[166] COG 2005, paras 9.15–9.18.
[167] *Ibid*, paras 9.46–9.53.
[168] *Ibid*, para 9.53.
[169] HSA 2001, Sch 6, para 6.

secure tenancy. Where a tenant has a short Scottish secure tenancy because it has been converted from a Scottish secure tenancy or where the ground for its creation was a previous anti-social behaviour or an anti-social behaviour order, there is an obligation to provide or ensure the provision of such housing support services as the landlord considers is appropriate to enable the tenancy to be converted to a Scottish secure tenancy.[170] The housing support services most relevant to short Scottish secure tenancies cover such things as "assisting the service user to engage with individuals, professionals and other bodies with an interest in the welfare of the service user" (7) "advising or assisting the service user with personal budget and debt counselling" (9) and "advising or assisting the service user in dealing with relationships and disputes with neighbours" (10).[171]

(7) Accommodation in property not owned by landlord[172]

As indicated, there may be no Scottish secure tenancy where the landlord does not own the property and is himself a tenant for a fixed period. In such circumstances the mid-landlord may choose to provide a short Scottish secure tenancy for a period up to but not exceeding the term of his own lease. The mechanism provided by the statute is the short Scottish secure tenancy with its guarantee of recovery to the landlord.

The relationship between Scottish secure tenancies and short Scottish secure tenancies

INTRODUCTION

Unlike the private sector regime where the assured and short assured are versions of the modern private tenancy there is an active relationship between the two kinds of tenancy available in social renting. Where there is a Scottish secure tenancy it can, in certain circumstances, be "downgraded" to a short Scottish secure tenancy. By the same token, by the passing of time, among other reasons, a short Scottish secure tenancy is "upgraded" to become a Scottish secure tenancy.

CONVERSION OF A SCOTTISH SECURE TENANCY TO A SHORT SCOTTISH SECURE TENANCY[173]

We look first to the reasons for a tenant losing the security of the Scottish secure tenancy. This can occur where the landlord serves a notice of

---

[170] HSA 2001, s 34(7).
[171] Housing (Scotland) Act 2001 (Housing Support Services) Regulations 2002 (SSI 2002/444).
[172] HSA 2001, Sch 6, para 7.
[173] *Ibid*, s 35 .

conversion where there has been an anti-social behaviour order in terms of the Antisocial Behaviour etc (Scotland) Act 2004.[174] This notice may be challenged by the tenant and the court may decide to grant a declarator that the order is of no effect. It will does this where it considers there are good grounds for doing so.[175]

CONVERSION OF SHORT SCOTTISH SECURE TENANCY TO A SCOTTISH SECURE TENANCY[176]

The situation where a short Scottish secure tenancy exists is rather different. Here, the change occurs where no anti-social behaviour by the tenant comes to the attention of the landlord. Where in the 12 months following the creation of a short Scottish secure tenancy the landlord has not served a notice seeking possession, the tenancy becomes a Scottish secure tenancy.[177] Where the landlord commences proceedings for possession but either the notice is withdrawn or it has ceased to be in force then the conversion takes place 12 months from either the date the notice was withdrawn or ceased to be in force or after 12 months, whichever is the later.[178] If possession proceedings against a tenant are raised unsuccessfully then the conversion takes place either on the date the proceedings are finally determined[179] or on the expiry of the 12-month period, whichever is the later.[180] Where a short Scottish secure tenancy does become a Scottish secure tenancy the landlord must inform the tenant of the fact and the date on which the tenancy became a Scottish secure tenancy.[181]

LANDLORDS' AND TENANTS' RIGHTS AND OBLIGATIONS

The principal issues which feature in relationships between landlords and tenants – rent; eviction; repairs; succession; relationship breakdown – are dealt with in other chapters in more detail. At this juncture, though, it is perhaps helpful to outline briefly the rights which are implied by the relationship of landlord and tenant as far as housing is concerned. In many situations, as we shall see, statutes provide the rules which might have been expected to be found in the contractual terms.

---

[174] Section 234AA of the Criminal Procedure (Scotland) 1995 and s 4 of the Antisocial Behaviour etc (Scotland) Act.
[175] HSA 2001, s 35(6).
[176] *Ibid*, s 37.
[177] *Ibid*, s 37(1).
[178] *Ibid*, s 37(2)(a).
[179] *Ibid*, s 37(3) – when the date for appealing has expired or if there is an appeal it has been withdrawn or decided.
[180] *Ibid*, s 37(2)(b).
[181] *Ibid*, s 37(4).

The landlord's duties

There are a number of duties which the common law has imported into all residential landlord and tenant contracts. In some instances, such as the obligation to provide habitable and tenantable property, the common law has been extensively supplemented by statutory provisions.

GIVE POSSESSION OF THE SUBJECTS AND MAINTAIN THE TENANT IN POSSESSION

This cardinal requirement at common law has been indirectly buttressed by the statutory duty to give and maintain the subjects leased in good condition throughout, whether the tenancy is assured[182] or secure.[183] The implications of failing to maintain the tenant in the property[184] and of the tenant failing to possess the subjects[185] are dealt with elsewhere.

HABITABLE AND TENANTABLE PROPERTY

The duty to provide property that is wind- and watertight and which is habitable and tenantable is encountered in the common law. Both Erskine[186] and Rankine[187] lay great store by this obligation and the statutory forms in which landlords' duties are now framed are discussed below.[188]

WRITTEN LEASE

The obligation to provide a written lease is relatively modern and applies in the social[189] and private rented sectors.[190] It does not seem to have generated much by way of litigation. Landlords who use professional advisers, in the author's experience, generally provide quite clear and appropriate documentation for their tenants. The newer breed of landlords who are buying to let as part of their retirement plans have tended often to borrow from the social rented sector and provide more generous rights than perhaps intended on such matters as the duty to repair when damage is caused by third parties. Rather than rely on common law and seek to exclude such damage, clauses are used which accept liability provided that the tenant reports the matter to the police within 24 hours of the incident. This is presumably on the basis that the damage will be covered

---

[182] HSA 2006, s 14.
[183] HSA 2001, Sch 4.
[184] See Chapter 4 below.
[185] See Chapter 6 below.
[186] Erskine 2.6.43.
[187] Rankine (1916) at 240ff.
[188] See Chapter 4 below.
[189] HSA 1987, s 53.
[190] HSA 1988, s 30.

by insurance policies if such procedure is followed. There does not seem to be much evidence of unfair terms being used which would be covered by unfair consumer contract regulations.[191]

RENT BOOK

The Rent Acts made this obligatory for regulated[192] and assured tenancies[193] and Pt VII contracts[194] where the rent is paid weekly.

SAFE GAS APPLIANCES

Any landlord providing gas appliances must ensure that they comply with the relevant Gas Safety Regulations[195] and that electrical equipment is safe.[196]

FIRE SAFETY AND FURNITURE AND FURNISHINGS

A major shift in the recent past has been the attention paid to fire safety in domestic situations. This has borne fruit in the obligations to comply with fire safety standards.[197]

SELL THE PROPERTY TO THE SITTING TENANT

Tenants in the private sector have the option to acquire ownership of the premises they rent where the property consists of crofting[198] or agricultural land[199] and tenancies-at-will.[200] The same kind of rights have yet to extend to private sector tenants in residential property. Such a right, however, does exist in the social rented sector. Since the Tenants' Rights etc (Scotland) Act 1980 came into effect, initially, tenants of local authority houses[201] and subsequently of housing associations were given the right to purchase the properties in which they had been living as their only or principal home for at least 2 years[202] prior to the application to purchase.[203]

---

[191] Unfair Terms in Consumer Contracts Regulations 1999 (SI 1999/2083) (as amended by the Unfair Terms in Consumer Contracts Regulations 2001 (SI 2001/1186) .
[192] RSA 1984, s 113.
[193] HSA 1988, s 30(4).
[194] RSA 1984, s 79.
[195] Gas Safety (Installation and Use) Regulations 1998 (SI 1998/2451).
[196] Electrical Equipment (Safety) Regulations 1994 (SI 1994/3260).
[197] Furniture and Furnishings (Fire) Safety Regulations 1988, 1989 and 1993 (1988/1324; 1989/2358 and 1993/207).
[198] Crofters (Scotland) Act 1993, ss 12–19 for individual crofters; Land Reform (Scotland) Act 2003 for crafting community bodies, Pt 3.
[199] Agricultural Holdings (Scotland) Acts 1991 and 2003.
[200] Land Registration (Scotland) Act 1979, ss 20–22.
[201] Housing (Scotland) Act 1986.
[202] Extended to 5 years by HSA 2001, s 42.
[203] HSA 1987, s 61(2)(c).

Discounts from the market value were given for such purchases. The discounts ranged from 32 per cent minimum for houses and 44 per cent for flats to 60 per cent for houses and 70 per cent for flats.[204] Certain properties were excluded from coverage as not being secure tenancies[205] – premises occupied under a contract of employment; temporary letting to a person seeking accommodation; temporary letting pending development; temporary accommodation during works; accommodation for homeless persons; agricultural and business premises; police and fire authorities accommodation; houses which are part of, or within the cartilage of other non-housing buildings.[206]

The Housing and Planning Act 1986 originally introduced the right to buy for housing association tenancies which were secure tenancies. New housing association tenancies entered into on or after 2 January 1989 were covered by the assured tenancy regime,[207] which does not include the right to buy, leaving pre-1989 tenants with a preserved right to buy. In due course, the right for housing association tenants to buy was revived by the transfer of social landlords into the Scottish secure tenancy regime on 30 September 2002 by the Housing (Scotland) Act 2001, subject to postponement.[208] Where the Scottish secure tenancy is created after 30 September 2002 then the right to buy does not apply for 10 years,[209] unless the RSL waives such period.[210]

Certain housing association properties were also exempt from the right to buy – RSLs with 100 houses or fewer;[211] co-operative housing associations;[212] RSLs which are charities;[213] and housing designed for people with special needs provided with or situated near special facilities for tenants or housing support services.[214] In addition, where the needs of any area exceed substantially or are likely to exceed substantially the amount of housing stock available, the local authority may apply for "pressured area" status to avoid selling off its stock.[215] The period for which this status operates preventing sales can be up to 5 years[216] and may be revoked upon the Scottish Ministers being

---

[204] HSA 1987, s 62.
[205] See above at p 86.
[206] HSA 1987, Sch 2.
[207] HSA 1988, s 43(2) and (3).
[208] HSA 1987, s 61A(3) (as inserted by HSA 2001, s 44).
[209] HSA 1987, s 61A(3)(a) (as inserted by HSA 2001, s 44).
[210] HSA 1987, s 61A(7) (as inserted by HSA 2001, s 44).
[211] HSA 1987, s 61(4)(c).
[212] *Ibid*, s 61(4)(ca).
[213] *Ibid*, s 61(4)(e).
[214] *Ibid*, s 61(4)(e)(ea).
[215] *Ibid*, s 61B(1) (as inserted by HSA 2001, s 44).
[216] HSA 1987, s 61B(2)(b) (as inserted by HSA 2001, s 44).

satisfied as to there being sufficient reasons.[217] The Housing (Scotland) Act 2010 lays the right to buy to rest.[218]

PROVIDE LOANS AND GRANTS

There is a right related to the tenant's right to buy by way of an obligation on local authorities to provide loans to those who have not been able to secure building society finance and who apply.[219] There is also a duty on local authorities to provide assistance by way of loan or grant where the owner is required to carry out work under a "work notice"[220] to improve, repair or maintain a house, bring it into or keep it in a reasonable state of repair, provide means of escape from fire and other fire precautions.[221] Where work is required to provide a house with one or more of the standard amenities to meet the needs of a disabled person[222] then the assistance must be by way of grant.[223] There is provision for regulations to specify those circumstances when assistance in other situations must be way of grant.[224]

NOT UNREASONABLY WITHHOLD CONSENT TO A DISABLED TENANT'S RIGHT TO ADAPT THE HOUSE[225]

Tenants of private-sector rented houses have the right to have adaptations which the tenant considers necessary for the purpose of making the house suitable for the accommodation welfare or employment of any disabled person living there or who intends to live their as their sole or main residence.[226] The landlord may consent; consent subject to reasonable conditions; or refuse consent, provided that it is not refused unreasonably.[227] There may be no contracting out of this obligation.[228]

Tenant's obligations

Just as the landlord must give possession and usually provide a written lease, so tenants must meet certain obligations even if the lease is silent on such matters. The lease might, for instance, merely indicate what the

---

[217] HSA 1987, s 61B(8) (as inserted by HSA 2001, s 44).
[218] HSA 2010, Pt 14.
[219] HSA 1987, s 216.
[220] HSA 2006, s 73(1)(a).
[221] *Ibid*, s 71(1)(b) and (2).
[222] See Chapter 4 below.
[223] HSA 2006, s 73(2).
[224] *Ibid*, s 73(4).
[225] *Ibid*, ss 52–54.
[226] *Ibid*, s 52(2).
[227] *Ibid*, s 52(5).
[228] *Ibid*, s 52(9).

rent is and not specify that rent is payable. That is, however, implied at common law.

NOT MAKE FALSE OR FRAUDULENT REPRESENTATIONS

The tenant may have his tenancy reduced where he makes false or fraudulent representations to obtain a tenancy. In the private sector the tenancy may be reduced[229] and in the social rented sector it is a discretionary ground of repossession.[230]

TAKE AND MAINTAIN POSSESSION OF THE SUBJECTS

Having been granted a tenancy, the tenant must take and maintain possession of the subjects.[231] This has been more of an issue in relation to "keep open" clauses in commercial tenancies[232] where commercial landlords consider that other tenants will be put off by the appearance of empty shop units. The issue in relation to residential properties centres around the maintenance of the fabric of the building through keeping it aired and fired. The guiding principle accepted from a shop tenancy case is that the premises should be kept in good condition.[233] Given the requirement that most current tenancies be the only or principal homes of the tenants, it is perhaps not surprising that modern authority is lacking.

CARE OF THE SUBJECTS

It is crucial that the tenant takes reasonable care of the leased subjects. Allowance for wear and tear will be made in determining whether or not any sum of money is forfeited at the end of the tenancy. The situation in commercial tenancies is much more fully elaborated than currently exists in Scottish residential leases. A significant number of landlords, in the author's experience, have tended to operate a simple policy of retaining deposits to cover damage both real and imagined. Proposals to provide for rent deposits to obviate this practice which features extensively in private-sector student tenancies have been put forward.[234]

---

[229] *Govanhill Housing Association* v *Palmer* 1997 Hous LR 133 at 140.
[230] HSA 2001, Sch 2, ground 6; see Chapter 6 below.
[231] Rankine (1916) at 233ff.
[232] *Retail Parks Investments* v *Royal Bank of Scotland (No 2)* 1996 SLT 669.
[233] *Whitelaw* v *Fulton* (1871) 10 M 27 at 29 – the interlocutor of the 2nd Division talks only of the tenant's obligation to keep the premises "habitable", although Sheriff Bell ordained the tenant to "keep proper fires lighted in the premises in question and air the same" – at 28.
[234] Rent deposit proposals were put forward by Shelter in 2005: http://scotland.shelter. org.uk/professional_resources/policy_library/policy_library_folder/a_rent_deposit_ protection_service_for_scotland.

PAY RENT

Unless the lease specifies otherwise, rent is one of the cardinal features of a tenancy without which there can be no real right for the tenant.[235] There are a number of situations when this might not apply. There may be situations where the tenant carries out tasks by way of services rather than paying an actual formal rent[236] or some other formulation[237] or where there is an obligation to maintain the subjects in repair. Although this issue has not been litigated, it seems likely that it would be treated as rent.

NOT INVERT THE SUBJECTS

It is implied that the tenant will use the premises only for the purposes contained in the lease.[238] If the lease is for residential use then commercial use is a breach of the probably express or implied terms of the lease and may result in the lease being irritated and the premises being repossessed.

GRANT ACCESS FOR REPAIRS

Any doubts which might have existed as to the nature of the right of the landlord to obtain access to carry out repairs have removed by the incorporation of this obligation into statutory form in 2001.

MOBILE HOMES

The position of those living in mobile homes has been conspicuous by its absence from many of the texts dealing with property and housing rights. Part of this may well be due to the extremely limited nature of the rights enjoyed by those in this kind of accommodation. Changes in the nature of the properties found on traditional caravan parks have altered the rights of some of the occupiers too. Many of today's "mobile homes" are by no means easily moved although they are usually still technically able to transferred by low-loader from one site to another. Contrast the kind of caravan occupied by Cathy and Reg in *Cathy Come Home* (1966) with those occupied by Sarah Tobias in *The Accused* (1989) and Mark, Ricky and Dianne Sway in *The Client* (1995). Standard Rent Act protection may be available where there is permanence and the services

---

[235] Robson and Halliday (2nd edn, 1998) at 1.20–1.23; McAllister (2002), Ch 1.

[236] *Scottish Residential Estates Development Co Ltd* v *Henderson* 1991 SLT 490 – here, the landlords were able to establish that other requirements of a lease were lacking to deny the occupier the status of tenant.

[237] *Smyth* v *Caledonian Racing (1984) Ltd* 1987 GWD 16-612 (£1 plus a share of turnover).

[238] Rankine (1916) at 236ff.

to the property occupied exist. The suggestion made over 25 years ago would seem applicable to many of today's mobile homes:

> "(w)here (the caravan) ... is rendered completely immobile, either by the removal of its wheels or by its being permanently blocked by some brick or concrete construction, then it is more likely to be regarded as a house in the same way as a bungalow or prefabricated dwelling would be".[239]

The kinds of questions which would be asked in relation to making a decision were proposed to make a decision between mobility and site permanence:

> "Are the wheels still on the vehicle? Are the stabilising struts of a permanent nature or of a kind ordinarily used by a caravan when moving from site to site? Are the services attached to the caravan? If so, are they of a fixed nature or readily detachable? Is the caravan ever moved? If so, for what purpose and with what facility?"[240]

The protections which have been introduced cover situations where mobile homes are the only or principal residence of the mobile home dweller.[241] It does not give protection to those who occupy merely at weekends or during holidays. Such occupiers can be charged very high prices for such things as bottled gas, without recourse to any form of independent arbitration.

Security of tenure

The Caravan Sites Act 1968 enacted protections against anyone who unlawfully deprived the occupier of occupation on a protected site. This was one which had been granted a licence for permanent and not holiday or otherwise temporary residence. This was applied to Scotland by the Mobile Homes Act 1975. It was extended by the Mobile Homes Act 1983[242] and has been amended by the Housing (Scotland) Act 2006.[243] Occupiers must be provided by the site owner with a written statement setting out the particulars of the agreement concerning the occupancy of the site, prior to the agreement being made.[244] In terms of the Housing (Scotland) Act 2006[245] a right is given to anyone entitled to park a mobile

---

[239] R v Rent Officer of the Nottinghamshire Registration Area, ex p Allen (1985) 52 P & CR 41 at 44.
[240] Ibid.
[241] West Lothian DC v Morrison 1987 SLT 361 – family of travelling showmen with a 52- week tenancy of a showground in Broxburn where the show lasted a week; Cooper v Fraser 1987 GWD 22-824 – caravan used for 2-year temporary work assignment.
[242] Mobile Homes Act 1983 (MHA 1983), s 5(1).
[243] Pt 6, ss 166–171.
[244] MHA 1983, s 1 (as substituted by HSA 2006, s 167).
[245] Housing (Scotland) Act 2006 (Commencement No 5, Savings and Transitional Provisions) Order (SSI 2007/270).

home on a protected site to be given these prescribed particulars covering both express and implied terms before making an agreement.[246] The information must specify the names and addresses of the parties, the particulars of the land where the mobile home is stationed, the express and implied terms. The implied terms are laid out in Sch 1 to the Mobile Homes Act 1983. They cover the duration of the agreement which must be for no longer than the period covered by the relevant planning permission.[247] Termination by the occupier shall be by written notice given to the owner of not less than 4 weeks.[248] The owner will be entitled to terminate the agreement for breach after serving a notice to remedy the breach as long as the court is satisfied it is reasonable to terminate,[249] or if the occupier is not occupying the mobile home as his only or main residence.[250] There is also provision for termination of an agreement where the court is satisfied that, having regard to its condition, the mobile home is having a detrimental effect on the amenity of the site or likely to have such effect in the future.[251] The court may make an order setting out the repairs to be carried out with a time-scale where the occupier indicates an intention to carry out repairs. This can occur where the court considers that it would be reasonably practicable for repairs to be carried out on the mobile home, having regard to the present condition of the mobile home. There may be no further proceedings in relation to the termination unless the court is satisfied that the specified period has expired and the repairs have not been effected.[252]

The implied terms of Sch 1, Pt II, as from 28 May 2007, are to be implied by the court on application by either party. Express terms may be varied or deleted by the court on application by either party.[253] The period for such application is within 6 months from the date when the agreement is made or 6 months after the date on which the statement is given if given after that date.[254] Any express terms not set out in the agreement are not enforceable.[255]

So the right to remain on the site subsists until the occupier gives 4 weeks' notice in writing, planning permission for the site use as caravan site expires or the owner's interest in the land expires[256] or the owner obtains a court order. A court order will be granted where the court is

[246] MHA 1983, s 1(2) (as substituted by HSA 2006, s 167).
[247] MHA 1983, Sch 1, paras 1 and 2.
[248] *Ibid*, Sch 1, para 3.
[259] *Ibid*, Sch 1, para 4.
[250] *Ibid*, Sch 1, para 5.
[251] MHA 1983, Sch 1, para 6 (as substituted by HSA 2006, s 169).
[252] MHA 1983, Sch 1, para 6 (as substituted by HSA 2006, s 169).
[253] MHA 1983, s 2(3) (as substituted by HSA 2006, s 168(b)).
[254] MHA 1983, s 2(3) (as substituted by HSA 2000, s 168(b)).
[255] MHA 1983, s 1(6) (as substituted by HSA 2006 s 167).
[256] MHA 1983, Sch 1, para 2.

satisfied that there has been breach of one of the terms of the agreement and the occupier has not complied with a notice requiring remedy of the breach within a reasonable time.[257] There is in addition a requirement that such an order be reasonable.[258] There may be suspension of an eviction order for a period not exceeding 12 months, subject to such terms and conditions as the court thinks reasonable.[259]

Where the court is satisfied that the mobile home is no longer being occupied as an only or principal home, there will be decree.[260] There is also a possibility that the agreement can be terminated at the end of 5-yearly periods where the court is satisfied that the mobile home is having a detrimental effect on the amenity of the site or is likely to have such effect before the expiry of the next 5-year period.[261] Where an occupier owns their mobile home they may lawfully sell it and assign their rights in the agreement and the consent of the owner may not be unreasonably withheld. The owner has 28 days to respond.[262] Approval may be subject to conditions which are reasonable and capable of being satisfied without varying or deleting any express term of the agreement.[263] There is appeal to the court if the owner fails to respond or decides not to approve the person or if the occupier is aggrieved by a condition imposed.[264]

The occupier is also entitled to give the mobile home, and to assign the agreement, to a member of his family approved by the owner, whose approval shall not be unreasonably withheld.[265] There are also succession rights to members of the family.[266] "Family" is defined as spouses and partners, parents, grandparents, children, grandchildren, siblings, uncles, aunts, nephews and nieces. Relationships by marriage, half-blood and step-relationships are treated the same as full-blood ones and illegitimate children are treated as the legitimate children of the mother and reputed father. The position of adopted children, civil partners and same-sex partners is not made explicit in the statute.[267] There are also a number of issues which may be implied.[268]

---

[257] MHA 1983, Sch 1, para 4.
[257] *Ibid.*
[259] Caravan Sites Act 1968, s 4.
[260] MHA 1983, Sch 1, para 5.
[261] *Ibid*, Sch 1, para 6.
[262] *Ibid*, Sch 1, para 8(1B) (as substituted by HSA 2006, s 169(3)).
[263] MHA 1983, Sch 1, para 8(1C and D) (as substituted by HSA 2006, s 168(3)).
[264] MHA 1983, Sch 1, para 8(1F) (as substituted by HSA 2006, s 168(3)).
[265] MHA 1983, Sch 1, para 9.
[266] *Ibid*, s 3.
[267] *Ibid*, s 5.
[268] *Ibid*, Sch 1, Pt II – 1. The right of the occupier to quiet enjoyment or, in Scotland, undisturbed possession of the mobile home. 2. The sums payable by the occupier in pursuance of the agreement and the times at which they are to be paid. 3. The review at yearly intervals of the sums so payable. 4. The provision or improvement of services available on the protected site, and the use by the occupier of such services. 5. The

Unlawful eviction

Although there may well not be a right to stay in the mobile home, mobile home residents still come within the coverage of "residential occupiers" and still enjoy statutory protection. Initially, it was provided that a person was guilty of an offence if, during the subsistence of a residential contract, he unlawfully deprived the occupier of his occupation on the protected site of any caravan which the occupier was contractually entitled to occupy as his residence.[269] A court order for eviction at the end of the contract was required.[270] It is also a criminal offence to harass the occupier into abandoning occupation of the caravan or into refraining from exercising any rights in respect of the occupation.[271] This covers any acts calculated to interfere with the peace or comfort of the occupier or persons residing with him. It includes persistent withdrawing or withholding of services or facilities reasonably required for the occupation as a residence on the site.[272]

Rent control

There are no controls over the rents which may be charged by mobile home site owners to those who own homes stationed on their sites or who rent such properties except where there is coverage by the relevant Rent Act legislation.[273] As indicated, it would seem, from the author's unsystematic but extensive survey of the kinds of properties found on sites in the 21st century, that most would be covered, albeit by the reduced rights available for leases from 1989 onwards.

---

preservation of the amenity of the protected site. 6. The maintenance and repair of the protected site by the owner, and the maintenance and repair of the mobile home by the occupier. 7. Access by the owner to the land on which the occupier is entitled to station the mobile home.

[269] Caravan Sites Act 1968, s 3(1)(a) (as applied by MHA 1975).

[270] *Ibid*, s 3(1)(b) (as applied by MHA 1975).

[271] *Ibid*, 3(1)(c) (as applied by MHA 1975).

[272] *Ibid*, s 3(1)(c) (as applied by MHA 1975).

[273] *R v Rent Officer of the Nottinghamshire Registration Area, ex p Allen* (1985) 52 P & CR 41 at 44.

4 HOUSING STANDARDS AND GOOD REPAIR

For those who occupy their property as owners, what state of repair they keep the property in was traditionally a matter for themselves to decide on. Since the middle of the 19th century, however, owners are required to meet the public health standards contained in the environmental protection legislation as well as to comply with any notices which the local authority may serve on them in pursuance of their duties to deal with sub-standard houses in its district.[1] The same rules apply to property which is rented out to tenants. Tenants, though, have rights stemming from the landlord and tenant contract. In theory, the law of contract and the common law provide redress for anyone whose landlord does not met the implied obligation in the lease to provide tenantable and habitable accommodation and the Institutional writers stated the law in unequivocal terms.[2] For Rankine, the question of whether a house was tenantable and habitable was one of fact to be determined on a proof or by remit to a man of skill.[3] For many tenants living in damp and insanitary houses, however, this proved hard to implement, with defences such as *volenti non fit injuria* and "obvious defect" being deployed.[4] Add to this the difficulty of accessing the courts for those with limited resources and tenants' chances of enforcing the common law were problematic.[5] In the 21st century, the common law has been largely supplanted. In both the social rented sectors as well as the private rented sector there are now clear statutory duties which encompass what was found in the common law and various earlier statutes. In simple terms tenants in social rented sector look to the Housing (Scotland) Act 2001, Sch 4 and private-sector tenants can use the Housing (Scotland) Act 2006, Pt 2. These incorporate the variety of related obligations and rights encountered in both the common law and earlier statutes.[6] Tenants may, of course, also seek to enforce any obligations undertaken by the landlords within any rent contract which provide more extensive rights. Experience, however, suggests that

---

[1] See below at p 131.
[2] Erskine, II, VI, 39 and 43; Bell, *Principles* 1253.
[3] Rankine (3rd edn) at 241.
[4] Robson (1979).
[5] See below at p 137.
[6] Robson and Halliday (1998) Chapter 3.

landlords initially often provided minimal rights in the terms of the lease. Since the introduction of implied statutory terms, landlords, especially in the social rented sector, have tended simply to replicate the terms of the statutory obligations within the lease.

There are, in addition, a range of statutes which lay an obligation on local authorities to maintain minimum standards. These require them to ensure that the properties in their area are of a tolerable standard [7] and are neither overcrowded[8] nor sub-standard[9] as well as enabling properties to be repaired,[10] closed and demolished.[11]

One might not expect owners of properties to require any form of compulsion to keep their property in good repair. It is broadly left to owners to decide the standards they wish to maintain if their accommodation is physically separate. The issue, though, is rather more complicated where people live in tenement flats or in terraces and any possible inaction would affect others. For owners of properties, then, there are direct and indirect methods of ensuring that they keep their property in a safe condition. These older forms of regulation are largely in the hands of local authorities and do not provide direct access to either the courts or any other forum for standards to be enforced.

What this chapter seeks to do is to provide an outline of the remedies available to individuals along with the role which can be played by local authorities in securing satisfactory housing standards for both individual houses and for areas. These remedies have developed in response to problems with common law and earlier statutory remedies as well as with the enforcement of rights in the past. The chapter outlines how the current law has developed in order to provide a context for understanding the range of current remedies. The focus is principally on landlord obligations and tenant remedies.

MODERN LEGAL REGULATION

Individual remedies

CONTRACTUAL AND COMMON LAW BASIS

As noted, in addition to the standard remedies for breach of the formal terms of the contract the common law has traditionally imposed an obligation on landlords to provide accommodation which is "tenantable and habitable".[12] While the common law has not formally been super-

---

[7] Housing (Scotland) Act 1987 (HSA 1987), Pt IV.
[8] *Ibid*, Pt VII.
[9] HSA 2006, Pt 1.
[10] HSA 1987, Pt V.
[11] *Ibid*, Pt VI.
[12] Erskine, II, VI, 43.

seded, the obligations imposed under common law for both social renting and private sector have been incorporated into the legislative provisions of the Housing (Scotland) Act 2001 and the Housing (Scotland) Act 2006 and can be regarded as no longer enjoying, in practice, a separate existence.

STATUTORY INTERVENTIONS

Until 2001 the same rules applied to all rental housing. The remedies were the same. The only major difference was that the nuisance provisions of the public health legislation were not applied to local authority housing. The system of parallel rights was complex and somewhat confusing but it applied across the board. The Housing (Scotland) Act 2001 altered that and split the applicable rules into social rented obligations and private sector. They are now covered by separate statutory regimes. In addition, the public health legislation continues to operate in respect of both social rented and private rented sector property. In practical terms, as noted, the nuisance provisions are applied only in the latter sector. There is statutory authority in England for the inapplicability of public health standards to local authority housing.[13] The Court of Appeal determined that there was no obligation on councils to make housing orders in respect of their own property.[14] There is no equivalent Scottish case but the practice of local authorities has been not to serve nuisance abatement notices on themselves.[15] Their tenants are likely to have drawn their attention to the defects.

SOCIAL RENTED HOUSING (PUBLIC SECTOR)

The Housing (Scotland) Act 2001 introduced a new framework for dealing with repair issues. A number of the rights which are now enshrined in this legislation stem from litigation between 1980 and the end of the 20th century. Until this date there had been no distinction between the tenant's right of repair and the kind of tenancy they held.

Basic repair obligations for Scottish secure tenancies

The landlord's obligations to repair a house let under a Scottish secure tenancy are covered by Sch 4 to the 2001 Act.[16] Schedule 4 provides a mixture of pre-existing common law and statutory rights along with

---

13 *R v Cardiff City Council, ex p Cross* (1983) 81 LGR 105.
14 By the time the case came to court the council had re-housed the affected tenants and disposed of the properties: *ibid* at 106.
15 Scottish Home Affairs Committee (1984) noted that, of the 6,233 notices served, for instance in 1981, none had been served on local authorities (para 57).
16 HSA 2001, s 27(1).

confirmation of some issues that had been successfully litigated and clarification of others where there was less certainty. What has been removed in this sector, however, is the obligation to keep in repair the structure and exterior of the property and the installations for the supply of gas, water, and electricity and for space and water heating found in Sch 10, para 3 to the Housing (Scotland) Act 1987. These standards incidentally remain in the private rented sector under the terms of the Housing (Scotland) Act 2006.[17]

WHAT STANDARD MUST BE MAINTAINED?

The landlord must ensure that the house is wind- and watertight and in all other respects reasonably fit for human habitation.[18] It must be in this condition at the commencement of the tenancy and it must be kept in this condition throughout the tenancy.[19] The standard is to be measured by looking at the extent to which the house falls short of the building regulations in force by reason of the disrepair or sanitary defects at issue.[20] Sanitary defects are defined drawing on the tests for the "tolerable standard".[21] These cover such items as lack of air space or ventilation, lack of lighting, dampness, absence of adequate and readily accessible water supply or of sanitary arrangements or of other conveniences, and inadequate paving or drainage of courts, yards or passages.[22]

PRE-TENANCY INSPECTION

Prior to the commencement of the tenancy, the landlord must inspect the house and identify any work necessary to bring it up to the wind- and watertight and "reasonably fit for human habitation" standard.[23] The tenant must be notified of such work.[24] Where the landlord is running the business professionally one would expect these inter-tenancy inspections to be carried out when the previous tenant vacated. Repairs would be made during the void period, obviating the need to tell subsequent tenants and providing them with a property that met the statutory standard.

WHEN DOES THE OBLIGATION TO REPAIR ARISE?

Whatever work is required to bring the house up to the statutory standard must be carried out within a reasonable time of either the tenant notifying

---

[17] HSA 2006, s 13(1).
[18] Sch 4, para 1(a).
[19] Sch 4, para 1(b).
[20] Sch 4, para 5(1).
[21] See below at p 131.
[22] Sch 4, para 6.
[23] Sch 4, para 2(a).
[24] Sch 4, para 2(b).

the landlord or the landlord otherwise becoming aware that the work is required.[25]

DAMAGE CAUSED DURING REPAIR WORK

While landlords would seek to carry out repairs with the minimum of disruption and without causing damage, the legislation does make clear that any such resultant damage is the landlord's responsibility.[26] Given the less than enthusiastic welcome given to the case which confirmed this in the 1980s, one might expect this to be an area of some contentiousness.[27]

NOTICE TO TENANT FOR ACCESS

The landlord may at any reasonable time enter the house to view its state and condition or to carry out any work necessary to meet the statutory repair standard.[28] Twenty-four hours' written notice must, however, be given.[29]

Qualifying repairs

The Act also makes provision for tenants to have "qualifying repairs" carried out in certain specified circumstances.[30] Regulations[31] specify the maximum amount for any single "qualifying repair" as well as the period within which the repair is to be completed and which repairs are covered.[32] Included as "qualifying repairs" are unsafe power or lighting sockets or electrical fittings; loss or partial loss of electric power; loss or partial loss of gas supply; blocked flue to open fire or boiler; insecure external window, door or lock; loss or partial loss of space or water heating where no alternative heating is available; toilets which do not flush (where there is no other toilet in the house); blocked or leaking foul drains, soil stacks or toilet pans (where there is no other toilet in the house); blocked sink, bath or basin; loss or partial loss of water supply; leaking from a water or heating pipe, tank or cistern; unsafe rotten timber flooring or stair treads; loose or detached banisters or handrails; and broken mechanical extractor fan in internal kitchen or bathroom. The financial limit was originally set back in 1994 at £250 but currently stands at £350.[33] Where

---

[25] HSA 2006, Sch 4, para 3(a).
[26] *Ibid*, para 3(b).
[27] *Little* v *Glasgow DC* (1991) 1 SHLR 195, adopting the approach in *Bradley* v *Chorley BC* (1985) 17 HLR 305.
[28] HSA 2006, Sch 4, para 4.
[29] *Ibid*.
[30] Section 27(2).
[31] Scottish Secure Tenants (Right to Repair) Regulations 2002 (SSI 2002/316) (originally the Secure Tenants (Right to Repair) (Scotland) Regulations 1994 (SI 1994/1046)).
[32] Section 27(3).
[33] Scottish Secure Tenants (Right to Repair) Regulations 2002 (SSI 2002/316).

landlords fail to meet their obligations in time, compensation is payable at the rate of £15 and £3 per every working day subject to a maximum of £100.[34]

Enforcement

The mechanism, however, for the enforcement of these standards remains the courts. Most of the pioneering litigation to ameliorate the living conditions of tenants during the 1980s to the present day has been in relation to social rented housing, principally the houses rented by local authorities in the west of Scotland and, to a lesser extent, in Aberdeen. From this litigation, much of it conducted by community law centres, it is possible to identify a number of chronic problems encountered in the social rented sector. The principal one has been dampness.[35] Landlords often sought to place the blame for the dampness on condensation caused by the lifestyles of the tenants. While this defence was successful in a number of cases, the Court of Session made it clear that any landlord contending that the cause of dampness was the result of the actions of the tenant had to be specific.[36] The matter can be broken down conveniently into four issues.

ESTABLISHING THE EXISTENCE OF DAMPNESS

The existence of a chronic problem rather than a temporary result of related work has been a factor, as where the cause of dampness has been disputed. Thus the evidence and credibility of the narratives of landlords and tenants have played a major part. In one case the cause of dampness on balance of probabilities was accepted as being penetration of cladding from high-pressure jets used to clean concrete slabs in high-rise flats prior to coating them with an impermeable membrane.[37] In another case the evidence of a pursuer was preferred as to the cold, damp, draught, condensation and mould between late 2000 and March 2004 despite his refusal to allow insulation to be applied. Tellingly, the problems were solved after introduction of a new heating scheme in February 2004.[38] Again, the credibility of witnesses has been crucial, along with an architect's report.[39] Nor is there a requirement to aver fault or "*culpa*" in these kinds of claims, since they are based on breach of contract.[40] Only a reasonable period to effect the repairs is allowed.

---

[34] SSI 2002/316, reg 12(2).
[35] See Brown and McIntosh (1987).
[36] *Guy* v *Strathkelvin DC* 1997 Hous LR 14.
[37] *Campbell* v *Aberdeen City Council* 2007 Hous LR 26.
[38] *Christian* v *Aberdeen City Council* 2005 Hous LR 71.
[39] *Galloway* v *Glasgow City Council* 2001 Hous LR 59.
[40] *Neilson* v *Scottish Homes* 1999 SLT (Sh Ct) 2.

CAUSE OF ESTABLISHED DAMPNESS

The cause of existing dampness has in the past revolved around whether this is principally a result of the design of the accommodation or how that accommodation is used. Landlords wishing to attribute the dampness to the lifestyle of the tenants through their failure to heat and ventilate must specify in what way the tenant has been deficient.[41] A bald assertion is no defence to a claim that the property is damp. It is now not possible simply to assert that the way the tenant lives is the root cause of the problem.[42] This is illustrated in a 2009 case from Glasgow sheriff court. Mary Deans sought damages from her landlords for loss and inconvenience caused by the property's disrepair and internal dampness.[43] The landlords argued that there was contributory negligence on behalf of the tenant through her failure adequately to heat and ventilate the property. Sheriff Mackenzie followed *Guy* in stating:

"I do not consider that it is sufficient for the defenders to baldly aver a duty incumbent upon the pursuers in such general terms ... the defenders would need to aver what degree of heating would have been necessary to eradicate or control the dampness complained of, that the pursuer, as tenant, had the capacity to achieve that level of heating and further that it would be a reasonable demand made upon her by the landlord to achieve that level of heating and maintain it."[44]

The landlords had stated that none of the other flats in the same block had the same problems. The sheriff did not think that this was enough.

The matters are often long running and involve more than simply blaming the tenants' lifestyle. They include efforts by landlords to improve conditions which can be taken as a crucial indicator as to the root of the problem.[45] In *Frankenberg*, for instance, there had been water penetration and condensation since 1996. New windows, installed in 1997, improved the wind- and watertight situation and a heating upgrade in 2001 made a significant improvement. The technical evidence of the council was preferred on the dampness issue, though.

---

[41] *Guy* v *Strathkelvin DC* 1997 SCLR 405; see also *McGuire* v *Monklands DC* 1997 Hous LR 41.

[42] See also earlier versions of this principle in the sheriff court: *Gunn* v *Glasgow City Council* 1992 SCLR 1018 (inadequate insulation of building and water penetration caused dampness and onus on council to establish tenant's lifestyle outwith the spectrum of what the council could reasonably have expected from their tenants) and *Burns* v *Monklands DC* 1997 Hous LR 34 (claimed LA failed to provide adequate structure and counterclaim of failure to heat and ventilate. Cause accepted as installation of double glazed windows without ventilation, as previously).

[43] *Deans* v *Glasgow Housing Association Ltd* 2009 Hous LR 82.

[44] *Ibid* at 85, para 21.

[45] *Frankenberg* v *Dundee City Council* 2005 Hous LR 55.

THE ROLE OF THE TENANT'S OBLIGATION TO HEAT AND THE EXTENT OF THE OBLIGATION

Complementing the landlord's obligation to provide habitable and tenantable accommodation, the tenant has an obligation not to mistreat the subjects. This common law obligation is expressed as the obligation to keep the property "aired and fired".[46] In older case law this was found in the duty not to leave the subjects empty during bad weather. A more modern expression of this has been the notion that there is an obligation on tenants to use whatever form of heating is supplied.[47] Landlords must provide heating rather than merely respond to complaints of excessive cost by removing it.[48] Using the heating provided must not involve excessive expenditure by the tenant.[49]

As noted, a claim that a tenant failed to heat and ventilate needed to be specific as to the degree of heating required to eradicate and control the dampness complained of.[50] Various attempts have been made to quantify the proportion of income that a tenant might be expected to apply to the property.[51] The figure of 7.5 per cent mentioned chimes in with the commitment to eradicate fuel poverty in Scotland. The Housing (Scotland) Act 2001 required the Scottish Ministers to prepare a statement on fuel poverty.[52] This was to set out the measures which they and local authorities had taken, are taking and intend to take to ensure, so far as reasonably practicable, that people do not live in fuel poverty. A target date within 15 years of the statement had to be specified.[53]

QUANTIFYING THE LOSS

While, of course, every case depends on the specifics of the property and the nature of the tenants and the efforts of the landlords to deal with perceived problems, some general guidance can be found in the following indications of the levels of awards in the past. The sums are not large and do not appear to have kept up with inflation in any way. It should be noted that the sums awarded for non-replacement items are not for "stress" but for "inconvenience". The term "solatium" is inappropriate and should not be employed.[54] The point was raised in a case since a claim for "mental or emotional reaction" constituting a claim for "personal injuries" would

---

[46] *Boyle* v *Weddell* (1870) 11 M 223.
[47] *Dover DC* v *Farrar* (1980) 2 HLR 32.
[48] *GLC* v *LB Tower Hamlets* 1989 (1983) 15 HLR 57.
[49] *McArdle* v *Glasgow DC* 1989 SCLR 19.
[50] *Deans* v *GHA* 2009 Hous LR 82.
[51] *Burns* v *Monklands DC* 1997 Hous LR 34; *McGuire* v *Monklands DC* 1997 Hous LR 41 at 44.
[52] Section 88(1).
[53] Section 88(3).
[54] *Mack* v *Glasgow City Council* 2006 SLT 556 (Extra Division) at 559.

have been time barred[55] as being brought in August 2004, more than 3 years after the tenants had ceased to occupy the damp flat in March 2001.[56] The Inner House determined that damages for living in a damp house were payable not because of an impairment of the tenant's physical or mental state but because they suffered "inconvenience".

Gunn v *National Coal Board*[57]

£582 award for about 10 months' occupancy of damp NCB premises – £300 of that for inconvenience.

Kearney v *Monklands DC*[58]

£600 per year for period when defects not remedied. The claim, after repeated complaints about mould affecting carpets, beds etc, was successful but the award was reduced by 60 per cent because of the tenant's refusal of the council's offer to "dry line" the flat 5 years after accepting that the problem was structural rather than caused by lifestyle.

Neilson v *Scottish Homes*[59]

Tenants in damp accommodation from April 1988 to November 1993 and claiming £7,500 to cover 5 years and landlord aware of complaints.

Galloway v *Glasgow City Council*[60]

£500 per annum for inconvenience over 5 years plus £250 for clothes, carpets and furniture.

Christian v *Aberdeen City Council*[61]

£2,750 for about 3.5 years of damp conditions.

Mack v *Glasgow City Council*[62]

Damages for breach of contract between January 1999 and March 2001 – £3,160 claimed, including £1,340 for discarded items.

Campbell v *Aberdeen City Council*[63]

£2,900 agreed for loss – period not clear.

---

[55] Prescription and Limitation (Scotland) Act 1973, s 17(2).
[56] *Mack* v *Glasgow City Council* 2006 SLT 556.
[57] 1982 SLT 526.
[58] 1997 Hous LR 39.
[59] 1999 SLT (Sh Ct) 2.
[60] 2001 Hous LR 59.
[61] 2005 Hous LR 71.
[62] 2006 Hous LR 2.
[63] 2007 Hous LR 26.

PRIVATE RENTED HOUSING

Background

The Housing (Scotland) Act 2006 introduced the "repairing standard" into private-sector residential tenancies. Tenancies with their own statutory regimes were not covered, including the Scottish secure and short Scottish secure tenancies,[64] tenancies on agricultural holdings under the Agricultural Holdings (Scotland) Act 2003,[65] crofts[66] and small landholding tenancies.[67]

The "repairing standard"

In the same way as occurred in the social rented sector in 2001, the 2006 Act gathers together the various standards previously in operation and incorporates these different issues into one single obligation.

The landlord must ensure that the house meets the repairing standard laid down in s 13 at the start of the tenancy and at all times during the tenancy.[68] This effectively puts an end to any temptation to cite the Edwardian child injury cases of *Mechan* v *Watson*[69] and *Davidson* v *Sprengel*,[70] suggesting that the tenant has been harmed by a defect obvious at the commencement of the tenancy. By the same token, pleas of *volenti non fit injuria* whereby a slow reaction from a landlord to a repair complaint shifted the burden back to the tenant, would also seem to be undercut.[71] What does remain an issue, of course, is the question of notice which is discussed below.

A house meets the repairing standard if:

- the house is wind- and watertight and in all other respects reasonably fit for human habitation;[72]
- the structure and exterior of the house (including drains, gutter and external pipes) are in a reasonable state of repair and in proper working order;[73]

---

[64] HSA 2006, s 12(1)(a).
[65] Section 12(1)(c).
[66] Section 12(1)(d).
[67] Section 12(1)(e).
[68] Section 14(1).
[69] 1907 SC 25.
[70] 1909 SC 566.
[71] *Webster* v *Brown* (1892) 19 R 765 and *Proctor* v *Cowlairs Co-op* 1961 SLT 434.
[72] HSA 2006, s 13(1)(a) – this was the old common law duty – *Wolfson* v *Forrester* 1910 SC 675 at 678 per LP Dunedin.
[73] Taken from the statutory implied terms of the successor to the 1962 and 1966 Housing (Scotland) Acts, the Housing (Scotland) Act 1987, Sch 10, para 3.

- the installations in the house for the supply of water, gas and electricity and for sanitation, space heating and heating water are in a reasonable state of repair and in proper working order;[74]
- any fixtures, fittings and appliances provided by the landlord under the tenancy are in a reasonable state of repair and in proper working order;[75]
- any furnishings provided by the landlord under the tenancy are capable of being used safely for the purpose for which they are designed; and[76]
- the house has satisfactory provision for detecting fires and for giving warning in the event of fire or suspected fire.

This last requirement, to have satisfactory fire alarms, is an innovation stemming from a recommendation of the review of Scots law undertaken by the Housing Improvement Task Force for the then Scottish Executive.[77]

The landlord's duty to repair and maintain includes a duty to make good any damage caused by carrying out any work to meet the repairing obligation.[78] This obligation takes on board the sheriff court decision in *Little* v *Glasgow District Council*[79] which followed a Court of Appeal decision[80] requiring the council, *inter alia*, to repaper the wall where new plaster had been put on following damp in the chimney breast.

The duty imposed under the repairing obligation arises only where the tenant has notified the landlord or the landlord "otherwise becomes aware". The requirement to notify is, on the face of it, reasonably straightforward as an issue of fact. There are, however, a number of instances in the post-1980s litigation against damp housing in the west of Scotland of tenants stating they had complained at a local office on a particular date and the local authorities having no record of this. Sheriffs tended to take a common-sense approach and were frequently less than impressed with council record keeping, preferring the evidence of the tenants.[81]

The question of when a landlord might "otherwise become aware" again seems to derive from a consideration of practical issues. At common law, the warrandice as to possession has always been absolute. This would

---

[74]   HSA 1987, Sch 10, para 3.
[75]   *Ibid.*
[76]   *Ibid.*
[77]   Stewardship and Responsibility: A Policy Framework for Private Housing in Scotland – The Final Report and Recommendations of the Housing Improvement Task Force (2003), para 68 – which incidentally rejected the suggestions that the tolerable standard should include thermal efficiency and this did not form part of the 2006 Act changes.
[78]   HSA 2006, s 14(2).
[79]   1991 1 SHLR 195 at 199.
[80]   *Bradley* v *Chorley BC* (1985) 17 HLR 305.
[81]   *Glasgow DC* v *McCrone* 1991 1 SHLR 45; *Barrie* v *Glasgow DC* 1991 1 SHLR 82; *McEachran* v *Glasgow DC* 1991 1 SHLR 149.

suggest that any failure to provide possession would give rise to a right to tenants to some kind of financial or other appropriate remedy. In similar vein, the requirement to deliver and maintain subjects in tenantable condition might imply an obligation to inspect the subjects let and ensure that they continued to be tenantable. Thus, in one Edwardian case a landlord carried out work on the landlord's lower flats, disrupting access via a common stair and causing structural damage.[82] The landlord was derogating from the grant of full possession and was liable when loss resulted to the tenant.[83]

In the 1970s this notion seemed to obtain support in an *obiter* statement in a Court of Session case involving flood damage from a defective drain on a neighbouring property. In *Golden Casket (Greenock) Ltd* v *BRS (Pickfords) Ltd*[84] Lord Dunpark remarked that there might be situations where a landlord might reasonably have known of the need for a repair. He did not specify what he had in mind but it might well encompass a tenant going on "rent strike". In addition, employing a surveyor to carry out a survey of the property with a view to establishing value would, one imagines, personally bar a landlord from later claiming that a defect had not been drawn to his attention by the tenant. The landlord might also be assumed to have knowledge where the landlord owned adjacent property and had actual personal knowledge of a mutual defect. Typically, where a landlord owned an upper flat and knew of water problems, whether from gutters or defective pipes, he could not rely on the need for the tenant to give notice. Establishing exactly when that knowledge is available could, however, prove problematic.

Avoiding the repair obligation

There are a number of situations where the landlord's repairing duty does not apply.[85]

TENANT ACCEPTS RESPONSIBILITY IN A 3-YEAR PLUS CONTRACT

In longer leases it was not uncommon for tenants to accept responsibility for repairs obligations. The legislation makes provision for this provided that the lease is for a period of not less than 3 years. A lease is for 3 years where neither party has a break option during the first 3 years of the lease. This mirrors the exceptions found in the previous legislation, the Housing (Scotland) Act 1987, which excluded leases of 7 years from the coverage of the implied repairs provision and leases of 3 years or more were not entitled to the coverage of the "fitness for human habitation" provisions.

---

82 *Huber* v *Ross* 1912 SC 898.
83 *Ibid* at 916 per Lord Johnston.
84 1972 SLT 146.
85 HSA 2006, s 16.

Such longer leases are frequently encountered in rural locations and tend to be for a longer period where there is an element of rebuilding and decoration work involved on the part of the tenant. In such situations the low level of the rent, in the writer's experience, reflects the "sweat equity" which the tenant is likely to have contributed. Such "repairing" tenancies are often between 5 and 20 years in duration.

TENANT'S FAULT

Any work occasioned by failure by the tenant to use the property in a proper manner is not the landlord's responsibility. The principle from the common law is explicitly included to prevent tenants who mistreat their property being entitled to have these depredations laid at the landlord's door. You cannot sell the lead off the roof and expect the landlord to pay for the resulting repair and damage.

FIRE, FLOOD OR INEVITABLE ACCIDENT

Rebuilding or reinstatement is not required where the destruction or damage is the result of fire or by storm, flood or other inevitable accident. What amounts to inevitable accident in the context of housing disrepair has been commented on in the past in the context of extremely cold weather: *Cameron* v *Glasgow District Council*.[86] The court did not accept that this amounted to any kind of act of God. The notion of inevitability is encountered where a landlord carried out a "temporary repair" and the pipe could have burst at any time in the 15 years between the repair having been effected and the actual flood: *Mearns* v *Glasgow District Council*.[87] Here, the council was liable.

LACK OF RIGHTS, INCLUDING ACCESS

There is no liability for failure to carry out a repair where the only reason is that the landlord lacks the necessary rights to carry out the repair, provided that the landlord has taken reasonable steps to acquire such rights. This might be through lack of access. The issue of effecting access is one which features extensively in landlords' anecdotes about "tenancy problems". The problem, in such situations, however, is usually a practical one rather than a lack of rights. A situation involving a lack of rights was encountered in one of the earlier cases to come before the PRHP,[88] where the landlord was caught between an unhappy tenant and a recalcitrant developer with contractor problems.

---

[86] 1991 1 SHLR 5.
[87] 2001 Hous LR 130.
[88] See below at p 129 – prhp/G1/6/07 – Ingram Street, Glasgow, application by Storm Huntley – Glasgow, 10 December 2007.

Prohibition on contracting out[89]

Any lease terms which purport to shift the responsibility from landlord to tenant in relation to the repairing standard are prohibited. This may occur through the tenant being required to carry out work, or pay a contribution to such work, or indirectly where the lease provides for termination of the tenancy or some kind of penalty if the tenant seeks to enforce the repairing obligation. There are, however, two situations where the tenant may assume the repairing obligation and this is enforceable. We have already noted the situation where leases are for a duration of 3 or more years.[90] In addition, there is provision for obtaining the express consent of the sheriff for such a shift of obligation.[91]

Contracting out with consent of the sheriff[92]

The sheriff may permit the repairing obligation to be excluded or modified provided that both the tenant and the landlord agree. The sheriff must consider that it is reasonable to make an order excluding or modifying the repairing obligation, having regard to the terms of the tenancy and all the circumstances. This mirrors the option for shrieval consent found in the previous legislation: the Housing (Scotland) Act 1987.[93] The author has never encountered such a situation. One assumes that this would usually be something which the landlord would seek as it is not entirely obvious what would be the benefit for the tenant in assuming this responsibility, other than some kind of initial financial inducement. As indicated, it might arise where a tenant was restoring a shell of a property in exchange for a nominal rent. In the author's experience, in such situations, the parties simply ignore the repairing obligation as it is not pertinent to their arrangement.

The operation of the "private rented housing panel"

The new obligations found in the Housing (Scotland) Act 2006 have a new method of swift and effective enforcement through the "private rented housing panel". The panel's operations are determined by Sch 2 to the 2006 Act and by regulations made under the 2006 Act.[94] Schedule 2 covers the basic structure. A tenant may apply, with reasons, to the private rented housing panel for a determination that the landlord has failed to

---

[89]   HSA 2006, s 17.
[90]   Section 16 and see also above.
[91]   Section 18.
[92]   Section 18.
[93]   HSA 1987, Sch 10, para 5(1).
[94]   Section 22(5) and Sch 2. Schedule 2, para 8 provides for further regulations which are currently Private Rented Housing Panel (Applications and Determinations) (Scotland) Regulations 2007 (SSI 2007/173), outlined below in Appendix 1.

meet the repairing duty. The tenant must first notify the landlord that work requires to be carried out. This right of application is not available where the landlord is a local authority housing accommodation[95] or for a Scottish secure tenancy or a short Scottish secure tenancy,[96] or an agricultural holding tenancy[97] or a croft.[98]

NOTIFICATION OF REFERRAL[99]

When a tenant applies, the PRHC must serve notice on the landlord and tenant as soon as practicable. No specific time frame is laid down but given that the issue is disrepair, this has, thus far, in practice, been a matter of days rather than weeks.

CONTENT OF THE NOTICE[100]

The notice must set out the details of the application and specify the day by which any written representations must be received or when a request for oral representations must be made. The minimum period is at least 14 days after the day on which the PRHC notice is served. There is room before that date for written representations or request for oral hearing to be altered at the request of either party. Both parties must be notified if such a change is made.

ENQUIRIES[101]

The committee has power to make such enquiries as it thinks fit for determining whether the landlord has complied with the requirement to meet the repairing standard. There is scope as to what these enquiries should cover. These range as wide as matters other than those to which the application refers. One might have imagined, for instance, the theme of affordability raised by sheriffs in cases in the 1990s being taken up.[102] Hence the level of benefits or income of tenants and actual and average costs of heating might be matters which might shed light on how effectively a property was tenantable. This does not appear in the decisions thus far reached. Essentially, though, this part of Sch 2 gives the PRHC the scope to be a truly investigative body in carrying out its tasks. This is a far cry from the restricted role that the Court of Session sought to impose on the

---

[95] HSA 2006, s 12(1)(b).
[96] *Ibid*, s 12(1)(a).
[97] *Ibid*, s 12(1)(c).
[98] *Ibid*, s 12(1)(d).
[99] *Ibid*, Sch 2, para 1.
[100] *Ibid*.
[101] *Ibid*, Sch 2, para 2.
[102] *McArdle* v *City of Glasgow DC* 1989 SCLR 19; *McGuire* v *Monklands DC* 1997 Hous LR 41 at 44; but contrast *Galloway* v *Glasgow City Council* 2001 Hous LR 59 at 75.

Rent Assessment Committee in *Albyn Properties* v *Knox*,[103] where it was limited in its deliberations to the evidence brought before it.

OBLIGATORY MATTERS[104]

The enquiries must cover certain matters, including consideration of any written representations of either landlord or tenant made within the time limit; hearing an oral representation where requested by one of the parties; and considering any report as to the state of repair of the house prepared by a third party.

TIMEOUS[105]

A representation is timeous if made by the day specified in the notification of referral or any later date specified by the committee.

EVIDENCE[106]

Oral

The committee has the power to require the landlord, tenant or any other person to attend a hearing of the committee to give evidence. They may not be required to answer any question or disclose anything which they would be entitled to refuse to answer or disclose on the ground of confidentiality in civil proceedings in the Court of Session. The kinds of matters would be matters such as the nature of business practices.

However, failure to attend a hearing or to answer any other question not covered by confidentiality or making false or misleading statements amounts to an offence liable to a level 3 fine on summary conviction. It is a defence to a charge of failure to attend a hearing or answering any question that the person had a reasonable excuse for refusing or failing to do so. Committees have not insisted on attendance by either side. Indeed, where the matter involved an ex-tenant, attendance at the inspection phase was not possible. The committee, nonetheless, proceeded to make a determination.[107]

Written

As far as documents are concerned, the committee can require the landlord, tenant or any other person to give the committee such documents as they may reasonably require by a specified date.

---

[103] 1977 SLT 41 at 44.
[104] HSA 2006, Sch 2, para 2(3).
[105] *Ibid*, Sch 2, para 2(4).
[106] *Ibid*, Sch 2, para 3.
[107] prhp/AB41/94/08 – Cassiegills Cottage, Ellon, 4 February 2009.

This does not include any document covered by the confidentiality exemption noted in relation to oral evidence. It is a defence to a charge of failure to give a committee any document that the person had a reasonable excuse for refusing or failing to give the document. In a somewhat different context the Criminal Law (Consolidation) (Scotland) Act 1995, s 52 (which consolidated earlier statutes) deals with vandalism. This involves the destruction or damage of property belonging to another, without reasonable excuse. The court must determine, in each case, whether an excuse is reasonable. In *MacDougall* v *Ho*,[108] the proprietor of a Chinese takeaway damaged the windscreen of a taxi because he believed (wrongly) that a person who had just broken his shop window was escaping in it. This was accepted as amounting to a reasonable excuse. The matter, the courts have been keen to emphasise, does depend on the particular facts and circumstances. For example, in *John* v *Donnelly*[109] the court determined that it did not amount to a reasonable excuse to hold a sincere belief that nuclear weapons were unlawful and had potentially appalling effects.

Failure to supply any document or information required by the committee or deliberately altering, suppressing, concealing or destroying any document sought is an offence punishable by a level 3 fine on summary conviction.

SATISFACTORY PROVISION FOR DETECTING FIRES AND GIVING WARNINGS AS AN ISSUE UNDER THE REPAIRING STANDARD[110]

Where the matter in the application relates to fire safety, the committee must consult with the chief officer of the fire and rescue authority in the locality of the property concerned.

EXPENSES[111]

Any person, other than the landlord, tenant or their representatives, is entitled to expenses for attending a hearing, providing a report or anything else they were requested to do by the committee. Reasonable travelling expenses are payable to anyone involved in a hearing of the PRHC.

RECORDING AND NOTIFICATION OF DECISIONS[112]

Decisions may be reached by a majority and must be recorded, giving a full statement of facts and reasons for the decision. In the days when the fair rent work of the Rent Assessment Committee flourished, reasons were provided only when specifically asked for. This was a reflection of

---

[108] 1985 SCCR 199.
[109] 1999 JC 336.
[110] HSA 2006, Sch 2, para 4.
[111] *Ibid*, Sch 2, para 5.
[112] *Ibid*, Sch 2, para 6.

the approach of the former Lord Chief Justice, Lord Widgery, in *Guppy's Properties* v *Knott (No 1)* where he took the view that, when deciding what a fair rent was, it was almost impossible to go beyond the bald statement that this was the figure the expert body has fixed on looking to all the evidence: "There will be many, many cases where all that the assessment panel can do is say 'Doing our best with the information provided, we think that the rent should be £x'."[113]

This obligation on the appellant to have to seek a full explanation rather than receive one as a matter of practice is also current in other hearings in the Tribunals Service, such as those dealing with Disability Living Allowance, Employment Support Allowance (formerly Incapacity Benefit) or social security issues where notes of reasons are given only where there is a specific request for them. These tend to be sought only where the appellant is both represented and does not receive the award they were seeking. Given the rather less procrustean nature of the repairing obligation test, compared with those mentioned above, it is likely that there would have been requests for reasons, had their provision not been obligatory.

The procedures which the Private Rented Housing Committees must follow are laid down in Sch 2 which provides for regulations to be made. These were brought into force on 3 September 2007. They cover a range of issues such as applications requiring to be in writing, provision for representation, evidence, inspections, hearings, decision and expenses.

The work of the PRHP

In the first couple of years of operation of the repair provisions of Pt 1 of the Housing (Scotland) Act 2006 the PRHP and its constituent committees dealt with a wide range of cases. The cases come from all parts of the country, both urban and rural.[114] There were, in the 20 months between 3 September 2007 and April 2009, some 175 applications. The level of application has been steady throughout this period across Scotland, at around eight per month. There is, on the face of it, a high level of success for tenants. Some 45 per cent of cases are withdrawn. This occurs principally where the repair has been completed or where it is under way. The remainder are "invalid" and this occurs chiefly where there has been no prior notification to the landlord as required. The landlords who have gone through the PRHP process have been principally individuals (75 per cent), followed by companies (20 per cent) and trusts (5 per cent). This contrasts with the breakdown of the private rented sector as a whole in Scotland.[115]

---

[113] [1978] EGD 255 at 259.
[114] See Appendix 2 below.
[115] Scottish Government (2009d).

DETERMINATIONS

The previous specialist tribunals dealing with the fixing of fair rents, the Rent Assessment Committees, were only required to provide written reasons for their decision on request by either of the parties. As indicated, the committees which determine repair issues are required to provide reasons for their decisions,[116] and these are available online.[117] A number of interesting practice points and distinct issues have been raised which are worthy of some attention.

The standard form

Unlike in other judicial bodies such as First Tier Tribunals in the social security system, there seems to have been no reticence in providing *pro forma* advice for those writing up decisions. This consistency of approach means that it is rather easier to follow the fact-finding process and trace how committees have treated the evidence before them. By examining all the decisions of the committees in Scotland for the first years of the operation of Pt 1 of the Housing (Scotland) Act 2006 the same basic outline appears with only minor variations in all decisions:

background;
inspection;
hearing
summary of the issues;
findings of fact;
reasons for the decision;
decision.

It is worth expanding a little on what is encountered under each of these headings.

BACKGROUND

In this section the date of the application to the PRHP is provided, along with a brief indication of the issues complained of, usually without reference to the specific subsections of s 13. Hence we find in a decision dated 20 July 2008:

"In her application the Tenant alleged that the landlord had failed to comply with the duty to ensure that the Property met the Repairing

---

[116] Private Rented Housing Panel (Applications and Determinations) (Scotland) Regulations 2007 (SSI 2007/173) reg 26(2).

[117] The PRHP website provides copies of the relevant papers. There is a suffix to indicate the stage – rseo (repairing standard enforcement notice); rro (rent reduction order); nla (notice to local authority; var (variation of rseo) – http://www.prhpscotland.gov.uk/prhp/221/html.

Standard (as defined in the Act). In particular the Landlord had failed to ensure that:–

(i)   The windows within the property were wind tight;

(ii)   The central heating system within the property was adequate and consequently it failed to heat the Property efficiently;

(iii) The Property was free of internal dampness."[118]

INSPECTION

When the inspection took place and who attended is noted here. There may be provided more extensive details of what the committee was able to observe at the inspection and what comments both landlord and tenant had on the issue. This is found in the very detailed and clear determination dated 18 December 2007 in relation to 13B Balfron Road, Killearn. This includes issues on which there was agreement that an issue had been resolved: "The parties advised that the [washing machine] had been replaced" and "The parties advised that the guttering had been repaired" to issues on which there were ongoing complaints:

> "The tenant showed the committee that the open, close and lock mechanisms of the windows in the kitchen did not work properly. Also the bottom hinge fixing of the main window in the master bedroom was broken."

HEARING

When and where the hearing took place is also noted, along with any issues of special note. In one set of reasons involving an unwilling landlord the determination notes:

> "The Landlord's representative ... attended. He confirmed that he was part owner of the house with his wife ... and that they were both partners in the firm of ... the Landlord specified in the RSEO ... [he] accepted that none of the said repairs specified in the RSEO had been carried out and he stated that he had no intention of completing these said repairs until after the Tenant had vacated the property."[119]

SUMMARY OF THE ISSUES

Here the committee sums up the formal legislative issues which are to be determined by it with reference to the legislation. Hence in a determination dated 27 March 2008 the matter is expressed succinctly:

> "The issue to be determined by the Rented Housing Committee is whether or not the Property meets the repairing standard in terms of Section 13(1)(a), 13(1)(b) and 13(1)(c) of the Act as at the date of the hearing."[120]

---

[118] prhp/G63/12/07 – 13b Balfron Road, Killearn.

[119] prhp/ML3/4/08 – 48 Central Avenue, Ardrossan.

[120] prhp/KW15/22/07 – Castlegreen, Carness Road, St Ola, Kirkwall.

One determination from 15 September 2008 breaks the issues down into their constituent parts rather more explicitly and helpfully for the non-specialist reader:

"(a) Whether the condition of the central heating system was such that it is in a reasonable state of repair and in proper working order as required by section 13(1)(c) of the Housing (Scotland) Act 2006.

(b) Whether the condition of the front and back door handles and the windows are in a reasonable state of repair and proper working order as required by section 13(1)(b) of the Housing (Scotland) Act 2006.

(c) Whether the condition of the piping under the bath and the toilet pan are in a reasonable state of repair and proper working order as required by section 13(1)(d) of the Housing (Scotland) Act 2006."[121]

FINDINGS OF FACT

These are the statements of what the committee is able to report as regards the issues complained of, and on which there is concrete evidence. In a determination dated 3 September 2008 the following were the findings of fact of the committee:

"9. A gas safety certificate in respect of the Property was available. In the circumstances the Committee accepted that installations in the house for the supply of gas and for space heating and water heating were in a reasonable state of repair and in proper working order.

10. The Landlord had failed to produce evidence that the electrical installations in the Property were in all respects safe. The Committee accepted that the Tenants evidence that there were loose sockets in the Property and that a number of light bulbs would blow on a regular basis. The Committee further noted that the gas safety certificate lodged by the Landlord indicated that the equipotential bonding of the gas installation was not satisfactory."[122]

REASONS FOR THE DECISION

In coming to their conclusions committees have varied in the details they have provided. In some instances they have been highly succinct, such as in the Cumbernauld decision noted from September 2008:

"11. The Committee were satisfied that there was a sufficiency of evidence to determine that the installations in the house for the supply of electricity were not in a reasonable state of repair or in proper working order."[123]

---

[121] prhp/KA3/39/08 – 2 Onthank Drive, Kilmarnock – where in due course a 65 per cent reduction in rent was ordered.
[122] prhp/G67/27/07 – 42 Glenhove Road, Cumbernauld .
[123] *Ibid.*

DECISION

The decision simply recites what the determination of the committee, on the evidence before it, amounts to. This is found at both the beginning and the end of committee determinations. The form is simple and, where failure to comply is found, links to the Repairing Standard Enforcement Order under s 24(2). The committee, when it finds that there is failure to comply, must by order require the landlord to carry out such work as is necessary for the purposes of ensuring that:

"(a) that the house concerned meets the repairing standard, and

(b) that any damage caused by the carrying out of any work in pursuance of that duty or order is made good."

The link between the decision and the RSEO is made clear in this determination from 20 July 2008:

"The Committee, having made such enquiries as it saw fit for the purposes of determining whether the Landlord has complied with the duty imposed by Section 14(1)(b) of the Housing (Scotland) Act 2006 ('the Act') in relation to the Property, and taking account of the written evidence given by the Tenant, the submissions made by both parties, and the evidence given by the Landlord at the Hearing unanimously determined that the Landlord had failed to comply with the duty imposed by section 14(1)(b) of the Act. The Committee therefore requires that the Landlord carry out such work as is necessary for ensuring that the property meets the Repairing Standards and that any damage caused by the carrying out of any work in pursuance of this order is made good. The Committee issued a Repairing Standard Enforcement Order as annexed to this Statement of Reasons."[124]

In this instance the RSEO indicated that the landlord had failed in the duty to ensure:

"(a) the bathroom window was water tight

(b) the radiators in the hall, the living room and the bedrooms are fit for their purpose."

The landlord was ordered to carry out such work as was necessary to meet the repairing standard and

"In particular the Private Rented Housing Committee requires the Land-lord:–

(a) to replace the window in the bathroom; and

(b) to remove the existing radiators in the hall, living room, and the bedrooms and replace them with radiators which are fit for their purpose."[125]

---

[124] prhp/DD8/33/08 – South Tarbrax Farmhouse, Inverarity, by Forfar.
[125] *Ibid.*

Contentious issues

LANDLORD NOT IN CONTROL OF THE REPAIR[126]

Where the landlord is not in a position to effect the repair through lack of rights of access or otherwise and has taken reasonable steps to obtain such rights, s 26(4) provides that the committee must serve on the local authority notice stating that the consider that the landlord is unable to comply. The statute is silent on the next step. This occurred in a property in Ingram Street, Glasgow, where the tenant complained that she could not use her parking space because of the dripping of corrosive liquid from a pipe. The repairs were being overseen by the developer who was in dispute with the contractors.

LANDLORD WANTS TO DEMOLISH RATHER THAN REPAIR[127]

In a case involving property in Kirkwall where the landlords were unwilling to engage in the expense of repair as they wished to repair, the committee determined that the obligations, nonetheless, fell to be carried out.

TENANT'S COMPLAINTS ARE EXCESSIVE[128]

In a number of instances the tenant has been successful in obtaining limited redress from a long list of complaints.

TENANT NO LONGER IN OCCUPATION[129]

The committee has made clear that under Sch 2, para 7(3)(b), the legislation allows it to make a determination where the tenant is no longer in the property. In this instance the tenant was keen to protect future tenants. At the hearing the landlord's agent would not permit the tenant and his wife into the property and "the Committee conducted the inspection outwith their presence".

Enforcement of RSEOs

On a number of occasions situations have arisen in practice which resulted in the committee imposing a rent relief order in terms of s 27 of the Act.

FAILURE TO REPAIR[130]

In the first case there seems to have been a breakdown in communication between the landlords, based in the south of England, and those carrying

---

[126] prhp/G1/6/07 – Ingram Street, Glasgow.
[127] prhp/KW15/22/07 – Kirkwall, 27 March 2008.
[128] prhp/DD8/33/08 – Inverarity, 20 July 2008.
[129] prhp/AB41/94/08 – Cassiegills Cottage, Ellon, 4 February 2009.
[130] prhp/G67/27/07 – Glenhove Road, Cumbernauld, 3 September 2008 – a certificate of completion was finally granted on 29 August 2009.

out work on their behalf, as well as a dispute over the extent of the electrical repair works required. Despite this the committee went on to make a rent relief order reducing by £200 the monthly rent of £425.

REFUSAL TO REPAIR[131]

A different reason led landlords in Ardrossan not to comply with an order from the committee in August 2008 in relation to window repairs. The landlords indicated at the hearing that they were not prepared to carry out the repairs until the tenant vacated the house. The monthly rent was reduced from £450 to £360. The problem was that the tenant was in rent arrears and landlord/tenant relations had broken down, apparently irrevocably.

FAILURE TO REPAIR TIMEOUSLY[132]

In a rather different case there seems to have been a problem in effecting repairs. These ranged from repairing electrical wiring, to the back-door lock not working, the shower unit water not draining away, a mixer tap not replaced and the kitchen oven not working. Both parties were at the original hearing, inspection, re-hearing and re-inspection. In the 10-week time scale provided, many of the repairs had been done either ineffectively or not at all. While the committee acknowledged that the landlord had made efforts in respect of the required repairs, it made a 50 per cent reduction in the rent

Nuisance provisions

Although the nuisance provisions of the Environmental Protection Act 1990 remain available to tenants in the private sector, it is hard to see why anyone would choose to use the environmental health route rather than the PRHP mechanism to secure repairs to a rented house.

The test as to whether a problem in a property amounts to a statutory nuisance is whether it is prejudicial to health. Is it injurious or likely to cause injury to health? This can be from the premises themselves or from any noise, smoke, gases etc on the premises.[133]

---

[131] prhp/KA/5/08/rro – Ardrossan, 14 August 2008 – this is the same case as that in n 119 above, which has a different reference.

[132] prhp/EH15/26/09 – 35 Southfield Farm Grove, Duddingston, Edinburgh, 5 November 2009.

[133] Section 79 – (a) any premises in such a state; (b) smoke emitted from premises; (c) fumes or gases emitted from premises; (d) any dust, steam, smell or other effluvia arising from an industrial, trade or business premises; (e) any accumulation or deposit; (f) any animal kept in such a place or manner; (g) noise emitted from premises; (h) noise emitted from or caused by a vehicle, machinery or equipment in a road; (i) any other matter declared by any enactment to be a statutory nuisance.

Statutory notices

There is also an indirect route to secure repairs through the service by the local authority of either a repairs notice or an improvement notice. Whether or not the local authority determines that such a notice is appropriate is a matter for its discretion and the courts will intervene only where the local authority acts in a way in which no reasonable authority would act.

Community regulation

Although anyone living in damp and unsatisfactory housing is understandably unlikely to be concerned as to whether they have public law remedies or whether their rights derive from private law, these two distinct sources do reflect the two principal routes society has opted to take in seeking to address the failure of the market to provide decent housing conditions for large swathes of the population. Community responses, both direct and indirect, have provided solutions which individuals have been unable to secure. They are based on seeking to bring houses up to a specified standard. This "tolerable standard" is defined in terms of a range of criteria encompassing freedom from dampness through having hot and cold water and a WC to having satisfactory facilities for the cooking of food within the house.[134]

The two avenues, however, provide alternative ways of achieving the same result. They complement each other but need to be separated out to provide a clear picture of how decent housing for all can be achieved. There is overlap in the alternative public and private enforcement mechanisms available for dealing with statutory nuisances. This issue is considered below in relation to individual remedies since it is directly available to tenants and property owners, although, strictly speaking, it is a public law remedy. The issues discussed now are different, in that they rely for their efficacy on action taken on behalf of the public by local authorities. There is detailed provision in the legislation for periods of notice within which to appeal against the making of an order and periods within which to carry out any requirements of the notice.[135]

---

[134]   HSA 1987, s 86(1) (as amended by the Housing (Scotland) Act 2006): (1) structurally stable; (2) substantially free from rising or penetrating damp; (3) satisfactory provision for natural and artificial lighting, for ventilation and heating; (3a) satisfactory thermal insulation; (4) an adequate supply of wholesome water available within the house; (5) a sink provided with a satisfactory supply of both hot and cold water within the house; (6) has a water closet available for the exclusive use of the occupants of the house; (6) has a water closet or waterless closet available for the exclusive use of the occupants and suitably located within the house; (7) has an effective system for the drainage and disposal of foul and surface water; (8) has satisfactory facilities for the cooking of food within the house; (9) has satisfactory access to all external doors and outbuildings; and (10) complies with electrical installation requirements.

[135]   See Pts IV, v and VI of the Housing (Scotland) Act 1987.

Local authorities have for some time had obligations to look to eradicating unhealthy housing from their areas. From 1969 they were to ensure that houses in their areas met the "tolerable standard". This somewhat anodyne term replaced the previous one of "fitness for human habitation" which was retained in England and Wales until 2006. It provided local authorities with a power to close houses, demolish houses or bring houses up to standard where they were deemed to fall below the tolerable standard.[136] This was a power, though, for use on areas rather than for individual houses. The Housing Improvement Task Force's recommendations resulted in changes to allow for action where houses were not only below the amended tolerable standard[137] but where their appearance or state of repair was adversely affecting the amenity of that locality.[138] The general duty in relation to sub-standard houses is further supplemented by powers to close houses below the tolerable standard[139] as well as to demolish such houses.[140]

CLOSING AND DEMOLITION ORDERS

The Housing (Scotland) Act 1987 is the most recent location for powers allowing local authorities to close and demolish buildings which had their origins in the Artisans and Labourers Dwellings Act 1868. Individual sub-standard houses can be either closed or demolished by authorities where the authority is satisfied that the building does not meet the tolerable standard and ought to be demolished.[141] If the house forms part of a building which comprises other houses *not* below the tolerable standard then a closing order will be made.[142]

REPAIR NOTICES

These were introduced to complement the more extensive activities of the closing, demolition and improvement orders in 1969 to allow individual houses which are in a state of serious disrepair to be brought up to such standard as is reasonable having regard to its age, character and location but disregarding the internal decorative repair, of the house.[143]

IMPROVEMENT ORDERS

Building on the concept of the "tolerable standard" from the 1960s, these orders, introduced in 1978, provide for buildings to be brought up to this

---

[136] Housing (Scotland) Act 1987, Pt IV, s 85.
[137] Housing (Scotland) Act 2006, s 11.
[138] *Ibid*, s 1(b).
[139] Housing (Scotland) Act 1987, Pt VI, s 114.
[140] *Ibid*, Pt VI, s 115.
[141] *Ibid*, s 115(a).
[142] *Ibid*, s 114(1).
[143] *Ibid*, s 108(2)(b).

standard. These are relevant where a house is outwith a housing renewal area.[144]

MAINTENANCE ORDERS

A maintenance order requires the owner of a house to prepare a plan to secure the maintenance of the house to a reasonable standard. Maintenance orders may be made only where the house has not been, or is unlikely to be, maintained to a reasonable standard.[145] These orders are intended to allow the addressing of problems encountered when recalcitrant fellow-owners block plans to undertake communal repairs and maintenance. Tenant management schemes were introduced by the Tenements (Scotland) Act 2004 as the default management scheme for all tenements in Scotland where no provision is made in the title documentation. Local authorities have the power to require that the owner of a house prepares a maintenance plan for securing the maintenance of a house to a reasonable standard within such period, not exceeding 5 years, as the order lays down.[146]

Indirectly accessible quality standards

This has been supplemented by a power to deal with emergency situations. The Civic Government (Scotland) Act 1982 introduced the power for local authorities to repair a property in the interests of health and safety or to prevent damage to any other property.[147] The problem with these mechanisms is, of course, that they are dependent on the local authority deciding to take action and do not provide a *locus standi* to individual complainants.

Finally, an overall obligation is now laid on local authorities and registered social landlords to meet the national Scottish Housing Quality Standard (SHQS). As was noted in the report on the future of housing standards in Scotland,[148] there had been discussion going back to the work of J B Cullingworth in the 1960s[149] of the "the need for a 'satisfactory standard', i.e. an aspirational standard that set a quality target for all houses towards which policy should be directed over the longer term". This was an issue which had been seen with the launch in England of the Decency Standard, with the objective that all public rented houses should meet this Standard within 10 years.[150] The National Assembly for

---

[144] Formerly "housing action area" and before that "treatment area".
[145] Housing (Scotland) Act 2006, s 42(2)(b).
[146] *Ibid*, s 42(1).
[147] Civic Government (Scotland Act) 1982, s 87.
[148] Scottish Government (2003a), para 45.
[149] Cullingworth (1968).
[150] "What is the Decent Homes Standard?": http://www.communities.gov.uk/housing/decenthomes/whatis.

Wales had also launched a Welsh Housing Standard.[151] In Scotland, in November 2002 the Minister for Social Justice announced the intention of developing a Scottish Social Housing Standard.

The SHQS which emerged, after consultation, requires that registered social landlords provide accommodation which reaches a quality standard as determined by the housing regulator. While this requirement has no formal legislative sanction attached, like a statutory duty, it seems clear that failure to meet the SHQS would result in action from the Scottish Housing Regulator (formerly Communities Scotland) whose role in relation to social landlords is to monitor their performance.

The standard derives from a consultation paper, *Modernising Scotland's Social Housing* (March 2003), and the work of the Housing Improvement Task Force. To meet the Standard, a house must be:

- compliant with the tolerable standard;[152]
- free from serious disrepair;
- energy efficient;
- provided with modern facilities and services;
- healthy, safe and secure.

These broad criteria are defined in terms of a detailed specification. The letter of 2 February 2004 from the then Scottish Executive setting out the SHQS noted the potential problem with all Scottish housing meeting these criteria and concluded: "The intention is that the Scottish Housing Quality Standard is relevant to the housing stock as a whole. Its application will, however, vary according to tenure."

As far as the social rented sector was concerned, it was expected that local authorities and registered social landlords would "ensure that their stock meets the standard by 2015". They were able to set their own "milestones" for making progress providing Standard Delivery Plans for submission to Scottish Ministers by April 2005 via Communities Scotland. Local authorities would update their Local Housing Strategies. Although this standard was to apply across the board, this was to be a matter of choice for owner occupiers.

> "Aside from instances where owners may be required to, for example, bring properties up to the Tolerable Standard or rectify serious disrepair that has been the subject of a statutory notice, it is ultimately a matter for individual owners to decide whether to make improvements if their properties do not meet the Standard ... local authorities ... will need to consider what

---

[151] For details of the Welsh Housing Quality Standard, see http://wales.gov.uk/topics/housingandcommunity/publications/whqsrevisedguide/.
[152] This now includes the requirement that the house has satisfactory thermal insulation: HSA 2006, s 11.

measures might be adopted to encourage private owners to undertake relevant works."

The details of the Standard indicate the following:

Housing quality criteria	Criteria definition	Criteria elements	Failure assessed by
Compliant with the tolerable standard	Tolerable standard	Below tolerable standard	Single primary failure
Free from serious disrepair	Primary building elements	Wall structures Internal floor structures Foundations Roof structure	Single primary element failure An element fails where it requires repair or replacement of more than 20 per cent
	Secondary building elements	Roof covering Chimney stacks Flashings Rainwater goods External wall finishes etc	Failure by *two* or more elements An element fails where it requires repair or replacement of more than 20%
Energy efficient	Effective insulation	Cavity insulation where technically feasible and appropriate 100mm loft insulation where appropriate Insulation of hot water tank and pipes (and cold water tanks as an ancillary measure)	Single element failure
	Efficient heating	A full-house central heating system that has an acceptable rating, or similarly efficient heating system that is developed in the future	Single element failure
Modern facilities and services Healthy, safe and secure		Bathroom amenities including WC, bath or shower and wash-hand basin Internal pipe work lead free Smoke detector Adequate lighting in common areas	

These criteria were clarified in a letter of 28 July 2004 as to what was meant by an element requiring repair or replacement of more than 20 per cent, for instance. This failure refers to the percentage of the item in question which is in disrepair for each individual dwelling. For example, disrepair to a roof covering is an area-based measure and the approach taken is to identify buildings where 20 per cent or more of the surface area of the roof is in disrepair. In contrast, disrepair to chimney stacks is assessed by identifying disrepair to each component of the chimney stack (cope, structure, finish, pots) and weighing the results to arrive at an overall repair score for the chimney, which again would be 20 per cent or more to trigger item failure.

POLITICAL, SOCIAL AND HISTORICAL CONTEXT OF THE DEVELOPMENT OF HOUSING STANDARDS

In his examination of the development of housing in Glasgow in the 19th century, John Butt counsels care when applying qualitative approaches when looking at earlier social conditions because of the absence of universally acceptable tests of validity.[153] Bearing that in mind, the statistics in relation to rates of death and levels of sickness are, nonetheless, a stark reminder that we are talking about more than the inconvenience of outside toilets and the absence of central heating when official reports tell us that much housing in both rural and urban areas was not in good repair.[154] Kelso's picture of the levels of disease in 19th-century Paisley is an eye-opener.[155] Gauldie similarly reports very high infant mortality rates.[156] Sanitary inspectors' reports paint a bleak picture[157] where the law was far from effective in ensuring that citizens lived in safe and sanitary housing.

Common law background

A pragmatic problem which was encountered by tenants extensively prior to the 20th century centred around the relative lack of bargaining power of tenants in relation to where they lived. This accommodation was for the most part rented from private landlords. Those properties which were constructed in the public sector were of a high standard

---

[153] Butt (1971) at 57.
[154] Royal Commission on the Housing of the Working Classes (1885) and Royal Commission on the Housing of the Industrial population of Scotland, rural and urban (1917).
[155] Kelso (1922).
[156] Gauldie (1974) at 101ff.
[157] Robson (1979) at 293–342.

suitable for "well-doing artisans" and can still be seen in such cities as Glasgow.[158]

The issue of the lack of quality and uninhabitability in the property occupied can be seen in the solutions sought by the better off. Those with greater ability to affect their adverse circumstances tended to move. The extent of moves for these reasons is not known but the kinds of issues can be guessed at from the 19th-century case law. Landlords had a number of weapons in relation to tenants. They could insist that tenants meet the terms of the contract by returning and living in the property after dealing with the defects. There are a number of examples of tenants being pursued in the courts on trying to bring their tenancies to an end prematurely on the basis of the landlord's failure to provide accommodation that was tenantable and habitable. This was the basic common-law obligation of landlords. The reasons were loss of significant forward revenue as tenancies of longish duration, such as 5 years, are reasonably common in the case law.

The approach of the courts was in some instances reasonably sympathetic to the plight of those suffering in unhealthy conditions. In *Kippen* v *Oppenheim*,[159] for instance, a tenant was able to give up a property infested with beetles and cockroaches, while a doctor who lost a child to typhoid fever was also not required to continue with the tenancy in *Scottish Heritable Security Co (Ltd)* v *Granger*.[160] The approach could also be "robust" and from 1892[161] it operated for over the next century the notion that the tenant could be personally barred from a claim through consent. Hence, as late as the 1960s in *Proctor* v *Cowlairs Co-operative Society Ltd*[162] we find the landlords successfully resisting a claim by the widow of a man dying after a fall on an unsafe common stair.

By their very nature, the solutions available to tenants through suing in terms of contract were limited. We occasionally get a glimpse into the lives of tenants in poor housing when an accident occurred. Hence in *Mechan* v *Watson* we come across a child being injured through slipping through a gap in the stairs in a Duke Street tenement.[163] More

---

158   Easily viewable are the houses built by the Glasgow Improvement Trust in Saltmarket erected in 1887 and the houses in the High Street north of George Street (1893). St George's Mansions at Charing Cross were also constructed at this time and bear the coat of arms of the city of Glasgow. This huge tenement block was built in 1902 to designs by the architects Burnet & Boston. It was built by the City Improvement Trust and one of its earliest occupants was the celebrated Oscar Slater. He lived at 69 St George's Road in a third-floor flat prior to his being convicted of the murder of Miss Marion Gilchrist.

159   (1847) 10 D 242.

160   (1881) 8 R 459; see also *McKimmie's Trustees* v *Armour* (1899) 2 F 156.

161   *Webster* v *Brown* (1892) 19 R 765.

162   1961 SLT 434.

163   1907 SC 25.

dramatically, a 2-year-old girl was burned to death through her nightgown catching fire in a Rose Street stair.[164] Neither case was successful as the courts accepted the notion that the cause of the accidents had been defects which were obvious at the start of the tenancy.

Alternative solutions were provided in both accessible mechanisms for use by the whole community through public health legislation as well as the introduction of statutory standards aimed to be more exacting than "tenantable and habitable".

Public health legislation

Apart from the possibilities of individual tenants taking action for breach of contract, two kinds of community involvement were available. From the middle of the 19th century some authorities, such as Glasgow and Edinburgh, used local Acts of Parliament to assist in dealing with insanitary slums.[165] Although this prefigured the concept of comprehensive redevelopment of the 20th century, the process tended to drawn out and expensive. Results were mixed, with both Greenock and Aberdeen spending most of their budgets on compensation to slum property owners.[166]

Rather less costly was the piecemeal process of taking action against individual "nuisances" by or on behalf of the public. The power for local authorities to employ sanitary officers was introduced in 1867.[167] It was not until 1887, however, that it became a duty to provide such services. Even when it was a duty, the operations appeared to have been relatively modest. Kelso talks about a town the size of Paisley employing his boss, himself and a clerk to deal with the problems of a town of more than 60,000 dwellings.[168] In Perth the post of sanitary inspector was one of the several tasks allotted to the Registrar of Births, Deaths and Marriages. A budget of £5 is recorded for the town of Arbroath. Those operating the legislation recognised in their conferences and reports to the Local Government Board that their efforts were puny in contrast to the problems of urban disease and squalor.[169]

"Fitness for human habitation"

In 1890 a slightly different approach was introduced. All residential properties which were leased required to be "fit for human habitation". The enforcement mechanism, was, however, through the courts. There seems to have been doubt as to the need for the introduction of a fresh

---

[164] *Davidson* v *Sprengel* 1909 SC 566.
[165] Gauldie (1974); Robson (1979).
[166] Robson at 343–361.
[167] Gauldie (1974).
[168] Kelso (1922).
[169] Robson.

statutory right for tenants. Rankine pointed out that there was already, in Scots law, a requirement for houses to be "tenantable and habitable".[170] Some decisions seem unusual, as where an invasion of sewer rats did *not* result in a house being declared unfit for human habitation.[171] The court explained that these occasional invaders could not be said to be located in the dwelling-house. Generally, though, the major reported cases do not provide an accurate picture of the problems encountered by tenants in slum housing at the end of the 19th century and the first half of the 20th century. Litigation appears to have been concentrated on public landlords. The reported cases are involved in looking to see where the boundary of "fitness for human habitation" is drawn and so we encounter relatively minor issues, such as broken windows in *Morgan* v *Liverpool Corporation*,[172] *Summers* v *Salford Corporation*[173] and *McCarrick* v *Liverpool Corporation*.[174] In Scotland, the same sort of boundary fixing is encountered where we see cases in the Inner House of the Court of Session about a jammed window in *Haggerty* v *Glasgow Corporation*[175] and in the sheriff court about a defective fire grate in *Hughes' Tutrix* v *Glasgow District Council*.[176] Of rather greater general impact was the cost of redecoration: *McCarthy* v *Glasgow District Council*.[177]

The "fitness for human habitation" test applied, however, in terms of the Housing of the Working Classes Act 1890 only to properties rented out at £4 or less. It was raised by the Housing, Town Planning etc Act 1909 and in due course in 1923 to £26 per year and covered at that time a large proportion of rental housing likely to have sanitary defects. As the years passed, however, levels of rents paid rose but the ceiling for applicability of the legislation remained fixed. There was, therefore, less coverage and the test fell into disuse. There were only a couple of reported cases in the post-War years.[178] It was not until the Housing (Scotland) Act 1988 that the application was recalibrated up to £300 per week.[179] This covered, for the first decade of its operation from 2 January 1989, almost all houses outwith the top end of the market where tenants were unlikely to be troubled by chronic damp or insanitary conditions.

---

170   Rankine (2nd edn, 1903).
171   *Stanton* v *Southwark* [1920] 2 KB 642.
172   [1927] 2 KB 131.
173   [1943] AC 283.
174   [1947] AC 219.
175   1964 SLT (Notes) 54.
176   1982 SLT 70.
177   1991 1 SHLR 181.
178   *Haggerty* v *Glasgow Corporation* 1964 SLT (Notes) 54; *Hughes' Tutrix* v *Glasgow DC* 1982 SLT 70.
179   Landlord's Repairing Obligations (Specified Rent) (Scotland) (No 2) Order 1988 (SI 1988/2155) as specified in Sch 8 to the Housing (Scotland) Act 1988, para 9, in terms of s 72.

There were, in effect, two alternatives for individual tenants taking action through the courts. They could continue in Scotland to use the common law. This required that any landlord of residential property had to provide, in return for charging rent, accommodation which was "habitable and tenantable". They might be covered by the statutory requirement that property be "fit for human habitation". From 1962, in addition there was a statutory "implied repairs provision".[180]

The implied repairs provision

This was introduced in the Housing (Scotland) Act 1962. This development, like the "fitness for human habitation" test, came from limitations experienced by tenants of poor-quality housing in England and replicates the tests introduced in the Housing Act 1961. From July 1962 there was an implied provision that the landlord would keep in repair the structure and exterior of the house, including the drains, gutters and external pipes, as well as keep in repair and proper working order the installations for the supply of gas, electricity, space and water heating.

POLITICAL CONTEXT

Although the state of repair of tenements occasionally made its appearance in documentary films,[181] the response to insanitary and untenantable conditions was slum clearance. The replacement of housing rather than its repair remained a standard solution until the 1970s. Of course, the development of the extent of the court remedies and the alternative public health approach addressed the problem of private landlords' unwillingness or inability to carry out repairs. As far as public-sector housing was concerned, the same kinds of profit constraints were not a factor. One would assume that property owned by the community for occupation by members of the community would be kept in good repair by the community through its executive arm, the council. This did not turn out always to be the case. Properties erected under some of the slum clearance programmes in the 1930s used cheap materials and had inadequate insulation for the Scottish climate. While, as Jonathan Mitchell pointed out in one "dampness" case, "it is possible to heat an igloo at the South Pole", this was not what was expected or required.[182]

---

180   Housing (Scotland) Act 1962.
181   Housing Problems (1935) Edgar Anstey and Arthur Elton – available at http://www.screenonline.org.film/id/513807/index.html.
182   *McArdle* v *City of Glasgow DC* 1989 SCLR 19.

APPENDIX 1: PRIVATE RENTED HOUSING PANEL REGULATIONS IN FORCE AT 31 MARCH 2010[183]

Applications to the panel

WRITTEN

Applications must be by written notice. They *may* be, but do not have to be, on the Panel's form.[184] They must include the names and addresses of the tenant and his representative, the name and address of the landlord and the nature of the work requiring to be done. This must include a statement that the landlord has been notified and reasons for considering that the landlord has failed to comply with landlord's duty. This failure to notify the landlord was the reason for the majority of cases which were rejected in the first year of operation of the legislation. Applications must also indicate whether the tenant does or does not wish to attempt to resolve the dispute by mediation.[185]

ATTACHMENTS REQUIRED

A copy of the lease, tenancy agreement or rent book, or as much information as the tenant can give, is required,[186] along with details of the manner in which the landlord has been notified that the work specified in the application requires to be carried out.[187]

REPRESENTATION

A person may act in person or be represented.[188] They must notify the committee and the other party when a representative starts to act for a party[189] and when they cease so to act and also of the name and address of a new representative (if known).[190]

Such notice may be provided orally if it is done at the hearing, otherwise it requires to be written.[191] The agent may do anything that the party may do under the regulations.[192]

The committee may refuse to permit a particular person to assist or represent a party at a hearing if it is satisfied that there is a good reason.[193]

---

[183] Private Rented Housing Panel (Applications and Determinations) (Scotland) Regulations 2007 (SSI 2007/173).
[184] Reg 3(1).
[185] Reg 3(2).
[186] Reg 4(1).
[187] Reg 4(2).
[188] Reg 5(1).
[189] Reg 5(2).
[190] Reg 5(4).
[191] Reg 5(5).
[192] Reg 5(3).
[193] Reg 5(6).

WITHDRAWAL OF APPLICATION

A tenant wishing to withdraw an application may do so orally at the hearing or in writing at any time by serving a notice of withdrawal. Notice of withdrawal may be made in writing and on a form obtained from the Panel offices.[194]

Processing the application

ACKNOWLEDGEMENT

This must be sent to the tenant on receipt of the application.[195]

Details to be entered in the register of cases and details of the case number to be provided to the tenant together with an address for delivery of communications to the Panel.[196]

Usually within 14 days for informing tenant that application is to be referred immediately to the committee, or rejected or deferred to allow parties to attempt to resolve the dispute.[197]

Where the president considers that further information is required and a decision cannot be made within 14 days, the tenant must be informed of that and given a further date by which time a decision may be made.[198]

RESOLUTION

The Panel Secretary must bring to the attention of the parties the availability of mediation as an alternative procedure for the resolution of the dispute and, if the parties consent to mediation, facilitate that mediation.[199]

ADDITIONAL APPLICATIONS/MULTIPLE PROBLEMS

Where the property fails to meet the repairing standard in more than one respect, the tenant may raise all the issues in a single application.[200]

ADDITIONAL WORK/FURTHER ISSUES EMERGE

The tenant may make a further application to include any issues which come to light in the course of the investigation by the committee. The landlord must be notified that further work requires to be done in order to comply with the landlord's repairing duty.[201]

---

194 SSI 2007/173, reg 17.
195 Reg 6(a).
196 Reg 6(b).
197 Reg 6 (c).
198 Reg 6 (d).
199 Reg 7.
200 Reg 8.
201 Reg 9.

These further issues must follow the same procedure as the original application,[202] although there may be shortening of timescales if both parties agree.

CONJOINING APPLICATIONS

Where two or more applications relate to the same property at the same time, the committee may direct that they be heard together.[203]

ENQUIRIES

Parties must be given not less than 10 working days' notice of any date specified for production of documents or information.[204]

DIRECTIONS[205]

The committee may give directions to the parties relating to the conduct or progress of the application either on application or on its own initiative.[206] Directions may be given orally or in writing.[207] They may relate to any matter concerning preparation for a hearing; specify the length of time for something to be done; vary any time limit of previous directions; provide for a matter to be dealt with as a preliminary issue; provide for a party to provide further details of his case or any other information which appears to be necessary for the determination of the application; witnesses to be heard (if any); and the manner in which any evidence is to be given.

The committee may require any party to lodge and serve statements of any evidence which will be put forward at the hearing; a paginated and indexed bundle of all the documents which will be relied on at the hearing; a skeleton argument summarising the submissions which will be made at the hearing and citing all the authorities which will be relied on, identifying any particular passages to be relied on; and a list of witnesses any party wishes to call.

When making directions the committee must take into account the ability of parties to comply with the directions.

EVIDENCE

Where the committee has set time limits for lodging and serving written evidence it must *not* consider any written evidence not lodged within those time limits *unless* satisfied that there are *good reasons to do so* (my emphasis).[208]

---

202   Reg SSI 2007/173, reg 10.
203   Reg 11.
204   Reg 12.
205   Reg 14.
206   Reg 14(1).
207   Reg 14(3).
208   Reg 15(1).

Originals may be required where a party seeks to rely on a copy.[209]

Clerical errors or omissions may be corrected by the chair of the committee and must be served on the relevant party.[210]

INSPECTIONS

An inspection may be made before or during the hearing or after an adjournment, at such stage as the committee shall decide.[211]

Further inspections may be made or commissioned as appropriate to enable the committee to determine whether or not work required by an RSEO has been completed adequately or to decide whether to grant a s 60 certificate.[212]

Any second or subsequent inspection may be made by the whole committee or by one member alone or by any person authorised by the committee to carry out such an inspection.[213]

The committee must give such notice in writing as it deems sufficient of an inspection to the parties and shall allow each party and their representatives to attend any inspection.[214]

HEARINGS

Where a party attends a hearing and is not represented by another person, the committee may assist that party to make the best of his case, without advocating the course that party should take.[215]

Not less than 14 working days must be given in writing to the landlord and the tenant of the date, time and place of the hearing.[216] Hearings are in public unless the committee otherwise decides "to ensure a fair hearing" – this may be on its own cause or on application by the parties. This does not affect a member of the council on tribunals attending.[217]

The committee may exclude from a any hearing or part of it any person (including a party or their representative) whose conduct has disrupted the hearing or whose conduct has otherwise interfered with the administration of justice.[218]

The committee must, apart from other considerations, have regard to the interests of the parties and in the case of exclusion of a representative whether the party will be adequately represented.[219]

---

[209] SSI 2007/173, reg 15(2).
[210] Reg 16.
[211] Reg 18(1).
[212] Reg 18(2).
[213] Reg 18(3).
[214] Reg 18(4).
[215] Reg 14(6).
[216] Reg 19(1).
[217] Reg 19(2).
[218] Reg 20(1) .
[219] Reg 20(2).

At the hearing a party may conduct his own case with or without a representative. The procedure is as determined by the committee, ie order of parties etc. Parties may call witnesses, give evidence on their own behalf and cross-examine any witness called by any other party.[220]

ADJOURNMENTS

Where a party applies for an adjournment he must:

(i)   notify all the parties of the application (if practicable);
(ii) show good reason why an adjournment is necessary;
(iii) produce evidence of any fact or matter relied upon in support of the application for an adjournment.[221]

The committee must not adjourn a hearing of an application at the request of a party unless satisfied that the application *cannot otherwise be justly determined*.[222] In particular, the committee must not adjourn in order to allow the applicant party more time to produce evidence unless satisfied that it relates to the matter in dispute, it would be unjust to determine the case without permitting the party a further opportunity to produce the evidence and where the party has failed to comply with directions for the production of evidence a satisfactory explanation for that failure has been provided.[223]

AMENDMENTS

At any time up to 5 working days prior to the date of the hearing, either party may amend his written representations. These changes must be made in writing and must be intimated to the other party on receipt by the committee.[224] If they are within the 5-day window there may be amendments only where the committee gives consent and subject to any conditions it thinks fit.[225]

When an amendment is made at a hearing it may be made orally in the presence of the other party and noted by the committee.[226]

The committee has discretion to allow evidence to be heard on any matter which it considers to be relevant, whether or not that matter has been specified in the written representations.[227]

---

[220] SSI 2007/173, reg 19(3).
[221] Reg 21(1).
[222] Reg 21(2) (my emphasis).
[223] Reg 21(3).
[224] Reg 22(1–3).
[225] Reg 22(4).
[226] Reg 22(5).
[227] Reg 22(6).

Where the effect of the amendment would be to introduce a new issue of disrepair, the committee must consent to such amendment.[228] In any event, the tenant must have notified the landlord as to the requirement to do further work.[229]

The landlord in such a case will be entitled to make written representations in response and have not less than 14 days from intimation of the service of amendment to make these.[230]

The tenant also may make further written representations or request the opportunity to make oral representations by the date specified for the landlord to respond to the amendment.[231]

The committee may change the date by which representations must be made at the request of either party to such date as it thinks fit and must notify the parties of any such change.[232] Where the amendment application is made by the landlord, the committee will allow such further time as it considers reasonable for the necessary work to be completed,[233] being not less than 21 days.[234]

If a party does not appear at the hearing the committee may proceed to deal with the case upon the representations and all the material before it, assuming that the relevant notice has been given as laid down in reg 19 (above).[235]

The committee may prohibit photography or any audio or visual recording of the proceedings except as required to make reasonable adjustments to accommodate the disability of a party or his representative.[236]

DECISIONS

The decision of the committee must be recorded in a document signed by the chair (or a substitute where the chair person is absent or incapacitated).[237] A statement of reasons "will be prepared" by the chair with the assistance of the other members of the committee and will contain references to the decision of the majority and in such a situation will "provide a brief note of the opinion of the minority".[238] Decisions and statements of reasons are publicly available.[239]

---

[228] SSI 2007/173, reg 23(1).
[229] Reg 23(2).
[230] Reg 23(3).
[231] Reg 23(4).
[232] Reg 23(5) and (6).
[233] Reg 23(7).
[234] Reg 23(8).
[235] Reg 24.
[236] Reg 25.
[237] Reg 26(1).
[238] Reg 26(2).
[239] Reg 26(3).

EXPENSES

Expenses are payable by way of reasonable travelling expenses for the landlord, the tenant or their representatives in terms of the Housing (Scotland) Act 2006, Sch 2, para 5.[240]

APPENDIX 2: PRHP APPLICATIONS

Cities and large towns – 94 (55 per cent)			
GLASGOW	29	FALKIRK	1
EDINBURGH	28	DUMFRIES	1
DUNDEE	12	GREENOCK	2
ABERDEEN	10	KILMARNOCK	3
STIRLING	5	PERTH	1
PAISLEY	4	HAMILTON	2
AIRDRIE	3	DUNFERMLINE	1
INVERNESS	2		

Small towns and rural locations			
ELLON	1	FRASERBURGH	1
CUMBERNAULD	3	GLENROTHES	3
MAYBOLE	1	ANGUS	1
BALLATER	1	COATBRIDGE	1
MAUCHLINE	1	FIFE	4
CALLANDER	1	SHOTTS	1
UPLAWMOOR	1	STEVENSON	1
MILLPORT	1	RENFREW	2
CARSTAIRS	1	CULROSS	1
NEWTON MEARNS	1	AUCHINLECK	1
LARBERT	1	SUTHERLAND	1
ALLOA	1	KIRKWALL	1
ELLON	2	KILWINNING	1
SAUCHIE	1	BALNACROFT	1
IRVINE	3	ARDROSSAN	1
PRESTWICK	1	ABERDEENSHIRE	1
KILLEARN	1	HELMSDALE	1
ABOYNE	1	DUNIPACE	1
KEITH	1	SPRINGSIDE	1
GOUROCK	1	ARMADALE	1
EAST KILBRIDE	2	MORAY	1
NEWTON STEWART	1	CASTLE DOUGLAS	1
CUPAR	1	NAIRN	1
INVERURIE	1	HOUSTON	1
NEWHAVEN	1	KINROSS	1
BROUGHTY FERRY	1	STRATHDON	1
FORFAR	1	BUCKHAVEN	1
SOUTH QUEENSFERRY	1		

---

[240] SSI 2007/173, reg 27.

5   PAYING FOR HOUSING

INTRODUCTION

There are four principal ways of occupying housing with different financial implications: owner occupation; private renting; social renting; and tied housing. As we have noted in Chapter 1, there has been a rise over the past century in the popularity of owner occupation, from 5 per cent to 65 per cent. A decline has occurred in the number of people renting from private landlords, from 90 per cent in 1909 to some 8 per cent in 2009.[1] The concept of renting from bodies which are publicly owned, such as local authorities or housing associations – social renting – has risen during this period from a mere handful to over 40 per cent in 1980. It has since fallen to 25 per cent through the process of tenants exercising their right to buy in local authority housing under the Tenants' Rights etc (Scotland) Act 1980. People occupying housing as a term of their employment is a small but interesting area which is less significant than it used to be, when employers such as coal owners and railway companies provided housing to their workers. The numbers have never covered more than 5 per cent of the housing stock.[2]

Irrespective of the kind of housing anyone occupies, they will find themselves paying for their housing throughout the period of their occupation through the method of partly funding local services. These payments come in the form of a property tax. The original system of rates based on the notional rental value of the property was controversially replaced in the 1980s by a poll tax – the community charge.[3] This was based on the numbers of persons occupying the property and its rationale was that the payments were for using the services provided by the local authorities, such as education, police and libraries. The current charge – the council tax – is a reversion to a tax based on property values.

---

1   Scottish Government (2009d).
2   *Ibid.*
3   Abolition of Domestic Rates (Scotland) Act 1987.

CURRENT MECHANISMS FOR DEALING
WITH HOUSING COSTS

Owner occupation

The traditional attraction of owner occupation has been the level of control it gives to occupiers over what they can do in their homes as well as the freedom from fear of eviction. As the various crises of world economies in the 21st century have made plain, however, lenders are no less liable to evict than landlords when the money which is owed them is not forthcoming.[4] In times of inflation, the process of property purchase also allows a buyer to, in effect, step off the rising price escalator. Allied to this, there has also been the attraction of windfall capital gains profits for those becoming property owners. Such gains have never fallen to be taxed where property is for the occupancy of the owner as their only or principal home. These advantages are moderated in times of nil inflation and deflation. Such periods have been limited in the past century to occasional temporary property slumps, as in 1973 and the early 1990s. For those who have no option but to sell because of changes in their family circumstances or employment status or location, they may end up realising less in their house sale than they owe on their mortgage. This experience of "negative equity" took place in the early 1990s and has been exacerbated by people either being granted mortgages in excess of the current market value of the property or taking out second mortgages so that the loans exceeded the equity in the property.[5]

The sector has in the past been encouraged to grow through four improvements providing direct benefits for those seeking to become owner occupiers. First, there was the Small Dwellings Acquisition Act 1899 which gave local authorities the power to make available to residents loans of up to four-fifths of the market value of the property for houses below a certain level, at modest rates. Although Rodger suggests that it was "a dead letter in Scotland",[6] it was still used by Edinburgh Corporation in the late 1960s for purchases of small tenement properties in places such as Watson Crescent, Foutainbridge, which building societies would not consider. An updated version of the legislation still operates in Ireland in the Small Dwellings Acquisition Act 1957.[7]

Second, there was the abolition in 1960 of Schedule A property tax for owner occupiers. This tax was estimated to yield to the Treasury some

---

[4] *Capitalism: A Love Story* (2010) – Michael Moore's documentary film makes this point graphically in the context of the latest crisis of capitalism.

[5] http://www.timesonline.co.uk/tol/money/property_and_mortgages/article4969314. ece.

[6] Rodger (1989) at 239.

[7] Norris and Redmond (2007).

£25 million per year.[8] Schedule A tax covers income from the rent from
residential property which is treated as unearned income. Expenditure
is usually allowed if "wholly and exclusively incurred" for such things
as repairs and maintenance (excluding improvements), property and
contents insurance, services provided to tenants, management costs,
including administration and bad debts and council tax paid on behalf
of the tenant.

Third, the opportunity for those paying interest on mortgages to receive
tax relief reduced the cost of borrowing. It was originally permitted on
interest on any loans but was restricted to mortgage loans from 1969.
There was no equivalent for those paying rent, and the benefit was highly
regressive in that it allowed higher-rate tax payers to receive allowances
to set against their higher tax band. In simple terms: the richer you were,
the more the community helped you to buy your property. Mortgage
interest relief was initially restricted to a ceiling of £30,000 and finally
was abolished in 2000. It is still possible to obtain some tax advantages
from property purchase since anyone paying premiums on a life insurance
policy receives an allowance in their tax return for such premiums. Buying
with an endowment mortgage rather than a repayment mortgage still
preserves an element of tax advantage since life insurance premiums can
be set against tax liability. This form of mortgage has, however, been less
sought since the problem emerged for some borrowers of endowments
with bonuses where the level of bonus did not meet the amount due at the
term of the mortgage because of falls in the value stocks and shares. The
Prudential ceased to sell such mortgage products in 2001.[9]

Finally, the exemption of their property from capital gains tax is an
important benefit for owner occupiers. Individuals who are resident or
ordinarily resident in the United Kingdom are subject to a capital gains
tax, charged at 18 per cent at the time of writing. The exceptions include
principal private residences. Every individual has an annual capital
gains tax allowance: gains below the allowance are exempt from tax, and
capital losses can be set against capital gains in other holdings before
taxation. All individuals are exempt from tax up to a specified amount of
capital gains per year. For the 2009/10 tax year this "annual exemption" is
£10,100. This exemption operates whatever the level of the capital gain
on the sale of any property that has been a person's main residence. Only
a property occupied as a principal residence can qualify for the exemption.
An investment property in which a person has never lived would not
qualify. "Occupying" as a residence requires a degree of permanence, so
that living in a property for a few weeks with a view to benefiting from

[8] Margaret Thatcher, "Do you qualify for a refund?" *Finchley Press*, 18 March 1960.
[9] Memorandum submitted by Prudential plc (12 January 2004) to House of Commons
     Committee on Pensions: http://www.publications.parliament.uk/pa/cm200304/
     cmselect/cmtreasy/275/275we32.htm.

the exemption is unlikely to work. The exemption includes land that is for "occupation and enjoyment with the residence as its garden or grounds up to the permitted area". The permitted area is half a hectare including the site of the property – about 1.25 acres. Larger gardens and grounds may qualify but only if they are appropriate to the size and character of the property and are required for the reasonable enjoyment of it. The test is an objective one of what was needed for the reasonable enjoyment of the property. Sale of part of the garden for development would also come within the exemption provided it comes within the permitted area. Anyone with one or more houses can only obtain the benefit in respect of one disposal and must make an election within 2 years of any relevant purchase of a second property. If no election is made, then the first property is treated as the main residence throughout, and any gain on this property would be wholly exempt and any gain on a second property would be wholly chargeable

The encouragement for the acquisition of dwellings by first-time buyers has recently found support in the Open Market Shared Equity pilot scheme.[10] There seems to be no likelihood that owner occupiers are likely to be asked to pay Schedule A tax. The nearest that there has been to a proposal to tax owner occupiers has been the suggestion in October 2009 from the Liberal Democrats that for properties over £1,000,000 an annual levy of 0.5 per cent would be introduced.[11] In the Party Manifestos for the 2010 Election this was notable by its absence.

Private renting

RENT CONTROL POLICY FOR PRIVATE TENANCIES ENTERED INTO ON OR AFTER 2 JANUARY 1989

Shortly before the General Election in February 1987, the then Minister of Housing, John Patten, talked on Matthew Parris's *Weekend World* television programme of how he wished to encourage the flourishing of the private rented sector. Renamed the "independent rented sector" to cast off the shadows of Peter Rachman and his like, this would be a new opportunity for tenants to rent from approved landlords with confidence. The sector would not be itself regulated and this would encourage the entry of investors into this market. When the Conservatives were returned for a third term in office, the newly appointed Housing Minister[12] introduced part of the Patten scheme. It was done in a way that did not threaten

---

10 Scottish Government (2010), para 5.
11 Liberal Party Treasury Spokesman Vincent Cable announcing a tax on properties worth more than £1m to raise tax – September 2009 (http://www.timesonline.co.uk/tol/news/politics/article6842800.ece (last consulted 20 July 2010)).
12 John Patten, Minister of State for Housing, was succeeded by William Waldegrave and Michael Howard in June 1987: http://www.parliament.uk/documents/commons/lib/research/briefings/snpc-04657.pdf.

existing tenants. Those with fair rent and security of tenure holding in terms of the Rent Act 1977 and the Rent (Scotland) Act 1984 were not affected. They retained these rights. There was no form of creeping decontrol or automatic decontrol which had done so much to encourage harassment and illegal evictions in the late 1950s under the Rent Act 1957.[13]

For new tenancies the new system looked at first glance as though it offered an element of protection from market forces. Tenants under the assured tenancy regime were subject to market rents. They did, however, enjoy security of tenure on broadly similar lines to the previous regime. There was also provision for a kind of tenancy where repossession at the end of the contract was automatic on notice. In such tenancies, however, there was a minimum term of contract of 6 months as well as the option to have excessive rents regulated by the Rent Assessment Committee. The subtle difference, however, in the role of the RAC under the 1988 legislation is the absence of any concept of scarcity disregard. The base line for determining whether rents are exorbitant is the level of rents charged in the market.[14]

RENTS IN SHORT ASSURED TENANCIES

For short assured tenancies entered into on or after 2 January 1989,[15] committees are required to consider rents only where there is a pool of comparables[16] and where the rent being paid by the tenant is significantly higher than the rent which the landlord might reasonably expect to be able to obtain having regard to comparables.[17]

The first part of this test provides a practical problem for many tenants who might wish to test out exactly how this process operates. In the early days of the operation of the legislation tenants required to establish the comparables themselves. There was an early suggestion that tenants needed to produce more than a solitary example to provide a "pool of comparables".[18] The impact of this approach has been modified in later decisions, with the committees taking a more active role in the process. Thus, a determination on a property in Inchinnan from 2007 recorded that "the Committee had not found any properties to lease in the locality of Inchinnan. They had found details of over thirty properties to lease

---

[13] Milner Holland Report (1965), Chapter 7, Abuses 162–178.

[14] See below at p 154.

[15] 15 January 1989 is the start date for England and Wales' equivalent: the shorthold assured tenancy. Since the coming into force of s 96 of the Housing Act 1996 the "default" tenancy in England and Wales is the shorthold assured tenancy.

[16] Housing (Scotland) Act 1988, s 34(3)(a).

[17] *Ibid*, s 34(3)(b).

[18] GWS 0003 (Glasgow Rent Assessment Committee, Statement of Reasons dated 2 February 1991).

in the neighbouring town of Renfrew but none of these properties were bungalows".[19] Another committee in 2007 also showed that the approach of more recent times has been for a more proactive committee role, rather than expecting the tenant to have such information available to produce. A non-determination from September 2007 records that "the Panel identified from internet sources and local newspapers" what rents were being paid in the area.[20]

The second leg of the test requires that the rent be significantly higher than rents of comparable properties in the area. Hence, where a committee had evidence from its own research that there were "a great number of similar houses available to let in the area" and that the rents for these houses "are similar to and often higher than the rent" under consideration, it made no determination.[21] Where there is evidence of levels of rents the committee indicated in one 2006 case that a difference between the rental level of £4,740 per annum and £4,500 per annum constituted "significantly higher" in terms of s 34(3)(b).[22] The evidence in this instance came from the tenant's submission. Committees have, however, drawn on "their own knowledge and experience" in making findings of rent levels. A differential between £750 being paid and a market rent of £700 was held in a case in 2007 to satisfy the "significantly higher" test – rent reduced from £9,000 per annum to £8,400.[23] Where the evidence of local market rentals has been somewhat imprecise, one committee used the capital return method to fortify its determination that a rent of £100 per week was significantly higher than the rent fixed of £78 per week.[24]

ASSURED TENANCY MARKET RENTS

As for those tenancies which operate as assured tenancies, the role of the private rented housing committee – previously the Rent Assessment Committee – is specifically to determine the rent which it considers the house would let for in the open market by a willing landlord once the contractual tenancy has been terminated.[25] There is no option for the tenant to have the rent considered *during* the term of the tenancy. Tenancies may or may not have increase mechanisms included in their

---

[19] RAC/PA4/S34, 29 October 2007.
[20] RAC/ML3/S33, 28 September 2007.
[21] *Ibid.*
[22] RAC/G40/S29, 12 December 2006.
[23] RAC/DD4/S31, 12 June 2007 – capital value £60,000 – 6% return with allowance for repairs, insurance premiums and factors' charges of £500 pa resulted in a reasonable market rent of £78 per week. Rents of comparable properties in the region of £60/80 per week accepted from tenant's CAB representative.
[24] RAC/DG9/S30, 30 April 2007.
[25] Housing (Scotland) Act 1988, s 25.

terms. If there is no such mechanism and the landlord is seeking an increase from a well-advised tenant he will require to terminate the contractual tenancy and utilise the mechanism provided in the Housing (Scotland) Act 1988 for increases in statutory assured tenancies.

This role for the private rented housing committee is only available for the fixing of market rents for statutory assured tenancies. These come into operation when at the end of the term of the tenancy the landlord serves notice on the tenant terminating the tenancy. At this point the tenant is reliant for his occupancy on the legislation and occupies as a statutory assured tenant. It is for these tenancies that the landlord may seek an increase in rent. The tenant may have this increase referred to the private rented housing committee. It is, however, limited to determining a rent which "the committee consider that the house might reasonably be expected to be let in the open market by a willing landlord under an assured tenancy".[26]

Matters to be ignored

In determining what amounts to a market rent committees are required to ignore any improvements made by the tenant,[27] such as decoration or installation of a wood-burning stove,[28] as well as the effects of any ill-treatment by the tenant in breach of the terms of the tenancy agreement.[29] Where the tenancy is granted to a sitting tenant this factor must also be disregarded.[30]

Inspecting the property

Committees use the visit to the property to see for themselves the condition of the property and to ascertain what works, if any, the tenant has carried out.[31] Both parties are entitled to attend at such a visit in order that each has the opportunity to respond to any comment by the other party and requests for a private meeting with the committee have been turned down as breaching this fundamental principle.[32]

Comparables

By the same token, if comparables are being relied on, the other side has a right to see these and claims of commercial sensitivity are irrelevant.[33]

---

[26] HSA 1988, s 25(1).
[27] Ibid, s 25(2)(b).
[28] RAC/AB21/A63 (2 March 2010).
[29] HSA 1988, s 25(2)(c).
[30] Ibid, s 25(2)(a).
[31] RAC/AB21/A63 (2 March 2010).
[32] Ibid.
[33] Ibid.
[34] RAC/DD1/A61 (9 November 2009); RAC/EH10/E60 (11 November 2009); RAC/KY12/A55 (6 March 2009).

Committees will use comparables supplied to them by either party,[34] although they may not necessarily find them helpful.[35] These comparables have included figures from the PRHP fair rent register where no deduction has been made for scarcity.[36] Where comparables are unavailable the committee has used comparables from as far away as 30 miles as well as drawing on its own "knowledge and experience".[37] Alternatively, they have perused local newspaper advertisements, or the solicitors' property centre and searched internet sites to find comparables to use.[38]

Adjustments from existing market rents

As far as making adjustments to reflect problems properties would have in attracting new tenants is concerned, committees have in the past made deductions for a whole range of problems. These include deductions to reflect matters integral to the property, such as an isolated location with no local amenities, schools or public transport as well an inadequate rural water supply and waste disposal system.[39] In urban locations factors which have predominated have been the lack of such items as double glazing, central heating, a modern kitchen and a modern bathroom,[40] as well the need for general upgrading in order to re-let.[41] Straightforward factors such as the condition of unmodernised bathrooms and kitchens and lack of central heating have been cited as discouraging prospective tenants and resulting in deductions from the "going market rate".[42] This need for market rents to reflect what tenants are actually expecting in the modern rental market was expressed by one committee thus:

> "The Committee recognised that prospective tenants would prefer a re-decorated, refurbished property which had a modern kitchen and bathroom. Moreover double glazing and central heating would add to the appeal of the dwellinghouse. Consequently the Committee considered it appropriate to take account of these factors and make an appropriate deduction of rent."[43]

Another committee explained how it had reached its deduction for modernisation by relying on its instinct as well as more technical calculations similar to those used in relation to regulated tenancies:[44]

---

[35] RAC/AB54/A54 (31 October 2008).
[36] RAC/G52/A53 (20 August 2008).
[37] RAC/IV40/A33 (10 June 2009).
[38] RAC/AB54/A54 (31 October 2008).
[39] RAC/IV63/A51 (17 November 2008).
[40] Ibid.
[41] RAC/AB21/A63 (2 March 2010).
[42] RAC/PH1/A58 (7 July 2009).
[43] Ibid – here a deduction of £125 per month from the £500 market figure.
[44] See below RAC/G12/689 (24 August 2009) 179 Hyndland Road, Glasgow.

"The Committee were of the view that the market rent for a property falling within this description could fairly be set at £575 per month. The Committee were of the view however that the Property in question was not in the best condition ... and would require modernisation to achieve a rental of £575 per month ... The Committee were of the view that a current market rent of £510 per month would be appropriate ... by way of explanation, the Committee were of the view that the landlords would require to spend circa £8,000 to bring the Property up to the standard to achieve the higher rental of £575. Rentalising this at 10 per cent would give a figure of £800 per annum and a monthly figure of just over £65. When deducting this from the figure of £575 per month, this gave a current market rent of £510 per calendar month which coincided with the Committee's view."[45]

Factors relevant for increases

Committees have also made increases on rental figures given by previous committees, to reflect general rental increases as well as landlord improvements such as rewiring.[46] Committees also rely on their own investigations into rental levels in the area.[47] The suggestion that there should be a deduction of 15 per cent from advertised rental rates to reflect the charges of letting agencies has been rejected as reflecting an avoidable cost.[48]

Conclusion

Centred as it is on what rent can be achieved in the market, the process involved in operating s 25 in respect of the fixing of market rents in terms of the Housing (Scotland) Act 1988 is one where it is important to obtain information on fluctuations in the market for rental properties wherever this is available. The more detailed and precise this evidence is, the better. One committee, in applying its "skill, knowledge and experience as best it could" explained that they felt that the factors of dated kitchen and bathroom fittings, absence of double glazing etc. had produced a lower figure than the previous year for what at this time of determination "might be a reasonable expectation of the open market rent".

> The Committee checked this rental figure by considering the rental increase sought by the landlord and whether it was roughly consistent with inflationary rental increases. Investigations into "Trends in Scottish Residential Lettings" produced by Citylets on their website www.citylets. co.uk for the first Quarter of 2009 showed that average rents in Glasgow fell over the first quarter of 2009 by 0.7 per cent with the Scottish Retail Index

---

[45] RAC/EH10/E60 (11 November 2009).
[46] *Ibid*; RAC/IV40/A33 (10 June 2009).
[47] RAC/AB21/A63 (2 March 2010).
[48] RAC/EH10/E60 (11 November 2009).

between the date of the last decision made by a Private Rented Housing Committee for this property in August 2008 and March 2009 decreasing from 109.6 to 107.6."[49]

REGULATED TENANCY RENTS

As indicated, the strategic masterstroke of the framers of the Housing (Scotland) Act 1988 and its English equivalent, the Housing Act 1988, was the decision not to seek to alter the rights and status of existing tenants. This largely deflected any criticism of the new scheme being introduced. In the debates in Westminster about the Housing (Scotland) Act 1988 there was, instead, a focus on the remit of Scottish Homes and the implications for tenants in Scottish Special Housing Association tenancies which were being transferred from social renting to this unaccountable *quango* rather than the likely impact of an unregulated market on tenants.[50]

Those in existing private-sector tenancies prior to 2 January 1989 continued to have their statutory rights under the Rent (Scotland) Act 1984. These included the opportunity at any time during their tenancy to apply to the Rent Officer to have a "fair rent" fixed. The system set up by the Rent Act 1965 made provision for a two-stage process to operate. In the first instance, a Rent Officer would fix what he considered to be the "fair rent" for the property. If neither party was happy with that figure, then there was provision for the issue to be determined by a three-person rent assessment committee. The rent fixed lasted for 3 years and at the end of that period the landlord would return to have a new rent set. Given that it has not been possible to create new protected tenancies under the Rent (Scotland) Act 1984 for over 20 years, all the decisions encountered today are for returns. The details can be found on the website of the Private Rented Housing Panel which now oversees both this area and the repairs rights under the Housing (Scotland) Act 2006.

The criteria for determining a "fair rent" were laid down in the original 1965 legislation and had been amended in some minor ways in the ensuing years. The current legislative provision reads:

"The Committee shall have regard to all the circumstances (other than personal circumstances) and in particular to apply their knowledge and experience of current rents of comparable property in the area, as well as having regard to the age, character and locality of the dwelling house in question and to its state of repair ... for the purposes of the determination it shall be assumed that the number of persons seeking to become tenants of similar dwelling-houses in the locality ... is not substantially greater than the number of such dwelling-houses in the locality which are available for letting."[51]

---

[49] RAC/G52/A57 (20 May 2009).
[50] HC First Scottish Standing Committee, col 761; 16 February 1988.
[51] RSA 1984, s 48.

The basis was that the rent fixer had to take into account a number of factors and ignore others. They had to have regard to the age, character, locality and state of repair of the property. In addition, they had to ignore any harm done to the property by the tenant or the value of any improvements to the property. The rationale was straightforward. Tenants were not to benefit from their misconduct nor were landlords to benefit from having conscientious "improving" tenants. There are two other crucial assumptions to be made. One is that the personal circumstances of the parties involved are to be ignored. This is a rent for the property, reflecting its good points and defects, rather than the need of the tenant for somewhere cheap to live or the landlord for a decent income.

The other is the issue which came to divide professionals and politicians alike. The soubriquet "fair" was justified by the exclusion of the factor of "scarcity". The rent fixer is required to assume that the number of people seeking to become tenants and the number of properties for rent are broadly in equilibrium. Put simply, they must assume that there is no scarcity factor involved which would allow the landlord to take advantage of the restricted market and charge more than where the supply and demand are balanced. In the absence of evidence being presented by either party on which to base a decision the legislation provides specifically for the committee to rely on its own knowledge and experience of rents in the local market. This will usually be informed by the inspection of the property in question, provided that access is possible.[52]

There are three principal ways in which this process operates. First, the rent fixer can have resort to the register of existing fair rents which have previously been fixed. The most helpful will be those which are for similar-sized properties of similar character and location. The more recent these are the more useful they are likely to prove. Alternatively, a return on the vacant possession capital value of the property can be calculated. This will be a percentage – traditionally in the reported cases[53] between 6 per cent and 8 per cent – to which sums are added to cover the costs of repair, management and insurance.[54] Since the introduction of the Housing (Scotland) Act 1988 there is now also a set of rents of assured tenancies which represent the market rent. The question which was initially raised in the English Court of Appeal was

---

[52] RAC/G3/705 (15 September 2009) re 4 Derby Street, Glasgow.

[53] *Learmonth Property Investment Co* v *Aitken* 1971 SLT 349; *Albyn Properties* v *Knox* 1977 SLT 41; *Western Heritable* v *Husband* 1983 SLT 578 (HL).

[54] The gross income return found in the Scottish Government Report was 4.9% – calculated by dividing the yearly rental income by the purchase price of the property – Scottish Government Review of the Private Rented Sector, vol 1 (2009, Scottish Government), para 2.19.

whether or not these involve an element of scarcity.[55] The issue has been taken up in the Scottish courts. The Court of Session has indicated that use of these as evidence of market rent is permissible but that there is no method to be regarded as the primary method.[56] In practice, the method chosen by the committee will depend in each case upon the evidence available.[57]

Comparables

Where comparable properties are produced committees will often use these as a baseline from which to make appropriate deductions reflecting differences between the properties. These may cover such distinctions as lack of central heating, modern kitchen or bathroom fittings or floor coverings.[58] These may expressed in broad terms:

> "The committee considered ... that the market rent of an improved property comparable to (the property) was £450 per month. The committee acknowledged that an adjustment was required to reflect the fact that the property was unimproved, with no modern bathroom or kitchen fitments, appliances, double glazing, decoration or floor coverings being supplied by the landlords. They also acknowledged that an adjustment was required to reflect the particularly poor condition of the common close. They considered that deduction of £1980 per annum was reasonable to reflect these differences."[59]

Capital return less scarcity

Although one of the recognised and accepted ways of reaching a rental figure, this method has been employed less in the recent past by committees in Scotland, for a range of reasons. One committee, for example, in 2010, indicated the problems of capital return at a time of financial crisis and concluded it was not a route to follow:

> "The Committee considered capital values, but given the diverging views on "appropriate return", ranging from bank base rate of 0.5 per cent, savings rates averaging 3 per cent to the Landlords' figure of 6 per cent, the Committee did not consider this was the preferred method for ascertaining a fair rent."[60]

Committees often note in their statement of reasons something along the lines of "No evidence was produced in relation to capital values. The

---

[55] *Spath Holme* v *Greater Manchester & Lancashire RAC* [1996] 28 HLR 107 at 121.
[56] *Western Heritable Investment Co* v *Hunter* 2004 SC 765 (23 March 2004).
[57] RAC/G12/694 (12 August 2009) re 5 Great George Street, Glasgow.
[58] RAC/DG1/703 (15 July 2009) re 86 The Grove, Heath Hall, Dumfries; RAC/G41/700 (23 June 2009) re 40 Apsley Street, Glasgow.
[59] RAC/G4/701 (23 June 2009) re 188 Albert Drive, Glasgow.
[60] RAC/G11/726 (5 March 2010) 93, Turnberry Road, Glasgow.

Committee decided it was therefore inappropriate to proceed on the basis of capital value".[61] If this method is employed there must be an appropriate deduction for scarcity. One other reason for the limited use of capital return is the volatility of property values:

> "The Committee then considered whether to calculate an appropriate return based on the capital value of the property. Taking into account the recent fluctuations (both upwards and currently downwards) in the capital value of property in Scotland and the lack of detailed information available to the Committee, the Committee did not consider it appropriate to assess the fair rent on the basis of a capital return to the landlords."[62]

Market rent less scarcity

Committees were left to their own devices in selecting between the different approaches to rent fixing.[63] It has been stressed, however, that while they do not require to have evidence directly produced before them by one of the parties and may rely on their own knowledge and experience,[64] they should proceed on the best available evidence, using other evidence as a cross-check wherever possible.[65] The indications from the committees are that assured tenancy rents are a source from which a discount for scarcity can be made.[66] These may be found in newspaper advertisements, or on the internet, and having made enquiries with letting agents. This can be seen in the decision where the previous annual rent had been £2,950 and the landlords were looking for an increase to £3,450. The Rent Officer had fixed a rent of £3,250 and the tenant had indicated that he was dissatisfied with this figure. The committee explained how it reached the figure of £3,180. This sheds light on both the method of assessing the rent and the role of research in coming to this figure.

> "Using its knowledge and experience and having regard to other properties available for let in the area the Committee considered that a market rent for a double glazed and centrally heated unfurnished three roomed flat in the locality of the present property would be a minimum of £550 per month. We arrived at this figure after researching the rental market through newspaper advertisements, the internet, and having made enquiries with letting agents."[67]

---

[61] RAC/DG1/703 (15 July 2009) re 86 The Grove, Heath Hall, Dumfries; see also RAC/G11/698 (12 August 2009) at para 12.
[62] RAC/AB55/691 (23 July 2009) re 1 Langstane Lane, Keith.
[63] *Mason* v *Skilling* 1974 SLT 42.
[64] This approach by the Inner House in *Albyn Properties* v *Knox* 1977 SLT 41 was displaced by the amendment to the then applicable Rent (Scotland) Act 1971 by the Tenants' Rights etc (Scotland) Act 1980.
[65] *Western Heritable Investment Co Ltd* v *Hunter* 2004 SC 765.
[66] RAC/EH8/707 (16 October 2009) re 130 Buccleuch Street, Edinburgh.
[67] *Ibid.*

In the absence of evidence being suggested as to comparables or capital return, committees will rely on their own knowledge and experience and make a calculation based on market rent less any scarcity which may be present.

> "The Committee from its own, experience, knowledge and information available on the internet and from local letting agents considered that comparable properties for the rental for 1 bedroom properties in the Partick area of Glasgow ranged from £350.00 pcm to £475.00 pcm. The Committee was of the opinion that the appropriate market rent in respect of this property, which had an internal kitchen rather than a dining kitchen and so was at the lower end of the rental price spectrum was £350.00 pcm."[68]

The process of starting with the market rent for a furnished property is what is the most likely situation in the urban rental market in the second decade of the 21st century. Whether or not the deductions are detailed or "guestimates" will vary. One Glasgow committee explained how it came to a figure of £600 pcm. for a property which it determined, using "its own knowledge and experience of the market", would usually have been rented at £670 pcm.

> "The Committee estimated that the cost of furnishing the property, installing central heating and double glazing, upgrading the kitchen and bathroom, purchasing and installing white goods and laying suitable floor coverings would be in the region of £20,750. The life expectancy of these improvements will vary, but we considered that, by taking a reasonable average, the total sum of these costs could reasonably be defrayed over a period of ten years ... having adjusted that figure to take account of all the above factors, we accordingly assessed the market rent for this property in the condition at which it must be valued as £600 p.c.m."[69]

State of repair

The committee may indicate the role of the state of repair in terms of a percentage deduction from what rent would usually be charged for a flat not in such a state of repair:

> "the reference property is in a deplorable state of repair. Dampness is seeping through the wall, a bedroom ceiling is in a precarious state and the kitchen and bathroom are barely functional. There is no central heating and no double glazing. The bathroom is functional but remains untiled after a period of three years. The kitchen is damp. We noted floor coverings would require to be provided by the Landlord. Numerous smaller repairs are required to the flat. Given the extremely poor condition of the flat we

---

[68] RAC/G11/698 (12 August) re 19 Vine Street, Glasgow.
[69] RAC/G12/689 (24 August 2009) re 179 Hyndland Road, Glasgow.

doubt if the landlord would find another tenant in the current market place. We considered a total of £285 per month should be deducted from the open market figure to take account of these factors leaving a rental of £265 per month".[70]

Related to the question of the state of repair is the issue of the changes in rental practices in the past 30 years. It is now much less common than it once was for properties in the private rental sector to be rented out unfurnished. Most tenants stayed between 6 months and 2 years in properties before moving on.[71] The tenants for whom the fair rent regime was introduced are long-term tenants occupying, for the most part, property which has not been modernised and which was let out unfurnished. In seeking to make use of the comparables available from the assured and short assured regimes which are let as market rents, committees have tended to make deductions to reflect the cost of installing the kinds of facilities which those seeking to rent in the modern private rental sector would expect and the absence of central heating, double glazing, modern kitchens and bathrooms, carpeting, white goods etc:

> "The Committee considered that a number of deductions should be made to take account of various factors. Prospective tenants are likely to be reluctant to incur high costs of laying floor coverings and installing white goods, and even more reluctant to meet the costs of modernizing the kitchen and bathroom. The Committee considered that these factors would adversely impact upon the level of rents likely to be achieved ... The Committee further considered that a deduction was appropriate of £1600.00 per year in respect of improvements required for the installation of central heating, double glazing, kitchen and bathroom fittings."[72]

Scarcity

This is a matter for the specific type of property so that there can be findings that where the relevant sources "produced an extensive list of available properties for rent in the area where the house is located ... there should be no scarcity deduction"[73] or where "the Committee was of the view that there was no scarcity in relation to properties similar to the dwellinghouse in its locality ... confirmed by the numbers of properties available to let in publications and in local Estate Agents".[74] This information which leads to such a finding includes a range of issues as to whether there is evidence of scarcity.

---

[70] RAC/EH8/707 (16 October 2009) re 130 Buccleuch Street, Edinburgh.
[71] Scottish Government (2009) Review of the Private Rented Sector, vol 2, 33, fig 5.1.
[72] RAC/G12/694 (12 August 2009) re 5 Great George Street, Glasgow at para 32.
[73] RAC/G81/702 (15 September 2009) re 7 Bon Accord Square, Clydebank.
[74] RAC/DG1/703 (15 July 2009) re 86 The Grove, Heath Hall, Dumfries.

"While travelling to the inspections the Committee was aware of 'To Let' signs in the area. Inquiries with West End letting companies produced a list of available properties for rent. Internet sources similarly produced a number of properties for rent of similar sizes to the flats in the Glasgow area. Taking into account the plentiful supply of three and four apartment flats in the area, the Committee concluded that at present there should be no scarcity deduction in the Glasgow area."[75]

One committee went as far as taking the view, in the middle of the 2008–09 recession, when property sales had plummeted, that "there appears to be a surplus over demand in relation to the availability of properties for rent".[76] Another noted that in January 2009 the RICS had indicated in a report that there continued to be an excess of supply of properties in the private rented sector in Scotland.[77] This situation is, of course, likely to be subject to local variations as well as being subject to alteration.

Personal circumstances

It might be argued that a tenant might not have the financial resources to cope with a proposed rent rise. These factors must be ignored, as required by s 48:

"The Committee considered the representations of the Tenant of the second flat. She had referred to her personal circumstances and her ability to pay the increased rent and her daughter's ill health ... these are matters which are personal to the Tenant's circumstances and therefore must be disregarded by the Committee in terms of section 48 of the 1984 Act."[78]

Locality

The area covered by this will depend on the rural or urban nature of the property in question. This is an area where the knowledge and experience of the committee will be particularly to the fore. Thus, a committee comparing two flats in the West End of Glasgow differentiated between one property in a poorer part of town from the other in the better area in terms of "popularity": "The flat in Oran Street is situated in the Maryhill part of the West End which is a location which is not as popular as Mingarry Street which lies in the North Kelvinside area."[79]

Decisions may be closer, as where another committee dealing with the West End of Glasgow accepted a flat in Hyndland as being an appropriate area for comparison with a flat in Maryhill Park, which, given

---

[75] RAC/G3/704 (15 September 2009) re 4 Derby Street, Glasgow.
[76] RAC/G12/699 (14 August, 2009) re 41 Crosbie Street, Glasgow.
[77] RAC/G42/686 (3 July 2009) re 10 Overdale Gardens, Glasgow.
[78] RAC/G3/705 (15 September 2009) re 4 Derby Street, Glasgow.
[79] RAC/G20/706 (29 July 2009) re 115 Oran Street, Glasgow.

the schooling placement requests situation and other social amenities in the two areas, is perhaps surprising.[80]

Social renting

The tradition in the United Kingdom has been for local authorities to be given discretion to charge an appropriate amount to their tenants. At the present time there are no external limitations on what the landlord body can charge its tenants. There have been times when housing associations fell within the remit of the private renting regimes and were covered by the Rent (Scotland) Act 1984's fair rent regime and the Housing (Scotland) Act 1988 market rent controls. South of the Border, the Housing Finance Act 1972 introduced the system of fair rents for local authority housing. The notion was to take away the perceived power of local authorities to charge low rents to their tenants as a price for their political support. The equivalent Scottish legislation, the Housing (Financial Provisions) (Scotland) Act 1972, sought to achieve the same kind of political impact through a slightly different way. Both approaches were short lived and local authority finances were returned to local control. In practice, however, the level of autonomy is limited by the level of contribution from central government. If the Scottish Government is unhappy with the level of rents, it has the option to restrict the size of the Housing Revenue Grant.[81] The most recent policy pronouncements do not lead one to suppose that this "hands off" approach is likely to alter.

Tied housing

The arrangements within tied housing vary from a specified rent, to the occupancy being made available without charge. The occupation is better seen as a part of the remuneration package. The important thing from the point of view of the occupier is that there is no process by which any charge can be reviewed. The availability of support through housing benefit depends on meeting the financial criteria for entitlement to that means-tested benefit.[82]

THE DEVELOPMENT OF POLICIES ON MEETING THE COST OF HOUSING

Controlling the private rental market charges

INTRODUCTION

The conflict between landlords and tenants in residential property centred initially on the question of rent. During the years before the First World

---

[80] RAC/G12/699 (14 August, 2009) re 41 Crosbie Street, Glasgow.
[81] McGarvey and Cairney (2008).
[82] Welfare Reform Act 2007, Pt 2.

War there were struggles involving rent strikes over the levels of rent.[83] The strikes themselves had an interesting side-effect, with the setting up of a Royal Commission in 1912. This had the effect of shelving the issue for the meantime and the Commission did not report until 1917.[84] By this time, a temporary solution had been provided which was pragmatic rather than principled[85] and had a major impact on how policy towards private renting subsequently developed.

FREEZING OF RENTS

The "temporary" solution fashioned in the early part of the Great War was neat and elegant. Different interpretations have been placed on the major driving forces at work which produced the first legislation.[86] Whichever narrative is most plausible, there is no question but that the legislation was not part of a grand plan for housing. The Government certainly took into account the impact of the rash of industrial action in support of tenants threatened with rent rises or eviction. The Hunter Committee examined the evidence. Although Lord Hunter and Professor Scott were of the opinion that the actual incidences of exploitation and eviction had been patchy, they provided a rationale for intervention.[87]

The President of the Board of Trade, Walter Long, explained the thinking behind the provisions of the Increase of Rent and Mortgage Interest (War Restrictions) Bill, introduced in November 1915, and the rents rises which had caused such uproar:

> "... if it were not for the special circumstances and if it were not for the fact that we are at war ... I do not think that I should propose legislation of this kind ... masses of people hold tenaciously to the view that the minority who happen to own houses, are taking advantage of war time to exploit the war for their own benefit ... The existence of that feeling is a danger to society, and ought to be removed, if it can be fairly and justly removed ..."[88]

The important point, though, about the 1915 Rent Act solution was its temporary nature. The legislation was passed on the specific promise that the freezing of rents was to extend only for the period of the War. The

---

[83] Melling (1983); Damer (1983); Bradley (1997); Petrie (2008).
[84] Royal Commission on Housing in Scotland (1917).
[85] Increase of Rent and Mortgage Interest (War Restrictions) Act 1915.
[86] Gauldie ascribes the legislation to fear of revolution at home (Gauldie (1974, 308); Damer and Melling stress the role of labour militancy (Damer, 1980; Melling, 1983) Englander locates the cause within the pre-War landlord and tenant struggles (Englander 1983) Daunton stressed the sacrifice of the landlord class to the national interest (Daunton, 1983) Holmans suggests that one should see rent control as part of the development of controls to run a war economy (Holmans, 1987).
[87] Hunter Scott, *ibid* at 5(v).
[88] HC, 25 November 1915, col 421.

legislation specifically provided that it would "continue in force during the continuance of the present war and for a period of six months thereafter and no longer".[89]

In terms of a long-term solution to the conflict between landlords' needs for an attractive return on their capital investment and the ability of tenants to afford the rents fixed by the market, this was not ever intended to do such a thing. The suspension of the market through freezing was reconsidered by Lord Hunter again towards the end of the Great War. His Committee's recommendations were unambiguous to continue the Rent Act restrictions for a further 3 years from the end of the War due to the mismatch between supply and demand for housing.[90]

As a result of the recommendations of various expert committees, the "temporary" concept of "frozen rents" was retained for the next 40 years.[91] The thinking was pragmatic. Just as an alternative to a market rent fixing mechanism had been adapted for English tenant farmers in the 1860s,[92] Irish tenant farmers in the 1870s [93] and for Scottish crofters in the 1880s,[94] an alternative was adopted in the British residential sector. The balance of political forces was, however, assessed somewhat differently in the inter-War period. The potential for "grave unrest" [95] was regarded as significant and landlords were not perceived as a coherent threat to those making these decisions.[96] The temporary nature of the Rent Acts was still acknowledged in this inter-War period. A member of the Marley Committee, the Mayor of Manchester, Sir E D Simon, did not see it as having any contribution in the broader attempt to deal with poor housing conditions – the "anti-slum campaign". Writing in 1933, he noted:

> "Rent restriction is a temporary phenomenon, which is only necessary on account of shortage of houses. The problem has therefore no special interest from the point of view of this book, as it will automatically disappear when the supply of houses becomes adequate."[97]

That said, he did wonder, in 1933, whether the confidence of Sir Hilton Young in bringing the Rent Restriction Act to an end by 1938 would be

---

[89] Increase of Rent and Mortgage Interest (War Restrictions) Act 1915, s 43.
[90] Hunter Report (1918) at 4(IV).
[91] See Barnett (1979) for a useful précis of the various Reports and legislative changes.
[92] Law Commission Report (2002).
[93] Newby (2007).
[94] Hunter (2010).
[95] Onslow Committee (1923) 7.
[96] Indeed there was a specific Report on the threats of the Rent Strikes in Scotland, particularly Clydebank – Constable Committee (1925). See also the tone and tenor of the debate in the Reports of the Marley Committee (1931) and Ridley Committee (1937).
[97] Simon (1933) at 42.

justified.[98] The assessment of the supply of rental and other housing had altered by the mid-1930s.[99] The Ridley Committee in 1937 outlined a final end to intervention.[100] The outbreak of war in 1939 resulted in an immediate re-imposition of a rent freeze on houses.[101]

Although furnished property had been excluded from the original coverage of the Rent Acts during the War, a new body was introduced to provide protection for tenants of such property. This was originally set up for Scotland in 1943[102] and the system was extended to England in 1946.[103] The subsequent loss of thousands of houses to bomb damage helped the reconstituted Ridley Committee to advise retention of control for at least another 10 years.[104]

The housing problem was perceived across the political spectrum to be a question of numbers rather than of house type: "An all-out housing policy will not only make a tremendous contribution to family life, but also to steady employment and to national health. All our energy must be thrown into it. Local authorities and private enterprise must both be given the fullest encouragement to get on with the job."[105]

The need for rent control was also accepted across the board: "So long as there is a serious shortage of houses, rent control must continue on houses controlled at present. The establishment of Tribunals throughout the country to fix fair rents as between landlord and tenant (as recommended by the Ridley Committee) seems to provide the best solution of a long-standing problem."[106]

It was not until the autumn of 1956 that Duncan Sandys announced the review of the rent control legislation which paved the way for the abolition of rent control.[107] Duclaud-Williams suggests[108] that he had taken the advice of a fellow politician:

> "Rent control in the words of a minister whom it would not be fair to name, has been regarded as a nettle to be seized only by a government with a large majority in its first year of office or by a doomed government in its last."[109]

---

[98]   Simon (1933) at 49. Young was Minister of Health from 1931 to 1935.
[99]   Ridley (1937) at 19ff.
[100] Ridley (1937).
[101] Rent and Mortgage Interest Restrictions Act 1939.
[102] Rent of Furnished Houses Control Scotland Act 1943.
[103] Furnished Houses (Rent Control) Act 1946.
[104] Ridley (1945) at 49.
[105] 1945 Conservative Party General Manifesto – Winston Churchill's Declaration of Policy to the Electors – http://www.conservative-party.net/manifestos/1945/1945-conservative-manifesto.shtml.
[106] *Ibid.*
[107] *The Times*, 12 October 1956.
[108] Duclaud-Williams (1978) at 65.
[109] *Manchester Guardian*, 4 November 1953.

What was most remarkable about the policy decision to end rent control was the absence of a non-political preliminary inquiry such as had occurred between 1918 and 1945. Duclaud-Williams ascribes this to Duncan Sandys' desire to follow a path he was not certain a committee of inquiry would recommend.[110] It was, after all, only 10 years since the Ridley Committee had stated: "We are emphatically of the opinion that ... the principle of decontrol on vacant possession should not be revived since the evidence shows that in the past this principle has been responsible for many of the hardships which have arisen."[111] This was a reference to among other things the commotion which had resulted in the 1920s when the first attempt at decontrol on vacant possession had occurred under the Rent Act of 1923. This had led to such civil resistance and unrest that a committee under A H B Constable had been set up to investigate. This had reported that the difficulties encountered in the industrial West of Scotland were due to the severe and prolonged industrial depression which made it difficult for many tenants to pay increased rent and rates with court actions for ejection the result.[112]

OPTIONAL "FAIR RENTS"

Fair rents were introduced in the Rent Act 1965 by the new Housing and Local Government Minister, Richard Crossman. Within a few years the concept was adopted by Edward Heath's Conservative administration as the "solution" to the perceived problem of council house tenant subsidy.[113] After only a dozen years one leading housing commentator regarded them as uncontroversial: "the Rent Act of 1965 gives every impression of having now become one of the foundation-stones of British housing administration".[114]

Within a further 10 years they had, in effect, been abolished. Before they fade into the mists of half-remembered concepts, it is worth examining in a little detail the contribution of politicians and the courts to this rise and fall of this attempt to address the politics of renting which had been such a thorny issue for at least 50 years and which lives on today in the battles over housing benefit.

When the Labour Party campaigned in the 1960s on housing one of its areas of focus was the abuse being suffered by tenants in the private sector as a result of the Rent Act 1957. This legislation took away security of tenure rights, leaving tenants with only the right to remain in the properties for as long as the lease contract lasted. It also returned fixing of rent levels to the mechanism of the market in place of the freezing of rents,

---

[110] Duclaud-Williams (1978) at 70.
[111] Ridley (1945) at 9.
[112] Constable (1925), para 73.
[113] DoE (1971); Housing Finance Act 1972.
[114] Duclaud-Williams (1978) at 83.

with repair additions, introduced in 1915 and 1939. The 1957 legislation allowed for the market mechanism to be imposed automatically for larger houses[115] and for smaller houses on vacant repossession. It marked the first instance in relation to 20th-century policy-making on rental housing where policy was not preceded by any kind of investigation. Instead, in the case of the Rent Act 1957 it followed the thinking of Enoch Powell when he started to look at the issue of the impact of regulation arguing from a political intuition that freeing rental housing from regulation would inject life into the rental market.[116]

The impact of the relaxation of control was rather different.[117] Rents doubled in those properties where tenants remained and tripled where there was a change of occupancy.[118] With the prospect of sale on vacant possession or higher market rents once existing tenants moved out, there were strong incentives for unscrupulous landlords to hasten this process of moving.[119] A White Paper in 1963[120] indicated that London needed to be examined as a special case. With the eruption of the Profumo scandal in the spring of 1963, the Housing Minister announced the setting-up of an inquiry into housing in Greater London in July 1963. As Barnett, Banting and most recently Davis have pointed out this problem had been festering for many months without attracting media attention. With the death in November 1962 of Peter Rachman, however, and the Profumo scandal proving such a media attraction,[121] the social problems were given an airing. This conjunction of a worthy social issue and titillating sexual scandal was expressed effectively in the satirical magazine *Private Eye*. The cover of the edition at the time of the Stephen Ward trial shows Mandy Rice-Davies suggesting "If it wasn't for me – you couldn't have cared less about Rachman".[122] While there is conflict as to the precise nature of the abuse which occurred – "sweating" buildings with maximum occupancy was what Rachman favoured, according to some, as opposed to emptying houses and selling – [123] there was, however, an impact on the Labour Party to produce some sort of policy response. The brief flirtation with the notion of municipalisation from the 1961 Party Conference was not pursued when Richard Crossman took the reins of the Ministry of Housing and Local Government after Labour's return to political office in October 1964.

---

[115]   Above the rateable value of £40.
[116]   HC Deb, vol 560, cols 1759–1777, 21 November 1956.
[117]   Rent Act 1957 Report (1960).
[118]   *Ibid*, 25; Milner Holland (1965), Appendix V, 358.
[119]   Milner Holland (1965), Appendix 4.
[120]   Ministry of Housing Local Government and Minister for Welsh Affairs (1963).
[121]   Davis (2001).
[122]   *Private Eye*, Friday 26 July 1963 – reproduced in Ingrams (1971) at 84.
[123]   Green (1979); Rent Act 1957 Report (1960); Barber (2009) 42 – the older man, Simon, who featured in the book and film, was involved with Rachman.

As Dunleavy has pointed out, the Civil Service numbers dealing with housing were limited[124] and were led by someone with an interest in planning rather than housing, Dame Evelyn Sharp.[125] Crossman was keen not to be simply controlled by the agenda of the Civil Service and used an alternative policy forum of selected extra-political experts.[126] What they produced between them was the "fair rent".

Subsequent politicians left the meaning of "fair rents" to the judges and two approaches emerged which received the backing of the courts. One approach adopted the spirit of the Crossman concept and produced a conceptually flawed but simple solution. The other used a formula never mentioned by Crossman but with which some valuers and lawyers were comfortable. That dual approach can still be encountered today in the work of the private rented housing committees discussed above.[127]

The first "simple" approach can be termed the "subjective" strategy. It centred on rooting out "abuse" of market position through employing as rent fixers the "right personnel". It is what Crossman and his adviser, Arnold Goodman, had in mind, as Crossman explained in the diaries he compiled at the time:

> "What we have said is that we would not try to define a fair rent by any normal method and we wouldn't relate it either to a fair return on the landlord's money or a standard rent or anything else. What Arnold Goodman has in fact said to me is, don't try to invent a formula. Get the right people and let them do the job of setting a series of precedents in the early decisions."[128]

The initial fair rents could be used as a database on which to fix subsequent rents and rents of similar kinds of properties. Lord Parker in the Court of Appeal explained how the process of using the Register of Rents would operate:

> "It must surely be the essence of this whole scheme that there should be uniformity, and no doubt as the volume of registered fair rents increases in the future no one will go to the market rent less scarcity, they will go straight to the enormous volume of fair rents that have been registered."[129]

Lest this should be thought to be a straightforward endorsement of the capital return method as the benchmark, Lord Widgery explained that, as far as giving reasons was concerned, it was not a question of using a formula: "There will be many, many cases where all that the assessment

---

[124] Dunleavy (1981) at 9–11.
[125] Sharp (1969).
[126] Crossman (1975).
[127] See above at p 154.
[128] Crossman (1975), vol 1, p 187 (24 March 1965).
[129] *Tormes Property Co Ltd v Landau* [1970] 3 All ER 653 at 655.

panel can do is say 'Doing our best with the information provided, we think that the rent should be £x'."[130] The alternative "objective" formula was the approach favoured by landlords in their submissions to reviews of the fair rents fixed by Rent Officers. In debates before the courts the success of the two approaches was mixed.

The politicians' level of interest in the minutiae of rental housing policy can be gleaned from the comments of some of the major players in the Labour administration which introduced the legislation. The Prime Minister, Harold Wilson, notes perfunctorily that the Government's plans included "repeal of the odious provisions of the highly controversial Conservative Rent Act of 1957".[131] He later notes among the things which pleased him in terms of social reform achievements was "the repeal of the Conservatives' Rent Act".[132] The issue does not feature in the political diaries of other major Labour figures of the time, such as George Brown, Roy Jenkins, James Callaghan and Barbara Castle.[133] Banting has characterised this policy as "simply a holding operation in a decaying sector of the housing market",[134] which seems unduly harsh and a little simplistic.

The reception was not universally applauded. One backbench Tory MP, with a legal background, suggested that, as the formula involved "considerable arbitrariness", it threatened to be "the very negation of legislation".[135] *The Times* dismissed the fair rent formula as "flexible nonsense".[136] Nonetheless, the concept was deemed sufficiently acceptable as to form the basis for fixing council house rents in terms of the Housing Finance Act 1972. This massive enterprise never got seriously under way before the return of Labour into office in February 1974 and the repeal of the Housing Finance Act's attempt to curb local authority autonomy in housing. As almost a side interest, the collapse of the Freshwater property empire in 1974 provided food for thought as to the wisdom of relying on fair rent returns that were linked to property values to expand a vast portfolio. This, though, was linked to the levels of gearing employed by Freshwater rather than the inherent low returns to be made through fair rents.

---

[130] *Guppys Properties* v *Knott (No1)* [1978] EGD 255 at 259.
[131] Wilson (1971) at 28.
[132] *Ibid* 54.
[133] Brown (1971); Callaghan (1987); Jenkins (1991); Castle (1993) were all silent on the question of the new Rent Act. Only Barbara Castle mentions the Rent Acts, echoing Wilson and noting that the "excellent things in the Queen's Speech (in October 1964) ... included the repeal of the Tory Rent Act of 1957 which had decontrolled rents (and incidentally forced Ted and me out of our Highgate flat as its rent skyrocketed)" – 352).
[134] Banting (1979) at 65.
[135] HC, *Hansard*, 30 June 1965, col 669 per tax barrister Margaret Thatcher.
[136] *The Times*, 24 March 1965.

While it is unlikely that legislators and policy-makers will be quite as frank as Lloyd George when he described his post-1906 Election social reform programme as "sops for Labour",[137] in published statements there is some evidence of the architect of the 1965 Act, Richard Crossman, being quite as concerned to put up a good show in Cabinet as with the problems of tenants.[138] He confessed that he had never really had any experience and could not relate to the problems of tenants in concrete terms. In addition, his own personal ambition seems to have been concerned to "do down" the Civil Service or at least establish his own advisorate's status as a source of policy for Ministers.

In the general rush to produce something that looked, and particularly *sounded*, impressive, it is undeniable that the 1965 Rent Act failed to address itself to the central issue of housing finance equity. This may have been as a result of a disinclination to be seen to be providing subsidies for landlords as well as a failure accurately to perceive the impact of this form of control on rental dwelling supply. It may be that we can see in the 1965 legislation an implicit acceptance of the "orderly" rundown line subsequently advocated by the RTPI.[139] However, before we can assume that Crossman was possessed of such Machiavellian cunning, it is worth examining the context and ambiguous content of the rent formulation designed to be fair to tenants and landlords alike.

FAIR RENTS IN PRACTICE

Interpreting the "fair rent"

A broad professional view was initially expressed in terms of the threat to professional standards in the overall field of valuation stemming from the unqualified nature of rent officers. However, the *Estates Gazette* took the view that they had to accept the new form of control and make it work. Their feelings about the likely impact of the legislation can be gauged from the attention accorded to the possibility of the introduction of a fully fledged subsidy for the poor tenant allowing the landlord the full fair rent. The fair rent was perceived as essentially unproblematic, in light of the experience of the courts' approach to local authority "reasonable rents".[140]

The problems for valuers were seen as creating initial anxiety due to failure to define a fair rent in the 1965 Act. Despite the actual difficulty of the wording of the fair rent section, the valuer's task was perceived as being to seize the nettle firmly and quickly, for sound pragmatic reasons:

---

[137] George (1908) – writing to his solicitor brother William in Welsh.
[138] *Crossman Diaries* (1975) 43.
[139] *Estates Gazette*, 4 October 1980, 39.
[140] *Estates Gazette*, 9 October 1965, 141.

"in the long term the method of applying section 27 (fair rent section) will obviously be by comparison with fair rents fixed for other accommodation by Rent Officers and Rent Assessment Committees and their decisions in early cases will become the yardstick by which later cases will be judged".[141]

The apparent doubts evident in the Civil Service and in Parliament[142] do not seem to have bothered all those involved. In some instances this convenient Nelson-like approach to the task of applying the fair rent formula stemmed from a desire to achieve a degree of professional kudos. We find a Senior Rent Officer outlining the breadth of the tasks entrusted to his rent officer colleagues, explaining their need to be polymaths able to value, conciliate, negotiate, as well as administrate and needing to be an expert in landlord and tenant law, building inspection techniques and quantity surveying.[143] The depoliticising impact of the rent machinery was taken as being a central concern:

"Having determined in his own mind an approximate figure he wishes to register as a fair rent ... the Rent Officer endeavours to obtain the consent of both parties to the amount he suggests. He persuades the landlords that any value that can be ascribed to the 'scarcity factor' must not only by law be discounted but that it is only common justice so to do; and he persuades the tenant that his idea of rental values is really very out of date and that the landlords is entitled to a fair return in accordance with the statutory definition."[144]

The difficulties of operating the legislation were also minimised by one of the most influential professional valuation advisers, Denis Pilcher, stressing the need for rents to "be related to fair value and not to be a mathematical formula".[145] He explained his conception of scarcity which caused advisers and economists so much difficulty since:

"... divide the housing field into three sectors. The one at the top is the highest priced and rented Sector – dwellings for people of substantial means. No one, I think pretends that they have not got a good choice. ... The next sector is the middle sector where supply and demand are in near balance, the sector which it is our vital job as a profession to identify. ... The third sector is that where the demand outstrips the supply and this is the sector which section 27 (i.e. fair rent formula) is designed to protect."[146]

Such a conception of the sensitivity of the market to demand seemed to be based on a common-sense notion of the rental market rather than any economic model but insofar as Pilcher appears to have been

---

[141]   *Estates Gazette* (196) 1965, 1141.
[142]   Banting (1979) at 52 and 58ff.
[143]   *Estates Gazette* (202) 1967, 977.
[144]   *Ibid.*
[145]   *Estates Gazette* (210), 71 at 72.
[146]   *Ibid.*

the major architect of this part of the new formula,[147] it is the one with which tenants, landlords and the rent fixers had to work from 1965.[148] It was clearly forged through his success at persuading his colleagues in Crossman's "outside" advisers of the viability of this notion. It is in the unlikely location of the courts that these problems have been argued over since 1965 as well as the committees. This is a relationship which merits examination.

While it is always somewhat dangerous to attempt to make inferences about the development of social policy from the unusual and exceptional eventuality which is constituted by reported cases, there is clear evidence that the series of cases which occurred in this sphere were largely the result of a deliberate attempt by certain property companies to establish the precise bounds of novel concepts such as fair rents.

The intention of Crossman, with his faith in the distilled wisdom of rent officers and Rent Assessment Committees, was no doubt genuine. It is apparent, though, from the litigation following the 1965 Act that the larger company landlords were less than enamoured of a wholly open-ended method of fixing fair rents. One strand of litigation kept going on for over a decade with landlords seeking to persuade the courts to light on one consistent method of fair rent fixing.[149] The method which was favoured by landlords was one which was specifically counselled against by Crossman, namely the return on the landlord's capital. The courts were somewhat equivocal on this issue. They consistently failed to make a firm recommendation one way or the other but were equally reluctant to "disqualify" any method from consideration. How individual rent assessment committees chose the method to be adopted was another issue which was the subject of apparently considerable regional variation.

Interpreting fair rents in the courts

AVOIDING INTERVENTION

Essentially, the first major case to be litigated the Divisional Court made no suggestion on the approach which a Committee was to favour. The Lord Chief Justice, Lord Parker, suggested that "evidence of capital value, though useful, was by no means conclusive".[150] His colleague, Lord Widgery, was rather more illuminating:

---

[147] Banting (1979) at 48.

[148] Francis Report supra at 59–62 indicates the genuine confusion of those operating the scarcity disregard.

[149] "Fair Rents, Ignoring the Experts", E Young and P Watchman, 1978 SLT 201; "Determining Fair Rents", P Robson and P Watchman, 1978 NLJ 1209 and "Fair Rents and the Judicial Control of Administrative Discretion", P Watchman, 1979 Conveyancer 205.

[150] Crofton Investment Trust Ltd v Greater London Rent Assessment Committee [1967] 2 QB 955 at 969.

"(fair return on … capital value of (the) investment … is rarely if ever put forward as providing an accurate guide to the rent which parties will agree in respect of a dwelling still less to what is a fair rent in the special circumstances of this Act … (this) tends to be a ceiling above which the rent should not go".[151]

Quite why Lord Widgery viewed the fair return as a ceiling, he did not explain. His colleague, Lord Parker, again indicated the fluidity of the rent determination process 2 years later when he commented on the of historic cost as a basis for a percentage yield:

"this is a quite novel method of valuation which the committee adopted. It is certainly one that I have never seen before … It may well be because there is no fixed yardstick by which a fair rent is to be arrived at, that this is a permissible method".[152]

This non-interventionist approach was expressed in a slightly more directive way in the English *locus classicus Tormes Property Co Ltd* v *Landau*.[153] The discretion of the committee was confirmed but a hint was given by Lord Parker again as to how this discretion might best be exercised:

"The committee have said they were not going to approach the matter on the basis of (a fair return on investment) but that they were going to go either to market value less scarcity or to the fair rent or other premises which had already been fixed by assessment committees."[154]

Noting that fair return could provide only a ceiling and that not much weight could be given to this approach, Lord Parker indicated that: "No doubt as the volume of registered fair rents increased in the future … (committees) will go straight to the enormous volume of fair rents that have been registered."[155] The discretion, though, was the committee's: "Without criticising (any) yardstick put forward … the committee are perfectly entitled to reject it and apply another yardstick."[156]

THE SCOTTISH APPROACH

In the Scottish courts, with exactly the same legislative provision, a rather different approach was taken. Drawing on the recent treatise on landlord and tenant which was published before any kind of pronouncements from the courts on the fixing of fair rents, the Court of Session, equivalent in

---

[151] [1967] 2 QB 955 at 970.
[152] *Anglo-Italian Properties Ltd* v *Greater London Rent Assessment Panel* [1969] 2 All ER 1128 at 1129.
[153] [1970] 3 All ER 653.
[154] *Ibid* at 654.
[155] *Ibid* at 655.
[156] *Ibid*.

rank to the Court Appeal, pointed out that when a fair rent was being fixed this involved fairness to both parties. Lord Clyde talked of the importance of "paying regard to the probable return of the landlord's capital as an important factor in fixing a fair rent. ... If the landlord is not a charitable organisation it is surely a material factor in fixing the rent that the landlord should receive a fair return on the capital value of his property".[157]

Lord Cameron echoed these sentiments in very similar language. He quoted with approval Paton and Cameron on *Landlord and Tenant* which suggested that "fairness *quoad* the landlord must involve securing for him a return on his property which will represent a reasonable alternative to an outright sale" and considered that:

> "Expected return on capital, though not specifically mentioned (in the fair rent section) is, in my opinion, an equally powerful and relevant consideration (as compared with market rents less scarcity)."[158]

This endorsement of the view that private renting was indeed a field for private profit led to use in Scottish Rent Assessment Committees of the "capital return" method. This emphasis on the economic *realpolitik* of the landlord's enterprise was again emphasised in *Skilling* v *Arcari's Executrix*:[159]

> "regard has to be had to all the circumstances ... 'market rents' constitute a circumstance to which the committee has to have regard, but expected return on capital is an equally powerful consideration".[160]

When the *Skilling* case reached the House of Lords, capital return was again approved as a method of calculation but in a less robust way: "A fair rent should be fair to the landlord as well as fair to the tenant and it can be regarded as fair to the landlord that he should receive a fair return on his capital."[161]

Lord Kilbrandon also gave approval to the notion of using capital return when he suggested the role of the capital return method:

> "Considering what net return a landlord might reasonably expect to get, looking at the house as an investment seems reasonable, since the 'fair rent' has got to be fair to the landlord as well as to the tenant."[162]

However, this approval of return on capital as a method was also coupled with approval of the use of comparables which had been built up since

---

[157] *Learmonth Property Investment Co Ltd* v *Aitken* 1971 SLT 349 at 352.
[158] *Ibid* at 355.
[159] 1973 SLT 139.
[160] *Ibid* at 141.
[161] 1974 SLT 46 at 47.
[162] *Ibid* at 50.

the Act's inception and in the words of Lord Reid: "this section leaves it open to the rent officer or committee to adopt any method or methods of ascertaining a fair rent provided they do not use any method which is unlawful or unreasonable".[163]

In view of the consistent line of approval given to the need for "fair" rents to be fair to both parties and to take account of the landlord's position as an investor, it was suggested, at the time, that the capital return method would be likely to find favour with many rent assessment committees. Some rent assessment committees took a rather different sort of view of the *Skilling* development. In a decision by the Aberdeen Rent Assessment Committee, the view was expressed:

> "The Opinions of the Judges in the House of Lords showed that the comparable method was preferable and that any formula based on capital value was regarded as an ancillary process to determine a fair rent."[164]

The landlords appealed on the ground that the committee had erred in law in "treating the capital value computation advanced in evidence before them as at best a process ancillary to the comparative method for the determination of a fair rent". The Court of Session took the slightly unusual step, at the time, of issuing an opinion of the court rather than individual judgments. This again confirmed the reliance which should be placed on the economic return to the landlord. The First Division of the Court of Session indicated that the *Skilling* case and the *Learmonth* case: "make it perfectly clear that in fixing a rent which is fair to both landlord and tenant, the probable return on the landlord's capital is an important matter".[165] Although stressing that any lawful reasonable method of valuation was possible, the court did point out that "consideration must be given to what would be required to allow to the landlord a fair return on his investment".[166]

Now, while these statements do not constitute in any way a rejection of comparables, they do not seem to indicate a consistent stress on the return to the landlord as a crucial factor in any method of decision-making. Not, as was suggested in *Crofton Investment Trust*, simply as an upper limit but it would appear a central concern. However, the apparent unwillingness of the courts (even Scottish) to *prefer* one method over another meant that the guidelines for rent assessment committees were a little confused.

The first major review of the operation of the Rent Acts, the Francis Report,[167] was singularly uninformative as to the resolution of this issue,

---

[163] 1974 SLT 46 at 47.
[164] Cited in *Albyn Properties* v *Knox* 1977 SLT 41 at 42.
[165] *Ibid* at 44.
[166] *Ibid*.
[167] 1971 Cmnd 4609.

of methods of determination. The report simply recited the methods generally used − comparables; market rents without scarcity and return on capital value etc − and blandly stated that "The fair rent seems to be an amalgam of the results produced by these lines of approach".[168]

RECONCILING THE CONFLICTING APPROACHES?

On one hand, then, we had English courts at Divisional level suggesting, without formally instructing, that comparables would tend to provide the best guide to fair rent fixing. On the other hand, the Scottish courts at Court of Session level advised the importance, without actually stating a preference, of return on capital. However, as the judgments on both sides of the Border made plain, the committees had the ultimate discretion on which line to take. The dichotomous position was highlighted, though, by the approach which some landlords pursued in a less direct manoeuvre. Rent assessment committees under the Rent Act 1965 were set up as "tribunals" within the meaning of the Tribunals and Inquiries Act 1971 (formerly the Tribunals and Inquiries Act 1958). As such, they required to give reasons for their decisions. Landlords tried to force the hand of the committees by pushing for clear and unambiguous reasons. Their argument, put crudely, was that it was all very well for committees to have the discretion to select a figure based on one or more methods of valuation but it was incumbent on such a committee to explain how its figure for fair rent had been arrived at. Again, the then common British legislation was accorded different interpretations in the courts in England and Scotland.

The issue of formality was discussed in the *Crofton Investment Trust* case where the pattern of the English response was set when the Lord Chief Justice in the Divisional Court stressed that the approach laid down by his predecessor, Lord Chief Justice Goddard, in a Rent Tribunal determination for furnished property on how a "reasonable rent was to be fixed was appropriate in "fair rent" problems dealt with by rent assessment committees:

> "I am quite satisfied that a committee ... under a procedure which is clearly intended to be informal and not to be carried through with the precision of a court of justice, is fully entitled to act ... in their own impression and on their own knowledge, it is idle in my view to think of gentlemen among this committee and sitting maybe day after day without acquiring knowledge and experience of conditions in the locality, and to say that they should shut their eyes to what they know of their own knowledge, and act only on such evidence as may or may not put before them, seems to me to reduce the matter to absurdity."[169]

---

[168]   1971 Cmnd 4609 at 59.
[169]   *Crofton Investment Trust Ltd* v *Greater London Rent Assessment Committee* [1967] 2 QB 955 at 967.

Although the remark was made *obiter*, Lord Widgery summed this approach up most felicitously in *Metropolitan Properties Ltd* v *Lannon*:

> "A judge in civil litigation who finds all the evidence unacceptable can retire behind the onus of proof and dismiss the plaintiff's claim: but the rent assessment committee, once it embarks upon its enquiry, must produce a fair rent at the end of it all, and if the evidence tendered proves unacceptable or unreliable, what else can it do but draw upon its wisdom, experience and judgment and do the best it can in all the circumstances."[170]

In addition, though tied only loosely to rigid rules of evidence and procedure in the conduct of their determination, the issue was raised as to how extensive the reasons given by the committees needed to be. The notion of committees being able to rely on their own storehouse of information on particular localities militated against a legalistic kind of procedure and approach at the hearing. This was extended to the written reasons in *Tormes Property Co* v *Landau* in 1970. Lord Parker indicated that he saw nothing wrong in a committee simply preferring one method of rent determination to another without explicitly indicating the reason for its preference:

> "the committee were perfectly entitled to do what they did. Without criticising the yardstick put forward by the landlords it seems to me that the committee were perfectly entitled to reject it … I do not think that the committee can be criticised for just saying that they were not going to go into (the)method of approach advanced by the landlords".[171]

His successor, Lord Chief Justice Widgery, took up this line of thinking in *Metropolitan Properties* v *Laufer*, where the landlords in effect were keen to find out the basis for the figure selected by the Committee as the "fair rent". This process might be less than illuminating because of the nature of the enterprise, Lord Widgery explained:

> "as so often happens in the typical simple case, the landlord's experts say that the rent should be X and the tenant's experts say that the rent should be X minus Y, if the committee thinks that neither figure is the right one not only can it choose a figure in between the two extremes but it should do so … in (such) a case there are no reasons the committee can give, save that it was not satisfied with either of the alternatives put forward in evidence and on its own expert knowledge preferred another figure".[172]

Lord Widgery became even more expansive in later cases: explaining the reasons for rejecting either party's arguments, his Lordship explained:

---

[170]   [1968] 1 WLR 815 at 831.
[171]   *Tormes Property Co Ltd* v *Landau* [1970] 3 All ER 653.
[172]   *Metropolitan Properties* v *Laufer* (1975) 29 P & CR at 177.

"There are plenty of judicial offices ... where reasons undoubtedly have to be given for every decision, but that does not mean that if the judge has two conflicting opinions put before him in evidence he has to explain why he chose one in preference to another. Such explanations are not possible. They are matters of judgment, impression and sometimes even instinct, and it is quite impossible to give detailed reasons to explain how the system of decision has worked and so with a rent assessment committee."[173]

This gradual drift into the notion of rent assessment committees as rent-fixing conjurers in England was paralleled by a development north of the Border which was far more akin to the sort of approach favoured by landlords and their agents. Again motivated by the Weberian need for predictability and rationality in the rent-fixing process, landlords had suggested that reasons for decisions should be clear and unambiguous.

In Scotland, while it was not fully appreciated at the time, the Court of Session in 1970 in *Learmonth Property* had taken a very different line in the duty to give reasons:

"If (the committee) are to proceed to make a computation ... independently of the contentions of both parties it is incumbent upon them to give details of how it was reached. Otherwise the parties cannot be satisfied of the fairness or reliability of the Committee's decision."[174]

The First Division of the Court of Session was more emphatic in a common judgment given a year later in the *Glasgow Heritable Trust* case. Stressing the importance of the need to make clear the basis on which a decision was reached, it suggested that a statement of reasons was inadequate where it contained "no statement of what facts the committee found to be proved and no indication whether the arguments of the parties were accepted as convincing or not ... (and) no indication of what scarcity allowance they considered reasonable still less of what estimate they allowed for it and why".[175]

This was translated into a positive duty to do all these things in an appeal again heard by the First Division some 5 years later in *Albyn Properties* v *Knox*:

"In order to make clear the basis of their decision a committee must state – (i) what facts they found to be admitted or proved; (ii) whether and to what extent the submissions of parties were accepted as convincing or not; and (iii) by what method or methods of valuation applied to the facts found their determination was arrived at. In short they must explain how their figures of fair rent were fixed."[176]

---

[173]   *Guppy's (Bridport) Ltd* v *Sandoe* (1975) 30 P & CR 69 at 74.
[174]   *Learmonth Property Investment Co Ltd* v *Aitken* 1971 SLT 349 at 352.
[175]   Unreported, cited in 1977 SLT 44.
[176]   *Albyn Properties* v *Knox* 1977 SLT 41 at 43.

CHOOSING BETWEEN THE ALTERNATIVES

What was interesting about this twin line of judicial interpretation is that it took place with minimal reference to the decisions in the other jurisdiction. This was most crucially highlighted in the *Albyn* and *Guppy's* v *Knott* cases. In neither of these cases was there any reference to the line of authority elsewhere in Great Britain despite the availability of this information. The reporting of *Albyn* south of the Border resulted in an attempt to bring the jurisdictions into line with each other effectively on the issue of what approach to adopt in rent assessment committees should be.

In the Divisional Court in 1980 the West of England property company Guppy's, under the direction of Leslie Parlett, managed to displace the traditional line (taken by Lord Parker and elaborated by Lord Widgery) in favour of an adoption of the Scottish approach.[177] The matter was complicated by the unusual status of the judge in the Divisional Court.[178] Sir Douglas cited the paragraph instanced above as his guiding light in approaching the issue of reasons. No mention was made in the judgment of the line of English authority from the Lord Chief Justices, although these cases were apparently cited in argument.[179]

Although one might see in this the beginnings of consistency between the jurisdictions, the Tenants' Rights etc (Scotland) Act 1980 altered the fair rent formula for Scotland by providing that in future, in addition to looking to all the circumstances etc, the committee "shall ... apply their knowledge and experience of current rents of comparable property in the area".[180]

The immediacy of the impact these two new policy thrusts can be inferred from the ways in which committees had previously interpreted their role.

THE ROLE OF LANDLORDS, THEIR PRACTICES AND PERSPECTIVES

One problem with looking at landlords as a homogenous group providing housing units, whose reaction to the restrictions on the operation of the market can be gauged in terms of a reaction to straightforward economic incentive, is that this is an inaccurate and misleading image of landlords in modern Britain. Accordingly, those projections which concentrate solely on the return of the landlord fail to take account of this important dimension to the problem. Put simply, the fact that there are a number of disparate sectors within the landlord group means that

---

[177] *Guppy's Properties Ltd* v *Knott (No 2)* (1981–82) 1 HLR 30.
[178] Seasoned commentator Trevor Aldridge suggested that this limited the value of the case at a Conference on the Fixing of Rents in London, May 1980.
[179] Mr Leslie Parlett of Guppy's was the source for this and much other background information on this issue.
[180] Section 48.

a variety of perceptions and responses are possible to alternations to legislation. Robson and Watchman's work in the early 1980s seemed to suggest that the issue of levels of return needed to be looked at critically before its alleged implications are assumed to be accurate. They made a clear distinction between the problems of small landlords and company landlords.[181]

Politicians were not the only individuals who had expressed doubts over the operation and nature of the rent-fixing provisions introduced in 1965 and operated by the Rent Registration Service. However, those directly affected by the levels of rental fixed by this new method had never been particularly clearly organised nor had they always spoken with one voice. This was less surprising given the very different sorts of problems and goals confronting landlords. It was estimated in 1980 that there were some 500,000 landlords of whom only about 20,000 belonged to any recognised organisation.[182] This had always been a bugbear of this form of enterprise and the cry that "Union is Strength"[183] has not always been heeded.

Those landlords whose properties were left under the old form of control, ie frozen rent with repairs additions based on expenditure which had existed from 1914 and 1939 until 1957, regarded themselves as comparatively so badly off compared with the fair rent system that they formed a Fair Rents Association in April 1966 which campaigned for their properties to be brought into line with registered or fair rents.[184] In spite of doubts, also about the logic and theoretical viability of the system, landlords and their advisers recognised early on that what would be crucial in the coming years was the level of rents initially set by rent officers and committees.[185] There seemed to have been a recognition that the major goal of Rent Acts was to weed out landlords who were "shockers" and "ensure that rapacious landlords would not be able to profit at the expense of their tenants".[186] However, over the years there was a continual flow of complaints about the kinds of return which landlords could expect to receive.[187] The actual evidence for these complaints was less than clear cut and it was suggested that most of the decisions in the courts on the approach of committees to rent fixing as well as the committee decisions available to Robson and Watchman suggested that many of the complaints of landlords and professional organisations were being met.

---

[181] See, for example, *Lost Property*, SLA Access TV programme, 25 March 1979.
[182] SLA evidence of 24 October 1980.
[183] Glasgow Landlords' Association AGM January 1883, Presidential Address cited in Robson (1979).
[184] *Estates Gazette* (201) 1967 at 445.
[185] *Ibid* at 153.
[186] *Estates Gazette* (200) 1966 at 981 per Sir Sidney Littlewood.
[187] The *Estates Gazette* correspondence columns reveal a fairly steady flow of dissatisfaction over the years.

It was clear that different committees in different parts of the country and different rent officers interpreted their duties in different ways. Thus, while it was possible to point to returns in line with the aspirations of individual landlords and their organisations in certain areas, this was no guarantee that landlords in other parts of the country could expect the same sort of treatment. The figures which the British Property Federation quoted and which the Small Landlords Association referred to in its publications[188] suggested wide differences between areas.

The Small Landlords Association asked in its compilation of letters from landlords: why do landlords not get fair rents? It attributed this process to the failure of the rent fixers to apply the law properly:

"When landlords quote the case of Mason and Skilling to Rent Assessment Committees it is usually greeted with a barely stifled yawn and the committee proceeds to ignore it and to determine the new rent on the basis of 'comparables'."[189]

However, the point here was that if this was how a significant section of the potential renting suppliers of rented property perceived the operation of Crossman's formula, this was a barrier to the legislation working to the mutual satisfaction of the various parties. The SLA, in its evidence to the Environmental Committee of the House of Commons in October 1980, talked of a yield of 2–3 per cent *gross* on fair rents. This was not entirely easy to square with the data from RACs which Robson and Watchman encountered.

The sort of return which the British Property Federation suggested would be acceptable in its evidence to the Department of Environment Consultation paper of January 1977 was in line with the Robson and Watchman figures: "In present circumstances the Federation would venture to suggest that 6 per cent nett of outgoings would be about right in the majority of cases."[190]

It should be noted that the BPF was "devoted to the interest of property owners and others with a major concern with property"[191] so that the interests of landlords were dear to their hearts. The Federation "prides itself on representing all property owners, large and small".[192]

The Rating and Valuation Association suggested that a figure of 8 per cent would be seen as nearer to what was required to allow for a proper return, bearing in mind capital improvement.[193] The Country Landowners Association suggested that fair rents should "bear a sensible

188   *Submission to Rent Act Review. Letters from Landlords.*
189   *Letters from Landlords,* p 10.
190   *Review of the Rent Acts* at 14.
191   *Ibid.*
192   *Ibid.*
193   *Estates Gazette,* 14 May 1977.

relation" to capital value while the Royal Institution of Chartered Surveyors considered that fair rents should be made more realistic, attracting potential investors into the rental accommodation field. However, again since it talked of a gross return in some cases of the order of 2 per cent, this had to be seen in this light.[194] Less encouraging even than these views for adherents of the Crossman approach was the view of the National Association of Estate Agents, which regarded the fair rent system as discredited: "... these rents have never been fair".[195]

In the late 1970s and the early 1980s there seemed to have been a resurgence of a degree of satisfaction with rent assessment committee practice, although their colleagues, the rent officers, were subjected to what one writer describes as "bashing".[196] Thus, one company landlord wrote that the level of success in appeals in late 1979 had given 152 successful increases out of 164 appeals, with 19 of these figures being higher than the figure actually asked for by the landlords.[197] Other landlords confirmed this. This was echoed by a director of the Guppys Property Group, Leslie Parlett, who suggested in March 1980 that there was nothing wrong with the systems but simply its administration: "The law is fair. What is unfair is the way it is implemented."[198]

The fault, Mr Parlett suggested, rested to some degree with property owners themselves in actually operating the system: "Nor would I suggest is any credit due to property owners who put up such a poor show at contesting rent assessments before committees ... A more supine and listless body would be hard to imagine."[199]

Later in 1980, though, he did suggest that:

"no informed person in his right senses would let his property where full Rent Act protection is entailed. Such lettings as these are generally conceived in ignorance or on a basis of trust or careful calculation of the risk".[200]

From other remarks made by landlords' agents, though, it was clear that satisfaction with the system was far from universal when the notion of capital return received little credence.[201] There then appeared to be almost two faces to the landlords' position on "fair rents". While, in their literature and evidence, the impression was conveyed of minimal returns on holdings, the aspirations of landlords were not necessarily far from actual practice.

---

[194] *Estates Gazette*, 14 May 1977.
[195] *Ibid.*
[196] *Estates Gazette*, 9 February 1980.
[197] *Estates Gazette*, 26 January 1980.
[198] *Estates Gazette*, 1 March 1980.
[199] *Ibid.*
[200] *Estates Gazette*, 25 October 1980.
[201] *Estates Gazette*, 5 January 1980.

A study undertaken by Robson and Nicoll for the Social Science Research Council in the early 1980s sought to obtain a clearer picture of the reality of the private rental market across Scotland. It looked at the kinds of landlords in the field as well their perceptions of legislation. It found that levels of ignorance of the legislation and its impact were high but that few were affected by its terms. Landlords in Glasgow, Dundee and Montrose operated on a small scale and had few problems with either returns or security of tenure. Their knowledge of the Rent Acts was at best sketchy.[202]

THE ROLE OF TENANTS AND THE FATE OF FAIR RENTS

As far as tenants were concerned, there was a paucity of evidence on exactly what perceptions tenants had of the whole control system erected ostensibly for their benefit. They had never been a well-organised grouping and their successes in the past had been confined to spectacular temporary gains in popular peasant movements following violence.[203] As far as the town dweller was concerned, the problem of permanent and common interests of residents had meant that tenants' groupings had been short lived, although often achieving specific gains. Their reactions as a whole to the 1965 legislation can be inferred from the level of applications for fair rents,[204] some attitudinal surveys and some material a study carried out in the mid-1980s.

One difficulty is that there are reasons why tenants may never operationalise the optional rent control legislation or even know of its implications and may appear content when their non-application to have a fair rent fixed reflect ignorance or fear of landlord reprisals. Alternatively, it was suggested that the relatively low use by tenants of what Crossman called the Tenants' Charter[205] stemmed from a rejection of external interference in a private agreement and on some occasions simply a desire for a quiet life:

> "lots of tenants in Kensington and Chelsea stay away from the Rent Officer not for any sinister reason but because they do not want to bother: or they may think that the landlord has never troubled them so why should they trouble him".[206]

The views of tenants as to various types of housing tenure have been the subject of study over the years. This data gives some indirect information as to tenants' views of the Rent Acts.

---

202 Nicoll (1985).
203 Hunter (2010); Newby (2007).
204 After an initial flurry in 1965–66 these dropped rapidly so that in 1972 and 1973 the applications by tenants comprised some 10 per cent down from over 60 per cent.
205 Crossman (1975).
206 *Estates Gazette* (1966), 141.

The 1976 DoE survey of the attitudes towards letting held by private landlords, private tenants and owner occupiers, indicated tenant satisfaction with rent levels.[207] Landlord satisfaction, even where rents were agreed privately outside the control or regulation system, was only just over half; while in the same category 83 per cent of the tenants were satisfied.[208] One might infer from this rather higher expectations from landlords. Only 28 per cent of those landlords with fair rents registered were satisfied with their returns by way of rent.

In the BMRB Housing Consumer Survey of 1976,[209] views were ascertained as to the various attitudes to tenures in general and the advantages of particular tenures. The major disadvantages with private tenancies were seen as being problems with repairs which 33 per cent of those actually in that sector mentioned.[210] This was followed by concerns over fear eviction mentioned by 19 per cent of the total sample and by 12 per cent of those actually in the private rented sector. Ten per cent spoke of high rents.

Insofar as the survey also covered aspirations of those surveyed, this seemed to indicate that the ideal choice of those renting privately was into either owner occupation (36 per cent) or into council property (17 per cent). Overall, of those only 8 per cent took as their ideal tenure private renting. Expectations as opposed to aspirations suggested that almost half of those in the private rented sector expected to move in the next ten years into owned housing (29 per cent) or council property (17 per cent) while 41 per cent expected to remain in their current tenure. At the end of the 1970s, then, the strength of attachment to this tenure then seemed weak and possibly reflective of low levels of satisfaction with the fair rent and security of tenure basis of the market. This was the context then in which a radical alteration to housing policy was introduced by the Conservative administration of Margaret Thatcher.

THE HOUSING ACT 1988 AND THE IMPACT ON "FAIR RENTS"

When the Conservative Party regained the reins of government at the end of the decade reform of private rental housing received less publicity than the dramatic changes to the rights of local authority tenants. The latter were given the opportunity to purchase their tenancies at significant discounts from 25 per cent to 60 per cent of market value under the Housing Acts of 1980. The existing position of private-sector tenants was left unaltered. The new opportunities provided in the 1980 legislation for landlords to invest without the prospect of tenants having security of

---

[207]   Paley (1978).
[208]   *Ibid* at para 3.15.
[209]   British Market Research Bureau (1977).
[210]   *Ibid.*

tenure beyond the contract term were coupled with the continuance of fair rents in these "shorthold" and "short" tenancies.

The investment in the new tenancies with automatic repossession was extremely limited and in February 1987 the then Minister of Housing John Patten indicated that the independent rental sector would be encouraged in a way which encouraged investment but which confronted the issue of bad landlords. In future, he suggested those operating in the sector would require to be approved and registered. They would, however be freed from control in terms of the rent they charged and the ability to regain possession.[211]

PERSONAL SUBSIDY APPROACH

Rent allowances, rent rebates and housing benefit

The initial impetus for the creation of social renting and the introduction of rent controls in the private rented sector were both intended to protect the mass of tenants from the vagaries of market forces. Both were relatively simple methods of ensuring that the expensive commodity housing could be occupied at a reasonable cost by the vast majority of the population living on modest incomes. Rather than provide support to the whole of the sector, an alternative form of subsidy has been adopted in the past 40 years – housing benefit.

Neither the functioning private rented sector nor the social rented sector is directly constrained by any legislation in the rents it charges.[212] The level of community support, then, is a difficult issue, once one has accepted the notion of minimum levels of income for all citizens and a decent quality of life for all as of right. How one does that with rents is trickier. It is a thorny issue which, hitherto, politicians have been unwilling to grasp. The problem in the private sector is how to avoid rents set at levels that do not allow landlords to receive additional income from the community where the tenants are having their housing costs met through local or national benefits. The solution thus far has been the local housing allowance. This works by fixing a level of rent which reflects what is being paid by willing tenants in the open market and using this as the basis for calculating means-tested benefits. It depends crucially for its effectiveness on there being a genuine market of willing tenants and landlords and having supply and demand in equilibrium. Which takes us back to how the Rent Acts came in, in the first place.

What determines the rents in the social renting sector is the historical levels along with peer developments and pressure from the Scottish

---

211 *Weekend World*, Matthew Parris, February 1987.

212 The wording of s 33 of the Housing (Scotland) Act 1988 and the resultant tiny number of applications in relation to rents "significantly in excess" of the market rent in the short assured tenancy sector means that market figures operate here with scarcely any need for constraint of excess – see above at p 154.

Housing Regulator. As we see below, there is a form of regulation in relation to the standards of service and cost of same which has been covered in the past 20 years by Scottish Homes, Communities Scotland now the Scottish Housing Regulator. Part of its remit is to determine whether or not social landlords are giving good value for money. Part of this involves the levels of rent being charged and the regulators have extensive powers to ensure that any social landlord conforms to the sector norm. The levels of rent, for instance, in social rented housing at the time of writing show considerable variation between sectors and within sectors. Average housing association rents varied in 2008–09 from £52 in the Scottish Borders to £63 per week in East Renfrewshire and local authority rents from £39 in Moray to £60 in Edinburgh.[213] The social rented sector has been transformed in Scotland between 1980 and 2010. According to the Scottish Government: "only a quarter of the housing stock is social housing and those entering the sector are likely to be on low incomes or not in work".[214]

Given the demise of rent control in the private sector and the constraints on social housing support, the future is uncertain. The only constraint on what people pay for modern rental housing in Scotland is what levels of support are available from the community to support those unable to afford the market or social rents which they require to pay. At the time of writing, one of the periodic moral panics about housing benefit is in full flow. What form the means testing of this form of support for living will take in the future remains to be seen, Since it is not a devolved function it is one over which the people of Scotland have rather less input than in other housing matters. The problem, though, of how to support the cost of an expensive commodity, shelter in a relatively hostile physical climate where decent housing is a necessity is not one which is new to Scots. Solutions though from earlier days, one fervently hopes will be resisted. The cost of housing the poor was viewed as a grim necessity by those raising the money to pay for such accommodation in the 19th century. It was, however, expenditure which was to be minimised. The pre-Victorian version of housing benefit was the alternative to the Workhouse, outdoor relief. As Gramsci reminds us, in the struggle for a better future, there is always a grim war of attrition to be fought to maintain what has been won. The cheeseparing, dismal days of yore are described eloquently in relation to outdoor relief in 19th-century Kilmarnock:

> "In calling general attention to the PARISH ROLL for the current year, the HERITORS and KIRK SESSION flatter themselves, that from the great diminution of expenditure, since the publication of last year's Lists, the inhabitants will be disposed to view with approbation, the measures

---

213   Scottish Government (2010).
214   *Ibid* at 16, para 16.

that have been pursued, and are still in progress, to mitigate the pressure of Assessment: and ameliorate the condition of the Poor, by throwing them more on their own resources, and the kind attention of their neighbours and relatives. The Ministers of Religion are loudly called on, to urge the obligations of private and public Benevolence: seeing the effects that have resulted from the salutary exertions of those entrusted with the Parochial Funds. The public may rest satisfied, that the determination of the Heritors and Session, to persevere in their present efforts, shall undergo no relaxation, till the sum, raised by Assessment from Town and Parish, shall be reduced to a mere trifle [Kilmarnock 10th January 1829]."

The circumstances of those without resources, then, is, at the time of writing, one where misfortunes of birth and skills are to an extent shared with the provision of minimum support for housing costs. It is, as ever, under challenge through crude misrepresentation.

6   LOSS OF HOUSING AND EVICTION

OWNER OCCUPATION AND LOSS OF PROPERTY

The principal psychological advantage of ownership of property as against renting property centres on the fact that there is no possibility of being evicted on the whim of some modern version of the top-hatted, cigar-smoking heartless landlord featured in silent film and the cartoons of the 1915 Rent Strikes.[1] Although it is true that there is no equivalent to the landlord able to evict a property owner, there are still circumstances in which property can be lost. Traditionally if a property owner had debts relating to the property such as repairs to common parts like the roof a creditor could raise an action of adjudication.[2] This meant that the owner could be forced to sell the property to meet the debts. This has been replaced by the process of land attachment.[3] At the time of writing the provisions of this legislation have not been brought into force due to concerns by the later minority administration that it would be used oppressively.

Not all property owners, however, own their properties outright. They have to borrow to buy the house or flat they live in. With property an expensive commodity in a country with a climate like that in Scotland, the loans are long term and secured over the value of the property. The extension of property ownership in the 20th century came about principally through the availability of long terms loans over property. Lenders could insist on the payment of the bond and it was partly to protect borrowers from such actions that the Rents Acts were introduced. The full title of the first legislation was in fact the Increase of Rent and Mortgage Interest (War Restrictions) Act 1915 and the protection of those with mortgages was in the title of all the legislation until the Rent Act 1957.[4] Originally

---

[1] The image derives from Great War images seen in Petrie (2008) cover, back, 61 and 62 and has appeared on the cover of the housing journal *Roof* portraying the threat of landlords at the end of the 20th century.

[2] Gordon (2nd edn) at 1.40–1.43 and 20.74.

[3] Bankruptcy and Diligence (Scotland) Act 2007, Pt IV.

[4] Increase of Rent and Mortgage Interest (Restrictions) Act 1920; Rent and Mortgage Interest (Restrictions) Act 1923; and Rent and Mortgage Interest Restrictions Act 1939.

in the form of a bond and disposition in security, modern mortgages have since 1970 come in the slightly different form of the standard security.[5] In the event of the borrower being unable to meet the payments on the loan then the terms of the mortgage agreement usually allow the lender to insist on full payment of the outstanding sum due on the loan. If the debtor was unable to meet this sum then they would have to sell the property.

The rights of borrowers in this process are limited by the contractual terms of the mortgages which the parties sign. The Conveyancing and Feudal Reform (Scotland) Act 1970 provided that where the occupier fell into arrears with the loan, the creditor had extensive rights to repossess the property to meet the debt having served the appropriate notices.[6] Repossession was almost always successful. The Mortgage Rights (Scotland) Act 2001 was introduced to enable the courts to suspend certain rights of mortgage lenders where the borrower was in default and to provide greater protection for tenants of borrowers in default. It provides powers for the sheriff court to suspend the enforcement process and apply its discretion. The circumstances where the court may apply its discretion are where the applicant might be able to repay the debt or arrears of fulfil the obligation in the standard security within a reasonable time so as to keep their home or to give the applicant and others staying in the property time to find alternative accommodation.[7] Whether or not they exercise this discretion depends on the nature of and reasons for the default, the ability of the applicant to fulfil within a reasonable time the obligations of the standard security and any action taken by the creditor to help in this respect and the ability to secure reasonable alternative accommodation.[8] The Home Owner and Debtor Protection (Scotland) Act 2010 received the Royal Assent in March 2010 and provides further protection for owner occupiers by requiring court proceedings and the satisfaction of the court that the lender has sought to avoid the repossession.[9]

In the event that there is loss of owner occupied accommodation, there are two forms of assistance available to those displaced from their homes. First, there is the mortgage to rent scheme. The Scottish Executive issued a draft consultation paper, *Mortgage to Rent*, in July 2000 outlining a possible voluntary scheme to allow those in mortgage difficulties the flexibility to change the tenure of their home from ownership to a tenancy in the social rented sector. This was found in the Mortgage Rights (Scotland) Act 2001 which provided a method of avoiding homelessness.[10] This is available nationally and provides a subsidy to those social landlords who participate

---

[5] Conveyancing and Feudal Reform (Scotland) Act 1970; Paisley (2002).
[6] CFRSA 1970, s 24.
[7] MRSA 2001, s 2.
[8] *Ibid*, s 2(2).
[9] HODPSA 2010, ss 1–6.
[10] MRSA 2001.

in the scheme. It was originally available from some social landlords such as Weslo as a service to property owners in their area who had exercised the right to buy and who had at later date been unable to meet mortgage payments.[11] Under the MTR scheme the property is purchased by a landlord such as Weslo and the owner reverts to paying rent. The great advantage for families is that there is no disruption by having to move or change schools at what is likely to be a stressful time in people's lives, anyway. Take-up was in initially patchy and the scheme at the time of writing was voluntary for social landlords.[12]

For those who are unable to take advantage of mortgage to rent, there is assistance available under the homelessness provisions of the Housing (Scotland) Act 1987 which require local authorities to secure accommodation becomes available for homeless applicants in priority need who have not brought their situation upon themselves by intentional acts or omissions.[13] Non-payment of mortgages is an issue which the Code of Guidance suggests should not be regarded as being intentional:

> "if ... a person's house was sold because he or she could not keep up the loan repayments ... because of real personal and financial difficulties (for example if he or she became unemployed, or is working part time, or has reduced income following death of a partner or relationship breakdown) their acts or omissions should not be regarded as having been deliberate".[14]

RENTED PROPERTY AND EVICTION

Introduction

Rented property throws up different rather problems. The threat of eviction at the hands of others, who have the right to eject someone from their home because they own the property, has always hung over tenants. It can occur without any misdemeanour or bad behaviour by the tenants. This is still the position today. The headline "You're Evicted" is the lead story in a local newspaper appeared in summer 2010. A family is described as devastated after being given 6 months' notice to leave the home they have rented for the past 15 years from a local company. The tenants worked as a social worker for vulnerable people and a district nurse. They had brought up their four children in the property and had fostered more than 30 youngsters there. When their eldest son returns from his third tour of duty to Afghanistan the house he was brought up in will no

---

[11] Between 2003 and 2010 Weslo had assisted over 50 home owners to remain in their homes through the mortgage to rent scheme – Weslo Annual Report 2010.
[12] Scottish Government (2009c).
[13] See Chapter 2.
[14] COG 2005, para 7.13.

longer be his home. The company wish to redevelop the site on which the property is located. They pointed out that they had extended the required notice term from 2 months to 6 months as a gesture of goodwill. The company regretted that their plans for the property will have an impact on the tenants but noted that the "current economic climate necessitates us reviewing our portfolio of property at this time".[15] This, then, in a nutshell, has been the dilemma facing tenants and landlords since the process of renting property began. The interests of the tenants to occupy their home contrasted with the right of the landlord to realise their asset and sell or redevelop the property. The conflict between the rights to a home and the right to property has been the core of political struggle throughout the past century. The struggle at the present time of writing largely favours property owners as we shall see, although for the most part social landlords are unlikely to have major changes in their policies to make. Housing Associations and local authorities are by their very nature in the business of renting the homes they construct or acquire. It is generally only private sector landlords who are likely to wish to diversify their activities and realise or develop their property assets.

Security of tenure

As indicated, in the past century the position of landlords to decide when they wish to obtain vacant possession without the need to have any reason to evict their tenants has been a fraught issue. The shift from a situation of simple market forces to one of severe restrictions on landlords' ability to regain possession of their properties has varied with the political exigencies of the day. At the present time tenants in the social rented sector have a significant degree of security of tenure while their fellow tenants of private landlords have rather less rights. The situation is, however, complex depending on when a tenancy was entered into as well as what kinds of technical arrangements were operative. This chapter seeks to give a comprehensible guide to the range of alternative situations in which tenants find themselves and to explain how the current convoluted situation has arisen.

One of the major aims of the rent legislation in Scotland since the Leases Act 1449 has been to provide a degree of security of tenure to those occupying property. Over the years as we have noted elsewhere, the level of security for tenants has varied.[16] The current statutes retain the concept of security of tenure and specify those situations where landlords can seek to have tenants

---

[15] *Wear Valley Mercury*, Issue 194, Friday June 11 2010 p. 1 – www.wearvalley mercury.co.uk – although this story related to property in the north east of England it could just as easily have come from any part of Scotland since the basic law on the subject is the same.

[16] See Chapter 3.

evicted. This contrasts with the position in the market where no reason was ever required by the landlord to regain possession of his property as long as the contract so permitted. The impact was neatly summed by the Ridley Committee which explained in 1945:

> "The Rent Restriction Acts achieve their purpose of preventing undue rise in rent, which may be caused by housing shortages, by limiting the rent a landlord may legally recover from a tenant, while at the same time giving security of tenure … Landlords who are restricted in this way are themselves given protection against undue increases in rates of mortgage interest and against the calling up of mortgages as they pay the restricted interest due."[17]

Under the assured tenancy regime, as with protected tenancies under the Rent (Scotland) Act 1984 and secure tenancies under the Housing (Scotland) Act 2001, there is a requirement that possession orders only be given on one or more of the grounds specified in the legislation. There are two sets of requirements. Grounds for possession must be established and proper notice given. There are also forms of private sector tenancy and social renting in which the landlord does not require to have a ground of repossession but can simply evict at the end of the contractual term or on raising an action thereafter. Here we look at the standard grounds of repossession and then at the situations where there is very limited security.

Grounds of possession

As the Appendix makes clear, there is considerable overlap between the rights of tenants in the private and social rented sector in relation to repossession. It is, however, hopefully less confusing to deal with each sector separately in terms of the grounds of repossession. We look first at the modern private rented and then the social rented sector.

ASSURED TENANCIES

Grounds for possession must be established

The most frequently encountered type of tenancy in the private rented sector is the assured tenancy. These are the only kinds of new tenancy which can be created on or after 2 January 1989. More than 20 years on they represent by far the most common rental contract.[18] Interestingly, only 50 per cent of tenants thought they had short assured tenancies.[19] Most of these assured tenancies are, however, the short assured version which has, as we shall see, rather easier possession arrangements for landlords. The sheriff has no power to make an assured tenancy possession order in any circumstances other than those laid down in Sch 5 to the 1988 Act. One or more of the

---

[17] Ridley Committee (1945), para 12.
[18] Scottish Government (2009d).
[19] *Ibid*, vol 2, 8.4 and fig 8.1.

grounds for possession must be established. There are two situations which can exist when a possession order is sought in the private sector. Under the discretionary grounds the sheriff has discretion and must be satisfied not only that the conditions in the ground are satisfied but also that it is reasonable to grant the order for possession. In situations where mandatory grounds are being invoked, if the ground is satisfied there is no element of discretion and the order must be granted. The statute states "the sheriff ... shall grant an order".[20] A statutory "notice of proceedings for possession" must be served before there can be an order for possession. By contrast, it must be remembered that in the social rented sector all the grounds require the sheriff to exercise discretion and no ground is automatic. The grounds under the Rent (Scotland) Act 1984 are now sufficiently rare that they are not covered in detail in a work of this type. It is crucial, though that anyone seeking to give advice on a repossession issue does not forget to check how long the tenancy has been operative in case the provisions of Sch 2 to the Rent (Scotland) Act 1984 apply. They are more extensive and restrictive on the plans of landlords than the Housing (Scotland) Act 1988, Sch 5 and are outlined in the Appendix to this chapter. Fuller coverage is provided in *Residential Tenancies* by Robson and Halliday.[21]

Necessity for inclusion of grounds in tenancy agreement

The Housing (Scotland) Act 1988 also provides that there can be no possession order while the contract runs under certain grounds unless the tenancy agreement specifically makes such provision. This seems to have the effect that where a short, perhaps amateur, lease agreement merely states the premises, term and rent, then during the contractual term the landlord may not use these grounds. The landlord would need to terminate the contractual tenancy at its term by giving Notice to Quit. This would prevent tacit relocation operating and the landlord would then be able to use one of the grounds in Sch 5 which are applicable to statutory assured tenancies. This requirement to incorporate the possession ground in the tenancy agreement is in addition to the need for a separate written notice of intention required for the certain grounds such as owner occupier's own use, former principal home, off-season holiday let and student lettings by specified educational institutions.[22] The grounds which must be specified are as follows:

(1) mortgage repossession;
(2) rent 3 months in arrears;
(3) persistent delay in paying rent;
(4) rent in arrears;
(5) breach of terms of tenancy (other than rent);

---

[20] HSA 1988, s 19(5).
[21] 3rd edition by Robson, Halliday and Vennard, scheduled for 2012.
[22] HSA 1988, Sch 5.

(6) deterioration of house or common parts;

(7) anti-social behaviour;[23]

(8) deterioration of condition of furniture.[24]

Mandatory grounds of possession

In addition to the automatic repossession ground available for short assured tenancies, there are a number of grounds of possession where, if established, there is no requirement for the sheriff to be satisfied that it is reasonable to grant possession order. It is important to stress that these grounds have no equivalent in the social rented sector in terms of the Housing (Scotland) Act 2001. In addition, some of the grounds may only be available after the specified time laid down in Sch 5 – off-season holiday lets – or where specific landlords are involved – lettings of student accommodation by specified educational institutions. The sheriff may not adjourn an action if it is a situation where the landlord is using one of the mandatory grounds of possession or if it is a "short assured tenancy". Where a possession order is granted for one of the appropriate grounds noted, such an order brings to an end the statutory rights of the tenant to remain in the property.

Prior notice

There are restrictions on some of the grounds by way of prior notice to the tenant at the commencement of the tenancy. This applies where the landlord wants to use the property for his own use or where the property was his former only or principal residence.[25] These two distinct reasons for repossession are, confusingly, included in a single ground. Also requiring notice to the tenant at the commencement of the lease are leases by tenants where the property is subject to a mortgage.[26] In the event of default by the landlord the lender may repossess without any need to show that the interests of the tenant have been considered and that it is reasonable for that person to be evicted. Off-season holiday lets – sometimes referred to as "winter lets" – also require to be notified to the tenant, as do lettings by specified educational institutions.[27]

Reasonable to dispense with prior notice

It may be that the landlord has drawn up the lease without proper professional advice and failed to include prior notice of a wish to use

---

[23] Stalker suggests that the amendments made by Antisocial Behaviour etc (Scotland) Act 2004, s 100, and the Housing (Scotland) Act 2006, s 180, do not achieve their goal of allowing sheriffs to grant possession orders when the term is not included in the tenancy agreement – 74–75. The points seem well made and it cannot be said with confidence that the courts will be willing to overlook the drafting limitations.

[24] HSA 1988, s 18(6).

[25] *Ibid*, Sch 5, ground 1.

[26] *Ibid*, Sch 5, ground 2.

[27] *Ibid*, Sch 5, grounds 3 and 4.

one the above-noted grounds. If, then, the requirements of notice are not satisfied, there is provision for the sheriff to dispense with such a notice. This applies to the owner occupier ground and the mortgage default grounds. There is, however, no possibility of the failure to provide notice being waived in the case of an off-season holiday let or a specified educational institution. The rationale would seem to be a recognition of a degree of sophistication in holiday letting and educational institutions enterprises where the landlords can be expected to be fully aware of the minutiae of legal procedure.

The test applied under the Housing (Scotland) Act 1988 is one of "reasonableness" rather than the "just and equitable" test previously applied in notice cases in the Rent Acts. The Court of Appeal have examined the provision in the Housing Act 1988 covering England and Wales in a case involving landlords who rented out property on the English equivalent of a short assured tenancy.[28] The landlords' plan was to work from their small country cottage but did not give written notice to the tenants of their London flat that they were intending to use the "principal home" ground. The husband got a job in London and wished to return to the London property. The oral notice given was accepted as adequate by the Court of Appeal and the need for written notice was dispensed with. Unfortunately, although this case gives an indication of the factors deemed relevant, the test in the Housing Act 1988 is "just and equitable". No Scottish decisions are known to the author on the issue of notice, the failure to give notice or waiving of the requirement to give notice. Given the propensity of landlords to opt for short assured tenancies even where they are renting out as ex-owner occupiers, mortgage holders or off-season holiday lessors it may well be that this will not become a litigated matter. Assistance on the interpretation of the test is also unlikely to come from England since, as from 28 February 1997, the "default" tenancy now provided in their legislation is the "assured shorthold" tenancy.[29]

The specific mandatory grounds of possession

THE LANDLORD FORMERLY OCCUPIED THE HOUSE AS HIS ONLY OR PRINCIPAL HOME[30]

This ground occurs where the landlord or one of the joint landlords occupied the house as his only or principal home and wants possession of the property. It should be noted that there is no need for the landlord to establish any need for the property provided that written notice is given at the commencement of the tenancy that possession might be recovered on this ground. While one might imagine that a landlord with a few properties might be able to use this mandatory ground for a small portfolio of properties a couple of matters need

---

[28] *Boyle* v *Verrall* [1997] 1 EGLR 25.
[29] HSA 1988, s 19A, inserted by s 96 of the Housing Act 1996.
[30] *Ibid*, Sch 5, ground 1(a).

to be borne in mind. First, the court would want to ensure that there was no evasion of the Rent Acts taking place through a landlord simply living for a few weeks in a property and claiming to be covered by this ground. Second, in order to establish one was genuinely occupying a property as an only or principal home the standard signifiers would require to be in place – bills, council tax, length of occupancy.[31] Finally, given the availability of short assured tenancies and their automatic right to repossession, this would be seem to be a waste of time and energy when the same result could be achieved by having slightly different paperwork and through service of an AT5. While it might appeal to a landlord keen to operate very short-term leases the same effect could be achieved with, I would suggest, more certainty by providing 6-month leases with break clauses available to tenants. This would satisfy the SAT requirements as well as allow tenants who chose a shorter period not to be disadvantaged.[32]

LANDLORD REQUIRES THE PROPERTY FOR HIS OWN HOME[33]

In addition, this ground is available where the landlord or one of the joint landlords requires the house as his or his spouse's only or principal home. Again there must be written notice at the start of the tenancy. This ground is not available to those who become landlords by purchase after the start of the tenancy. There is no requirement that the landlord "reasonably" require the premises. "Require" does not imply any element of necessity nor that it is reasonable to regain the property. It is simply that, in the judgment of the landlord, regaining the property fits into his plans. Any other reading would seem to go against the "laissez faire" approach of the 1988 legislation. It might be argued that in terms of plain meaning "requires" implies an element of need. The dictionary does give the meanings "to need" and "to necessitate". It gives these however, after "to ask", "to demand" ,"to exact", "to direct", "to call for" and "to request". There is no case law which relates to this specific ground. It is enough if the landlord states that the property is required for occupation for himself or his spouse's only or principal home. In certain circumstances it is hard not to imagine the court rejecting the ground as a sham. In a pre-1988 Act instance, a Minister had retired to rural Perthshire and rented out a flat in Garnethill, Glasgow. He sought to repossess this flat, claiming he required it for his own occupation. This kind of scenario might well be rejected as so improbable as to amount to an attempt to evade the Rent Acts. To grant the order the court would need to be entirely satisfied that the intention was to move back to urban living with its access to hospitals, cafes and shops and the matter would be down to credibility. The Court of Appeal suggested in a case involving the phrase "required as a residence"

---

[31] *Roxburgh DC* v *Collins* 1991 SCLR 575.
[32] See Chapter 3.
[33] HSA 1988, Sch 5, ground 1(b).

that, while this did not mean more than wants, there had to be a *bona fide* intention to return.[34] There had to have been a good reason, in the view of Megaw LJ for the omission of the word "reasonably".[35]

DISPENSING WITH NOTICE

The sheriff can dispense with the need for notice if it is considered reasonable to do so. As noted the test is whether it is reasonable to dispense with the notice. As noted in *Boyle* v *Verrall*[36] the Court of Appeal looked at the position of owner-occupier landlords who purported to rent out on a short assured tenancy but failed to serve the necessary formal notice that the tenants'rights were limited. Thinking that the tenants had no security of tenure the landlords did not, of course, serve a ground 1 notice. The Court of Appeal were of the view that it was "just and equitable" to dispense with this notice looking to all the circumstances. These included informal conversations about the landlords reoccupying the rented property and early written notice that the property would be required. Also of relevance were the respective needs of the parties – the landlords' alternative accommodation was not really satisfactory for someone who needed to work in London. The tenants, for their part, had no particular need to live in that particular area of London and their lack of income would be met by housing benefit wherever they stayed, in the view of the Court of Appeal.

MORTGAGE DEFAULT[37]

This ground is available where a heritable security over the house existed before the creation of the tenancy and where the property is being repossessed following default by the debtor. The tenant must have been given written notice that possession might be recovered under this ground although the sheriff has the power to dispense with this requirement where he considers it reasonable. Problems have arisen where lenders are keen that Housing Associations should incorporate this ground into their agreements while the Associations are not keen to do so.

This is an example of a case where the contractual rights of the tenant may not be fulfilled because of the owner losing his/her rights due to the lender repossessing. Where the landlord has unlawfully leased property without the written consent of the creditor, it is likely that a sheriff will dispense with the requirement for notice. Where a creditor recovers possession against a defaulting landlord only to find that an unauthorised tenancy exists, the creditor institution has two options. It can raise an action to have the unlawful tenancy reduced, or it can raise an action for

---

[34] *Kennealy* v *Dunne* [1977] QB 837, dealing with the test under the protected tenancy regime per Stephenson LJ at 850.
[35] *Ibid* at 851.
[36] [1997] 1 EGLR 25.
[37] HSA 1988, Sch 5, ground 2.

recovery of possession under this ground. The Home Owner and Debtor Protection (Scotland) Act 2010 provides that for the circumstances of persons such as spouses and partners where repossession is threatened, this coverage does not extend to unlawful tenants.[38] The repossession must proceed using s 18.[39] No notice to quit is required where the lease is being irritated[40] although the terms of the irritancy clause must be complied with. The tenant is entitled to have the grounds of repossession either repeated as they stand or at least a version of them.[41]

OFF-SEASON HOLIDAY PROPERTY[42]

This is designed for properties rented out "between seasons" which aims to guarantee that the property will be available for renting out for the next season. It is available where property is rented out for a period not exceeding 8 months and was at some time within the 12 months prior to the start of the tenancy occupied for a holiday. The same conditions as regards notice at the commencement of the tenancy apply here too but may not be dispensed with by the sheriff. This means that the landlord must start out using the property as a holiday let prior to renting out in the off-season to be in a position to take advantage of this ground.

For the purposes of this ground the tenancy is treated as not exceeding 8 months if it can be terminated at the option of the landlord before the expiry of 8 months from the start of the tenancy. Where there are options for renewal by the tenant which if added to the original length of the tenancy exceed 8 months then such an agreement is regarded as exceeding 8 months. The term "holiday" has been interpreted flexibly in relation to Rent Act evasions to include "working" holidays.[43]

EDUCATIONAL BODY NON-STUDENT TENANCIES[44]

This ground is more restricted than simply student tenants. That is not enough, although the author has come across landlords who went to elaborate lengths to claim to be some kind of college to come within what they understood to be this exception. It covers rentings to those not exempted by Sch 4.[45] This

---

[38] HODPSA 2010, s 5.
[39] *Tamroui* v *Clydesdale Bank plc* 1997 SLT (Sh Ct) 20.
[40] *Cameron* v *Abbey National Building Society* 1999 Hous LR 19.
[41] *RBS* v *Boyle* 1999 Hous LR 42 and 67.
[42] HSA 1988, Sch 5, ground 3.
[43] *Buchmann* v *May* [1978] 2 All ER 993; *McHale* v *Daneham* (1979) 249 EG 969; see also T Lyons, "The Meaning of 'Holiday' under the Rent Acts" (1984) *Conveyancer and Property Lawyer* 286.
[44] HSA 1988, Sch 5, ground 4.
[45] For the purposes of para 7 of Sch 4 to the Housing (Scotland) Act 1988 (tenancies granted to a person who is pursuing or intends to pursue a course of study which cannot be assured tenancies), there are specified the following educational institutions and bodies of persons or classes thereof: (a) any university, university college and any

took tenancies rented to students by recognised educational institutions outwith the scope of the 1988 legislation. Educational institutions, in addition, are encouraged to rent out out of term. If they have been renting out accommodation in the previous 12 months to a student then they may rent out to a non-student and rely on the mandatory ground to gain repossession. Such a tenancy must not exceed 12 months. As indicated the landlord must be one of the educational institutions specified in the Act.[46] The non-student tenant must be given notice at the commencement of the tenancy. There is *no* provision here for the sheriff to waive the requirement if the landlord fails to provide proper notice to the tenant.

MINISTER/LAY MISSIONARY PROPERTY[47]

The interests of clerical personnel to have access to convenient accommodation are reflected in this ground. It arises where the property is held for occupation by a minister or full-time missionary as a residence from which to perform the duties of the religious office and where the property is required for occupation by a minister or missionary. There must be prior written notice to the tenant that possession might be recovered on this ground and there is no provision for the landlord's failure to comply being waived by the sheriff.

DEMOLITION OR RECONSTRUCTION WORK[48]

This ground covers any landlord seeking to carry out substantial demolition and construction work. Its main use was expected to be by housing associations.[49] Before the 1988 Act housing associations had experienced some problems in this area with tenants in decants.[50] It is available where any landlord, including Housing Associations, intends to demolish or reconstruct or carry out substantial works on the house or building of which it forms part and the proposals are likely to be hampered by the tenant. This ground is only available to landlords who owned the property before the tenancy was created. The landlord must establish that he cannot reasonably carry out the intended work without the tenant giving up possession of the property, This ground may be brought into play by a landlord where the work can be carried out only if the tenant accepts a variation in the terms of the tenancy or accepts

---

constituent college, school or hall of a university; (b) any central institution within the meaning of s 135(1) of the Education (Scotland) Act 1980; (c) any college of education within the meaning of that section; (d) any institution for the provision of further education within the meaning of that section which is administered by an education authority; (e) any association approved by the Secretary of State under reg 8 of the Further Education (Scotland) Regulations 1959; and (f) The Royal College of Surgeons of Edinburgh.
46 Assured Tenancies (Exceptions) (Scotland) Regulations 1988 (SI 1988/2068).
47 HSA 1988, Sch 5, ground 5.
48 *Ibid*, ground 6.
49 HC First Scottish Standing Committee, col 697; 16 February 1988.
50 *Charing Cross and Kelvingrove Housing Association* v *Kraska* 1986 SLT (Sh Ct) 42.

an assured tenancy of part of the house or both of these and the tenant refuses to accept such a change. In addition the ground is available where the work cannot be carried out even if the tenant accepts a variation in the terms of the tenancy or an assured tenancy of only part of the house or both. Although this ground is one where the law-abiding, rent-paying tenant has no inkling that there might be a possibility of eviction, it seems to be a situation where the greater "good" of improving the property can override the tenant's normal right to continue in occupancy even where there has been no misconduct.

TENANCY INHERITED UNDER A WILL OR ON INTESTACY[51]

Where under the will of the tenant or where there is no will, on intestacy, the tenancy passes to another party the landlord may get the property back provided that proceedings are started not later than 12 months after the death of the former tenant. The sheriff may direct that this 12-month period be computed from the date when the landlord became aware of the former tenant's death. There is no indication as to what criteria should be used by a sheriff in making such a decision and it will be up to the landlord to establish the circumstances in which he failed to be aware of the tenant's death. The statute specifies that acceptance of rent from a new tenant is not to be regarded as creating a new tenancy unless the landlord agrees in writing to a change in the amount of rent, the period of the tenancy, the premises which are let or any other terms of the tenancy – as compared with the tenancy prior to the death. The policy behind this ground was expressed during the passage of the Housing (Scotland) Bill in 1988 as being the need to encourage the growth of investment by removing a right to succession.[52] It should be noted that succession to residential tenancies during the 20th century has generally been in terms of the statutory succession provisions of the various Rent Acts. These rights to succession to the family home were in effect ended in the Housing (Scotland) Act 1988 which only belatedly recognised the right of the surviving spouse to succeed to an assured tenancy,[53] which specifically exempts such succession from being covered by ground 7.[54]

3 MONTHS' RENT ARREARS[55]

3 months' arrears at the date of s 19 notice AND date of hearing[56] There has not been much discussion of this in the case law but there is the dual requirement which must be satisfied that "at least 3 months rent lawfully due from the tenant is in arrears":

---

[51] HSA 1988, Sch 5, ground 7.
[52] HC First Scottish Standing Committee, col 700; 16 February 1988.
[53] HSA 1988, s 31(1); see also Chapter 7.
[54] *Ibid*, s 31(3).
[55] *Ibid*, Sch 5, ground 8.
[56] *Ibid*.

at the date of service of the notice of proceedings for possession under s 19;
at the date of the hearing.

Possession, then, may be recovered where the tenant is at least 3 months
in arrears with the rent at both the date of service of the notice and at
the date of the hearing. The original wording in the Bill was changed to
make it clear that a full 3 months' arrears was required rather than what was
originally proposed which was simply "some rent lawfully due … more
than 3 months in arrears".[57] Solicitors have indicated that they have not
used this ground with any confidence that possession will be secured since
it is always vulnerable to the tenants reducing the arrears prior to the court
appearance. McAllister suggests that tenants will have limited room for
manoeuvre as they will receive only a s 19 notice of proceedings of possession
of 2 weeks.[58] Where, however, the lease does not specifically provide for the
tenancy automatically terminating by irritancy in this situation, a notice
of irritancy will be required. This would seem to be a prudent course of
action to ensure the tenant is aware that the lease is being brought to an
end and the reason for same. The English equivalent ground for monthly
and weekly tenancies was reduced to 2 months' arrears in 1996.[59]

The question of rent arrears due to problems with housing benefit
payments was at one time highly problematic.[60] The Homelessness etc
(Scotland) Act 2003 gave sheriffs in possession cases under this ground
discretion to not make an order where the rent arrears were the result of
a delay or failure in the payment of housing benefit not as a result of the
tenant's acts or omissions.[61]

In addition, in many instances of large arrears there is a dispute about
the level of services or quality of the accommodation behind the non-
payment rather than simply wilful refusal to pay and the issue of abatement
may well be relevant.[62] In such circumstances the tenant could hardly be
regarded as being in arrears of rent "lawfully due".

Discretionary grounds of possession

Introduction

The nine grounds in Pt II of Sch 5 to the Housing (Scotland) Act 1988
are discretionary. Here the sheriff may order possession. If the sheriff is
satisfied that any of the grounds in Pt II are satisfied she must not make
an order unless she considers it reasonable to do so. The discretion of the

---

[57] HC First Scottish Standing Committee, col 702; 16 February 1988.
[58] McAllister (2002) at 15.43.
[59] Housing Act 1996, s 101.
[60] On the previous situation on housing benefit arrears, see *Razack* v *Osman* [2001] 9 Ch
      426 and Mitchell (2002).
[61] HSA 2003, s 12, amending ss 18 and 20 of the HSA 1988.
[62] On abatement in the modern era, see *Renfrew DC* v *Gray* 1987 SLT (Sh Ct) 70.

sheriff, then, is a positive one. The sheriff must address the question of reasonableness rather than them be taken to have been satisfied. This is an issue which has been clearly established in case law in relation to the similarly worded discretionary powers in relation to repossession of social rented tenancies[63] and was required in the old "controlled rent" regime.[64]

The sheriff must be satisfied about overall reasonableness before granting a possession order under one of the grounds in Pt II of Sch 5. It involves taking into account every relevant circumstance affecting the interests of the parties such as their conduct and any possible hardship which might result if the order were to be made as a well as the interests of the public.[65] The question of the possibility of the tenant obtaining other accommodation is relevant as well as any rights under statute such as legislation for homeless persons. The steps to be followed before a case comes to court and the various procedural issues which will enable a successful recall of any decree are outwith the scope of this text and are dealt with admirably elsewhere.[66]

ALTERNATIVES AVAILABLE TO THE COURT

The Housing (Scotland) Act 1988 makes provision for the sheriff to adjourn, sist, suspend or postpone possession.[67] Where the landlord is seeking possession under one of the discretionary grounds the action can be postponed or sisted. Even where a possession order is granted it is possible; for the sheriff to postpone the date when the eviction is to take place. Alternatively, conditions can be set concerning payment of rent arrears or about any other conditions.

POSTPONING EXECUTION OF A POSSESSION ORDER

The sheriff can exercise the option to halt execution of the possession order or postpone the date. The sheriff also decides how long the period of these postponements is to last. Most postponements are for up to 1 month. Conditions are also frequently imposed as to rent payments and arrears in this context. In practice it may be that if the tenant keeps to any

---

[63] See *Midlothian DC* v *Drummond* 1991 SLT (Sh Ct) 67; *Midlothian DC* v *Brown* 1991 SLT (Sh Ct) 80; *Renfrew DC* v *Inglis* 1991 SLT (Sh Ct) 83; *Gordon DC* v *Acutt* 1991 SLT (Sh Ct) 78.

[64] *Smith* v *Poulter* [1947] KB 339 – even where the issue of rent arrears was not raised the court was required to do so.

[65] *Minchburn Ltd* v *Fernandez* [1986] 2 EGLR 103 – a tenant of 24 years' standing being evicted to a different flat to allow upgrading. The decision should have addressed the length of time of possession and the effect on the tenant's personal situation; the landlord's reason for deciding to obtain possession. Only the comparison of noise in the new place, raised by the tenant, was considered. Case remitted back for further consideration.

[66] See Stalker (2007); Mitchell (2002); Collins and O'Carroll (1997).

[67] HSA 1988, s 20.

other conditions imposed the possession order may not be operated and the assured tenancy continues. Typically this would occur where a schedule of repayments of arrears of rent is fixed and the tenant keeps to this.

IMPOSING CONDITIONS IN ADJOURNMENTS OR POSTPONEMENTS

When adjourning any possession action or postponing the operation of possession the sheriff is required by the Act to impose conditions where tenants are in arrears or there are payments due for occupation after the end of the tenancy.[68] There is an exception if the sheriff considers that to impose conditions would cause exceptional hardship or would otherwise be unreasonable.[69] The sheriff has discretion to impose any other conditions which he thinks fit such as concerning behaviour or treatment of the premises where the tenant's past behaviour or treatment of the premises is the ground for possession.[70]

CANCELLING A POSSESSION ORDER

The sheriff may cancel a possession order in the same way as under the Rent (Scotland) Act 1984 if the tenant abides by the conditions which they have imposed. This would apply where either rent arrears are cleared or where a tenant whose actions caused a nuisance is able to show that there has been a change in behaviour.[71]

RIGHTS TO SISTS AND POSTPONEMENTS OF MEMBERS OF THE FAMILY, SPOUSES/ COHABITANTS

If there is a spouse or cohabitant with occupancy rights living in the premises when possession proceedings are started, those partners have the same rights to get sists or postponements in the possession action.[72] No distinction is made between spouses and cohabitants in the legislation. The view has been adopted that the occupancy rights of spouses are the same as the rights of cohabitants to apply to have their rights determined by the courts.[73] This appears to be a somewhat doubtful proposition.

Specific Discretionary grounds

SUITABLE ALTERNATIVE ACCOMMODATION[74]

Although the availability of alternative accommodation is less likely in the private sector than in social housing this ground was encountered

---

[68] HSA 1988, s 20(3).
[69] *Ibid.*
[70] *Ibid.*
[71] *Ibid*, s 20(4).
[72] *Ibid*, s 20(5).
[73] *McAlinden* v *Bearsden and Milngavie DC* 1986 SLT 191.
[74] HSA 1988, Sch 5, ground 9.

from time to time during the period when the protected tenancy regime under the Rent (Scotland) Act 1984 covered private rented housing. There is extensive case law from this period although the issue does not appear to have been a feature of the assured tenancy operations. This may be attributed to the fact that the vast majority of landlords have very small property portfolios. As we note elsewhere, 75 per cent of landlords are individuals and the average property holding is 1.3 dwellings.[75] Since most landlords operate on a part-time basis the chances of them having suitable alternatives properties to offer are not high. In addition, two out of three dwellings are owned by landlords who started renting in the last decade and who tended to buy one or two properties as a way of ensuring they had income in their retirement.[76] Landlords may regain their property where they are able to offer accommodation broadly equivalent to the existing tenancy or where generally satisfactory conditions are on offer. This accommodation may come from the local authority. Here a certificate that the accommodation will be provided is conclusive as to its suitability.[77] If the landlord is supplying the accommodation, however, the criteria are that the sheriff must be satisfied that the accommodation is reasonably suitable to the needs of the tenant and his family.[78] This is determined by looking at proximity to the place of work[79] and if it is reasonably suitable to the means of the tenant and to the needs of the tenant and his family as regards extent and character.[80] This covers certain aesthetic elements but does not cater to the specific lifestyle requirements of the displaced tenant.[81] There is an overall requirement as to reasonableness which must also be satisfied which can include quite individualised matters such as the specific needs of tenants to have disabled relatives visit and lack of any particular reason for another tenant to occupy the property in question.[82]

TENANT WITHDRAWS A NOTICE TO QUIT[83]

There may be a number of very good reasons why tenants might withdraw a notice to quit such as where a job offer falls through or family circumstances change. The ground applies where the tenant has given notice to quit but stays on after this has expired in either the whole or part of the premises. In addition proceedings for possession must have been started by the landlord within 6 months of the expiry of the tenant's notice to quit as

75   Scottish Government (2009d) .
76   *Ibid*, para 2.18.
77   HSA 1988, Sch 5, Pt III, paras 1 and 3(2).
78   *Ibid*, para 3.
79   *Yewbright Properties Ltd* v *Stone* (1980) 40 P & CR 402; *Minchburn* v *Fernandez* (1986) 19 HLR 29.
80   HSA 1988, Sch 5, Pt III, para 3(b).
81   *Redspring* v *Francis* [1973] 1 All ER 740; *Siddiqui* v *Rashid* [1980] 1 WLR 1018.
82   *Trustees of Kinrara Estate* v *Campbell* 1999 Hous LR 55.
83   HSA 1988, Sch 5, ground 10.

well as there not being a new tenancy either expressly or impliedly entered into. This ground does not apply if a new tenancy has been entered into.[84] There have never been any reports of this ground being an issue in practice although its rationale was discussed in the Salisbury Report where its introduction received approval.[85]

PERSISTENT DELAY IN RENT PAYMENT[86]

This was a ground new to the Rent Acts in 1988 and was originally to have been one of the mandatory grounds of possession and appeared as such in the first version of the Bill. No assistance can be gained from the business tenancy sector since the element of discretion given to sheriffs in this ground has no parallel in commercial leases. In the debates on the ground it was suggested that persistently meant "repeatedly" or "over a long time".[87] For this ground to be satisfied all that is required is that "the tenant has persistently delayed in paying rent which has become lawfully due" even if at the date on which proceedings for possession are begun there are no rent arrears. This has not been extensively used on its own due to the problem of determining what is meant by "persistently delayed paying rent". Since this is a discretionary ground ie the sheriff must be satisfied on the overall ground of reasonableness, it is hard to imagine a sheriff being happy to evict someone from their home where the landlord has merely been inconvenienced. One Housing Association with whom the author was in touch in the 1990s was keen to evict a tenant who always paid late. They surmised he did this to annoy them and he had succeeded. They did not go ahead with seeking to evict on this ground.

It is not necessary that the rent be in arrears when the proceedings are begun. However, one of the problems which has bedevilled the rental market since its introduction has been the delays and difficulties experienced by tenants since housing benefit was introduced by the Social Security and Housing Benefits Act 1982. Drawing a parallel with the treatment of like issues under the homeless persons legislation, such a problem, being outwith the control of tenants, would not amount to persistent delay. It lacks the conscious element implied. In the 1990s landlords in the private sector, as Jonathan Mitchell pointed out, did, then, have the option to insist on direct payment of housing benefit where there are rent arrears of at least eight weeks. The authority had the discretion to pay direct where there are either no arrears or less arrears. Housing benefit is now paid direct to tenants and this particular issue should resolve itself. If the rent is in arrears as a consequence of a delay or failure in the payment of relevant housing benefit, then the sheriff

---

[84] HSA 1988, Sch 5, ground 10(d).
[85] Salisbury Report (1923), para 21.
[86] HSA 1988, Sch 5, ground 11.
[87] HC First Scottish Standing Committee, col 704; 16 February 1088.

must not make an order for possession unless he considers it reasonable to do so.[88]

Nor would the ground cover non-payment by tenants done in pursuance of legal rights. This occurs where tenants use their right to withhold rent to put pressure on landlords to carry out repairs or as a tactic in a dispute over the obligations of the parties under the lease. One might expect that with the introduction of the private rented housing committee and its work dealing swiftly with disputes over repairs,[89] withholding of rent would become a tactic less required.

RENT DUE[90]

This was treated as part of the breach of tenancy obligations under the Rent (Scotland) Act 1984 but was separated out for assured tenancies. Two elements are required in this ground of possession.

(1) rent must be unpaid at the date when the action for recovery is started;

(2) rent must also be in arrears at the date of service of notice. The need for this second element is, of course, not necessary where the sheriff dispenses with the need for service of the notice of proceedings for possession.

This is the principal ground of possession used against tenants in the private sector.[91] Due to the problems with payments for housing benefit there will be situations where the arrears are "technical" and sheriffs will need to be satisfied as to reasonableness before granting an order for possession in terms of s 12 of the Homelessness etc (Scotland) Act 2003.

BREACH OF OBLIGATIONS OF TENANCY[92]

Establishing that there has been a breach is the first step in this two-stage process which involves, significantly, looking at reasonableness. It comes into play where any obligation of the tenancy has been broken or not performed. Breach needs to be material, involving something more than a triviality. A condition banning any pets would, for instance, be breached by a tenant having a dog in the premises but a goldfish would surely be dismissed as irrelevant. The presence of a parakeet or budgie, however, would be of significance for a landlord looking to evict on breach. The presence of a single pet, where the conditions forbids pets in the plural, is still a breach of the tenancy conditions.[93] The fact that a

---

88 Homelessness etc (Scotland) Act 2003, s 12.
89 See Chapter 4.
90 HSA 1988, Sch 5, ground 12.
91 Report on the Private Rented Sector (2009); interestingly, though, given the difficulties of determining the meaning of "persistent", Stalker (2007) reports that this ground is in practice often combined with "persistent delay in payment" – ground 12–177.
92 HSA 1988, Sch 5, ground 13.
93 *Glasgow DC* v *Murray* 1997 Hous LR 105.

dog had been purchased for the protection of the tenant's wife during the Yorkshire Ripper's years of activity did not assist a tenant whose tenancy agreement forbade such animals – the court did note that the Ripper had been imprisoned and that the tenant and his wife had divorced.[94] The absence of an equivalent to the special repossession head in the public sector has led housing associations to use this head of possession when tenants have given false or misleading information to obtain tenancies with mixed success. This is likely to be used rather than reduction since following an Outer House decision, the landlord would still need to satisfy a sheriff in terms of the Schedule that the granting of possession order was reasonable.[95]

The breach must also be a term of the tenancy rather than a breach of a collateral personal agreement. The kind of term found in commercial tenancies that the existence of a breach is in the sole judgment of the landlord is not conclusive insofar as the sheriff still requires to be satisfied as to the reasonableness of granting a possession order.[96] The suggestion based on case law from the commercial rented sector that the bankruptcy of a tenant[97] of residential accommodation could amount to breach in terms of ground 13 seems to the author somewhat doubtful[98] since there are in existence mechanisms to ensure that the rent of those with limited funds is paid through Housing Benefit. It is not a term in residential leases which has been encountered extensively. The existence, however, of such a lease condition did occur in relation to a purported short tenancy under the Rent (Scotland) Act 1984 and its efficacy was not an issue which was raised in that instance.[99]

CONDITION OF HOUSE DETERIORATED[100]

Many of these grounds have their origins in earlier legislation. This ground appeared in the first emergency rent legislation, the Increase of Rent and Mortgage Interest (War Restrictions) Act 1915 and there is a modified version covering protected tenancies.[101] It was expanded to take in an issue which was introduced when public sector tenants were given security of tenure in the Tenants' Rights etc (Scotland) Act 1980, namely common parts such as stairways, lifts and halls. Establishing deterioration in connection with individual houses may be possible on failure to use a reasonable degree of diligence to preserve the property from harm such as damp by heating the property. One

---

[94] *Green* v *Sheffield City Council* (1994) 26 HLR 349.
[95] *Govanhill Housing Association* v *Palmer* 1997 Hous LR 133.
[96] HSA 1988, s 18(4).
[97] *Cadogan Estates Ltd* v *McMahon* [2001] 1 AC 378.
[98] Gordon and Wortley (2009) at 594.
[99] *William Grant & Son Distillers* v *McClymont* 2009 SCLR 388.
[100] HSA 1988, Sch 5, ground 14.
[101] Rent Act 1984, Sch 2, case 3.

would expect the problem for the future increasingly to centre around putting this notion into practice. There are real problems involved in heating and ventilating property with poor thermal qualities as expressed in the U-value. Since the *Gunn* decision in the Inner House[102] and *Guy* in the Outer House,[103] the landlord can no longer simply blame the tenant as some public sector landlords tried to do in the past. *Gunn* goes further in making it clear that landlords who blame the tenant must specify exactly how the tenant's actions have caused the condition of the property to deteriorate.[104] So as indicated above landlords wishing to attribute the dampness to the lifestyle of the tenants through their failure to heat and ventilate must specify in what way the tenant has been deficient.[105] A bald assertion is no defence to as claim that the property is damp. It is now not possible simply to assert that the way the tenant lives is the root cause of the problem. This is illustrated in the *Deans* case of 2009 from Glasgow Sheriff Court.[106]

As for common parts, in the absence of effective control through door-entry systems one could imagine landlords experiencing evidential problems in convincing sheriffs that the poor condition of common stairs is caused by specific tenants.[107]

NUISANCE, ANNOYANCE ANTI-SOCIAL BEHAVIOUR AND ILLEGAL/IMMORAL USE OF PREMISES[108]

Losing one's tenancy as the result of nuisance or annoyance was also a feature of the first Rent Act in 1915 in a truncated form covering nuisance or annoyance.[109] The conviction for illegal or immoral purposes was added in and was included in all such legislation from 1920.[110] As this is the same as the ground found in the Rent (Scotland) Act 1984[111] and the Housing (Scotland) Act 2001 for regulated and secure tenancies the precedents which

---

[102] *Gunn* v *Glasgow City Council* 1997 Hous LR 3.

[103] *Guy* v *Strathkelvin DC* 1997 SCLR 405.

[104] See Chapter 4.

[105] *Guy* v *Strathkelvin DC* 1997 SCLR 405; see also *McGuire* v *Monklands DC* 1997 Hous LR 41.

[106] *Deans* v *Glasgow Housing Association Ltd* 2009 Hous LR 82.

[107] *Pace Glasgow City Council* v *Al Abassi* 2001 Hous LR 23 at 27 – here part of the tenant's unacceptable behaviour was keeping a lit barbecue on the common stair. It was reportedly used to heat the flat. The report does not make clear whether this was a single instance or standard practice.

[108] HSA 1988, Sch 5, ground 15.

[109] The original wording was simple. There could be no repossession "except on the ground that the tenant has committed waste or has been guilty of conduct which is a nuisance or annoyance to adjoining or neighbouring occupiers" – IRMIWRA 1915, s 1(3).

[110] Increase of Rent and Mortgage Interest (Restrictions) Act 1920, s 5(b). The Salisbury Committee wished to expand the wording to cover those who were "of immoral, drunken, or disorderly habits" – para 17.

[111] RSA 1984, Sch 2, case 2; HSA 2001, Sch 2, ground 8.

have emerged are relevant The first point to be made is that the courts have in the past taken the view that the tenant is responsible for all the activities of other occupants of the premises. Tenants have been evicted where they failed to control their families while living in the property,[112] while in prison[113] or when they were physically incapable of restraining the nuisance behaviour.[114] The protection for joint tenants is that the sheriff must be satisfied as to overall reasonableness.

Where there are criminal activities going on in the premises the precedents suggest a broad interpretation on this head of possession. Frequent or continuous use is not required, but a single conviction would probably be insufficient – although where the issue involved, say, drug-pushing as opposed to individual use, this could result in the exercise of the discretion against such a tenant. Where the tenant argues that the landlord has forfeited the right to seek repossession through acquiescence in the conduct or that this has been condoned, such a claim must be clearly demonstrable. It is not enough simply to indicate that there has been acceptance of rent after the alleged conduct.

The ground required that the tenant, a person residing or lodging with the tenant or *a person visiting the house* has acted in an anti-social manner in relation to a person residing, visiting or otherwise engaging in lawful activity in the locality or pursued a course of anti-social conduct in relation to a person residing, visiting or otherwise engaging in lawful activity in the locality. This ground has been altered substantially since it was introduced into the law, replacing the narrower Rent (Scotland) Act 1984 test covering "conduct which is a nuisance or annoyance to adjoining occupiers".[115] The case law, again stems principally from the social rented sector where the provisions are identical and provide a useful guide as to how the courts react.[116]

This has been expanded in terms of persons liable, those affected, the relevant locale and the nature of the activities.

- It now covers tenants, lodgers, residents or persons visiting the house acting in an anti-social manner.
- It covers not just neighbours but also anyone visiting, or otherwise engaged in lawful activity.
- It covers not just the property or adjoining property but the "locality".

---

[112] *R* v *Salford City Council, ex p Davenport* (1984) 82 LGR 89; *Glenrothes* v *Graham*, unreported, 14 Dec 1994.
[113] *SSHA* v *Lumsden* 1984 SLT (Sh Ct) 71; *R* v *Swansea City Council, ex p Thomas* (1982) 9 HLR 66.
[114] *R* v *Swansea City Council, ex p John* (1982) 9 HLR 58.
[115] RSA 1984, Sch 2, ground 2 (my emphasis).
[116] See below at p 217.

- It is no longer restricted to illegal or immoral activities but covers anti-social behaviour – defined as an action or course of conduct causing or likely to cause alarm distress nuisance or annoyance – and harassment.

The wording in the Housing (Scotland) Act 2001 dealing with repossession of social rented housing is very much the same, as the Appendix to this chapter shows. In the absence of case law dealing with assured tenancies, reference can usefully be made to the decisions discussed below. The major difference is the absence of any specific guidelines as the factors to be considered by the courts in determining whether to grant a possession. As is discussed below such matters as the nature, frequency and duration of anti-social activities, who carried out the offensive conduct and the effect on other people are all matters specifically mentioned in the social rented legislation.[117] The case law from the social rented sector, then, discussed below is worth examining.[118]

DETERIORATION OF FURNITURE[119]

This ground was introduced into rent legislation when previously unprotected tenants of furnished property were given the same protection as tenants of unfurnished property in the Rent Act 1974. There is little evidence of its use in the past which may stem from practical considerations. Landlords do not always provide an inventory of what furniture is provided in furnished premises. If they do there may be no indication as to its condition. In cases of deterioration, often known as "wear and tear", as opposed to destruction, establishing ill treatment rather than fair wear and tear may be a problem. In accounting practice it is standard practice to "write down" the value of new stock such as furniture over a number years by way of depreciation. This recognises that chairs, beds and bedding only have a finite life and at the end of a tenancy a landlord cannot reasonably expect the tenant to renew such items.

EX-EMPLOYEE TENANT[120]

This ground appears as a discretionary ground rather than as a mandatory one in the legislation. It allows individuals who have taken a tenancy as part of the terms of employment with their landlord in essence to argue that it is not reasonable for the landlord to obtain a possession order. The landlord will have to indicate why the property is required and a possession order would, presumably, not be granted simply without a good reason being given such as re-housing a relative. The availability

---

[117] HSA 2001, s 16(3).
[118] See below at p 217.
[119] HSA 1988, Sch 5, ground 16.
[120] *Ibid*, ground 17.

of properties to landlords for their own or a spouse's use is dealt with in ground 1 above. It is not necessary that there be a new employee requiring to be housed by the landlord.

It might be though that where occupancy derives from a contract of service rather than a lease such occupiers are not tenants but service occupiers and, hence, are not covered by the Rent Acts. It is not easy to see how this notion is compatible with the existence of ground 17. The case authority for the service occupancy as something other than a form of tenancy is of limited assistance. These cases address the issue of whether or not the more limited occupation rights of a service occupancy can be inferred from the nature of the employment conditions.[121]

The National Health Service and Community Care Act 1990 specified that tenancies entered into on or after 1 April 1990 were no longer to be treated as exempt from the coverage of the Housing (Scotland) Act 1988. This applies to many doctors and nurses *working*, for the National Health Service. This has meant that in the past 20 years or so such landlords have required to get to grips with the intricacies of grounds of repossession. In those instances which have come to the attention of the author the kinds of leases and their provisions have varied considerably. Some contain almost no clauses other than the designation of the parties, the property and the payment due. Others more closely resemble modern day tenancies. This is understandable since many of the leases were drawn up simply to reflect the temporary occupancy of doctors and nurses while working in a particular hospital in whose grounds the accommodation was located. They were rather like temporary on-site caretakers' houses and, as such, not expected to house the tenants for any great length of time.

SHORT ASSURED TENANCIES

Introduction

While the law relating to recovering possession of assured tenancies is complex and involves satisfying different tests most tenancies encountered in practice are in fact a "lite" version of the assured tenancy, the short assured tenancy. These lack security of tenure beyond the contractual term. The removal of security of tenure and return to market principles was never announced by the Government when introducing the short assured tenancy. Provided that the proper notices are given there is no need for the landlord to satisfy the sheriff that it is reasonable to grant a possession order. The landlord may, alternatively, use the standard assured tenancy possession grounds. The right to evict on notice, then, is in addition to the availability of the various conduct grounds of possession in Pt II of Sch 5 and any of the special mandatory grounds found in Pt I.

---

[121] See Chapter 3.

Requirements for an SAT possession order on notice

There are four formal requirements laid down in the legislation[122] about which a sheriff must be satisfied:

The short assured tenancy has reached its ish[123]

The automatic repossession option is not available *during* the tenancy so that any decision that it would be convenient for the landlord's financial situation to sell the property with vacant possession, for instance, would need to wait until the tenancy had run its initial or current term.

Tacit relocation is not operating[124]

There is in Scots law a need to serve a notice to quit to prevent any tenancy simply continuing by operation of the doctrine of tacit relocation.[125] If this is not done then a typical 6-month short assured tenancy would simply continue for a further 6-month period. The maximum period for which there can be tacit relocation is a year.

No further contractual tenancy is in operation[126]

If there has been a fresh contract entered into of the same property and with the same parties then this would have superseded any earlier contract and prevent the possession order.

The landlord has given the tenant notice that he requires possession of the house[127]

There must, in addition to a notice to quit be service of some kind of notice by the landlord on the tenant. The legislation does not specify a form and while the AT6 form used for assured tenancies is not really appropriate, it is required as an SAT is an assured tenancy. There is no sense in which the landlord has to be seeking the property for his use or that he has an objective "need" for the property rather than he would merely like to have it. The period of notice is to be either 2 months or such longer period as may have been specified in the tenancy agreement.[128] The section talks of when the notice must be "served" and from this one infers that it must be written rather than merely verbal.

In terms of issues which have arisen in interpreting this repossession *carte blanche* for landlords there is very limited Scottish case law which has come to the author's attention. What has been reported seems to be somewhat dubious. In *Johnstone* v *Finnernan* Sheriff Principal Bowen allowed a

---

[122] HSA 1988, s 33(1).
[123] Section 33(1)(a).
[124] Section 33(1)(b).
[125] See Chapter 3.
[126] Section 33(1)(c).
[127] Section 33(1)(d).
[128] Section 33(2).

repossession of a short assured tenancy commenced in 2000 where the court was satisfied after 5 days of evidence that the appropriate notices had been served.[129] Prior to the short assured tenancy, however, the tenant had been in occupation under some other arrangement. She claimed that this amounted to an assured tenancy which had not been properly terminated. The sheriff principal, however, was not persuaded that there had been contracting out of the Rent Acts. It seems reasonable to suppose that this had occurred since there was no suggestion that the previous arrangement was a short assured tenancy. The default position would then be an assured tenancy with its greater security of tenure rights. The other authors on this topic do not discuss this case.[130]

Scottish secure tenancies

INTRODUCTION

The single social tenancy was introduced by the Housing (Scotland) Act 2001, built on the foundations of the Housing (Scotland) 1987 and the Act which introduced security of tenure into the social rented sector for the first time, the Tenants' Rights etc (Scotland) Act 1980. The major distinction between this sector and the private sector is the requirement that the sheriff consider the issue of reasonableness in all instances. The 2001 statute is expressed slightly differently from the 1988 Act. It states that the court must make an order for possession if it appears that the landlord has a ground of possession and it is reasonable to make the order. The sheriff must actively consider the question of reasonableness, even if the action is not defended.[131] The sheriff must consider all issues. Those issues which have been mentioned in court deliberations have been many and various – the age of the tenant;[132] the hospital needs of a tenant's child;[133] the efforts of a tenant to make her house into a home;[134] the risk of further violence from an ex-partner;[135] the problems of the tenant in securing alternative accommodation;[136] loss of contact with a child;[137] and the effect on the tenant and the family.[138] No one factor is conclusive.

---

[129] 2003 SCLR 157.
[130] Gordon (2009); Stalker (2007).
[131] *Midlothian DC* v *Drummond* 1991 SLT (Sh Ct) 67; *Midlothian DC* v *Brown* 1991 SLT (Sh Ct) 80; *Renfrew DC* v *Inglis* 1991 SLT (Sh Ct) 83 and where the action was not defended – *Gordon DC* v *Acutt* 1991 SLT (Sh Ct) 78.
[132] *Battlespring* v *Gates* (1988) 11 HLR 6 at 11).
[133] *Govanhill HA* v *Malley* 1996 Hous LR 61.
[134] *Falkirk DC* v *McLay* 1991 SCLR 895 at 897.
[135] *Ibid.*
[136] *Minchburn* v *Fernandez* [1986] 2 EGLR 103.
[137] *Fife Council* v *Buchan* 2008 Hous LR 74 at 78.
[138] *Ibid* at 77; *West Lothian Council* v *Reape* 2002 Hous LR 58 at 60.

GROUNDS OF POSSESSION

Rent lawfully due or any other obligation of the tenancy broken[139]   The rent must be lawfully due. Here there have been disputes about entitlement to housing benefit leading to apparent rent arrears. In the assured tenancy regime in the private rented sector there is now a requirement that prior to making a decision to evict under the mandatory 3-month rent arrears ground that the sheriff must consider the question of reasonableness.[140] In the social rented sector – local authorities and housing association tenancies – all the grounds of possession require the sheriff to be satisfied that a possession is reasonable. There is also only one version of rent arrears available, namely that "(r)ent lawfully due from the tenant has not been paid".[141] Case law under the terms of the Housing (Scotland) Act 2001 has been limited in the Scottish courts. In one case there were significant rent arrears of just under £1,500. The tenant's rent was around £240 per month and the tenant earned that same sum when in employment. She had failed persistently over a period of years to make rent payments or any arrears payments and this factor told against her and eviction was ordered.[142] In another instance a tenant was in substantial rent arrears but there was an appeal pending about whether there should have been a cut in housing benefit. There was a possibility that the appeal tribunal might accept the tenant's claim which would result in a substantial reduction in the rent arrears to under £100. Here the sheriff chose to continue the case for 8 weeks awaiting the outcome of the tenant's housing benefit appeal. In the end, apparently, the council agreed to make a backdated payment of housing benefit and the housing benefit appeal and eviction action were rendered unnecessary.[143]

ILLEGAL/IMMORAL USE OF PREMISES[144]

It is worth looking at the elements in this ground in some detail. Ground 2 mirrors the old private-sector ground from as far back as the 1920 Rent Act. There are four elements

[1] house used for immoral purposes   This has not been used for many years and reflects the language of the previous century rather than modern day approaches to what tenants do in their properties. There is authority to suggest that there are no actual offences of using premises for immoral purposes which are not also illegal.[145] If, however, some newfangled

---

[139]   HSA 2001, Sch 2, ground 2.
[140]   Homelessness etc (Scotland) Act 2003, s 12.
[141]   HSA 2001, Sch 2, ground 1.
[142]   *Angus Housing Association Ltd* v *Fraser* 2004 Hous LR 83.
[143]   *Renfrewshire Council* v *Hainey* 2008 Hous LR 43.
[144]   HSA 2001, Sch 2, ground 2.
[145]   *S Schneiders & Sons Ltd* v *Abrahams* [1925] 1 KB 301 (CA).

form of lawful but immoral behaviour emerges then the statute has this covered.

[2] house used for illegal purposes   The older authorities suggest that the fact that a house is the site where an offence was committed such as an assault or possession of cannabis does not bring this ground into play.[146] It is rather different if it established that it is the site from which dealing is organised or takes place.[147]

[3] offence committed in the house   The seriousness of the offence has been discussed in the case law along with whether there are the limitations where there is only single offence in the context of reasonableness. The more serious an offence is, the greater likelihood of a single instance satisfying the "reasonableness" test.[148]

[4] offence committed in the locality of the house   Although the original legislation talked specifically of "adjoining occupiers", the whole scope has been extended in the modern versions of the repossession ground. What amounts to the locality has not been specifically discussed although "adjoining" was interpreted as meaning those who might be affected who are "sufficiently close or related, so that the behaviour or conduct of the tenant of the one affects the access to, or the occupation, or enjoyment of the other by its occupiers".[149]

There is the possibility of continuing the action pending behaviour of the tenant – in a case in early 2009 this action centred around loud music and parties. There was a 21-year-old tenant with a 16-month-old daughter. There were convictions for low-level drug dealing and cannabis possession. The neighbours wanted the tenant moved out although there had been no acts of antisocial behaviour since 6 May 2008. The sheriff, in deciding to adjourn the case for 6 months, stressed that this was *not* a decision on reasonableness *per se*.[150]

DISPUTING THE FACTS

The issues include "straightforward" actions involving the ranging of contradictory and conflicting evidence. In one case there were 4 days of proof with evidence about the noise and disturbances over a 3-year period at a property in Milton, Glasgow, especially between 2 am and 4.30 am. Eleven members of the neighbour relations officers team – including

---

[146] *Abrahams* v *Wilson* [1971] 2 All ER 1114.
[147] *South Lanarkshire Council* v *Nugent* 2008 Hous LR 92.
[148] *Fife Council* v *Buchan* 2008 Hous LR 74 – possession of firearms and forgery equipment leading to a 3-year 9-month jail sentence.
[149] *Cobstone Investments Ltd* v *Maxim* [1985] QB 150.
[150] *Glasgow Housing Association* v *Hetherington* 2009 Hous LR 28.

members of the "out of hours service" – gave evidence, with one ex-neighbour now residing at an undisclosed address.[151]

These have included the mental illness of the tenant. In *Langstane Housing Association* v *Morrow*[152] there was an action of repossession on grounds of anti-social behaviour by a tenant with mental health problems. In granting this the sheriff weighed the interests of other residents as well as noting that a reasonable offer of alternative accommodation had been declined by the tenant. The effect on the schooling of children of an eviction has been raised – *Glasgow Housing Association* v *Marshall*[153] – this was rejected in a rather cavalier manner on the grounds that not being "academically gifted" little was expected of her "scholastically" and it could not be said that her future prospects would be damaged by a change of school or indeed home. Where a child was diagnosed as suffering from attention deficit disorder this did not prevent repossession since it was pointed out that the pattern of complaints continued beyond the commencement of the treatment.[154]

ASSESSING REASONABLENESS

There are three issues which should be noted here in looking at whether it is reasonable to grant a possession order. The sheriff must not make an order on the discretionary grounds "unless he considers it reasonable to do so".[155]

All factors   In previous litigation on the operation of the Rent Acts it has been stated that in making a decision on reasonableness that all factors fall to be considered.[156]

The statutory "factors" (where social rented housing is involved)   Adopting the list of factors suggested as being worth considering in *Glasgow DC* v *Lockhart*[157] the Housing (Scotland) Act 2001 specifies a number of factors relating to the social context of the conduct complained of. When deciding whether it is reasonable to make an order "the court is to have regard, in particular to":

---

151 *Glasgow Housing Association* v *Marshall* 2006 Hous LR 56.
152 2005 Hous LR 103.
153 2006 Hous LR 56.
154 *City of Edinburgh Council* v *HT* 2003 Hous LR 74.
155 Housing (Scotland) Act 1988, s 18(4) [assured tenancy regime]; the requirement in the Housing (Scotland) Act 2001 [Scottish secure tenancies] is that the sheriff must make an order where the ground is satisfied and "it is reasonable to make the order" [s 16(2)(a)(ii)].
156 See above at p 216.
157 1997 Hous LR 99.

(a) the nature, frequency and duration of the relevant conduct;
(b) the extent to which that conduct was that of persons other than the tenant;
(c) the effect of the conduct on others;
(d) any action taken by the landlord to stop the conduct.[158]

It has been suggested that this list is not an exhaustive one and that rather it "no more than instances of the type of considerations which arise in the assessment of the reasonableness of eviction".[159] As far as anyone seeking possession under an assured tenancy is concerned, these would seem factors worth considering to point a decision about reasonableness in a structured way to likely issues of relevance. As Sheriff Holligan pointed out, the list does not include the question of the effect of the repossession on the tenant or his or her family,[160] although this was a factor in determining overall reasonableness.

The most reasonable course or any one of several competing reasonable courses Although there seems to be a plethora of individual factors surrounding an action for repossession from which a sheriff might determine that it is reasonable to make such an order the question has been raised as to whether or not the sheriff should be seeking out the most reasonable course or simply adopting one of several reasonable alternatives. This issue was raised where a tenant was convicted of supplying diamorphine from the property where she lived with her daughter.[161] The daughter as a member of the family aged over 16 was served notice of the proceedings for repossession as a "qualifying occupier".[162] The daughter knew of her mother's addiction to drugs but claimed she knew nothing of dealing. The decision centred on the credibility of the daughter's account as well as weighing the community interest of "zero tolerance" against the interests of daughter and the 8-month-old child. It was suggested that what the sheriff should do, in determining what was a reasonable course, was opt for the *most reasonable course* comparing all the possible outcomes. The alternative was that he might choose one of several equally reasonable but conflicting courses. An order, the solicitors agreed, should be made only if it is the most reasonable outcome overall. Sheriff Ross indicated that it was undoubtedly reasonable to attempt to evict a convicted drug dealer. Although the sheriff was not unequivocally of the view that the "most reasonable course" approach was always to be adopted he applied it in this instance.[163]

---

[158] HSA 2001, s 16(3).
[159] *Glasgow Housing Association* v *McNamara* 2008 Hous LR 38 at 41 per Sheriff Ross.
[160] *Fife Council* v *Buchan* 2008 Hous LR 74 at 77.
[161] *Glasgow Housing Association* v *McNamara* 2008 Hous LR 38.
[162] HSA 2001, ss 14 and 15.
[163] 2008 Hous LR 38 at 41, para 28.

CRIMINAL BEHAVIOUR

The issues of anti-social and criminal behaviour are rolled into each other in the social rented cases in relation to drugs as we have noted in relation to questions of reasonableness. There are other issues of criminality, though where the courts have considered the question of criminal convictions. The legislation is the same in the private and social rented sector:

> "The tenant, a person residing or lodging with the tenant or subtenant or a person visiting the house has –
>
> (a) been convicted of-
>
>   i. using or allowing the house to be used for immoral or illegal purposes; or
>
>   ii. an offence punishable by imprisonment committed, in or in the locality of, the house."[164]

The question of the location of the offence has been raised in a drug case where the conviction was based on dealing in a pub where the tenant was arrested for dealing in a public house.[165] Drugs and drug paraphernalia were found in house – electric scales, a knife, chopping board and cling film. No evidence was led about of dealing from the house and the neighbours had not complained. The sheriff accepted, however, that the tenant was "warehousing" large quantities of illegal drugs on the tenancy property.

The seriousness of gun offences was illustrated in *Fife Council* v *Buchan*[166] where the tenant was convicted of possession of a revolver and counterfeiting equipment. He received a sentence of 3 years and 9 months for the former and 1 year for the latter offence. The sheriff went through the "statutory factors" of s 16(3) of the Housing (Scotland) Act 2001 but noted that there might be other factors which would weigh more heavily in determining reasonableness.[167] These would include consideration of the effect on the tenant and his family.[168] The weighing-up of the seriousness of the offence and the desire of the landlords to improve the area against the impact on the life of the tenant and his family was a balancing act in which the sheriff was prepared to grant the order.

Condition of house deteriorated[169]

Where the landlord can satisfy the court, just as in the private sector, that the condition has been made worse by the tenant then this ground is available. The nature of social rented sector tenancy practice is such that

---

[164] HSA 2001, Sch 2, ground 2.
[165] *South Lanarkshire Council* v *Nugent* 2008 Hous LR 92.
[166] 2008 Hous LR 74.
[167] *Ibid* at 77.
[168] *Ibid*.
[169] HSA 2001, Sch 2, ground 3.

deterioration usually comes to light after the termination of the tenancy and the move or demise of the tenant.

Condition of furniture deteriorated[170]

Similarly, where furniture is supplied by the landlord this provides a ground for repossession. Although it is not usual to provide furniture in the social rented sector, this is done in some interim homeless accommodation. In such cases, however, the tenancy provided would usually be a short Scottish secure tenancy. As is noted below, this tenancy does not come with security of tenure.[171]

Tenant absent for at least 6 months[172]

This is different from the administrative abandonment procedure which is also available in the social rented sector but not extensively used.[173] This is a ground which is not available in this form in the private rented sector. Where there is no reasonable cause for this absence then the social landlord is entitled to recover the property. The courts have taken a fairly broad view of acceptable reasons for absences ranging from going to live with a partner for a period of around 18 months prior to their break-up[174] through to moving into a nursing home and staying on three occasions for a total of 12 months between 1997 and early 1999. Here it was deemed possible to retain the intention to possess the property.[175]

Tenant obtains tenancy fraudulently[176]

Where the tenant induces the landlord to grant the tenancy by a false statement made either knowingly or recklessly then there may be recovery. Even, however, where that has been a tenancy obtained by deception the landlord may necessarily not regain possession. As with all the grounds of possession in secure tenancies this is a discretionary ground. So the fact, for instance, that a tenant has obtained accommodation through claiming to have no accommodation when they have an existing tenancy, this is not always fatal. We can see this operating in one such deception case where the court took into account the personal circumstances of a young mother and the needs of her young child.[177] The same principle of concern by a mother

---

[170]   HSA 2001, Sch 2, ground 4.
[171]   See below at p 224.
[172]   HSA 2001, Sch 2, ground 5.
[173]   *Ibid*, ss 17–21; *Smith* v *Dundee City Council* 2003 Hous LR 55 on the limitations of the "short cut statutory procedure".
[174]   *Crawley Borough Council* v *Sawyer* (1988) 20 HLR 98.
[175]   *Hammersmith and Fulham LBC* v *Clarke* (2001) 81 P & CR DG 20 but see also *Islington LBC* v *Demetriou* [2001] CLY 4216 – albeit a county court decision.
[176]   HSA 2001, Sch 2, ground 6.
[177]   *Falkirk DC* v *McLay* 1991 SCLR 895.

for her 5-year-old child and the need to get away from damp property with problem neighbours would have produced the same result in a similar later case, had the sheriff required to rule on the matter.[178]

Tenancy overcrowded[179]

Although not in the modern private regime this is a ground for protected (pre-1989 private) tenancies. This has never been encountered in the author's experience. The nearest we come to is in one English Court of Appeal case on the rental of a very small property. The landlord sought to ensure that the tenant did not have a tenancy by requiring him to vacate the property for 90 minutes each day. While the tenant was successful in persuading the court that this arrangement was a sham, he still ended up losing the accommodation due to the local authority placing a closing order on the property as being unfit for human habitation. The room in question measured 12 feet 6 inches by 4 feet 3 inches.[180]

Designed/adapted for occupation by a person with special needs[181]

This ground applies where there is no longer a person with special needs in occupation but where the landlord has someone else with such needs whom they wish to accommodate. There is again an equivalent ground in the Rent (Scotland) Act 1984 covering protected tenancies[182] but not in the 1988 assured tenancy regime.

House part of group designed or adapted for special needs[183]

This covers such situations as occur where there might be a dedicated warden service for a cluster of houses and/or special warning lights available. Again the ground may be used where there is no longer such a person in occupation but the landlord requires it for someone else with such special needs. Again an equivalent in the Rent (Scotland) Act 1984 covering protected tenancies exists but not in the 1988 assured tenancy regime.

Landlord's leasehold interest terminated or due to[184]

Clearly if the landlord no longer owns the property there is a problem for the tenant and possession may be ordered. It is not clear what would

---

178 *West Lothian Council* v *Reape* 2002 Hous LR 58.
179 HSA 2001, Sch 2, ground 9.
180 *Aslan* v *Murphy* (No 2) [1990] 1 WLR 766 – reported along with *Aslan* v *Murphy (No 1)* and *Duke* v *Wynne*.
181 HSA 2001, Sch 2, ground 11.
182 RSA 1984, Sch 2, case 20 – although here it is a mandatory ground.
183 HSA 2001, Sch 2, ground 12.
184 *Ibid*, ground 13.

be the effect of a sheriff deciding that it was not reasonable to do so. No equivalent ground exists in the private rented sector and no instances of this have been encountered by the author. It covers situations where the landlord's own lease has either terminated or is due to terminate in the 6 months following the raising of the possession proceedings.

Islands Council exemption [185]

Where an Islands Council – Orkney Islands Council, Shetland Islands Council or Western Isles Council – holds a property as part of its education function and requires the property for a person who will be employed in education. This operates where the property is currently occupied by someone who used to be so employed or has succeeded to such a tenancy. The Council must satisfy the court that it cannot reasonably provide a suitable alternative house to the incoming teacher/ janitor.[186] There is no equivalent in the private rented sector.

Inter-spousal/partner transfer [187]

The landlord can seek to have a transfer approved by the court which results in the loss of the specific accommodation by the tenant. This occurs where the landlord wishes to transfer the tenancy to the tenant's current or former spouse or civil partner or cohabitant of 6 months' standing,[188] where there has been application for transfer and where one of the parties to the relationship no longer wishes to live together with the other in the house. There is a requirement that the local authority provide other suitable accommodation for the partner being evicted.[189] There is, again, no equivalent in the private rented sector.

SHORT SCOTTISH SECURE TENANCIES

Repossession in the case of short Scottish secure tenancies is intentionally very straightforward. It should, be noted, however, that such tenancies only come about in special circumstances. As we saw above,[190] they are confined to tenancies of a specified term of not less than 6 months. The tenancy automatically converts to a Scottish secure tenancy after 12 months if the landlord does not follow through on any repossession action which has been raised or if this unsuccessful.[191] If the landlord does, however, raise a

---

[185] HSA 2001, Sch 2, ground 14.
[186] *Ibid*, ground 14(b).
[187] *Ibid*, ground 15.
[188] Including same-sex partners – *ibid*, ground 15(b).
[189] *Ibid*, s 16(2)(c).
[190] See Chapter 3.
[191] HSA 2001, s 37.

repossession action and the appropriate procedure in terms of the legislation is adhered to,[192] the court must make an order for repossession if:

The short Scottish secure tenancy has reached its ish [193]

As in any tenancy the automatic repossession option is not available during the tenancy so that any decision that it would be convenient for the landlord's strategic plans to repossess the property would need to wait until the tenancy had run its initial term.

Tacit relocation is not operating [194]

There is in Scots law a need to serve a notice to quit to prevent any tenancy simply continuing by operation of the doctrine of tacit relocation.[195] If this is not done then a further short Scottish secure tenancy would continue for a further period. Unlike the short assured tenancy, however, this converts after 12 months into a Scottish secure tenancy.[196] As has been pointed out elsewhere, strictly speaking, this provision is otiose since the normal rules of Scots common law would not seem to apply to this statutory creature.[197]

No further contractual tenancy is in operation [198]

If there has been a fresh contract entered into of the same property and with the same parties then this would have superseded any earlier contract and prevent the possession order.

Notice has been given that the landlord requires possession of the house [199]

There must, in addition to a notice to quit, be service of a notice by the landlord on the tenant in the form specified under the statute. The period of notice is to be either 2 months or such longer period as may have been specified in the tenancy agreement,[200] or the date when the tenancy could have been brought to an end had it not been a short Scottish secure tenancy.[201] The section, like the Housing (Scotland) Act 1988 on which it modelled, talks of when the notice must be "served" and from this one infers that it must be written rather than merely verbal. There has been no case law which has come to the attention of the author at the time of writing.

---

[192] HSA 2001, s 36.
[193] *Ibid*, s 36(5)(a).
[194] *Ibid*, s 36(5)(b).
[195] See Chapter 3.
[196] HSA 2001, s 37.
[197] See annotations to Housing (Scotland) 2001 Act by Robson and Halliday (2001).
[198] HAS 2001, s 36(5)(c).
[199] *Ibid*, s 35(5)(d).
[200] *Ibid*, s 36(2) and (3).
[201] *Ibid*.

UNLAWFUL EVICTION AND HARASSMENT

Unlawful eviction

All occupiers of residential property are protected against unlawful eviction. This covers tenants as well as owners. It does not matter whether one is an assured tenant, protected tenant, sharing with a landlord or occupying under a licence, the provisions of the Rent (Scotland) Act 1984 are applicable. This would also include anyone occupying a matrimonial home who had had their occupancy rights declared as well as someone occupying prior to their seeking occupancy rights.[202] It would include any owner occupier or tenant who was the butt of attempts to have them move out of a property such as an ex-prisoner.[203] The legislation states that if any person deprives the residential occupier of any premises of his occupation of the premises or attempts to do he shall be guilty of an offence.[204] There is a defence where the accused can prove he believed and had reasonable cause to believe that the residential occupier had ceased to occupy the premises.[205]

The offence also covers situations where any person seeks to cause the occupier to give up occupation of the premises[206] or refrain from exercising any right or pursuing any remedy in respect of the premises.[207] If convicted a person shall be liable on summary conviction to a fine or to imprisonment for up to 6 months[208] and on conviction on indictment to a fine or imprisonment for a term not exceeding 2 years or both.[209]

In addition, even where the occupier has limited rights of security of tenure where there is a residential landlord it is made an offence for an owner to enforce his right to recover the premises other than by proceedings in court. As noted above, the tenant in such circumstances is only entitled to "reasonable notice", but may not be evicted by force.[210] It should be emphasised that the offences can be carried out by not only the landlord himself but by any other person.[211] This was the traditional

---

[202] See *McAlinden v Bearsden and Milngavie DC* 1986 SLT 191.

[203] Paedophile is hounded out – the flat where a former BB officer lived after release from jail for offences involving over 31,000 images of children was targeted, with windows smashed and "beast" daubed on the wall. The occupant duly left after his whereabouts had been reported in a national tabloid and he had been recognised by a neighbour – *Falkirk Herald*, 28 August 2008.

[204] RSA 1984, s 22(1).

[205] *Ibid.*

[206] *Ibid*, s 22(2)(a).

[207] *Ibid*, s 22(2)(b).

[208] *Ibid*, s 22(3)(a).

[209] *Ibid*, s 22(3)(b).

[210] *Ibid*, s 23(1).

[211] *Daily Mail*, 8 April 2010, reports a court case in which a JP, Stephanie Lippiatt, along with a bulky 6-feet 7-inch accomplice, evicted a tenant, smashing the furniture,shouting "It's my fucking furniture, I can break it if I want to".

mode of landlords like Rachman and Hoogstraten to employ others to do the actual intimidation and eviction.[212] It has also been used alongside the more subtle forms of persuasion known as "winkling". Here, the occupier is not threatened or abused but bought off with money.[213] Stalker has suggested that to persuade a tenant to accept the lesser rights of a short assured tenancy in place of a regulated or assured tenancy would be "winkling".[214] As indicated elsewhere, the case law suggests this would be problematic.[215] Whether or not providing a financial inducement would mean the new contract offered was acceptable has yet to be decided. One imagines this is an issue which is quantifiable in monetary terms. In the author's experience, decent law-abiding landlords who require to downsize and move back to a rental property themselves can calculate what kind of sum is needed to get back into the property. If they face a recalcitrant tenant and are law-abiding then the tenant is in a powerful position. The author has encountered a number of situations where the tenants were not money-fixated but were simply happy where they were in familiar surroundings. In such circumstances even "winkling" has its limits, as Donald Trump discovered in his Aberdeenshire golf project.

Harassment

As we can see in other parts of this work, there are various situations where harassment comes into play between neighbours, partners and ex-partners. The protections of the law in terms of non-harassment orders, ASBOs and matrimonial interdicts are covered elsewhere in the text.[216] We are concerned here principally with situations where landlords seek to cause an occupier to give up the occupation of the premises. Certain kinds of actions amount to harassment and give rise to a claim for civil damages as well the possibility of the perpetrator being jailed where unlawful eviction is concerned. Originally, the temporary "holding" legislation, introduced by the first Wilson Government, proscribed eviction without a court order and made it a criminal offence.[217] It also covered situations where the landlord withheld or withdrew services or furniture.[218] The test used

---

Her fines and costs amounted to over £9,000 – http://www.dailymail.co.uk/news/article-1264194/Magistrate-ordered-pay-9-000-illegally-evicting-Romanian-tenant.html.

[212] The most sympathetic fictional portrayal of such an individual can be found in Stephen Frears' *My Beautiful Laundrette* (1990) where Johnny (Daniel Day Lewis) is employed by Omar's Uncle, Nasser Ali (Saeed Jaffrey), to clear houses of unwanted occupiers. The process is referred to as "emptying".

[213] Nelken (1982) at 57ff.

[214] Stalker (2007) at 88.

[215] *Milnbank Housing Association v Murdoch* 1995 SCLR 684.

[216] See Chapter 10.

[217] Protection from Eviction Act 1964, s 1(3)(a).

[218] *Ibid*, s 1(3)(b).

in the subsequent the Rent Act 1965 covered situations where landlord had done things with "intent to cause" the occupier to give up occupation of the premises.[219] That test remains and there is in addition a somewhat broader offence introduced by the Housing (Scotland) Act 1988. This makes it a criminal offence if the landlord does "acts calculated to interfere with the peace and comfort of the residential occupier or members of his household".[220] Conduct is also proscribed where a landlord does an act which "knowingly or having reasonable cause to believe … is likely to cause the residential occupier of any premises" to give up occupation of the premises or cease to exercise any rights relating to such premises.[221]

Damages for unlawful eviction

One of the problems encountered by tenants and their advisors in the 1970s and 1980s was the incentives which landlords had to carry out unlawful eviction. The difference between the value of a property with vacant possession and one with a tenant with a regulated tenancy was considerable. In monetary terms the property was a lot less attractive. The tenant not only had the right to apply for a fair rent and to stay as long as they paid rent and kept to the terms of the lease, but there could succession to the tenancy on up to two occasions. This combination of restrictions on income stream and availability of the property for many years down the line meant a significant difference between the vacant possession price of a property and a similar one with a young sitting tenant, particularly a fit and healthy one with a family. This was recognised in the Housing (Scotland) Act 1988 where the measure of damages payable by a landlord who did unlawfully evict was fixed at the difference between the value of the landlord's interest with a sitting tenant and with vacant possession.[222] In a time of property appreciation and an undersupply of houses to rent this means a payment which can be significant. There is a corollary to this which was experienced in the early 1990s and at the end of the decade ending in 2009. When, for a range of reasons, there is less demand for rental property and landlords are competing for tenants the value of a property with a sitting tenant can outweigh that of a property with vacant possession. One assumes, though, that in such circumstances there would be no financial pressure on a landlord to unlawfully evict should they need to realise their assets. In this scenario the financially prudent course of action would be to leave the tenant where they are. If, however, for whatever reason, there were an unlawful eviction, the measure of damages would be problematic.

---

[219]　Rent Act 1965, s 30.
[220]　HSA 1988, s 38 (inserting s 22(2A) into the Rent (Scotland) Act 1984).
[221]　HSA 1988, s 36(2).
[222]　*Ibid*, s 37(1).

BACKGROUND

Prior to the first emergency Rent Acts legislation in 1915 tenants relied on their contracts for the rights they had to remain in the rented property. The concept of security of tenure had already been encountered in agricultural tenancies so that the notion of a split between property rights and the concept of a home had been pre-figured.[223] Although, the debates and comments at the time recognized this conflict, the operative assumption seems to have been that commercial private renting would continue to be the source of people's housing and what landlords wanted were steady tenants rather than great flexibility to liquidate their assets and re-invest elsewhere.

The simple notion that there was an untrammelled market in operation should not disguise the fact that access to housing had been an issue of difficulty for tenants for various reasons. First, there was the requirement to commit to a contract of greater length than the likely security of employment. This was an issue which exercised tenants and on which there had been conflict in Scotland. Tenants of poorer dwellings had obtained a measure of relief from the market in Scotland. The practice had been for annual lets agreed around February with entry at Whitsunday in May. The House Letting and Rating Act 1911 permitted monthly lets.[224] In addition, access to housing was affected by the power of landlords to select tenants who were compliant. This depended on them having recommendations from their previous landlords. It was not enough to be in waged work or have a character reference from one's local church it seemed. The crucial requirements were recommendations known as "factors' lines".[225]

While the Rent Acts have always contained the twin restrictions on levels of rent along with limitations on when landlords can evict tenants, it has been an issue which has exercised some landlords more than others. For landlords whose "lifeblood is property" and who are in the long-term business of renting out property, the fact that they cannot evict at will is of limited concern.[226] What they are concerned with is the steady throughput of adequate rentals. On the other hand, one of the complaints of landlords in published and televised material had been the inability of landlords effectively to control their own property.[227] The source of these complaints has been psychological rather than substantial when one looked at the wide

---

[223] Counterposing the notion of the "home" and "property rights" is discussed in a set of essays covering family law, land law and planning. Rights of residential tenants do not figure in the 15 essays – Hudson (2004).

[224] Damer (1983) at 89.

[225] Sim (1995) at 47–55.

[226] Harloe, Isaacheroff and Minns (1974).

[227] Letters from Landlords Small Landlords' Association 1980; submission to the House of Commons Environmental Committee, 24 October 1980.

range of situations when possession orders were available to landlords.[228] The situation before 1974 had afforded landlords rather greater flexibility in allowing them to decide the level of security of tenure of their tenants based on a limited amount of furniture. The specific situation, however, of the harassed private property owner unable to live in his own property had long been a myth.[229] The Francis Report did, however provide an indication of how perceptions of reality could arise. They noted although the legislation provided for a Rent Tribunal to postpone a notice to quit for up to 6 months to allow a displaced tenant to find accommodation there had been successive grants of such stays. There were odd examples of these 6-month extensions being granted for up to 3 years and exceptionally up to 10 years.[230] From this sprang the notion of all tenants as fixtures.

Despite this and the mandatory grounds for possession introduced in 1974[231] to allow owner occupiers, retired couples and off season holiday properties to be reclaimed without the need to satisfy the burden of reasonableness or the greater hardship rule, the ideological and mythological power of tenants to remain for ever in *all* property became prevalent. While no one denied that in certain circumstances the rights of tenants were extremely strong, the exceptions were sufficient to accommodate the short-term occasional renting of property particularly where the landlord's house exceeded his space requirements or where he was expecting to be out of the country for a period of time.

The problem of treating landlords as having identical interests ignored the specific perceived difficulties of those very suppliers of rental housing. These were centred on flexibility rather than levels of return. The structure of the Crossman legislation was geared in favour of landlords able to take advantage of economies of scale in preparation of submissions to rent officers and rent assessment committees.[232] Similarly, there is additional flexibility afforded to larger landlords who are able to take advantage of the alternative accommodation section to upgrade and rationalise their property holdings.

Elliott and McCrone noted, over 30 years ago, the active nature of the management and turnover of property required to make good returns for small landlords.[233] This process included block purchases, rental sales, student letting and bedsitter accommodation, resale and reinvestment. Essentially, what Elliott and McCrone described as the typical form of Edinburgh landlordism – "small time, local ... with special expertise in and knowledge of Edinburgh's housing".[234] This continues to be the situation in the second

---

228 Rent (Scotland) Act 1971, Sch 3.
229 Salisbury; Onslow; Marley; and Ridley Reports on owner occupier repossession.
230 Francis Report at 150ff.
231 Rent Act 1974, s 3.
232 Harloe, Isaacheroff and Minns (1974).
233 Elliott and McCrone (1975) 539.
234 *Ibid* at 553.

decade of the 21st century[235] and is how much housing in Scotland for rent during the nineteenth century was provided with the associated problems of return and tenant problems.

The tendency of market orientated commentators has been to assume that in the period prior to the introduction of control landlords experienced no problems in respect of rental returns[236] or obtaining vacant possession of their properties. This was a feature of renting at the lower income levels in 19th-century Britain.[237] Other commentators have also tended to lump the problems of the landlord/tenant relationship together with the specific impact of the Rent Acts on security and levels of rent and assume that the one flows directly from the other. Thus, one respected newspaper provided a report which mirrored the complaints of the Small Landlords' Association. They reported that the Rent Act was to blame for tenants doing £4,000 worth of damage to rented property raiding the meters and causing the landlord to develop ulcers and two heart attacks. The role of the Rent Acts in this scenario is irrelevant but that was where the blame was laid.[238] As the ASBO statistics make clear, anti-social behaviour is by no means confined to tenants and certainly not those in the private rented sector.[239]

---

[235] Private Rented Housing in Scotland (2009).
[236] Chapman (1971); Englander (1983).
[237] Robson (1979).
[238] *Sunday Times*, 8 September 1978 and 15 October 1978.
[239] Scottish Government (2009d).

APPENDIX 1: GROUNDS OF POSSESSION

Protected Tenancies	Assured Tenancies	Scottish Secure Tenancies
Rent (Scotland) Act 1984, Sch 2	Housing (Scotland) Act 1988, Sch 5	Housing (Scotland) Act 2001, Sch 2
Rent arrears		
Where any rent lawfully due from the tenant has not been paid .... [1]	Some rent lawfully due from the tenant – (a) is unpaid on the date on which the proceedings for possession are begun; (b) was in arrears at the date of service of the (s 19) notice (Notice of proceedings for Possession) [except where sheriff waives NPP requirement] [12]	Rent lawfully due from the tenant has not been paid [1]
	Whether or not any rent is in arrears on the date on which proceedings for possession are begun, the tenant has persistently delayed paying rent which has become lawfully due [11]	
	Both at the date of service of the notice under s 19 [NPP] relating to the proceedings for possession and at the date of the hearing, at least 3 months' rent lawfully due from the tenant in arrears [8]	

	and [the sheriff is satisfied] BUT (b) that rent is in arrears as mentioned ... as a consequence of a delay or failure in the payment of relevant housing benefit [amended by s 12 HSA 2003] – "reasonableness test" required		

Breach of terms of tenancy

Where ... any obligation of the protected or statutory tenancy ... has been broken or not performed (1)	Any obligation of the tenancy (other than one related to the payment of rent) has been broken or not performed (13)	... any other obligation [not rent arrears] of the tenancy has been broken (1)

Immoral or illegal purposes

Where the tenant or any person residing or lodging with him or any sub-tenant of his ... has been convicted of using the dwelling-house or allowing the dwelling-house to be used for illegal or immoral purposes (2)	The tenant, a person residing or lodging with the tenant or a person visiting the house has – (b) been convicted of – i. using or allowing the house to be used for immoral or illegal purposes; or ii. an offence punishable by imprisonment committed, in or in the locality of, the house (15)	The tenant (or any one of joint tenants), a person residing or lodging in the house with, or subtenant of, the tenant, or a person visiting the house has been convicted of – (a) using the house or allowing it to be used for immoral or illegal purposes, or (b) an offence punishable by imprisonment committed in, or in the locality of, the house (2)

Anti-social behaviour

Where the tenant or any person residing or lodging with him or any sub-tenant of his has been guilty of conduct which is a nuisance or annoyance to adjoining occupiers[2]	The tenant, a person residing or lodging with the tenant or a person visiting the house has – (a) acted in an anti-social manner in relation to a person residing, visiting or otherwise engaging in lawful activity in the locality or (b) pursued a course of anti-social conduct in relation to [a person residing, visiting or otherwise engaging in lawful activity in the locality][15]	The tenant (or any one of joint tenants), a person residing or lodging in the house with, or any subtenant of, the tenant, or a person visiting the house has – (a) acted in an anti-social manner in relation to a person residing in, visiting or otherwise engaged in lawful activity in the locality or (b) pursued a course of conduct amounting to harassment of such a person, or a course of conduct which is otherwise anti-social conduct in relation to such a person, and it is not reasonable in all the circumstances that the landlord should be required to make other accommodation available to the tenant[7]	"anti-social", in relation to an action or course, means causing or likely to cause alarm, distress, nuisance or annoyance, "conduct" includes speech, and a course of conduct must involve conduct on at least two occasions "harassment" of a person includes causing the person alarm or distress (Protection from Harassment Act 1997, s 8)
		The tenant (or any one of joint tenants), or any person residing or lodging with, or any subtenant of, the tenant – (a) has been guilty of conduct in the vicinity of the house which is a nuisance or annoyance, or	

		(b) has pursued a course of conduct amounting to harassment of a person residing in, visiting or otherwise engaged in lawful activity in the locality and in the opinion of the landlord it is appropriate in the circumstances to require the tenant to move to other accommodation (8)
Condition of house deteriorated		
Where the condition of the dwelling-house has, in the opinion of the court, deteriorated owing to acts of waste by, or the neglect or default of, the tenant or any person residing or lodging with him or any sub-tenant of his and, in the case of any act of waste by, or the neglect or default of, a person lodging with the tenant or a sub-tenant of his, where the court is satisfied that the tenant has not, before the making of the order in question, taken such steps as he ought reasonably to have taken for the removal of the lodger or sub-tenant, as the case may be (3)	The condition of the house or any of the common parts has deteriorated owing to acts of waste by, or the neglect or default of, the tenant or any one of joint tenants or any person residing or lodging with him or any subtenant of his; and in the case of acts of waste by, or the neglect or default of, a person lodging with a tenant or subtenant of his, the tenant has not, before the making of the order in question, taken such steps as the tenant ought reasonably to have taken for the removal of the lodger or sub-tenant (14)	The condition of the house or of any of the common parts has deteriorated owing to acts of waste by, or the neglect or default of, the tenant (or any one of joint tenants) or any person residing or lodging with, or any subtenant of, the tenant; and in the case of acts of waste by, or the neglect or default of, a person residing or lodging with, or sub-tenant of, a tenant, the tenant has not, before the making of the order in question, taken such steps as the tenant ought reasonably to have taken for the removal of that person (3)

Condition of furniture deteriorated

Where the condition of any furniture provided for use under the tenancy has, in the opinion of the court, deteriorated owing to ill-treatment by the tenant or any person residing or lodging with him or any sub-tenant of his and, in the case of any ill-treatment by a person lodging with the tenant or a sub-tenant of his, where the court is satisfied that the tenant has not, before the making of the order in question, taken such steps as he ought reasonably to have taken for the removal of the lodger or sub-tenant, as the case may be [4]	The condition of any furniture provided for use under the tenancy has deteriorated owing to ill-treatment by the tenant or any other person residing or lodging with him in the house and, in the case of ill-treatment by a person lodging with the tenant or by a sub-tenant of his, the tenant has not taken such steps as he ought reasonably to have taken for the removal of the lodger or sub-tenant [16]	The condition of any furniture provided for use under the tenancy, or for use in any of the common parts … has deteriorated owing to ill-treatment by the tenant (or any one of joint tenants) or any person residing or lodging with, or sub-tenant of, the tenant; and in the case of ill-treatment by a person residing or lodging with, or subtenant of, a tenant, the tenant has not, before the making of the order in question, taken such steps as the tenant ought reasonably to have taken for the removal of that person [4]

House required by landlord for own occupation

Where the dwelling-house is reasonably required by the landlord for occupation as a residence for – (a) himself, or (b) any son or daughter of his over 18 years of age, or (c) his father or mother, or (d) if the dwelling-house is let on or subject to a regulated tenancy, the father or mother of his wife or husband [8]	The landlord who is seeking possession, or in the case of joint landlords seeking possession, at least one of them requires the house as his or his spouse's only or principal home, [and not a landlord by purchasing for value] [1(b)] *ALSO AVAILABLE* At any time before the beginning of the tenancy, the landlord who

is seeking possession or, in the case of joint landlords seeking possession, at least one of them occupied the house as his only or principal home [1(a)]		

Landlord induced to grant tenancy by false statement

The tenant is the person, or one of the persons, to whom the tenancy was granted and the landlord was induced to grant the tenancy by a false statement made knowingly or recklessly by the tenant [6]	*Falkirk District Council v McLay* 1991 SCLR 895 / *West Lothian Council v Reape* 2002 Hous LR 58

House overcrowded

Where the dwelling-house is so over-crowded as to be dangerous or injurious to the health of the inmates, and the court is satisfied that the overcrowding could have been abated by the removal of any lodger or sub-tenant (not being a parent or child of the tenant) whom it would, having regard to all the circumstances of the case, including the question whether other accommodation is available for him, have been reasonable to remove, and that the tenant has not taken such steps as he ought reasonably to have taken for his removal [10]	The house is overcrowded within the meaning of s 135 of the 1987 Act, in such circumstances as render the occupier guilty of an offence [9] [see s 139 of 1987 Act – "the occupier of a house who causes or permits it to be overcrowded is guilty *A house is overcrowded … When the number of persons sleeping in the house is such as to contravene – (a) the standard specified in s 136 (the room standard) (b) the standard specified in s 137 (the space standard)*]	*Aslan v Murphy* [1990] 1 WLR 766

Demolition or substantial work on house

	The landlord who is seeking possession ... intends to demolish or reconstruct the whole or a substantial part of the house or to carry out substantial works on the house or any part thereof ... NB Not available to purchasing landlords Only if work cannot be carried out without tenant giving up possession – v complex provision [6]	It is intended within a reasonable period of time to demolish, or carry out substantial work on, the building or a part of the building which comprises or includes the house, and such demolition or work cannot reasonably take place without the landlord obtaining possession of the house [10]

Special Needs adaptation

Where a dwelling-house has been designed or adapted for occupation by a person whose special needs require accommodation of the kind provided by the dwelling-house and – (a) there is no longer a person with such special needs occupying the dwelling-house and – (b) the court is satisfied that the landlord requires it for occupation (whether alone or with other members of his family) by a person who has such special needs [20]		The house has been designed or adapted for occupation by a person whose special needs require accommodation of the kind provided by the house and – (a) there is no longer a person with such a need occupying the house, and (b) the landlord requires it for occupation (whether alone or with other members of the person's family) by a person who has such special needs [11]

		The house forms part of a group of houses which has been designed, or which has been provided with or located near facilities, for persons with special needs, and – (a) there is no longer a person with such a need occupying the house, and (b) the landlord requires it for occupation (whether alone or with other members of the person's family) by a person who has such a need [12]

Absence from house

Statutory tenancy continues "so long as he retains possession of the dwelling-house" – English case law on the requirement for "residence" has allowed for extensive absences where there was an intention to re-occupy and a degree of physical occupation – contrast *Brickfield v Hughes* [1988] 1 EGLR 108 and *Duke v Porter* [1986] 2 EGLR 101	ONLY OR PRINCIPAL HOME THROUGHOUT TENANCY under s 12 but no specific periods in statute Statutory assured tenancy continues "so long as he retains possession of the dwelling-house" – allows for temporary absences if there is an intention to re-occupy	The tenant and – (a) the tenant's spouse, or civil partner or (b) any person with whom the tenant has, for a period of at least 6 months immediately prior to the commencement of the (absence), been living in the house as husband and wife or in a relationship which has the characteristics of the relationship between civil partners

have been absent from the house without reasonable cause for a continuous period exceeding 6 months or have ceased to occupy the house as their principal home [5]

Tenancy transfer

The landlord wishes to transfer the tenancy of the house to –

(a) the tenant's spouse (or former spouse or former civil partner), or

(b) a person with whom the tenant has, for a period of at least 6 months immediately prior to the date of application for transfer, been living in the house as husband and wife or in a relationship which has the characteristics of the relationship between civil partners

who has applied to the landlord for such a transfer; and the tenant or (as the case may be) the spouse or together with the other in the house [15]

APPENDIX 2
SUITABLE ALTERNATIVE ACCOMMODATION

The legislation also provides for landlords being able to offer different accommodation to their tenants. It must be stressed, again, that this is a ground which requires the sheriff's satisfaction as to reasonableness. There is little evidence that it is an option available to many landlords and it appears to be seldom encountered in practice.

The criteria for landlords regaining their property when they provide the sitting tenant with suitable alternative accommodation are on the same lines as those provided in the Rent (Scotland) Act 1984 and the Housing (Scotland) Act 2001. This can stem either from a local authority certificate of suitability or from being deemed by the sheriff to be suitable.

LOCAL AUTHORITY CERTIFICATE

Although conclusive evidence of suitability, these certificates are rarely used in the author's experience, although they have been encountered in the case law. If the public authority where the premises are situated certifies that suitable alternative accommodation will be provided for the tenant, this is conclusive proof that such accommodation will indeed he available. It applies to Local authorities. The court must then determine whether or not the alternative accommodation offered is similar to the accommodation in the certificate provided by the local authority in respect of similar-sized families.

DEEMED SUITABLE BY SHERIFF

Alternatively, the sheriff must be satisfied as to the level of security of tenure being offered. If there is no certificate then accommodation is to be regarded as suitable as far as security of tenure is concerned if it consists of either separate premises let on an assured tenancy (with certain important exceptions mentioned below) or a short assured tenancy or a tenancy which the sheriff considers will give the tenant reasonably equivalent security of tenure to the assured tenancy mentioned here. The assured tenancies which are excluded from this paragraph are those covered by the mandatory grounds of possession 1–5 where notice has to be given to the tenant:

(a) property is the landlord's former principal home;
(b) mortgage on the property before the lease;
(c) off-season let of holiday property;
(d) lease by educational body to non-student;
(e) lease to minister or full-time lay missionary.

CRITERIA FOR SUITABILITY

The sheriff must be satisfied that the accommodation is reasonably suitable to the needs of the tenant and his family. Three issues have to be addressed. First, the question of proximity to work must be considered. This must be satisfied along with one of two additional tests. The initial issue, which has never been encountered by the author, is whether the tenancy is similar as regards rental to equivalent public-sector housing. The alternative test is whether the accommodation is reasonably suitable to the means and needs of tenant. Given that most post-1988 tenancies in the private rented sector have been short assured tenancies there has been no case law emerging under the 1988 Act on suitable alternative accommodation and the provisions of the pre-1988 regime are relied on.

PROXIMITY TO PLACE OF WORK

This is determined by looking to the reality of the situation and the practicability of travelling between home and work. Where a person has a number of places of work to visit in the course of his work there will be difficulties in deciding which is the place of work. The issue of doing some work at home will also be a factor in deciding whether the proposed alternative accommodation is suitable are regards proximity to work.

SIMILAR AS REGARDS RENTAL AND EXTENT TO THE ACCOMMODATION

This is looked at in terms of what is offered in social renting in the neighbourhood to persons whose needs are similar as regards extent of accommodation in the view of the sheriff. In order to decide whether or not property is similar to that provided by a public authority a certificate from that body as to the extent of accommodation provided for a given size of family and the rent charged is conclusive of these facts. Again, this is a test which has not been encountered in the case law nor in the experience of the author.

REASONABLY SUITABLE TO THE MEANS OF THE TENANT AND TO THE NEEDS OF THE TENANT AND HIS FAMILY AS REGARDS EXTENT AND CHARACTER

This is the main issue which has been litigated under the Rent Acts and an objective test has emerged. Suitability goes beyond mere size of accommodation. It does not, however, cover lifestyle. The standard of housing is judged rather than ancillary personal interests or "fads, fancies and preferences". If a landlord offers accommodation which is overcrowded this cannot be deemed suitable to the needs of the tenant and his family. The test for overcrowding is found in Pt VII of the Housing (Scotland) Act 1987.

7 SUCCESSION

BACKGROUND

Most of the coverage of succession in this chapter relates to the rules developed under the statutory rules constructed and interpreted over the past century in relation to succession to tenancies. Those developing the rules have attempted to balance the competing notions of home and property. We have a set of rules which recognise not simply the rights of property owners to deal with their property as they see fit but which also recognise that the tenants who rent their properties have a stake in that property too, principally as a family home. The result has been a fascinating view of the changing notion of what amounts to a "family" over the past century, as well as shifts in the level of rights property owners have enjoyed as compared with those of their tenants.

Succession to owner-occupier property appears on the surface to be somewhat less complex. Anyone choosing to leave their property in a will has almost complete freedom to dispose of the accommodation as they wish, although only some 37 per cent of people in Scotland make wills.[1] There has, though, always existed in Scots common law a recognition of the importance of certain members of the immediate family. Prior to 1964, although the heritable property of someone dying intestate passed to male descendants, widows enjoyed a liferent[2] of one-third of the heritable property of their deceased husband, called "*terce*".[3] This right was superseded by the rules for intestate succession laid down in the Succession (Scotland) Act 1964 which introduced "prior rights". These entitled the surviving spouse or civil partner[4] to certain rights before the free estate of the deceased was distributed. These comprised the right to succeed to any house forming part of the deceased's estate, up to the value, in 2010, of £300,000; furniture and plenishings up to the value of

---

[1] Hiram (2007); citing figures from the Scottish Consumer Council Report *Wills and Awareness of Inheritance Rights in Scotland* (2006).

[2] The right to use and enjoy the property during her life but not to dispose of it.

[3] The "equivalent" right for widowers was a liferent of all the heritage of the late wife – called "courtesy".

[4] Succession (Scotland) Act 1964, ss 8 and 9 (as amended by Civil Partnership Act 2004, Sch 28, Pt 1).

£24,000; and a financial sum from the remaining estate of £42,000. The financial sum is £75,000 if the intestate dies without issue. Cohabitants have a right to apply for a share of the deceased cohabitant's property where the deceased dies intestate. The court may, after having regard to the size and nature of the deceased's estate and any benefit received by the survivor in consequence of the death, as well as the nature and extent of other rights and claims on that estate, make "such order as it thinks fit".[5] The cohabitant cannot received more than if he had been a spouse or a civil partner.[6]

It is, of course, possible to avoid a surviving spouse enjoying such rights by making a will. In Scotland, though, the testator can only make provision for the "dead's part", ie that part of the estate after the "legal rights" of surviving spouse and issue have been dealt with. These traditional common-law rights protecting the family are drawn from moveable property. They exist irrespective of any will which may have been made. The surviving spouse or civil partner is entitled to one-third of the moveables and the children one-third: the surviving spouse's share is increased to one-half if there are no surviving children.[7] This means that the statutory rules and common-law framework operating in Scotland have in the past recognised and now continue to recognise the centrality of the family in people's lives. In 1990 the Scottish Law Commission took the view that this structure provided "a very complicated answer to the simple question of how a person's estate should be divided when he or she dies intestate and ... [was] ... needlessly complicated".[8] The major change since the system's introduction in 1964 has been the extension, as indicated, of prior rights to civil partners. It is, therefore, possible to ensure that a surviving spouse or children receive nothing on death by transferring all one's property into heritage and making a will. In crude terms, it can be said that the underlying assumption encapsulated in these rules is that someone who died without leaving a will would have intended their surviving spouse to have inherited the family home. The Mackintosh Committee had noted, in 1951, that "the provision made by our existing law for the surviving spouse in the case of intestacy was quite inadequate in the circumstances of the present day".[9]

Rights under a residential lease were originally not transmissible on death because of the doctrine of *delectus personae* whereby "the choice of tenant made by a landlord was regarded as exclusive".[10] That ceased to be

---

5   Family Law (Scotland) Act 2006, s 29.
6   FSA 2006, s 29(4).
7   See Hiram, Chapter 4.
8   *Report on Succession* (Scot Law Com No 124, 1990), para 2.5.
9   Mackintosh Report (1951) at 14.
10 Rankine (3rd edn, 1916) at 157.

the common law position by the end of the 18th century.[11] Unfurnished residential leases form part of the estate of the deceased and vest in the executor for transmission either in terms of the will or under the law of intestacy. The doctrine of *delectus personae* still applies where the lease is furnished. Prior to the introduction of the Rent Act in 1915, any restrictions on the right to succeed to a tenancy were based on provisions in the lease contract. There seems to have been little use of such clauses. With the dominance of private renting, the flexibility of relatively short leases operated by most tenants allowed appropriate downsizing of property when the tenant died. While tenancies of 5 years were encountered, leases were in most working-class districts weekly or monthly and only a year for "tenants of better class workmen's dwellings".[12] Thus, while tenancies passed like any other property right on the death of the tenant, what was passed was of relatively limited value. Since tenants enjoyed the contractual rights in the tenancy only so far as the tenancy extended, what could be passed on for most residential tenants was the right to stay for a few months. They then might be able to arrange a further tenancy but had no right to insist on renewal of the existing tenancy. Where there was a joint tenancy, the surviving joint tenant carried on *qua* tenant.[13]

The coming of the Rent Acts and the expansion of municipal housing after the First World War radically transformed this scenario. The early Rent Acts recognised the importance of the family in its provision that a landlord could recover possession of a rented property if it was required for occupation of a member of the landlord's family.[14] This principle of members of the family of the landlord "trumping" tenants' rights remained a feature of the legislation throughout the 20th century until the radical break in 1988 and the return to rights determined solely by market forces. In addition, of more direct benefit to tenants from the Increase of Rent and Mortgage Interest (Restrictions) Act 1920 was the right of succession to a tenancy.[15] This notion was unprecedented and provided that where a tenant died their widow could succeed to the tenancy. In the event of there not being a widow the tenancy could pass to a member of the family. In times of chronic housing shortage this right was particularly valuable and extensive litigation followed between 1920 and the present day.

---

[11] Rankine (3rd edn, 1916) at 157.

[12] Guthrie Report (1907) at 3.

[13] See also *Young* v *Gerard* (1843) 6 D 347 which concerned a coal lease which was expressly granted to tenants and their heirs and successors. Here, one of the joint tenants became bankrupt and renounced the lease, leaving the sisters of his deceased ex-partner to exercise their right to carry on the lease to term.

[14] Increase of Rent and Mortgage Interest (Restrictions) Act 1920, s 12(1)(g) – "landlord" repossession in the Increase of Rent and Mortgage Interest (War Restrictions) Act 1915 operated only for occupation by the landlord himself or "some other person in his employ" – s 1(3).

[15] Increase of Rent and Mortgage Interest (Restrictions) Act 1920, s 12.

Essentially, what was provided in the legislation from 1920 onwards was a recognition that a tenancy was not simply a limited and finite contractual right but rather provided a home for a group of people which should be given formal recognition and protection.

This tension between the home of the tenant and the landlord's property rights and own family responsibilities was retained in the private rented arena between 1915 and 1988 in private-sector tenancies. The range of people to benefit from the protection given to the concept of "home" by means of the right of succession was expanded from the original wording of the legislation which, looking beyond the widow, talked simply of a "member of the family".[16]

There has been a general reduction in the nature and quality of the rights of private-sector tenants since 1988 in Britain as part of the policy against regulation of the Thatcher administrations. There are in Britain in the early 21st century three major separate statutory tenancy regimes with different approaches to succession.[17] Each of them has a separate legislative history and there is limited overlap as far as statutory provisions and case law are concerned. Their development, which is examined in some detail below, illustrates the tensions of competing social and political visions which for much of the time politicians left to the courts to adjudicate. The results in the case law and the terms of the decisions also provide a fascinating insight into the changing role of the judiciary in our system as well as the operation of precedent in 20th-century jurisprudence.

MODERN LEGAL FRAMEWORK

Two very different sets of rights are currently available for those living in rented accommodation. One reflects the notion of a tenancy as a lesser property right and the dominance of ownership. The other emphasises the idea that where people live is their home and deserves a measure of respect and protection. As we have noted, these two conflicting ideas have operated in tension with each other throughout the last century of modern residential renting.

Private-sector tenancies

ASSURED TENANCIES

The Housing (Scotland) Act 1988 provides for a limited right of succession to assured tenancies. There is provision for succession to the tenant's spouse where, immediately before the death, the survivor was occupying the house as his only or principal home.[18] The surviving spouse is entitled

---

16 Increase of Rent and Mortgage Interest (Restrictions) Act 1920, s 12.
17 See Chapter 3 above for a fuller picture of the range of tenancy types extant.
18 HSA 1988, s 31(1).

to retain possession of the house as a statutory assured tenancy.[19] This means that there is a good degree of security of tenure for the successor who complies with the terms of the tenancy, although, as has been noted above,[20] there are more extensive grounds of possession available to landlords in the assured tenancy regime than in the previous protected tenancy provisions. Most of the grounds are discretionary[21] and would require the sheriff to be satisfied that repossession was "reasonable".[22] A range of mandatory grounds is available,[23] including where the landlord has been the owner occupier of the property in the past.[24] In addition, there may be repossession where the landlord requires the property for his own occupation.[25] Again, here we see a shift in the balance of rights between the landlord and the tenant from what operated previously. The landlord merely has to demonstrate that he was previously an owner occupier. Alternatively, he can show that he "requires" the property as his only or principal home. The wording here is interesting since it does not state that the property is "needed". Nor does the landlord have to show that the desire to regain the property is "reasonable" in any way. What is required is a bona fide intention to occupy the property as a home.[26]

There is no provision for the transmission of an assured tenancy to any other member of the family in the event of there being no surviving spouse or that spouse declining the tenancy. The succession rights are quite narrowly prescribed. The deceased tenant must have been a sole tenant.[27] Succession does not apply where the deceased was a tenant by dint of having succeeded to the tenancy under the legislation.[28] There must be a surviving spouse. This includes a person who was living with the tenant at the time of the tenant's death as his or her wife or husband and who is treated as the tenant's spouse.[29] The spouse or cohabitant does not have to have been living with the tenant at the time of the tenant's death,[30] provided that they were occupying the house as their only or principal home.[31] They must, however, retain possession of the house.[32] This can be done where there is other accommodation elsewhere occupied on a

---

[19] HSA 1988, s 31(1)(c).
[20] See Chapter 6 above.
[21] HSA 1988, Sch 5, Pt II.
[22] *Ibid*, s 18(4).
[23] *Ibid*, Sch 5, Pt I.
[24] *Ibid*, ground 1.
[25] *Ibid*.
[26] *Kennealy* v *Dunne* [1977] QB 837 on the equivalent phrase "required as a residence" under the regulated regime at 850 per Stephenson LJ and per Megaw LJ at 850.
[27] HSA 1988, s 31(1)(a).
[28] *Ibid*, s 31(1)(c).
[29] *Ibid*, s 31(4).
[30] *Ibid*, s 31(1)(b).
[31] *Ibid*.
[32] *Ibid*, s 31(1).

temporary basis, such as for a part-time job,[33] or where a person has left the principal home, intending to return in the fullness of time. In the vast majority of cases the decision will be straightforward since there cannot be the concept which operated under the Rent Act (Scotland) 1984 of two homes.[34] Deciding the question of whether a property is the only or principal home, where regular or habitual residence is absent, depends on asking certain questions, according to Sheriff Principal Nicholson:

> "the questions which must be asked in cases where such residence is lacking is: On the facts of the case, did the person concerned have such a real, tangible and substantial connection with the house in question that, it rather than any other place of residence, can properly be described as having been his only or principal residence during the relevant period".[35]

If all these requirements are satisfied then the spouse or cohabitant is entitled to a statutory assured tenancy of the house.[36]

While these rights are significantly less than those existing under the previous legislative regime, they represented an improvement on what had been proposed in the Bill. When the legislation was originally introduced no provision was made for the transmission of assured tenancies to either spouse or any member of the family. Following extensive lobbying by, *inter alia*, SHELTER, this right was introduced at the Report stage in the House of Lords and accepted without debate.[37]

Whether or not a "spouse" covers those in a same-sex relationship was canvassed extensively by the House of Lords in *Fitzpatrick* v *Sterling Housing Association*.[38] Their Lordships were not persuaded that living in a relationship with the characteristics of the relationship between husband and wife except that the parties were of the same sex was equivalent to the parties living together as husband and wife.[39] The changes wrought in the rights of tenants in the social rented sector by the Housing (Scotland) Act 2001,[40] covered below, do not directly extend to the private sector.

PROTECTED TENANCIES

As is briefly outlined below, the succession rights which were operative from 1920 onwards in relation to the previous Rent Act regimes were extensive and are encapsulated in the Rent (Scotland) Act 1984. The succession rights were available to both succeeding spouses and members

---

[33] *Hampstead Way Investments Ltd* v *Lewis-Weare* [1985] 1 EGLR 120.
[34] *Brickfield* v *Hughes* [1988] 1 EGLR 108; *Duke* v *Porter* [1986] 2 EGLR 121.
[35] *Roxburgh DC* v *Collins* 1991 SCLR 575 at 578 D–E.
[36] HSA 1988, s 31(1).
[37] *Hansard*, HL, vol 499 (6 July 1988).
[38] [1999] 4 All ER 705.
[39] See below at p 258.
[40] HSA 2001, s 108.

of the family. There was provision of succession on two separate occasions. This recognition of the private rented property as a home was, however, significantly curtailed by the Housing (Scotland) Act 1988.

For deaths of tenants on or after 2 January 1989, an order of succession for two distinct scenarios in the 1988 Act is laid down for such protected tenancies. What such a successor is entitled to was a different kind of tenancy. In place of the protected tenancy with a right to have fair rent fixed, full security of tenure and with further succession rights, he now succeeds to a statutory assured tenancy covered by the Housing (Scotland) Act 1988. This means that the rent regulation provisions, further succession rules and the repossession rights of the protected tenancy regime under the previous legislation[41] do not apply. Instead, there is no protection as to levels of rent, no possibility of a further succession of the tenancy and the less valuable rights of Sch 5 to the Housing (Scotland) Act 1988 apply.

Death of the original tenant

The legislation provides an order of succession giving priority to the tenant's spouse or cohabitant.[42] Thereafter there is provision for succession by a member of the tenant's family who has been residing for the 2 years immediately preceding the tenant's death.[43] In the event of a competition, the sheriff decides.[44]

Death of original tenant's first successor

There is also provision for succession by anyone who was a member of the original tenant's family or of the successor's family, where that person was residing with the first successor for 2 years immediately prior to the tenant's death. The sheriff determines in cases where more than one person qualifies.[45]

One would not expect to come across such situations very frequently in practice, since it has not been possible to create protected tenancies for over 20 years. It is clear, though, that some protected tenancies still exist and of these there will be some occupants with their limited rights to succeed for some time to come.

Social rented tenancies

The rights of tenants in the former public, local authority, sector were until 1980 entirely dependent on the lease contract. Just as tenants had no

---

41 Rent (Scotland) Act 1984 (for Scotland) and Rent Act 1977 (for England and Wales).
42 RSA 1984, Sch 1A, para 2(1) (Housing (Scotland) Act 1988, s 46, inserting s 3A into the Rent (Scotland) Act 1984, and Sch 6).
43 RSA 1984, Sch 1A, para 3.
44 *Ibid*, Sch 1A, para 3(b).
45 *Ibid*.

rights beyond their contractual term in relation to repossession, neither did they have any automatic right to succeed to a local authority tenancy. The Tenants' Rights etc (Scotland) 1980 altered this situation and introduced the statutory scheme which is the basis of the current set-up found in the Housing (Scotland) Act 2001 which applies to tenants of local authorities and registered social landlords such as housing associations.

On the death of the tenant of a Scottish secure tenancy there is provision for the tenancy to pass by operation of law to a qualified person, unless the survivor is the author of the tenant's demise.[46] There is also provision for a further succession on the death of the first successor.[47] When the second successor dies, the tenancy is terminated[48] unless there is a surviving joint tenant who continues to use that house as his only or principal home.[49] If there is, either no qualified person or that person declines the tenancy, the tenancy is terminated.[50] Where a qualified person in occupancy declines a tenancy they must do so in writing within 4 weeks of the tenant's death.[51] They must vacate the house within 3 months of that written notice.[52]

QUALIFIED PERSON[53]

Schedule 3 to the Housing (Scotland) Act 2001 lays down who are qualified persons for the purposes of succession to a Scottish secure tenancy. Only people in this category have a right to succeed and the landlord must notify them in writing of their status.[54] The changes introduced by the 2001 Act recognise the caring role which involves many family members giving up accommodation to live with a relative. When that relative dies they are now included in the ranks of those who can succeed to the tenancy.

- The tenant's *spouse*, provided the house was their only or principal home at the time of the tenant's death.[55]

---

[46] HSA 2001, s 22(1); if the death has been at the hand of the successor the courts will determine whether or not that tenancy can pass – *McCreight* v *West Lothian DC* 2009 SCLR 359 – the Lands Tribunal was required to sist an application to purchase a property which had passed to the applicant before his role in the death of his ex-partner was known. The forfeiture rule would seem almost certain to apply where the would-be tenant was guilty of homicide – *Burns* v *Secretary of State for Social Services* 1985 SC 143.

[47] HSA 2001, s 22(2).

[48] *Ibid*, s 22(4).

[49] *Ibid*, s 22(8).

[50] *Ibid*, s 22(3).

[51] *Ibid*, Sch 3, para 11(1).

[52] *Ibid*, Sch 3, para 11(3)(a).

[53] *Ibid*, s 22(5).

[54] *Ibid*, Sch 3, para 10.

[55] *Ibid*, Sch 3, para 2(1)(a)(i).

- The tenant's *partner*,[56] provided that the house was their only or principal home throughout the period of 6 months ending with the tenant's death.[57]
- Surviving *joint tenant*.[58]
- *Member of the tenant's family* aged at least 16, where the house was the person's only or principal home at the time of the death of the tenant.[59]
- *Carer* providing or who has provided care for the tenant or a member of the tenant's family – provided that the carer is at least 16, the house was the carer's only or principal home at the time of the death of the tenant and the carer had an only or principal home which was given up.[60]

ORDER OF SUCCESSION BETWEEN QUALIFIED PERSONS

Where there is more than one "qualified person" entitled to succeed to the tenancy, the order of precedence laid down in the legislation will be observed:[61]

- spouse or partner or joint tenant;[62]
- member of tenant's family;[63]
- carer.[64]

If there is more than one "qualifying person" in a group and there is no agreement between such individuals, then the landlord selects.[65]

Where, following possession proceedings, a Scottish secure tenant is required to move to another property which is also a Scottish secure tenancy, both tenancies will be treated as a single tenancy for the purposes of succession. This occurs where the local authority has provided other accommodation – in cases of nuisance or annoyance; overcrowding; special needs adaptation no longer appropriate; landlord's interest in property ceases; or educational function.[66]

---

[56] HSA 2001, Sch 3, para 2(1)(a)(ii).
[57] *Ibid*, Sch 3, para 2(2).
[58] *Ibid*, Sch 3, para 2(1)(b).
[59] *Ibid*, Sch 3, para 2(3).
[60] *Ibid*, Sch 3, para 4.
[61] *Ibid*, Sch 3, paras 6–9.
[62] *Ibid*, Sch 3, para 2.
[63] *Ibid*, Sch 3, para 3.
[64] *Ibid*, Sch 3, para 4.
[65] *Ibid*, Sch 3, para 9.
[66] *Ibid*, s 22(10).

THE DEVELOPMENT OF PROPERTY RIGHTS AND THE CONCEPT OF "HOME"

The Increase of Rent and Mortgage Interest (War Restrictions) Act 1915 provided that landlords could evict only where a tenant had failed to pay rent or had breached the terms of the tenancy. There was to be no removal simply because the contract had reached its termination date. There was, however, an exception where the property was required for the use of the landlord or a member of his family. This was a short-term pragmatic solution to a problem which was threatening the war effort of the time. Nonetheless, the response recognised that rented properties were not simply limited contracts but were the homes of the people occupying them as well as potentially those of the landlord's family.

The rationale for this protection, then, was to provide protection to family homes – whether they be those of the tenant or the landlord. When the temporary legislation was extended at the end of the Great War this notion was clarified specifically to extend coverage of the rights beyond the contractual period to widows and members of the family. This recognition of a "home" as a worthwhile value to protect can be seen in the exception granted to landlords to recover where the family was involved.

Succession and the expanded family

This balance between the home of the tenant and the landlord's wider family responsibilities was retained between 1915 and 1988. The range of people to benefit from the protection given to the concept of "home" by means of the right of succession has been expanded from a narrow view of the family to a rather more expansive one in the intervening years. The original wording of the legislation giving landlords a right to recover possession talked simply of a "member of the family".[67]

Initially, landlords during the First World War could recover only their properties if the tenant was guilty of breach of the terms of the tenancy or if the landlord required the property for occupation by himself or a member of his family. Essentially, eviction on commercial grounds that a tenant paying a higher rent might be obtained was outlawed. This availability for landlords to obtain their property for a member of their own family does not appear to have been particularly controversial. Its impact has been limited and it has never figured as a ploy to avoid the Rent Acts. Weighing the competing interests of the existing tenant with the needs of the incoming member of the landlord's family has on occasion produced controversial decisions.[68] This stems from the wording of the provisions

---

[67] Increase of Rent and Mortgage Interest (Restrictions) Act 1920, s 12.
[68] *Hodges* v *Blee* [1987] 2 EGLR 119.

for landlords in regulated tenancies which provided a double test. First, the landlord required to show that the property was "reasonably required" for a restricted cohort of the family – son or daughter over 18 years of age or his father or mother.[69] In addition, the court was not to make an order for possession where, having regard to all the circumstances,[70] greater hardship would be caused by granting the order than by refusing to grant it.[71]

The rights of spouses and family members to succeed to tenancies which have existed since 1920 have been rather more expansive. As noted, commitment to the market in the provision of goods and services led to a general reduction in the nature and quality of the rights of private-sector tenants from 1988 in Britain as part of the policy of de-regulation of the Thatcher administration. For the purposes of the development of the case law we look at the private sector era where the issues were raised. Given the limitation of assured tenancy succession rights to spouses, the recognition to same-sex relationships given in the *Fitzpatrick*[72] case is of only limited practical significance for private-sector tenancies. It is in the statutes that we finally find equal treatment for cohabitation and same-sex relationships. The nature and tone, though, of the Court of Appeal and House of Lords pronouncements in *Simpson*[73] and *Fitzpatrick* suggest that, had there not been parliamentary intervention, the process of social change in the interpretation of the statutes would have provided the same result in due course.

Having their origin in the earliest Rent Acts, the succession rights for tenants of protected tenancies have undergone considerable change since their first version. The Increase of Rent and Mortgage Interest (War Restrictions) Act 1915 covered the question of recovery of possession in only a truncated manner and made no mention of succession to such a tenancy. Given that the legislation was scheduled to "continue in force during the continuance of the present war and for a period of six months thereafter and no longer"[74] no doubt led to this view of the Act as being a merely temporary measure. Things had altered somewhat by the time the legislation was consolidated in the Increase of Rent and Mortgage Interest (Restrictions) Act 1920, so that the protections afforded to tenants were extended to

> "The widow of a tenant dying intestate who was residing with him at his death, or, where a tenant dying intestate leaves no widow, or is a woman,

---

[69] Rent (Scotland) Act 1984, Sch 2, case 8.
[70] Including whether other accommodation was available for the landlord or the tenant.
[71] RSA 1984, Sch 2, Pt III.
[72] *Fitzpatrick* v *Sterling Housing Association* [1999] 4 All ER 705.
[73] *Harrogate BC* v *Simpson* (1984) 17 HLR 205.
[74] Increase of Rent and Mortgage Interest (War Restrictions) Act 1915, s 5(2).

such member of the tenant's family so residing as may be decided in default of agreement by the [county] court."[75]

The order of precedence of "widow – family" was introduced, then, in 1920. The specific right of widowers to succeed, *qua* widower, to tenancies in the names of their wives was formally instituted in 1980. In the intervening period they succeeded as a "member of the family". This was recognised in the early case of *Salter* v *Lask*, presided over, ironically, by a Judge Salter. Some 50 years later his widow was involved in a major case on the same question of the meaning of "member of the family".[76] In the case *Salter*[77] v *Lask*,[78] while accepting as axiomatic that a widower "is clearly a member of the family of the deceased wife", his colleague, MacKinnon J, did note, presaging the problems that were to emerge, that "[t]he language used in this Act resembles that of popular journalism rather than the terms of art of conveyancing".[79]

WIDOWS AND WIDOWERS

As indicated, the original succession rights were limited to widows. Tenancies in the names of women were not unknown. They were, however, rare.[80] As the practice of joint tenancies and tenancies in either spouse's name grew, the law on succession was amended to include widowers and thenceforth to cover spouses in 1980.[81] Until the introduction of the Housing (Scotland) Act 1988 the right, then, applied to spouses provided that the dwelling-house in question was the only or principal home at the time of the tenant's death. Prior to the 1988 Act, there was also provision for a second succession to take place, provided that there was another family member who met the requirements.[82]

"MEMBER OF THE FAMILY"

Membership of the family of the tenant was examined in the inter-War period in a case involving close family members including not just husbands but also a brother and sister.[83] The court noted that the word "family" includes brothers and sisters living with the deceased at

---

[75] Increase of Rent and Mortgage Interest (War Restrictions) Act 1915, s 12(1)(g).
[76] *Joram Developments* v *Sharratt* [1979] 1 WLR 3 – I am grateful to my colleague Alan Paterson for drawing my attention to this point.
[77] The surnames of the judge and the landlord were both, by coincidence, Salter.
[78] [1925] 1 KB 584.
[79] *Ibid.*
[80] SHAC Report (1980).
[81] Tenants' Rights etc (Scotland) Act 1980, s 56.
[82] *Sefton Holdings* v *Cairns* [1988] 1 EGLR 99.
[83] *Price* v *Gould* [1930] All ER 389 – although Miss Gould was evicted 6 weeks later, as the owner succeeded in satisfying the ground that she required the property for her own occupation as a residence.

the time of her death and that "that meaning is required by the ordinary acceptation of the word". While not specifying "precisely what may be the full extent of the word 'family'", the High Court took the view that "the legislature has used the word 'family' to introduce a flexible and wide term".[84]

When considering the position of an informally adopted child in 1949, Cohen LJ, in the Court of Appeal, suggested that there were two ways one might be regarded as a member of the family of the tenant. First, there was the primary meaning of "relations by blood or marriage". There was also the very broad notion of "household" including all living on the premises – relatives , servants and lodgers. The latter were not covered by the legislation. There was, however, a third way of construing "family". The approach, which had been mentioned in the High Court in the *Price* v *Gould* brothers and sisters case, led Cohen LJ to formulate the test: "Would an ordinary man, addressing his mind to the question whether Mrs Wollams was a member of the family or not, have answered 'yes' or 'no'?"[85]

The Court of Appeal looked at the issue after the Second World War in rather more contentious relationships. It adopted the "ordinary man" test adumbrated by Cohen LJ in *Brock* v *Wollams*. The courts looked at the applicability of the "ordinary man" test in a range of different situations during the post-War period. It was successfully argued for in a case involving a niece who looked after her aged aunt and uncle for some 18 months until the death of the tenant.It was noted that while not all nephews and nieces by marriage would count, the crucial issue here was the behaviour of the niece.

> "Here the defendant, the niece of the tenant's wife, assumed...out of natural love and affection, the duties and offices peculiarly attributable to members of a family of going to live with her uncle and aunt to look after them in their declining years. On those facts, I think that, if it were asked in ordinary conversation whether the defendant was a member of the tenant's family, an affirmative answer would be given."[86]

Using this benchmark, a number of other relationships were satisfied involving other relatives not covered by blood, such as brother[87] and niece by blood;[88] brother-in-law;[89] niece by marriage;[90] illegitimate child;[91]

---

[84] *Price* v *Gould* [1930] All ER 389 at 391.
[85] *Brock* v *Wollams* [1949] 2 KB 388 at 395.
[86] *Jones* v *Whitehill* [1950] 2 KB 204.
[87] *Donald* v *McKenzie* 1949 SLT (Sh Ct) 75.
[88] *Tandy* v *Bamford* [1929] *Estates Gazette Digest* 216.
[89] *Stewart* v *Higgins* [1951] CLY 2901.
[90] *Jones* v *Whitehill* [1950] 2 KB 204.
[91] *Jones* v *Trueman* (1949) 99 LJ 541.

step-child;[92] adopted child;[93] and grandchild by adoption.[94] The mere existence of a caring relationship between relatives, however, did not allow a family to be formed between first cousins who lived together for 29 years[95] – again applying the Cohen LJ's test of the "ordinary man".

The crucial point, though, of the Cohen LJ test which was used was the flexibility and apparent potential for variability of the criterion adopted as appropriate. This can be seen in the developments in relation to alternatives to formal marriage which developed in the post-War era.

COHABITANTS

The wording of the relevant statute has not been altered in this area but the courts have taken the view that a cohabitant could count as a member of the tenant's family and hence inherit the tenancy. In the years from 1920 the courts shifted from their view of unmarried couples as "living in sin"[96] in the 1950s to a full acceptance of this as a form of family life which is both accepted[97] and popular.[98] The birth of children outside marriage fell in Scotland, for example, in a single decade from 77 per cent in 1987 to 62 per cent [99] How the courts shifted in 25 years, almost seamlessly, from pride in those "living in sin" being denied the benefits of succession to their partners to accepting, as a matter of course, cohabitation is instructive.

One of the less discussed aspects of the impact on ordinary people's lives of the Second World War was the expansion in the numbers of marriage breakdowns and formation of households with illegitimate children.[100] Such were the changes in the nature of the family that cohabitation became a choice for a significant minority of couples. By the end of the 20th century the percentage of different-sex couples cohabiting had reached somewhere between 17 per cent[101] and 33 per cent.[102]

The case of *Gammans* v *Ekins*[103] first addressed the cohabitation issue in 1950. What was crucial here was the adoption of the "ordinary man"

---

[92] *Jones* v *Trueman* (1949) 99 LJ 541.
[93] *Ibid.*
[94] *Shepherd* v *Naylor* (1948) 98 LJ 603.
[95] *Langdon* v *Horton* [1951] 1 KB 666.
[96] *Gammans* v *Ekins* [1950] 2 KB 328 at 331 per Asquith LJ.
[97] *Dyson Holdings Ltd* v *Fox* [1976] 1 QB 503 at 512 G–H.
[98] *Fitzpatrick* v *Sterling Housing Association* [1999] 4 All ER 705 at 715e per Lord Slynn.
[99] Scottish Office, *Improving Scottish Family Law* (March 1999), Annex B at 51.
[100] Fitzpatrick (1999) 46.
[101] Office for National Statistics, *Regional Trends 33* (Stationery Office, 1998).
[102] *Fitzpatrick* v *Sterling Housing Association* [1999] 4 All ER 705 at 715e per Lord Slynn.
[103] *Gammans* v *Ekins* [1950] 2 KB 328.

approach to determining the meaning of "family". Although the tenant's partner was unsuccessful in his claim to be a member of the family of the deceased, the scene was set for developments in relation to cohabiting couples. Two of the judges noted that where there were children of a cohabiting relationship, the situation could be different.[104] The rights of "consorts" were considered by the Master of the Rolls and he was rather less antipathetic than his colleagues, suggesting that one should simply adopt the ordinary use of language as to the meaning of "family". He was, however, fortified in rejecting Mrs Gammans' claim that by denying recognition to the instant relationship "it is shown that, in the Christian society in which we live, one, at any rate, of the privileges which may be derived from marriage is not equally enjoyed by those who are living together as man and wife but who are not married".[105]

The mere existence of a child, mentioned in *Gammans*, did not, however, affect the decision of the Court of Appeal hearing a year later in a situation where the unmarried couple did have a child. The fact that the father had taken no steps to adopt the child after the mother's death indicated that, there, no family relationship had been formed. If he had maintained the child while the mother was alive, or if he had contributed financially to the upbringing of the child, the possibility of recognition of this as a "family" would have been rosier.[106] The interpretation of family was treated very much as one of fact. Hence, where a mother lived as a man's mistress for some 12 years prior to his death and had two children by him, her claim was successful.[107] The court was impressed by the fact that "they all lived together as a family". Mere cohabitation and common children would not have been enough, however:

> "The fact that someone living in a house, possibly as one of a number of domestic servants, has had a child by the tenant and the tenant makes provision for the child would not in itself … constitute the father and the mother of the child a family."[108]

In between this era with its use of the term "mistress" and the legislative changes in the 1980s, the courts attempted to work within the framework of precedent while recognising the sociological phenomenon of the decline in the popularity of the formal family. The results, from the point of view of practitioners, were less than satisfactory. In 1975 the Court of Appeal was faced with a long-term childless cohabitation case. Recognising

---

[104] *Gammans* v *Ekins* [1950] 2 KB 328 at 332 per Jenkins LJ.
[105] *Ibid* at 334 per Evershed MR.
[106] *Perry* v *Dembowski* [1951] 2 All ER 50 – given the problems of child support in the 1980s from fathers, this now seems less surprising – *Children Come First* (Cm 1264, 1990), para 1.5.
[107] *Hawes* v *Evenden* [1953] 2 All ER 737.
[108] *Ibid* at 738.

the rights of the surviving cohabitee, the majority rejected the views in *Gammans* v *Ekins* but recognised that the crucial term "family" had changed since its meaning since 1949.[109] It was noted that the "popular meaning of 'family' was not fixed once and for all time" and that with the passage of years it had changed. Lord Justice Bridge talked of a "complete revolution in society's attitude to unmarried partnerships ... [with] ... [t]he social stigma that once attached to them ... almost, if not entirely disappeared".[110] Accordingly, applying the test of Lord Justice Cohen, the test was satisfied. The matter was complicated by the presence on the Bench of one of the few "maverick" English judges, Lord Denning. He went further than simply adapting the Cohen test and held that the original decision had been wrong to make a distinction between a couple with children who could be a family and one without who could not.[111] The protection did not apply in every instance of cohabitation, however. It required that the couple, to borrow a phrase from the disapproving Lord Justice Asquith in 1949, "masquerade ... as husband and wife".[112] Where they did not hold themselves out as a married couple and retained their individuality and a degree of independence there was at that time no right to succeed to the partner's tenancy.[113] This disqualifying notion was also expressed in terms of "a sufficient state of permanence".[114]

The matter was discussed further by a decision in the supreme civil tribunal, the House of Lords, in a case involving two unrelated people who lived together in a platonic relationship for a period for 18 years. The tenant, Lady Nora Salter, the widow of the judge in *Salter* v *Lask*, at the age of 75 met a 24-year-old man, Frank Sharratt, who shared her interests in politics and the theatre. He resided with her – rent free after the first 3 years. In rejecting the claim of Mr Sharratt, their Lordships affirmed the approach to the family adopted back in 1949 in *Brock* v *Wollams*[115] by Cohen LJ. They considered that it was almost impossible for someone to establish a "familial nexus" – the kind of link one can only find within a family – by their actions alone.[116] This has been confirmed more recently at the end of the 1980s in the context of a woman living with the family of her deceased ex-fiancé.[117] The final clear rejection of the marriage-oriented approaches of the 1940s and 1950s arrived in a decision in 1980

---

[109] *Dyson Holdings* v *Fox* [1976] 1 QB 503 at 511F and 512G.
[110] *Ibid* at 512.
[111] *Ibid* at 509G.
[112] *Gammans* v *Ekins* [1950] 2 KB 328 at 331.
[113] *Helby* v *Rafferty* [1978] 3 All ER 1016 at 1020f.
[114] *Ibid* at 1024g.
[115] [1949] 2 KB 388 at 395.
[116] *Carega Properties SA (formerly Joram Developments Ltd)* v *Sharratt* [1979] 1 WLR 928 at 1087b per Lord Diplock – drawing on *Ross* v *Collins* [1964] 1 All ER 861 at 866 per Russell LJ.
[117] *Sefton Holdings Ltd* v *Cairns* [1988] 1 EGLR 99.

when the Court of Appeal upheld the right to succeed of a man who lived with a woman without children and without taking advantage of the opportunity to marry.[118] The meaning of the word "spouse" itself was extended to include cohabitants in the Housing (Scotland) Act 1988, specifying that a person living with original tenant as his or her wife or husband shall be treated as the spouse of the original tenant.[119]

SAME-SEX RELATIONSHIPS

The question of same-sex relationships in the context of housing rights was raised in the 1980s with the claim that a woman was entitled to succeed to the housing association secure tenancy of her same-sex partner of 15 years.[120] For the purposes of succession, although there are different statutory provisions dealing with the rules, these distinctions are not of great significance in the context of this discussion. The *Simpson* case was unsuccessful in establishing that Ms Simpson could be considered part of her same-sex partner's family. The Court of Appeal was of the view that this was a matter for Parliament to deal with.[121]

The House of Lords, in the mid-1980s, had been unwilling to consider the issue as an appeal.[122] With the passage of time, however, it was prepared to accept the notion that the meaning of "family" was capable of different meanings at different times. In the circumstances of the relationship being long term, stable and loving, the majority took the view that there was no reason, in principle, why such a relationship could not involve the partners being regarded as constituting a family.

The Fitzpatrick *decision and its rationale*

The problem facing any judge seeking to effect seamless change within a common-law system is how to fit the past forensic discourse into the strictures of precedent. Reading the judgments in the *Fitzpatrick* case, it becomes clear that the social goal of recognition of same-sex partnerships required a way to be found to distinguish between a gay/lesbian couple and other same-sex pairings. In order to distinguish between gay and lesbian couples and "spinsters" or "bachelors", *sex* or *the potential for sex* seemed to become the key differentiating features. The criteria which were fashioned to achieve this and adapt the family to the end of the 20th century are highly flexible. They derive from a formulation of the nature

---

[118] *Watson* v *Lucas* [1980] All ER 647.
[119] Housing (Scotland) Act 1988, s 46 (Sch 6, para 2(2), inserting Sch 1A into the Rent (Scotland) Act 1984).
[120] *Harrogate BC* v *Simpson* (1985) 17 HLR 205.
[121] *Ibid* at 215.
[122] *Ibid* – the court, according to Lord Fraser of Tullybelton, did not feel "the country was ready for it" (interview with the author in October 1986).

of a cohabiting heterosexual couple. The *Fitzpatrick* decision paved the way for the courts, failing Parliament, to give same-sex couples the same status as different-sex cohabitants.

THE GOALS OF THE LEGISLATION

The very broad and original purpose of the statute, as interpreted, was described as rewarding a range of relationships – close blood, remote blood, marriage, in-laws, step-children and lovers.[123] This meaning involves a continuum. The crucial notion which provided the *entrée* into a variable perspective on the family was accepted by a number of the judges: "A belief which represented unquestioned orthodoxy in year x may have become questionable by year y and unsustainable by year z."[124] An example derived from empirical observation was the cohabiting couple. No longer was the talk of the man and his "mistress" and their "bastard offspring" but a clear and popular version of the family: "I would have no hesitation in holding today that when, it appears, one-third of younger people live together unmarried, that … Each can be a member of the other's family."[125]

THE HALLMARKS OF THE NEW FAMILY

The notion of the family was constructed as being different from "living together as man and wife" for same-sex couples, where marriage and blood ties were absent:

> "Essentially the bond must be one of love and affection, not of a casual or transitory nature, but in a relationship which is permanent or at least intended to be so. As a result of that personal attachment to that other, other characteristics will follow."[126]

He specified the separate elements or *indiciae*: degree of mutual inter-dependence; sharing of lives; caring; love; commitment; and support. This involves a stable, loving and caring relationship which is not intended to be merely temporary where the couple live together broadly as they would if they were married. This applies to those of the same sex, although the onus on one person claiming that he or she was a member of the same-sex original tenant's family will involve that person establishing rather than merely asserting the necessary *indiciae* of the relationship. Certain relations are excluded, as where there is a transient, superficial relationship even if it is intimate or mere cohabitation by

---

[123] *Fitzpatrick* v *Sterling Housing Ltd* [1999] 4 All ER 705.
[124] *Ibid* at 715, quoting Lord Bingham with approval.
[125] *Ibid*.
[126] *Ibid*, per Lord Clyde at 737.

friends as a matter of convenience.[127] The mutual support element was seen as crucial: "readiness to support each other emotionally and financially, to care for and look after the other in times of need, and to provide a companionship in which mutual interests and activities can be shared and enjoyed".[128]

SOCIAL RATIONALE

The implications not just of changes in the meaning of words but of changes in the broader nature of society were seen as crucial too:

> "The courts have given a wide and elastic meaning to family in the present context ... if family were given a narrow or rigid meaning ... [such] a meaning would fail to reflect the diverse ways people, in a multicultural society, now live together in family units."[129]

The underlying legislative purpose was to provide a secure home for those who share lives in the manner which characterises a family unit irrespective of the morality of this relationship.

SIGNIFICANCE OF SEX

In addition to the fact that family membership would be difficult to establish without the couple living together in the same house, the majority in the House of Lords indicated that where a same-sex couple were living together in order to come within the ambit of "family" they required an active sexual relationship or at least the potentiality of such a relationship. It may also well be relevant that a couple have or care for children *whom they regard as their own.* This would make the family designation more immediately obvious

Lord Hutton found it difficult to see why two elderly spinsters who lived together for mutual support and companionship in old age without any sexual element in their relationship and who gave each other devoted care should not qualify as members of the same family. The sexual relationship between a couple was, he accepted, a very important and enriching part of their life together but he was "unable to accept that there is such a distinction between an elderly homosexual couple who once had an active sexual relationship and two elderly spinsters who never had a sexual relationship".[130] He was concerned that the same-sex couple should be regarded as members of each other's family and the spinsters should not.

---

[127] *Dyson Holdings Ltd* v *Fox* [1975] 3 All ER 1030 at 1035.
[128] Per Lord Clyde at 727j.
[129] Per Lord Nicholls of Birkenhead at 720b.
[130] *Ibid* at 740 per Lord Hutton.

REJECTING SAME-SEX RELATIONSHIPS AS EQUIVALENT
TO LIVING TOGETHER AS MAN AND WIFE

The rejection of same-sex couples living together as man and wife is merely asserted. There is no argument and the *indiciae* of family are the same as "living together as man and wife". Absence of coherent reasons, or more usually simple bigotry masquerading as reasons for legal decisions, is not unknown in the forensic history. In the realm of landlord and tenant law the hardships meted out in the name of freedom of contract in the 19th and 20th centuries are legion.[131]

The nature of the dominant discourse in *Fitzpatrick* means that the way would have been open for a future group of judges simply to accept that as many same-sex couples bring up or adopt children, have surrogate children etc this would allow them to be seen as meeting the one crucial attribute of different-sex couples. The meaning of the concept of "living together as man and wife" fulfills any set of criteria involving mutual love and support.

The heterosexual nature of living together as man and wife was asserted in two different ways. Lord Slynn relied on the notion of parliamentary intention. He suggested that *prima facie* it involved a man and a woman, and the man must show that the woman was living with him as "his" wife. He did not think that Parliament as recently as 1988 intended that these words should be read as meaning "my same-sex partner". If that had been the intention it would have been spelled out.[132] Lord Hobhouse of Woodborough simply rejected such a notion out of hand as being a clear usurpation of the legislative function.[133]

His colleague, Lord Hutton, was content to rely on plain assertion, albeit using the words of a Court of Appeal judge in the *Harrogate* v *Simpson* case:

> "A person can only live with a man as his wife when that person is a woman ... a person can only live with another person as a husband when that other person is a woman.
>
> I am in agreement with the opinion of Ewbank J at page 210 [Simpson (1984)] that:
>
> > 'The essential characteristic of living together as husband and wife is that there should be a man and a woman ...'"[134]

---

[131] Robson (1979) at 115–187.

[132] Per Lord Slynn at 710h.

[133] "As regards ... that he was Mr Thompson's "spouse" or was living with Mr Thompson "as his or wife or husband" "[t]o accept the submission of Mr Fitzpatrick would be an exercise of legislation, not interpretation" (at 745f).

[134] *Ibid* per Lord Hutton at 733g.

The recognition of same-sex relationships by the legislature for the purposes of succession in landlord and tenant cases[135] has rendered these debates of historical interest but by no means merely for academics. They demonstrate how recently the shift in judicial thinking was and how, having apparently taken the lead ahead of the legislature in recognising same-sex relationships as "familial", their various reasons for rejecting the equality of such same-sex relationships with marriage have themselves been rendered obsolete.

The House of Lords itself subsequently examined the issue in the context of discrimination under the Human Rights Act 1998. Articles 8 and 14 of the European Convention on Human Rights required legislation not to draw a distinction on the ground of sexual orientation without good reason. There was no justification for treating same-sex couples differently from heterosexual ones, the House of Lords determined.[136] Wearing Privy Council hats, their Lordships rejected the policy of Gibraltar's Housing Allocation Committee to exclude same-sex couples by refusing to grant such couples joint tenancies and thereby deny the survivor protection in the event of the tenant dying. Although, here, childless heterosexual couples were also denied such a right, they had the possibility of having children while same-sex couples would never be able to meet the criterion. This was, in the words of Lady Hale, a "form of indirect discrimination which comes as close as it can to direct discrimination".[137]

The same line of reasoning recognising same-sex relationships as giving rise to the same succession rights as marriage as far as tenancies are concerned is found in a number of cases heard before the European Court of Human Rights. The denial of succession rights was rejected in an Austrian case in 2003 and in a Polish case in 2010 which raised interesting individual points. First, the Court rejected the argument that it was possible to look back for the meaning to the time when discriminatory legislation was passed.[138] More recently, it made it clear that it did not matter that the rationale for discriminatory practice arose from terms of the Constitution ensuring the protection of the family founded on a "union of a man and a woman".[139]

---

[135] Housing (Scotland) Act 2001, s 108.
[136] *Ghaidan* v *Godin-Mendoza* [2004] 2 AC 557.
[137] *Rodriguez* v *Minister of Housing of Gibraltar* [2009] OKPC 52, para 19.
[138] *Karner* v *Austria* (2004) 38 EHRR 24.
[139] *Kozak* v *Poland* (2010) 51 EHRR 16.

8   REGULATION OF HOUSING

Regulation, in the form of limitations on what may be done by property owners, has a long history in relation to property. For centuries, there have been, for instance, restrictions on what kind of buildings may be erected and on how property owners may treat their tenants. Buildings required to conform to the rules of the precursors to building regulations, the Dean of Guild Court,[1] as well as with what restrictions might be imposed by feudal conditions.[2] There were also, until 1914, limitations on how some landowners could dispose of their property in terms of the entailing of land.[3] This was finally laid to rest in the Abolition of Feudal Tenure etc (Scotland) Act 2000. Using one's land to the detriment of others has long been prohibited in the concept of not acting maliciously against one's neighbour – *aemulatio vicini* – and through the common law rules on nuisance.[4] For their part, landlords have long been constrained by the terms of the Leases Act 1449 which gives tenants the right to remain in their property irrespective of a change of landlord for the term of their leases.[5] These limitations were principally restrictive and did not require property owners to do anything other than abstain from unlawful action. The difference with the modern forms of regulation is that owners and landlords require to play an active role in meeting certain standards and tests. Advisers of landlords could in the past expect to be asked to deal with problems after they arose, whereas in the 21st century their role has changed to a proactive one, advising on what requirements must be satisfied by landlords in terms of housing conditions prior to leasing property, the process of registration and the role of landlords in ensuring they avoid being subject to anti-social behaviour notices in respect of their tenants. There are further obligations for landlords who rent out what until recently would have been standard tenancies but where the number of tenants sharing takes the tenancy into the coverage of the

---

[1]   *Encyclopaedia of the Laws of Scotland* (1928), vol 5, pp 424ff.
[2]   Reid and Gretton (2008).
[3]   Burns (1938), Ch XXV; an international issue which also features in Maycombe, Alabama in *To Kill a Mockingbird* (1962) and is the key to the lynch mob deciding to back off when Scout raises the issue.
[4]   Paisley (2000) at 4.13–4.15.
[5]   See Chapter 6.

separate and quite onerous regime covering houses in multiple occupancy. This number of unrelated sharers which makes a property subject to the multiple occupancy control regime is now only three.[6]

LEGAL REGULATION

Common law basis

At common law tenancies were simply contracts entered into for a period of time granting the right to use heritable property for a fixed term. There have traditionally been a couple of distinctive rules allowing tenancies to continue beyond their termination date, or *ish*, if neither side had given a notice to quit to the other party. The doctrine of tacit relocation means that the tenancy continues for either the length of the original lease or a year, whichever was the shorter period.[7] In addition, where the subjects of the tenancy were residential, the landlord has always had an obligation to provide property that was tenantable and habitable.[8]

Statutory interventions

The expansion of social renting, the introduction of the Rent Acts in 1915 and the continued regulation of the levels of rents and security of tenure mean that there is now a range of different tenancy types.[9] There are two basic tenancy regimes. One operates where the landlord is a private individual or commercial organisation. The legal regimes here depend on when the tenancy commenced and what kind of lease is offered. Tenancies entered into before 1989 will be covered by the Rent (Scotland) Act 1984. Subsequent tenancies are covered by the Housing (Scotland) Act 1988 and are either assured tenancies or short tenancies. In the social rented sector there is a single social tenancy available to landlords who are either local authorities or registered social landlords. Within social renting there are two types of tenancy which are encountered – the Scottish secure tenancy and the short Scottish secure tenancy. The legislation which covers the creation and termination of these tenancies is the Housing (Scotland) Act 2001. The details of how these provisions operate are dealt with in the appropriate chapter. It is, however, important to note that in considering the nature of interventions in the market in relation to pricing, allocation and conditions that competing political visions of the nature and function of the role of government in housing have played a major role for the past century. Lack of faith in the ability of market forces to provide decent housing

---

[6] See Chapter 9.
[7] Rankine (3rd edn, 1916), at 598ff.
[8] See Chapter 4.
[9] See Chapter 3.

at a price working people can afford and in the places where they would wish to live has led to conflicting policies. These are reflected in the level and nature of Government regulation which has been encountered at various times during the past century.

There has been, then, indirect regulation in the rental market in these fields from 1915 until the present day. The major distinction is that there now requires to be active property management by the landlord as well as their needing to meet a threshold of respectability.

Regulation was first encountered in relation to rents from 1915, with the freezing of recoverable rents from that date. In terms of tenants rights to financial assistance in meeting their rent obligations, the Welfare Reform Act 2007 replaced the means-tested housing benefit payment for new claimants. The assistance is now paid at fixed rates depending on the area and household size rather than on the basis of the rent actually payable. This might be expected to have an impact on the rents set by landlords who can access the figures electronically. For instance, in June 2010 the rent payable for a two-bedroom property in the most expensive area in Scotland, Aberdeenshire, was £155.77 while in Edinburgh and the Lothians the figure was £144.23 and in Greater Glasgow it was £126.92. The cheapest accommodation of such a size was to be found in Dumfries and Galloway and the Borders, at £98.08.[10]

The most noticeable incursion into owners' traditional rights to do with their property as they chose was the introduction of security of tenure for life for the law-abiding rent-paying tenant back in 1915. This limited the landlords' rights to repossess property to specified grounds such as requiring the property for one's own occupancy or for a member of the family. Tenants who did not pay their rent or who breached the terms of their leases were not, however, protected. In addition, it was possible for a member of the family to succeed to the tenancy of what had been their home.[11]

Replacing the crude rent freeze of the Rent Acts prior to 1965, the fair rent system also limited the rents landlords were able to charge. Although no regulated tenancies have been created since 1989 they are still encountered. Governed by the Rent (Scotland) Act 1984, they give a right to seek to have a fair rent set along with extensive security of tenure rights to the immediate tenant and any spouse or partner living in the property. The rights of tenants, though to have a fair rent fixed were entirely optional. There was no requirement for landlords to seek a certificate of fair rent prior to renting out their property. Nor was there was obligation on tenants, who discovered that they were paying in excess

---

[10] http://www.scotland.gov.uk/Topics/Built-Environment/Housing/PrivateRenting/ rent-registration-service/setting-lha – consulted on 15 June 2010.

[11] See Chapter 7.

of what a fair rent would be, to approach the authorities. Where a claim for housing benefit to the local authority was involved the matter was taken out of the tenant's hands by the local authority. Landlords were, however, limited to this fair rent figure if the tenant sought to enforce their rights and could be required to pay back excess rent which had been paid in ignorance by a tenant provided the claim was made within 2 years of the date of payment.[12]

As far as security of tenure rights go, it should also be pointed out that tenants were under no obligation to enforce these rights. Numerous instances occurred in the 1970s and 1980s where tenants who sought advice had been asked by their landlords to leave their rented property so that the owners could sell in order to arrange their finances on relationship breakdown. Some tenants, advised of their rights as "sitting tenants", opted to exact a premium from the landlords for providing vacant possession and giving up their statutory security of tenure rights. Others were happy to move and seek accommodation elsewhere, recognising that the request for vacant possession was not mere caprice. The only group who have, in essence, been *required* to stay and defend their position have been those threatened with homelessness by an impending eviction.[13] The House of Lords made it clear in an early hearing under the Housing (Homeless Persons) Act 1977 that applicants should stay until as late as possible before seeking accommodation from the community,[14] rather than anticipate matters and give up accommodation prior to the possession order. This applied whether or not there was any colourable defence to the possession proceedings.[15]

There was no requirement on landlords in private residential tenancies prior to 1989 to provide written leases and many landlords did not do so or provided a skeleton lease identifying only the property, the names of the parties, the initial period of the lease and the rent payable. When the Housing (Scotland) Act 1988 was introduced it applied only to future tenants. The assured tenancy regime closely resembled the protected tenancy set up with controls over rents and security of tenure. The changes were, however, of major significance. In the first place there was a requirement that there be a written lease.[16] This obligation to provide a written document stating "the terms of the tenancy" at no cost to the tenant[17] included a sanction. Where either no lease was provided, or it

---

12   RSA 1984, s 37, discussed in *North* v *Allan Properties (Edinburgh) Ltd* 1987 SLT (Sh Ct) 141.
13   See Chapter 2.
14   *Din* v *Wandsworth LBC* [1981] 3 All ER 881 at 895.
15   The issue sometimes has been clouded as in cases where the tenancy was a tenancy that went with employment – a service occupancy: *R* v *Portsmouth City Council, ex p Knight* (1982) LGR 184.
16   HSA 1988, s 30(1).
17   *Ibid*, s 30(3).

failed to reflect the existing terms of the tenancy, the sheriff had to draw up such a document.[18]

There were also other differences. In tenancies entered into on or after 2 January 1989 where one person rents out to another a property which is that person's only or principal home the basic assured tenancy provides full security of tenure. It does not provide the option to have the rent changed by a rent officer or rent assessment committee.

As noted above,[19] there is another variant of the assured tenancy: the short assured tenancy. Here, two additional tests must be satisfied. First, the tenancy must be for a minimum of 6 months. Second, a special form, the AT5 notice, must be served, indicating to the future tenant that this was a special kind of tenancy in which the landlord had a "special right to repossess" the property. In effect, the tenancies provide no security of tenure beyond the term of the lease.[20] There is, however, a right to have an application to the rent assessment committee where the rent being charged is significantly higher than current market rents.[21]

As we explore in some greater detail elsewhere, there are detailed protections in place for properties in multiple occupancy.[22] Traditionally, those occupying in this part of the sector have been most vulnerable, with limited bargaining powers over their living conditions and the rent they pay. In addition, the presence of multiply occupied property has been seen as less desirable in neighbourhoods with its association with transient tenants and anti-social behaviour. Accordingly, much more detailed regulatory powers are available in this sector of the private market, covering tenancy terms, housing conditions and fire regulations.

A new form of direct regulation of who can be a landlord was added by the Antisocial Behaviour etc (Scotland) Act 2004. Part 8 of the Act makes registration of landlords compulsory for most commercial private rentals.

Private landlord registration

The need for private landlords to be on a register of approved landlords was introduced in Pt 8 of the Antisocial Behaviour etc (Scotland) Act 2004. It was originally intended as a pilot project. The process was conceived of as a service available on-line. After major delays due to software problems the registration part of the Act came into effect on 30 April 2006. It provides for a 3-year period of registration. There are essentially two types of registration. The first occurs where a person already owns

---

[18] HSA 1988, s 30(2).
[19] See Chapter 3.
[20] See Chapter 6.
[21] HSA 1988, s 34 – see, for greater detail, Chapter 5. The rent assessment committee is now the private rented housing committee.
[22] See Chapter 9.

property which they wish to let out, which involves specifying details of both landlord and the properties involved. In addition, there are situations where a person is thinking of renting in the future, perhaps with a "buy to let" mortgage. It might well be advisable to check that the proposed landlord meets the statutory criteria and will be able to rent out legally.

Each local authority must prepare and maintain a register of landlords. This was originally to be available for public inspection. It is not currently available to the public.[23] Instead, people can apply for details of a particular house, owner and agent.[24] The register is of houses where there is a lease or an occupancy agreement by virtue of which an "unconnected person" may use the house as a dwelling.[25] This broad terminology, including "occupancy agreements", means that anyone using any of the Rent Act evasions[26] should be covered. There is no requirement to register when renting out to members of the family. There does not appear to be a definition of the "family" within the 2004 Act nor is there any reference to a definition in any other legislation. There is a definition of "family member" in s 83 of the Housing (Scotland) Act 1987 which might be appropriate. It covers spouses, parents, grandparents, brothers, sisters, nieces, nephews, uncles and aunts. Cohabiting and same-sex partnerships and civil partnerships are given full legal recognition. It also makes no distinction between those of the whole blood or half blood or treated as family members or those adopted.[27]

The registration process is significantly cheaper than the HMO process since the level of intervention by the local authority is minimal.[28] There

---

23   ASBSA 2004, s 82 – repealed by Housing (Scotland) Act 2006, s 176.
24   HSA 2006, s 88A.
25   ASBSA 2004, s 83(1)(b).
26   See Robson and Halliday (1998) at 42ff.
27   "(1) A person is a member of another's family for the purposes of this Act if – (a) he is the spouse [or civil partner] of that person or he and that person live together as husband and wife [or in a relationship which has the characteristics of the relationship between husband and wife except that the persons are of the same sex]; or (b) he is that person's parent, grandparent, child, grandchild, brother, sister, uncle, aunt, nephew or niece.
     (2) For the purposes of subsection (1)(b) – (a) a relationship by marriage [or by virtue of civil partnership] shall be treated as a relationship by blood; (b) a relationship of the half-blood shall be treated as a relationship of the whole blood; (c) the stepchild of a person shall be treated as his child; and (ca) a person brought up or treated by another person as if the person were the child of the other person shall be treated as that person's child; (d) a child shall be treated as such whether or not his parents are married.
     (3) Except in subsection (1)(a), references in this Act to a person's spouse include references to [that person's civil partner or to] another person living together with that person as husband and wife or in a relationship which has the characteristics of the relationship between husband and wife except that the persons are of the same sex."
28   See Chapter 9.

is a fee payable for registration.[29] This is fixed centrally by the Scottish Government although the original idea in the first regulations was for local authorities who administer the scheme to set this figure. The figure at the time of writing is £55 for the first property and £11 for each subsequent property. There is a 10 per cent discount for on-line registrations, 100 per cent discount for charities. Late applications require to pay double. There is a discount for multiple authority applications.

EXEMPTIONS

Apart from the limited category of family members there is a list of bodies whose are specifically exempted from the requirement to register as landlords. The intention of the legislation is to root out those "bad apple" exploitative landlords as well as cover only appropriate and permanent accommodation.[30] The list of exempt properties covers care home service or school care accommodation, independent health care service accommodation, secure accommodation service. There are also exemptions for a range of situations where the standard commercial tenancy does not apply. These cover properties which are the only or main residence of the landlord and properties which are holiday lets only. Although distinct from a tenancy, the legislation makes clear that any occupancy under a liferent is also exempt. The aim of the legislation is to combat exploitation and bad management in the residential renting sector and so landlords of tenanted farms and/or crofts are not required to register. The first consultation on the operation of the legislation identified a number of scenarios where there might well be temporary rental arrangements where it would be onerous and inappropriate to require registration. The kinds of "transitory ownership" whose situation was clarified were rentals up to a period of 6 months by an executor holding pending transfer to beneficiary; heritable creditors in possession; insolvency practitioners.

The rest of the exemptions are a mixed bunch of properties where one might reasonably assume that the landlord is unlikely to exploit their position. This covers property owned by a local authority or registered social landlord who are assumed to have the best interests of their tenants at heart. As was pointed out in the minority Report of the Royal Commission on Housing in Scotland back in 1917, the dissatisfied tenant has an element of political control through the ballot box if the social rented landlord is not operating satisfactorily.[31] As we see later in this chapter, the level of bureaucratic regulation on behalf of social rented sector tenants is now considerable. Also, where local authorities have a

---

[29] SSI 2005/558, SSI 2006/28 and SSI 2008/403.
[39] ASBSA 2004, s 84(6).
[31] Royal Commission Minority Report (1917) *The Voting Power of the Municipal Tenant* at 393, para 214.

control order in force in terms of the Housing (Scotland) Act 1987[32] there is again no requirement for them to register.[33]

In addition, if there is a religious use and the property is occupied by a leader or preacher of that faith or occupied only by members of a religious order then there is no need for the religious order to be an approved landlord.[34] Again, here, the absence of an exploitative relationship is the key. This same notion accounts for why lets to members of landlord's family are also excluded. There does not, however, appear to be any definition in the Antisocial Behaviour etc (Scotland) Act 2004 of what constitutes a family. As mentioned above, one might assume that the definition found in the Housing (Scotland) Act 1987 might be used although it should be noted that this states that it is operational "for the purposes of this Act".[35] These exempt categories can be altered by the Scottish Ministers.[36]

THE REGISTRATION PROCESS[37]

There is certain information laid down in the legislation which an applicant must provide. This includes the name and address of the applicant, the address of each rented house (if any) within the area of the authority and the name and address of any agent acting for applicant.[38] There is provision for further information to be prescribed. This occurred in relation to the requirement to provide a correspondence address. In order for contact to be made with the landlord or his agent a correspondence address must now also be supplied. This gap was identified prior to the passage of the Housing (Scotland) Act 2006 which introduced this change.[39]

CRITERIA FOR A "FIT AND PROPER PERSON"[40]

One policy possibility which has existed since the days of Peter Rachman in the 1960s and of Nicolas Hoogstraten in the 1980s has been to regulate the sector by rewarding and acknowledging good practice or by requiring minimum standards of conduct. It is possible to have an approved landlord standard akin to that for hotels, guest houses and restaurants where the public can get some guidance from a system of quality standards. This would support landlords with demonstrably good standards of accommodation and service to tenants. A more minimalist approach would be to penalise or exclude those whose conduct is questionable. The

---

[32] HSA 1987, s 178.
[33] ASBSA 2004, s 83(6)(c).
[34] *Ibid*, s 83(6)(b).
[35] HSA 1987, s 183 (as amended).
[36] ASBSA 2004, s 83(7).
[37] *Ibid*, s 83(1)(a) and (b).
[38] *Ibid*, s 83(1)(c).
[39] *Ibid*, s 88A (as inserted by HSA 2006, s 176).
[40] *Ibid*, s 85.

2004 legislation adopts a strategy towards realising the goal of minimum standards while encouraging local efforts to adopt good practice.

In relation to minimum standards, the legislation requires a landlord to be a "fit and proper person".[41] Akin to the kind of regulation available in company law with the possibility of someone being excluded from being a director of a company for unfitness,[42] this allows local authorities to make a judgment as to suitability of an applicant to act as a private sector landlord. In deciding whether or not an applicant or any agent being used is a "fit and proper person" the local authority must have regard to a number of issues.

First is whether the applicant or agent has committed any offence involving fraud or other dishonesty or violence or drugs.[43] The link between this kind of behaviour and the likelihood of the landlord being a potential exploiter of tenants is clear. So too is the requirement for the local authority to consider whether an applicant has contravened any provision of the law relating to housing law or landlord and tenant law. Without going into the question of how exactly these fields of law are identified, this provision has a clearly protective goal. If a landlord has been engaged in unlawful eviction or failing to effect repairs in the past then this is at least an indicator that you would not want them as your landlord in the future. To this end, decisions of the private rented housing panel appear on the register in relation to repairs and any acts or omissions of the applicant or agent in relation to anti-social behaviour relating to the house including failure to comply with anti-social behaviour notices.[44] In the same vein, the local authority may look at any contravention of the letting code provided for in the Antisocial Behaviour etc (Scotland) Act 2004.[45] The local authority also have the option to look at the terms of any agreement between the landlord and their agent which might indicate whether or not the landlord is adopting good practice or seeking to exploit his position.[46]

Slightly less directly connected with the likely tenant experience but nonetheless one of the criteria laid down for deciding about fitness as a landlord is the issue of whether the landlord has practised unlawful discrimination on grounds of sex, colour, race, ethnic or national origins or disability in, or in connection with the carrying on of any business.[47] Again the assumption seems to be that to have a landlord who is racist is likely to lead to a bad experience for tenants. While the connection for

---

[41] ASBSA 2004, s 84(3).
[42] Company Directors Disqualification Act 1986, s 7(1) on unfitness; see Boyle and Birds (2009).
[43] ASBSA 2004, s 85(2).
[44] *Ibid*, s 87A – introduced by HSA 2006, s 175.
[45] *Ibid*, s 92A – introduced by HSA 2006, s 175.
[46] *Ibid*, s 85 and ss 3A and 4A – introduced by HSA 2006, s 175.
[47] *Ibid*, s 85(2).

anyone of the ethnicity approved of by the landlord might be perfectly fine, such behaviour in a multicultural society is to be discouraged. The same thinking lies behind the inclusion of disability awareness and acceptable practice. Acting prejudicially against people with disabilities may well be irrelevant to the experience of the tenants a landlord accepts. The negative attitude towards this issue is however, indicative of an unwelcoming attitude to an already disadvantaged sector of the community.

The local authority must look at the issues indicated and gather material in relation to the application. It might, for instance, gather information from local newspaper reports, for instance, where tenants are suing for the return of deposits. The material they look at is relevant if it appears relevant to the authority to the question of whether the applicant or agent is a fit and proper person.[48]

NOTIFICATION[49]

Where a local authority registers or refuses to register a person the authority must, as soon as practicable after doing so, give notice of the fact to the person. This notice must also be sent to all addresses of the property owner.

REMOVAL FROM THE REGISTER[50]

Where a person is registered and the person is no longer a fit and proper person there is provision for them to be removed from the register. This applies to those who apply in relation to specific property as well as those who merely seek to be approved landlords. The notification of such removal is to be by recorded delivery to the person and, where relevant, agent.

APPEAL AGAINST NON-REGISTRATION
OR REMOVAL FROM REGISTER[51]

There is provision for summary application to the sheriff by any person who has either been refused entry onto the register or whose name is to be removed from same. The sheriff may make an order requiring the authority to enter the person in the register or retain the person's name on the register. There is further appeal within 21 days from the date of decision to the sheriff principal whose decision shall be final.

CRIMINAL OFFENCES[52]

It is an offence to rent out accommodation to an unconnected person where a landlord is not registered by the local authority. It is also an

---

[48] ASBSA 2004, s 85(4).
[49] *Ibid*, ss 90 and 91.
[50] *Ibid*, s 89.
[51] *Ibid*, s 92.
[52] *Ibid*, s 93.

offence to "communicate with another with a view to entering into a lease or occupancy agreement". An "unconnected person" is a person who is not a member of the family of the relevant person.[53] It is not an offence to rent out or seek tenants where application for registration has been made and a decision is pending. There is a defence for a person to show that there was a reasonable excuse for acting in the way charged. If convicted there is a fine not exceeding level 5.[54]

CIVIL CONSEQUENCES – THE RENT PENALTY NOTICE[55]

Where there is an unregistered property or one has been removed from the register the local authority may decide "it is appropriate … having regard to all the circumstances" to serve a notice that no rent nor any other consideration shall be payable. Where the authority cannot identify the landlord, it may serve notice in two or more newspapers to include a local one. There is provision for appeal within 21 days to the sheriff. The owner must notify the tenant that a rent penalty notice has taken effect and that no rent is now payable. If he fails to do so, then he cannot claim back any rent if the rent penalty notice is revoked or overturned on appeal.

IMPACT OF THE REGULATION LEGISLATION

The legislation was all rather a surprise, coming, as it did, fully formed rather having been piloted. There was a delay in being brought into force until 30 April 2006 and the regulations made in respect of fees which had been made were amended prior to coming into effect. There have been some minor tidying up issues dealt with in the Housing (Scotland) Act 2006. A further consultation document was published in 2008.

There were some 87,875 applications in the first year of the legislation's operation and this had reached 138,194 applications for registration by February 2009, covering 193,170 properties.[56] Around 83 per cent had been assessed by February 2009. Local authorities received initial central Government funding of £5.2 million and the actual local authority expenditure on the scheme amounted to £6.6 million. Fees brought in £5 million and an approximate annual income of £1.7 million was expected.[57]

A Shelter report on the first 3 years of registration of landlords from April 2009[58] noted that 15 per cent of all landlords are not registered. This amounted to some 25 per cent of private rented properties. Its findings

---

[53] See above at p 272.
[54] ASBSA 2004, s 93.
[55] *Ibid*, s 94.
[56] Scottish Government (2009d), para 5.62.
[57] *Ibid*.
[58] Landlord Registration in Scotland: three years on (2009) – available at www.shelter.

suggest that Councils are not applying the "fit and proper" test and not using available sanctions to stop landlords indulging in bad practices like illegal evictions. There is in addition a problem with a lack of tenant awareness. The Scottish Government Private Rented Sector Report on the state of the private rented sector suggested in 2009 that only 4 tenants in 10 had heard of landlord registration.[59]

Antisocial behaviour notices

Part 7 of the Anti-social Behaviour etc (Scotland) Act 2004 introduced a new responsibility onto landlords in respect of the behaviour of their tenants. Part of the strategy to deal with anti-social behaviour available to local authorities and RSLs is the possibility of seeking ASBOs against their tenants. Landlords in the private sector have no such opportunity. Part 7, however introduces the ASBN – anti-social behaviour notice. In simple terms, ASBOs are served on individuals committing antisocial behaviour – loud music; noisy pets; inappropriate behaviour – by the local authority.[60] ASBNs are served on landlords whose *tenants* have been guilty of anti-social behaviour – by the local authority. The intention is to encourage landlords to ensure, insofar as they are able, that tenants behave appropriately meeting the terms of their tenancy agreements.

Where it appears to the local authority that a person is engaging in anti-social activity at or in the locality of a house in their area it may serve an anti-social behaviour *notice* on the landlord of the house.[61] The notice describes the anti-social behaviour that has been engaged in and requires the landlord to take within a specified period such action as may be specified. The landlord may be instructed to get the tenant to comply with the terms of the lease contract or in serious instances to seek repossession. The notice states the consequences of failure to take the action specified. There is a right to review.[62] If a landlord requests review then the local authority must review the notice. The request for review must be made within 21 days from service. The review must be carried out by person who had no involvement in making the ASBN in question, and who is senior to the person responsible whose decision is being appealed. The review may confirm, vary any part, suspend or revoke the notice. The affected person must be notified. There is no duty to carry out a further review.

This is an entirely new departure in terms of landlords' responsibilities. Previous to this, any landlord could take the view that while the behaviour of tenants might annoy others, as long as the rent was paid on time and the property was not damaged, then how their tenants behaved was not

---

[59] Scottish Government (2009d) at 6.
[60] See Chapter 6.
[61] ASBSA 2004, s 68.
[62] *Ibid*, s 69.

really their problem. The possibility of the ASBN alters this. If there are problems of compliance, these might be expected to arise through miscommunication. Where the landlord is living abroad or a goodly distance from the property then their response might be tardy. They might see the property simply as a cash cow rather than something requiring the investment of time and energy required for proper management. If that is the case and there is a failure by the landlord to comply with notice then there are potentially serious consequences.[63]

Rent income suspension

A rental income suspension notice may be served on the landlord and the occupants that no rent nor any other payment is payable by any occupant. This will be done where the sheriff is satisfied that the landlord has not taken timeous action in relation to matters specified in the ASBN and, having regard to all the circumstances relating to the house, it would have been reasonable to take action. The lease remains valid so that the tenant whose actions are at the heart of the problem remains unscathed for the meantime. There may be an appeal against a rental income suspension order. Any appeal against the sheriff's decision must be made to the sheriff principal within 21 days from date of decision appealed against.[64] The appeal must also be notified to the occupant tenant in prescribed form. In the event of failure to do this and the appeal succeeding then a tenant who had not been notified would not be due back rent. There is provision for further regulations specifying circumstances where no rent payable. The decision of the sheriff principal on the appeal is final. Where an order is made suspending rent, the local authority or landlord may apply to the sheriff to revoke, or suspend the order where the landlord has taken the action specified in the ASBN or having regard to all the circumstances it would be unreasonable for the order to continue to have effect.[65] This might occur if the tenant had moved away either voluntarily or had been incarcerated on some unrelated issue.

Management control order

Worse lies in store for a recalcitrant landlord who ignores the relevant correspondence from the landlord and local authority. If the sheriff is satisfied that the landlord has not taken action specified in the ASBN, and, having regard to all the circumstances, it would be reasonable for the landlord to take such action and, to enable the anti-social behaviour described in the notice to be dealt with, then the sheriff may feel it necessary to make a "management control order".[66] This is a more drastic

---

[63]   ASBA 2004, s 71.
[64]   *Ibid*, s 72.
[65]   *Ibid*, s 73.
[66]   *Ibid*, s 74.

sanction than the rent suspension order. The effect of the Management Control Order is to transfer, for a period not exceeding 12 months, the rights and obligations of the landlord to the local authority for existing and new occupants. The legislation, therefore, seems to suggest that the local authority can enter into new arrangements which will bind the landlord once the control order comes to an end. The local authority may recover rent or other consideration paid for occupancy during the period from the landlord and must keep accounts. The rights of the occupants causing the trouble are not affected.[67] Furthermore, where an MCO is in force the local authority may not only ingather rents but carry out repairs deemed necessary. The landlord is liable for the expenditure incurred by the local authority. The local authority or the former landlord may apply to sheriff for revocation of the MCO where action required under the ASBN has been taken or it would be unreasonable for the ASBN to continue to have effect. There are further consequences where a landlord fails to comply with an ASBN. It is a criminal offence where a local authority serves an ASBN and the landlord fails to take the specified action timeously. The landlord guilty of such an offence is liable, on summary conviction, to a fine not exceeding level 5 on the standard scale. It is a defence if the landlord can show that there was a reasonable excuse for the failure in question.[68] If, for instance, an agent who was managing the property had absconded leaving a trail of debts this could well be deemed a reasonable excuse. One would not expect ASBNs to be a major feature of the housing scene, given their powerful incentives to action by landlords. That said, simply doing as one correspondent recorded his client doing and just stuffing the official letters in a drawer in his desk is likely to bring on these serious sanctions.

SOCIAL RENTING

Background

There was initially no regulation in one part of the social rented sector, while regulation has been a standard feature of the other part. Local authorities were, until 1980, afforded extensive discretion in how they operated in relation to housing. They were obliged to assess the housing conditions in their area and the need for further housing accommodation.[69] They had to power to provide housing accommodation in a range of ways.[70] In terms of management of whatever stock they held and developed, they were, in essence, free to rent out to whom

67 ASBA 2004, s 74(3) and Sch 3.
68 *Ibid*, s 79.
68 Housing (Scotland) Act 1966, s 137.
70 *Ibid*, s 138.

they chose and with no restrictions on their right to evict.[71] The form of their tenancy was a matter for them and approaches varied enormously. Housing Associations, on the other hand, were regulated by the Housing Corporation which had been set up under the Housing Act 1964 and by the Registrar of Friendly Societies under the Industrial and Provident Societies Act 1965. This was subsequently covered by the Housing Act 1985 which covered Great Britain. From this period there has been a series of moves to bring these two parts of social renting into a common regulatory framework.

The Tenants' Rights etc (Scotland) Act 1980 most dramatically introduced the obligation on local authorities to sell their stock at large discounts to sitting tenants of 2 years' standing.[72] Less controversially, it brought in the concept of security of tenure for local authority tenants. Any landlord seeking, henceforth to evict a tenant had to satisfy the sheriff that it was reasonable to do so. The only grounds for repossession were laid down in Sch 2 to the 1980 Act. Limitations on the allocation of local authority housing were also introduced.[73] Initially, however, this was the extent of regulation. Rents were still a matter for local authority discretion.

Following a consultative paper in May 1987, the White Paper *Housing: The Government's Proposals for Scotland*[74] was published. The centrepiece of the White Paper was the introduction of the assured tenancy regime in the private rented sector. As far as the social rented sector was concerned, a new strategy was envisaged. Local authorities were to become enablers rather than direct providers of housing. So it was that, when the private rented sector was returned to be determined by market forces in 1988, a new body, Scottish Homes, was set up to take over the regulation of social rented housing. This body was responsible to the Secretary of State for Scotland. Most of its objectives were broadly political housing goals[75] but included "contributing to improved quality in housing and management".

Scottish Homes

The Housing (Scotland) Act 1988 accomplished two major tasks in relation to social renting. It transferred the business of the Scottish Special Housing Association[76] to the new body taking over the functions

---

[71] Cochrane (1976) at 101–102.
[72] See Chapter 3.
[73] See Chapter 2.
[74] Cm 242 (1987).
[75] For 1994–97 the other objectives were promoting home ownership; promoting the development of a more diverse rented sector; making an effective contribution to community regeneration strategies; assisting with housing needs; making an effective – Scottish Homes Strategic Plan 1994–97, quoted in Robertson (2001) at 115.
[76] See Begg (1987) on the history of the SSHA.

of the Housing Corporation as from 1 April 1989. Scottish Homes' dual role was summed up crisply by Douglas Robertson when he described it as an "interventionist body with a privatising purpose".[77] This latter function, involving the disposal of the SSHA's 85,000 houses, dominated discussion of the role of Scottish Homes. Its monitoring role was, on the face of it, rather more prosaic although of great political significance. It has been suggested that it went beyond the normal scope of monitoring in seeking to offer 'comfort' to private investors.[78] The different context produced by the introduction of private finance into this arena shifted, it is argued, to a kind of regulation "based on private sector notions of performance culture".[79] Monitoring became a much more intrusive issue and looked at the internal operations of housing providers.[80] Performance standards were introduced for housing associations which became the basis of the triennial monitoring visits,[81] altering, it was claimed, the role and scope of the housing association voluntary committees.[82] Seen as an instrument of Conservative housing policy, Scottish Homes was replaced after Labour came into office in May 1997.

Communities Scotland

A new regulatory framework encompassing housing associations and local authorities was set up in the Housing (Scotland) Act 2001. This made provision for a new concept, the registered social landlord. This covered housing associations and other bodies providing social housing. The regulation regimes for the new RSLs was to be the same for local authorities. The message of the Housing (Scotland) Act 2001 appeared to be simplification – a single social tenancy, a single regulatory framework and a single regulatory body.

Part 3 of the 2001 Act transferred the regulatory function from Scottish Homes to a new body – Communities Scotland. Scottish Homes had been a "quango" at arm's length from Government but with its membership and terms of reference determined by the then Scottish Office. Communities Scotland was an executive agency. This meant that it reported direct to Scottish Ministers and was accountable, through them, to the Scottish Parliament. A number of specific statutory functions were made its responsibility[83] by the Scottish Ministers who took over from Scottish Homes:[84]

---

[77] Robertson (1992) at 37.
[78] Robertson (2001) at 123.
[79] Ibid.
[80] Robertson and Bailey (1994).
[81] Scottish Homes (1995).
[82] Robertson and Bailey (1994).
[83] Housing (Scotland) Act 2001 (Commencement No 2, Transitional Provisions, Savings and Variation) Order 2001 (SSI 2001/397).
[84] HSA 2001, s 84.

* to maintain a register of social landlords[85] and to set criteria for admission of organisations to that register;[86]

* to agree performance standards to ensure the delivery of good quality housing and related services.

In addition, there was provision for a statutory Code of Good Practice[87] to provide national housing management standards. These Performance standards were to ensure that tenants and others in housing would be aware of the standards of service they can expect from all RSLs and local authorities. The housing and regeneration function of Scottish Homes was transferred to Communities Scotland. When they were abolished and their regulatory role was transferred to the Scottish Housing Regulator, these financial and strategic functions were transferred for a short period "into the core of Scottish Government".[88]

The Scottish Housing Regulator

The most recent incarnation of regulation in the Scottish social rented sector is to be found in the renaming of Communities Scotland with a more indicative title: the Scottish Housing Regulator. Its framework and guidance was hugely complex and involved extensive detailed information on a wide range of issues. It was centred around meeting peer group performance standards. The Ministerial Code of Practice from 2008 gave a clear indication of the key principles to be followed:

(a) equality of opportunity exists across all aspects of social housing and related services;

(b) tenants and other service users are encouraged and supported to participate in the management of the service they receive;

(c) regulated bodies to provide high quality services;

(d) regulated bodies observe the highest ethical standards and operate in an open and accountable manner; and

(e) value for money is achieved.[89]

The Scottish Housing Regulator was originally established as an executive agency of the Scottish Government in terms of the Scotland Act 1998 and the staff were civil servants.[90] It was to operate impartially carrying out its regulation and scrutiny of the housing sector while it remained directly accountable to the Scottish Ministers.[91] This situation

---

85 HSA 2001, s 57(1).
86 *Ibid*, s 61.
87 *Ibid*, s 80.
88 Scottish Housing Regulator Framework Document (2008d).
89 Scottish Government Code of Practice (2008b) at 5.3.
90 *Ibid* at 7.1.
91 *Ibid* at 2.1.

was changed with the enactment of the Housing (Scotland) Act 2010. This established the Scottish Housing Regulator as a body corporate[92] independent from Ministers who must not give directions nor seek to control the performance of the Regulator's functions.[93] Its membership consists of a chief executive and such other members (minimum three) as Ministers think fit.[94] The objective of the Regulator is to safeguard and promote the interests of persons who are or may become tenants of social landlords or recipients of the housing services of social landlords.[95]

The chief executive, who is responsible for the management, performance and future development and day to-day operational responsibilities, is to be a person with knowledge and skills relevant to the functions of the Regulator.[96] The Regulator is entitled to charge fees for the functions in relation to social landlords which was proposed in the original Bill.[97]

Performance assessment of social landlords

The Housing (Scotland) Act 2010 provides that the Regulator may set performance improvement targets specifying the level or quality of housing services or the standard of housing activities which social landlords must aim to provide by a specified time. Different performance improvement targets, or different times, may be set for different social landlords or for different areas, or cases.[98]

The Scottish Social Housing Charter

The standards and objectives which social landlords should aim to achieve when performing their housing activities are to be laid out in a Scottish Housing Charter and involve certain "outcomes".[99] This is expected to be effective from April 2012 after discussions with stakeholders in 2010, a discussion paper in spring 2011 and formal consultation on a draft Charter in late summer/autumn 2011.[100] The "outcomes" may relate to:

(a) the housing needs for which social landlords should provide;

(b) the prevention and alleviation of homelessness;

(c) the provision and management of sites for gypsies and travellers, whatever their race and origin;

---

[92] HSA 2010, s 1.
[93] *Ibid*, s 4.
[94] *Ibid*, s 7.
[95] *Ibid*, s 8.
[96] *Ibid*, s 13.
[97] Housing (Scotland) Bill, s 14.
[98] HSA 2010, s 34.
[99] *Ibid*, s 32.
[100] Scottish Government Policy Memorandum (2009) at para 48.

(d) the acquisition and disposal of housing accommodation;

(e) the allocation of housing accommodation;

(f) the terms of tenancies and the principles upon which levels of rent should be determined;

(g) the condition and quality of housing accommodation;

(h) the maintenance and repair of housing accommodation;

(i) the contribution of registered social landlords and local authority landlords to the amenity of the areas in which housing accommodation is situated;

(j) the contribution to and promotion of the environmental well-being and regeneration of the places in which housing accommodation is situated;

(k) the prevention of harassment or anti-social behaviour;

(l) the provision of information to the public by registered londlords or their services and governance arrangements;

(m) the participation of tenants (and bodies representing tenants) in formulating social landlords' proposals concerning the provision of housing services;

(n) the procedures for dealing with tenants' complaints about social landlords and for resolving other disputes between social landlords and their tenants.[101]

There may be different outcomes set for different social landlords or for different areas or cases.[102]

The Performance Standards operational from 2006 have involved 20 Guiding Standards and 33 Activity Standards. The Activity Standards relate to the major functional areas – housing management; property maintenance; property development (where appropriate); homelessness; services for owners; services for Gypsies/Travellers (local authorities only) and wider role (RSLs only).[103] The Guiding Standards focus on planning and managing performance; social inclusion; service delivery and communication and RSL governance and financial management.[104] This becomes clearer if one takes an instance of how the Guiding Standard is expressed in relation to social inclusion:

"GUIDING STANDARDS 2: SOCIAL INCLUSION

GS 2.1 *Equal opportunities* We embrace diversity, promote equal opportunities for all and eliminate unlawful discrimination in all areas of our work

[101] HSA 2010, s 30(1).
[102] *Ibid*, s 30(2).
[103] Scottish Government (2006) at para 11.
[104] *Ibid* at para 10.

GS 2.2 *Tenant participation*   We have published and are implementing a sound strategy for encouraging and supporting tenants, residents and service users to participate actively in all areas of our work. We support tenants to take an active interest in managing their homes.

GS 2.3 *Sustainability*   We ensure that our policies and actions are under-pinned by our commitment to sustainability. We consider the impact we can have in improving the economic, social and environmental circumstances of the wider community."[105]

The Activity Standards set out the standards that housing providers should be achieving in specific functional areas and activities. In assessing performance the focus is on outcomes, achieving good practice and how well the Guiding Standards are being mainstreamed into each activity such as how well the Guiding Standard on equality of opportunity is being met in relation to allocation, for instance.[106] The Activity Standard in relation to services for owners gives a flavour:

"ACTIVITY STANDARDS 5: SERVICES FOR OWNERS

AS 5.1 *Sales*   We sell houses fairly and efficiently through the Right to Buy. We follow the terms of the tenancy agreement and relevant legislation.

AS 5.2 *Factoring*   We are fair, efficient and effective factors for other property owners. We manage factoring funds on behalf of owners in a proper and accountable manner.

AS 5.3 *Care and repair*   (RSLs where applicable) We provide and/or manage a good quality care and repair service."

These standards are aimed to allow RSLs and local authorities to self-assess and make progress towards providing the levels of service envisaged by the Regulator. In order to provide an incentive in this process there is provision for inspections to take place of landlords in the social renting sector. Powers to inspect originally derived from the Housing (Scotland) Act 2001,[107] and are now found in the Housing (Scotland) Act 2010. The 2010 Act requires the SHR to publish performance reports on social landlords.[108] These must cover whether or not social landlords achieve the outcomes of the Scottish Housing Charter and meet any relevant performance improvement targets.[109]

---

[105]   Scottish Government (2006) at para 10.
[106]   *Ibid* at para 12.
[107]   HSA 2001, s 69.
[108]   *Ibid*, s 41.
[109]   *Ibid*, s 41(1)(a)(i) and (ii).

INSPECTION

The frequency, depth, scope and focus of inspections was based on assessment of risk and was proportionate as to how the SHR views performance.[110] These inspections were not completed at standard three or five year intervals and the whole approach became more about setting out expectations than being prescriptive.[111] A judgement was made on how good the organisation and services currently were and on how well they were being managed for improvement.[112] On the basis of the evidence gleaned the Regulator graded in the past RSLs and local authorities on how well they met the Performance Standards. The grades ranged from Grade A (excellent) through Grades B (good) and Grade C (fair) to Grade D (poor). There was an overall grade for the organisation. There had been in the past also grades for individual matters – landlord services; housing management, property maintenance and asset management; homelessness services.[113] These no longer figured from 2009. Smaller RSLs with stock of fewer than 250 houses were unlikely to be inspected and the approach was described as "less onerous".[114]

Prior to inspection there was an inspection submission with key information to be provided in a self-assessment document over a period of around 4 weeks.[115] The kind of information that was covered includes the extent, nature and turnover of stock as compared with peer group and national figures. The percentage of rental income deriving from housing benefit tenants was, for example, provided.

This covered key performance trends. This was then reviewed by the SHR and followed by a meeting with people from the organisation.[116] This involved a number of staff from the SHR visiting the RSL and asking questions and examining the procedures and processes on the ground. This took place over a period of several days. A draft Report followed on which the RSL could comment. This was principally to allow for errors of fact to be corrected prior to the publication of Final Report. The inspection sought to answer a couple of key questions looking both to current performance and future. How good are the services inspected? How well are these services being managed for improvement? In order to answer these questions the inspectors spoke to tenants, service users, staff and governing body members. They also asked other partner organisations such as local authorities with which the housing body interacted. They visited homes and local areas as well as seeing and testing how well the

---

[110] Scottish Government (2008b) at para 2.3.
[111] Scottish Government (2008d) at para 2.4.
[112] Scottish Government (2008b) at para 3.1.
[113] *Ibid* at paras 3.4 and 3.5.
[114] *Ibid* at para 9.1.
[115] *Ibid* at para 3.10.
[116] *Ibid* at para 3.11.

services were being delivered. There was also an examination of the key policies, publications, information and the self-assessment submitted by the organisation under inspection. They also analysed published performance such as rent loss and financial information.

The headings indicate the general thrust of the exercise. Much of the report was descriptive. In addition to an Overview summarising the findings and decision of the SHR as to grading, four separate chapters followed. One covered the context of the organisation – its current and future tenants and its housing stock. The report went on to look at how well the organisation was delivering including such matters as tenants' satisfaction, neighbourhood management, investment and repair response practice. The report then looked at management for improvement looking at such issues as strategic planning, risk and performance management, equalities and diversity practice and value for money. This was a public document and was published online and included recommended areas for improvement, where appropriate.[117] One way in which there might be assistance was in the field of "post-inspection improvement plans".[118] These were asked for where a local authority or RSL was graded C or D.[119] Improvement plans would usually address the weaknesses identified within 2 years[120] and would include such matters as revising policies, reviewing methods of service delivery, improving information for service users and increasing the use of performance information and management.[121] If no improvement plan was forthcoming, action was taken in line with the SHR's Intervention Strategy.[122] Intervention was based on the powers granted in the Housing (Scotland) Act 2001.[123] This ranged from appointing persons to the governing body of an RSL,[124] appointing a manager to an RSL[125] or requiring the RSL to appoint a manager,[126] instructing a statutory inquiry into the affairs of the RSL[127] and (if required) a related extraordinary audit of its finances.[128] There was also power to declare a moratorium on creditors' rights of 56 days in the event of RSL insolvency.[129] This would allow the SHR to enter into

---

[117]   Scottish Government (2008b) at para 3.13.
[118]   Scottish Government (2008a).
[119]   *Ibid* at para 5.
[120]   *Ibid* at para 7.
[121]   *Ibid* at para 9.
[122]   *Ibid* at para 17.
[123]   Section 63; s 71 (Appointment of manager – RSL); s 75 (Appointment of manager – local authority).
[124]   Schedule 7 (Pt 2, paras 5 (Industrial and provident society) and 6 (Company)).
[125]   HSA 2001, s 71(1)(a).
[126]   *Ibid*, s 71(1)(b).
[127]   *Ibid*, Sch 7 (Pt 4, para 16).
[128]   *Ibid*, Sch 7 (Pt 4, para 17).
[129]   *Ibid*, Sch 8.

negotiations with secured creditors to agree proposals for the future and management of the assets of the RSL.[130]

The predecessor to the Scottish Housing Regulator, Communities Scotland indicated that the intervention strategy would only be used where performance problems were serious and the service provider was not willing to take action, or its actions had failed or would not succeed without external intervention.[131] The kinds of circumstances leading to statutory intervention were likely to be the failures of corporate governance or management such as mismanagement or serious misconduct by an RSL's governing body of senior staff; mismanagement by a local authority's members or senior staff in relation to the authority's housing, homelessness or factoring functions; serious problems in a service provider's senior management arrangements, if these were impairing the performance of the organisation or service; sustained failure by the service provider to address underperformance in service delivery, in meeting Performance Standards, or in meeting its statutory obligations or serious cause for concern about an RSL's financial performance.

Regulatory intervention

The Housing (Scotland) Act 2010 provides for a similar range of interventions. These include submission of a performance improvement plan.[132] This is appropriate where the Regulator considers that a social landlord is or is at risk of failing to achieve an outcome set out in the Scottish Social Housing Charter or to meet its performance improvement target.[133] There may also be intervention where there has been misconduct or mismanagement of a registered social landlord's financial or other affairs or where any other conduct by a social landlord justifies it being required to submit and implement a performance improvement plan.[134] This plan must indicate how and by when the social landlord will rectify or avoid the failure or other problem.[135] Such a plan may be approved or rejected.[136]

There is also provision for the Regulator serving an enforcement notice where there has been failure to meet a performance improvement plan and the interests of a social landlord's tenants need protection or the social landlord's assets need protection or the financial viability of the

---

[130] Col 2319, Social Justice Committee 17th Meeting 2001, per Deputy Minister for Social Justice, Margaret Curran.
[131] Communities Scotland (2004), para 28.
[132] HSA 2010, s 55.
[133] *Ibid*, s 55(1)(a).
[134] *Ibid*, s 55(1)(b) and (c).
[135] *Ibid*, s 55(2).
[136] *Ibid*, s 55(5).

social landlord is in jeopardy or any other conduct justifies the service of an enforcement notice.[137] The enforcement notice requires the social landlord to rectify or avoid a failure or other problems.[138] The notice must set out why the notice has been served and by when the landlord must take action.[139]

The most extreme step is the appointment of a manager for housing activities[140] or for financial or other affairs.[141] In addition officers may be suspended[142] or removed from office[143] and new officers appointed in their stead.[144]

GOOD PRACTICE

The Scottish Housing Regulator and its predecessors undertook research into the sector as a whole. This was to enable them to identify areas of weaker performance, develop an understanding of good performance work, test out their benchmarks and produce guidance or self-assessment frameworks for the sector.[145] Such thematic work has included work on homelessness,[146] evictions[147] and equality.[148]

Assessing regulation in the social rented sector

It seems evident from the changes in title and relationship that the issue of regulating Scottish social housing is a major contrast with the regulation of the private sector. The RSL sector owns just under 270,000 homes and 5,000 bedspaces in Scotland, amounting to some 11 per cent of all Scotland's homes.[149] In January 2009 the Scottish Housing Regulator reported that of the 81 RSLs inspected under the Housing (Scotland) Act 2001, nearly 63 per cent were providing good or excellent services, 30 per cent fair services and 8 landlords were poor in terms of landlord services, governance or financial management.[150] Five of these underperforming landlords had been re-inspected and improvement was found.

---

137   HSA 2010, s 56.
138   *Ibid*, s 56(2)(c).
139   *Ibid*, s 56(3).
140   *Ibid*, s 57.
141   *Ibid*, s 58.
142   *Ibid*, s 61.
143   *Ibid*, s 62.
144   *Ibid*, s 65.
145   Scottish Government (2008b), para 7.1.
146   Communities Scotland (2005).
147   Communities Scotland (2005a).
148   Communities Scotland (2002 and 2006).
149   Scottish Housing Regulator (2009), p 2.
150   *Ibid* at 4.

Statutory powers have been used from time to time. During 2008/09 Board appointments were made to the Boards of five organisations,[151] and in two of these instances support was given to transfer to other housing associations.[152]

The future

As far as the general future of housing in Scotland is concerned, the situation of the regulation of rental housing is undergoing further change. The Housing (Scotland) Act 2010 makes changes to the formal structure and the role of the Scottish Housing Regulator.[153]

The private rental sector in Scotland is smaller than that in most other European countries.[154] The Scottish Government hopes that a National Voluntary Landlord Accreditation Scheme will allow landlords to follow best practice.[155] It is instructive to contrast the position in England and Wales with whom we shared the regulatory regime of the Housing Act 1985. Until recently housing associations in England and Wales were regulated by the Housing Corporation which also provided their funding. Following the recommendations of the Cave Review[156] the funding and regulation functions were split. The regulatory role has now been taken over by the Tenants Services Authority from 1 December 2008 under the Housing and Regeneration Act 2008 while funding duties lie with the new Homes and Communities Agency. The current remit of housing associations is to expand to cover local authorities and ALMOs in April 2010.[157]

As indicated, the social rented regulatory system in Scotland, though, is undergoing change at the time of writing with the Housing (Scotland) Act 2010. The Scottish Government's discussion document on the future of housing in Scotland, *Firm Foundations*,[158] talked of "(m)odernising the regulation of social housing through the creation of a new regulatory function that is focussed on protecting and promoting the interests of current and future tenants, that reduces the burden of regulation and inspection on local authorities and housing associations, and that exercises its powers independently of Ministers".[159] All this in the overall context of "fostering the development of the private rented sector and reinvigorating

---

[151] Scottish Government (2009) at 24 – St John (Glasgow) HA; Moray Housing Partnership; Four Walls Housing Co-operative; Forth Valley HA; Cumbernauld Housing Partnership.
[152] *Ibid.*
[153] HSA 2010.
[154] Scottish Government (2007), Chart 8 at 27.
[155] *Ibid* at 28.
[156] Cave (2007).
[157] Tenant Services Authority (2010).
[158] Scottish Government (2007).
[159] *Ibid* at 5.

social rented housing".[160] This involves "providing sufficient safeguards for tenants while, at the same time, avoiding excessive regulation which could put people off remaining as private landlords".[161] In the future the Government proposes that "social housing regulation should be more explicitly focussed on regulating for the benefit of consumers of housing and related services, with an explicit duty to promote their needs and interests"[162] This involves reducing the regulatory burdens on social housing providers and ending the cyclical programme of inspections once there has been a baseline inspection.[163] The starting point for the process is to be self assessment. The key for the future is "lighter touch regulation for the better performers" and "(i)ntervention ... at the minimum level necessary to ensure the desired outcome".[164] The Consultation document on the future of housing in Scotland poses a number of questions in pursuit of these overall strategic goals. The period of consultation is now over and detailed decisions are awaited.

SUMMARY OF REGULATION

As noted above, the intervention of Government into the field of residential housing involved controls on rents and security of tenure in the dominant private rented sector from 1915 onwards in Britain. This stemmed from the threats to wartime production by those resisting the rent rises and evictions which landlords were seeking to obtain in the early days of World War I. The chronic underinvestment of private sector landlords in providing a supply of housing for the whole population meant that the Royal Commission's Report of 1917 recommended that municipal housing would need to be provided on a wide scale.

The housing sector that emerged in Scotland encompassed, then, a highly regulated private sector and rather different social renting arrangements. Government provided the framework of rights for private-sector tenants by way of rents frozen as at 3 August 1914 and the requirement for landlords to obtain a possession order from the courts on showing good cause only for the next 40 years. There was, however, no direct intervention by way of a special rent fixing mechanism or housing courts to determine whether there might be repossession or not. These only emerged in the furnished sector in 1943 and in the rest of the market in 1965 following the Rachman scandal.

The provision of a service to fix rents which was provided in unfurnished accommodation from 1965 was a voluntary system, however. No one

---

[160] Scottish Government (2007) at 7.
[161] *Ibid* at 30.
[162] *Ibid* at 54.
[163] *Ibid*.
[164] *Ibid* at 55.

was obliged to have a fair rent fixed and the system operated mainly, as Crossman had hoped, to weed out particularly exploitative landlords.

Tenants of social landlords until 1980 relied on the very nature of municipal housing to provide them with protection against exploitation. Although such tenants had no formal protection against rent rises or against being evicted, the need for such rights was seen as irrelevant, given that housing provided by councils had no other purpose than to house residents of the area. There was no alternative profit motive to be pursued by way of selling of housing assets and diverting into other forms of investment as a private landlord might seek to do. By the same token the rents were not subject to any need to meet capital return targets.

A major impact on the social rented sector which transformed its very nature and threatened to reduce it to a low-quality residual location for those with no money to buy into the dream of owner occupancy has been the right to buy. Described as socially responsible, this notion provided tenants in the social rented sector with the opportunity to buy community owned property which had been built to meet general housing need. By providing discounts in terms of the Tenants' Rights etc (Scotland) Act 1980 and its successor, the Housing (Scotland) Act 1987, to sitting tenants, the policy had the effect of drastically reducing the stock of property made available to local authorities to meet housing need in their areas.[165] Prior to 1980, local authorities had the option to sell properties to their tenants and some sought permission to do so where it fitted in to their overall housing development policy. With the introduction of the right to buy, however, any element of planning in this process was taken away from the authority. If a tenant had a minimum of 2 years as a tenant in the local authority sector then they could buy the property which they occupied. Housing associations were initially exempted from this sale of communal assets.

The rather different emphases which were encountered in the 1960s and 1970s in relation to owner occupation and municipal housing provision were not a feature of the debates in the 1940s and 1950s. The common problem was perceived to be the "housing crisis" and the solution included both kinds of housing. The issue was always described as how to provide numbers of houses as opposed to a particular kind of housing. That started to change, however, in the White Paper of 1970 in which the value of owner occupancy and its identification with good citizenship[166] was contrasted with the "dependency culture" of the Welfare State.[167] The different forms of subsidy provided to the different sectors from the public purse were seen differently. The mortgage interest relief provided to those buying their houses and removing themselves from the property market

---

[165] Jones (2001) (in Jones and Murie (1999)).
[166] DOE (1970) at para 16.
[167] *Ibid.*

price escalator was treated as simply a tax relief no different from the personal allowance or the allowance for charitable covenants. The Central Government subsidy to local authority Housing Revenue Accounts to keep rents affordable for the majority of waged tenants was, however, seen in a rather different light. The former was encouraged through there being even higher tax reliefs being available to those paying tax at higher rates than the standard rate. The attempts to curb the power of local authorities through removing their power in relation to offering low rents was challenged increasingly with reductions in the subsidy available for municipal housing.[168] With faith in home ownership dented in the 2008 crisis, the future is uncertain.

---

[168] Murie (1983).

9 SHARED HOUSING AND HOUSES IN MULTIPLE OCCUPATION

Prior to the 21st century it was far more common for people to share facilities when they occupied properties. The notion of regulation of these kinds of living arrangements emerged in the middle of the 19th century, with the "ticketing" of houses in Glasgow for maximum occupancy rates from 1868.[1] This is an area where regulation and control have, however, been characterised by complexity and neglect over the years and one where the prospects of successful intervention in this part of the market have, hitherto, not been marked by conspicuous success. The latest system, introduced under the Housing (Scotland) Act 2006, and amended by the Housing (Scotland) Act 2010, makes serious attempts to redress this neglect.

It is worth setting this part of the private rental market into the context of the private rented sector generally. The private rented sector as a whole in 2009 accommodated approximately 233,000 households.[2] This market as a whole is not characterised by significant holdings of individual properties. In 2008 over nine in every ten landlords were private individuals, couples or families, with most of them owning just one property and operating part time.[3] The numbers of HMOs is probably higher than the 10,200 licences in force at 31 March 2008 due to avoidance of regulation, whether by accident or deliberately. This was a significant increase on the number the previous year and 2008 experienced a sharp rise in applications. This reflects the changes in enforcement policies as well as new entries into the market.[4] Students in the private rented sector are likely to live in HMOs. Some eight out of ten student households reside in such shared accommodation.[5] The rise in the number of HMOs has led to concerns about the impact on local amenities and a number of local authorities have introduced planning policies to control the density of HMOs in a given area, where planning permission is required for an HMO. This is only

---

[1] Butt (1971); The Burgh Police (Scotland) Act 1903 extended this to all parts of Scotland.
[2] Scottish Government (2009d), vol 1, para 3.2 – drawn from the Scottish Household Survey.
[3] *Ibid* at para 2.7.
[4] *Ibid* at para 2.21.
[5] *Ibid* at para 3.23.

required where use as an HMO is considered to constitute development.[6] While HMOs may strike neighbours as being undesirable, the Scottish Government has reminded local authorities that HMOs can play an important part in meeting the housing needs of certain groups such as students and young people.[7] Revised guidance on planning for HMOs expected in the spring of 2009 was not available at the time of writing.

MODERN LEGAL FRAMEWORK

Social landlords – local authorities and Registered Social Landlords – meet the needs principally of families and individuals with individual and joint tenancies. There is provision for taking in a lodger in the social rented sector, provided that the tenant obtains the landlord's consent.[8] Local authorities then have the capacity to control the density and nature of occupancy of their stock. Similarly. owner occupiers have that ability.

For the most part, the issue of multiple occupancy arises in the private rented sector. In the 21st century we do not encounter so much sharing between tenants and their landlord in the style of 1970s sitcoms.[9] The protection provided to those who do share with their landlords is now minimal. There is now no protection against eviction for such tenants. They are excluded from the coverage of the assured tenancy regime under the Housing (Scotland) Act 1988 and have only the most basic of rights against unlawful eviction and harassment.[10] No new Pt VII tenancies can be created from 1989 onwards. Since usually shared accommodation does not come within the phrase "let as a separate dwelling-house" it does enjoy the benefits of a 4-week minimum notice to quit. What tenants are entitled to is such notice as is laid down in their rental agreement. The basic minimum is to what is "reasonable notice". It had been suggested that hostel dwellers could be entitled to little by way of notice and, in effect, to be evicted "*brevi manu*".[11] An Extra Division of the Court of Session, however, overturned this ruling, stating that there were "common law rights

---

[6] Scottish Government (2009d).

[7] http://www.scotland.gov.uk/Publications/2008/25092557/0 (para 87) (last consulted 23 June 2010).

[8] HSA 2001, s 32.

[9] *Man About the House*, with landlords George and Mildred Roper (Brian Murphy and Yootha Joyce) and their three unrelated tenants, Robin Tripp (Richard O'Sullivan), Chrissie Plummer (Paula Wilcox) and Jo (Sally Thomsett) (1973–76); *Rising Damp* with landlord Rupert Rigsby (Leonard Rossiter) and his three unrelated tenants, Miss Ruth Jones (Frances de la Tour), Alan Moore (Richard Beckinsale) and Philip Smith (Don Warrington) (1974–78).

[10] See Chapter 6.

[11] *Conway* v *Glasgow City Council (No 2)* 1999 SCLR 1058 per Sh Pr Bowen at 1065; *Denovan* v *Blue Triangle (Glasgow) Housing Association Ltd* 1999 Hous LR 97.

not to be evicted without reasonable notice".[12] Two aspects of the case have, however, been addressed in legislation. The Housing (Scotland) Act 2001 makes provision for regulations from the Scottish Ministers. covering persons living in hostels and other short-term accommodation. Only draft regulations had been produced at the time of writing.[13] In addition, the Bankruptcy and Diligence etc (Scotland) Act 2007 provideds that decrees for eviction are unlawful before 8 am or after 8 pm, on Sundays or on local public holidays.[14]

There are two principal forms of regulation of private rented accommodation which is shared with other tenants – registration and licensing. Registration has been available since 1966 and provides valuable information to the local authority in relation to services required and to inform planning decisions.[15] Licensing was introduced in 1991 and became mandatory in 2000.[16]

Registration

Local authorities have powers to compile a list of properties in multiple occupancy in terms of Pt VIII of the Housing (Scotland) Act 1987.[17] The principal problem with the previous use of registration alone was that this merely provided local authorities with information. It did not require them to actually take action to ameliorate the conditions of those living in sub-standard accommodation. The powers to regulate have always been pretty extensive. These have provided local authorities with powers to make control orders.[18] In the event of failure to comply there was provision for local authorities to take over properties and manage these. Although this happened in fictional scenarios,[19] it was extremely rare in real life.

---

[12] *Conway* v *Glasgow City Council* 2001 SLT 1472. Stalker (2007) at 192 rightly points out that the case does not provide any definitive answers to the issues raised by the hostel cases. The affirmation of the "reasonable notice" concept is at least clear.

[13] HSA 2001, s 7(1); Terms of Occupancy of Residential Accommodation (Scotland) Regulations 2005 with a 5-day period proposed as a minimum (reg 14).

[14] BDSA 2007, s 217.

[15] Housing (Scotland) Act 1966.

[16] Civic Government (Scotland) Act 1982 (Licensing of Houses in Multiple Occupation) Order 2000 (SSI 2000/177).

[17] HSA 1987, s 152.

[18] *Ibid*, Pt VIII, ss 178–185.

[19] *Sitting Targets* (BBC) with Phyllis Logan in 1985. This involved a fictionalised Rachman/Van Hoogstraten landlord figure seeking to get tenants to leave flatted accommodation in London through cutting off their communal heating. The climax comes when the barrister "discovers" the provisions of the Housing Act 1974 dealing with HMOs and the local authority is browbeaten at a public meeting into agreeing to take over the properties. The properties did not seem like HMOs but rather flats with separate facilities and sharing only a central heating system.

Currently, the local authority must keep a register of HMO licences and applications for them in its area[20] available for public inspection at all reasonable times.[21] It must include details such as the name of the applicant, address of the living accommodation and any agent as well as the decisions and conditions relating to those applications.[22] It must exclude any information that is likely to jeopardise the safety or welfare of any person or the security of any premises.[23] Women's refuges are an example where such information would be kept confidential, as well as any other possibly sensitive proposals.

LICENSING

From 1991 onwards, local authorities could license houses in multiple occupation, using powers in the Civic Government (Scotland) Act 1982. This legislation has been used to cover such activities as booking offices and tattooing.[24] The requirement to have a licence for an HMO property was introduced by statutory instrument in 2000.[25] This was extended in 2002[26] and 2003.[27]

The regime making provisions for standards to be maintained and enforced was effectively optional. The practice of different authorities varied since the concentrations of this kind of housing were mainly in the principal urban centres of Glasgow, Edinburgh, Dundee and Aberdeen where three-quarters of the licences were held.[28]

HMOs and the Housing (Scotland) Act 2006

The Housing (Scotland) Act 2006 brings together the regulation of HMOs into a single piece of primary rather than secondary legislation. It comes into force on 31 August 2011. Minor changes were introduced through the Housing (Scotland) Bill 2010 to allow for additional categories of multi-occupancy living accommodation to be added as

---

[20] HSA 2006, s 160(1).

[21] *Ibid*, s 160(4).

[22] *Ibid*, s 160(2).

[23] *Ibid*, s 160(3)

[24] Civic Government (Scotland) Act 1982 (Licensing of Booking Offices) Order 2009 (SSI 20092/145); Civic Government (Scotland) Act 1982 (Licensing of Skin Piercing and Tattooing) Order 2006 (SSI 2006/43).

[25] Civic Government (Scotland) Act 1982 (Licensing of Houses in Multiple Occupation) Order 2000 (SSI 2000/177).

[26] Civic Government (Scotland) Act 1982 (Licensing of Houses in Multiple Occupation) Amendment Order 2002 (SSI 2002/161).

[27] Civic Government (Scotland) Act 1982 (Licensing of Houses in Multiple Occupation) Amendment Order 2003 (SSI 2003/463) – disregarding the landlord when calculating the numbers sharing a property where the landlord was himself an occupant of the properties à la Rigsby and the Ropers (see n 9 above).

[28] Scottish Government (2009d), vol 1, para 2.21.

licensable HMOs.[29] A new discretion is also given to local authorities to refuse to consider an application for an HMO licence if the local authority considers the occupation of the accommodation as an HMO would be a breach of planning control.[30]

Licensing of HMOs

Every house in multiple occupation must now be licensed by the local authority.[31] This licence authorises occupation of living accommodation as an HMO.[32]

Fees

The local authority has the power to charge a fee for an application as well as for issuing a certified copy of the licence.[33] There is power for the Scottish Ministers to make an order about fees. These may prescribe the amount or maximum amount of fee; how such fees are to be arrived at; and specify the circumstances when no fee is payable and when there are to be refunds.[34] At the time of writing, local authorities charges vary. Glasgow charges £887 for 3 years,[35] while Aberdeen's charges start at £1,200 per property and depend on the number of properties owned.[36] Other fees encountered can be as low as £493 in West Lothian. The charges in Edinburgh are more for new applications than for renewals and, again, depend on the number of occupants.[37]

Meaning of "house in multiple occupation"[38]

The HMO regulatory regime comes into play when there are three occupants or more in living accommodation where they come from

---

[29] These proposals were postponed.
[30] HSA 2006, s 129A.
[31] *Ibid*, s 124(1).
[32] *Ibid*, s 124(2).
[33] *Ibid*, s 161(1).
[34] *Ibid*, s 161(2) and (3).
[35] http://www.merchantlettings.com/landloards/informationpack.
[36] Table of HMO Licence Fees (Effective from 1 April 2010):

Number of tenants	Licence fee (£)
3 – 10	1200
11 – 20	1250
21 – 40	1500
41 – 100	2000
101 – 250	3000
251 – 500	4500
Over 500	6000

[37] *Renewal*: 3 Occupants – £330; 4 Occupants – £370; 5 and 5+ Occupants – £410. New: 3 Occupants – £505; 4 Occupants – £545; 5 and 5+ Occupants – £585.
[38] HSA 2006, s 125.

more than two families.[39] A property occupied by three unrelated people renting would count as an HMO as they comprise three families. If, however, four people, comprising two couples, occupied accommodation, this would not be covered as an HMO as they comprise only two families.

The accommodation which is covered may consist of a house or premises where the occupants share one or more of the "basic amenities" with each other.[40] "Basic amenities" are a toilet, personal washing facilities and facilities for the preparation of cooked food.[41] In essence, this covers sharing a bathroom and/or kitchen. A person is, however, not treated as sharing a basic amenity where there are more than one of such basic amenities and that person has exclusive use of at least one of them.[42] If, for example, there was a shared flat where one of the occupants had their own en-suite bathroom and kitchenette, this would not count as a shared amenity.

A person is treated as occupying living accommodation only if it is their "only or main residence".[43] Hence, normal stays in hotels or boarding houses with shared amenities would not be covered. Those who had no other accommodation would seem to be covered.[44] Full-time students during term time are specifically treated as occupying that living accommodation as their "only or main residence".[45] Any patient in a health service hospital[46] is, however, not treated as occupying that hospital accommodation as their "only or principal residence".[47]

Members of the same family

People are to be treated as being in the same family and as being related to each other in terms of the operation of HMOs if they are a couple or are a relative or a relative of either member of a couple.

A couple covers those who are married or are civil partners or who live together as husband and wife or in an equivalent relation or same-sex relationship.[48] A "relative" is defined as meaning parent, grandparent,

---

[39] HSA 2006, s 125(1).

[40] *Ibid*, s 125(2).

[41] *Ibid*, s 125(3).

[42] *Ibid*, s 125(4)(d).

[43] *Ibid*, s 125(4)(a).

[44] Although it seems improbable that Terence Rattigan's Major Pollock, Sybil Railton-Bell or her mother (*Separate Tables*, 1958) or Miss Tibbs and Miss Gatsby (*Fawlty Towers*, 1975–79) would enjoy the benefits of their lodging being treated as HMOs. It would depend on the extent of the sharing of facilities, about which we have limited information.

[45] HSA 2006, s 125(4)(b).

[46] National Health Service (Scotland) Act 1978, s 108(1).

[47] HSA 2006, s 125(4)(c).

[48] *Ibid*, s 128(2).

child, grandchild, brother, sister, uncle, aunt, nephew or niece.[49] Half-blood relationships are treated as a relationship of the whole blood[50] and stepchildren as children.[51] In addition, anyone brought up by another person as if they were that person's child is to be treated as if they were that person's child.[52] This includes any foster children[53] in terms of the Children (Scotland) Act 1995.[54]

HMOs exempt from the requirement to be licensed[55]

A wide range of properties which are in fact occupied by more than three unrelated people do not require to be licensed and are outwith the regime. The categories specified in the legislation may be added to, removed or varied through statutory instrument.[56] In addition, the Scottish Ministers have the power to designate HMOs which may be exempted from the requirement to be licensed,[57] and local authorities have the power to put such exemptions into effect in their area, if they so choose.[58]

The current exempt categories specified in the legislation are:

1. Property occupied by the owners of the HMO and any others, whether family members or from two other families.[59] This means that three families in total are permitted.
2. Care home.[60]
3. Independent health care.[61]
4. School care accommodation.[62]
5. Secure accommodation under the Regulation of Care (Scotland) Act 2001.[63]
6. Armed service accommodation owned by the Crown.[64]
7. Prison accommodation, including young offenders institutions and remand centres.[65]

---

[49] HSA 2006, s 128(2)(b).
[50] Ibid, s 128(2)(c).
[51] Ibid, s 128(2)(d).
[52] Ibid, s 128(2)(e).
[53] Ibid.
[54] CSA 1995, s 26(1)(a).
[55] HSA 2006, s 126.
[56] Ibid, s 126(2).
[57] Ibid, s 127(1).
[58] Ibid, s 127(2).
[59] Ibid, s 126(1)(a).
[60] Ibid, s 126(1)(b)(i).
[61] Ibid, s 126(1)(b)(ii).
[62] Ibid, s 126(1)(b)(iii).
[63] Ibid, s 126(1)(b)(iv).
[64] Ibid, s 126(1)(c).
[65] Ibid, s 126(1)(d).

8. Religious order accommodation.[66]
9. Property subject to an anti-social behaviour management control order in terms of s 74 of the Antisocial Behaviour (Scotland) Act 2004.[67]
10. Co-operative Housing Association accommodation managed by general meeting in terms of the Housing (Scotland) Act 1987, s 300(1)(b).[68]

The process of application[69]

Applications for an HMO licence may be made only by an owner of the living accommodation concerned,[70] using the written form of the local authority.[71] The local authority may grant the licence (with or without conditions) or refuse it.[72] There may be an oral hearing.[73] If the local authority holds an oral hearing it must invite the applicant and each respondent who has made a valid written representation which it intends to consider, as well as any other person it thinks fit to make oral representations.[74]

Suitability of licence holders[75]

Local authorities must refuse an application for an HMO licence if any applicant or their agent is considered not a fit and proper person to be authorised to permit people to occupy any living accommodation as an HMO.[76] Where the applicant or agent is not an individual then they must direct their minds to who is the director, partner or other person concerned in the management of the property.[77] The criteria to be applied are the same as those for deciding whether or not a person is a fit and proper person to be a private landlord.[78] These are, briefly, whether or not the person in question has:

(i) committed offences involving fraud, dishonesty, violence or drugs;
(ii) practised unlawful discrimination on the grounds of sex, race, nationality; or

---

[66] HSA 2006, s 126(1)(e).
[67] Ibid, s 126(1)(f).
[68] Ibid, s 126(1)(g).
[69] Ibid, s 129.
[70] Ibid, s 129(1).
[71] Ibid, s 129(3) and Sch 4, para 1.
[72] Ibid, s 129(2).
[73] Ibid, Sch 4, para 7(1).
[74] Ibid, para 7(2).
[75] Ibid, s 130.
[76] Ibid, s 130(1)(b).
[77] Ibid, s 130(2)(c).
[78] Ibid, s 130(3), specifying s 85 of the Antisocial Behaviour etc (Scotland) Act 2004 (as amended by, s 175 of the Housing (Scotland) Act 2006).

(iii) contravened any provision of housing or landlord and tenant law.

They must also look at whether there have been acts or omissions in relation to anti-social behaviour affecting houses rented out or managed by him – typically failure to heed an anti-social behaviour notice.[79] Where living accommodation is owned jointly by two or more persons, applications may be made by one owner or by the owners jointly.[80]

Suitability of living accommodation [81]

Unlike the regulation of private renting, the question of the suitability of the accommodation as well as that of the landlord is a factor in deciding whether or not an HMO licence is granted. The local authority may grant an HMO licence only if it considers that the living accommodation concerned is either suitable for occupation as an HMO or can be made so by including conditions in the HMO licence.[82] In deciding the question of suitability of living accommodation as an HMO, the local authority must consider:

- its location;
- its condition;
- any amenities it contains;
- the type and number of persons likely to occupy it;
- the safety and security of persons likely to occupy it; and
- the possibility of undue public nuisance.[83]

These issues reflect some of the problems mentioned above in terms of the past letting out of insanitary and unsafe premises to vulnerable tenants as well as the likelihood of increased noise and to-ing and fro-ing where there is a large number of transient occupiers. They also reflect elements of "nimbyism" where, for instance, residents assume that a property rented out, for instance, to tenants requiring support, living in shared facilities with some supervision are "undesirable". In addition, of course, authorities may take into account any other material which they reasonably consider relevant.

Restriction on applications

Where a local authority refuses a licence it may not consider a further application by the same applicant in relation to that property within a

---

[79] See Chapter 8.
[80] HSA 2006, s 164(1).
[81] *Ibid*, s 131.
[82] *Ibid*, s 131(1).
[83] *Ibid*, s 131(2).

year from the date of refusal. This applies whether the refusal is related to the inadequacy of the property or where the applicant is deemed not a fit and proper person to be an HMO licence holder.[84]

Terms of an HMO licence[85]

As indicated, licences may be granted with such conditions attached as the local authority thinks fit.[86] If the condition requires work to be done, it must be specified when that work is to be carried out[87] and it must be within a timescale that is reasonable.[88] There is power for the Scottish Government to require specific conditions to be included.[89]

Duration of an HMO licence[90]

The licence lasts either 3 years or such shorter period as is specified, subject to a 6-month minimum period.[91] The period starts from when the decision to grant is served on the licence holder.[92] Some councils, such as Edinburgh, have opted to have annual licences while others, such as North Lanarkshire, have opted to offer 3-year licences. The rationale for the longer period was expressed thus. "It is considered that these fees will adequately cover operational costs, while at the same time being set at a reasonable level, which will not place an unreasonable burden on owners of HMOs."[93]

Where there is a change of ownership, the licence transfers to the new owner on the date on which ownership passes and is treated as though it had been granted to the new owner.[94] It expires 1 month after the date when the ownership of the living accommodation is transferred.[95]

Appeals

There is provision for appeal by summary application to the sheriff[96] within 28 days of receiving notice of the decision.[97] The sheriff may

---

84 HSA 2006, s 132.
85 *Ibid*, s 133.
86 *Ibid*, s 133(1).
87 *Ibid*, s 133(4).
88 *Ibid*, s 133(5).
89 *Ibid*, s 133(2).
90 *Ibid*, s 134.
91 *Ibid*, s 134(1).
92 *Ibid*, s 133(2)(a).
93 North Lanarkshire Council Report, 12 August 2003: Planning and Environment (Protective Services) Sub Committee per Director of Planning Environment, para 3.3 – this proposed shifting from a flat rate of £300 per year per application to £800 for a 3-year licence.
94 HSA 2006, s 136(1).
95 *Ibid*, s 136(2).
96 *Ibid*, s 159(1).
97 *Ibid*, s 159(4).

confirm the decision of the local authority (with or without variations);[98] remit it (with reasons) to the local authority for reconsideration;[99] or quash the decision.[100] There is provision for appeal against the sheriff's determination to the sheriff principal within 28 days of the determination.[101] The sheriff principal's decision is final, although, as ever, subject to judicial review.[102]

The local authority is given discretion to operate the HMO licensing scheme and any challenge must meet the *Wednesbury* standard of reasonableness,[103] ie that no reasonable council could have come to the decision on the facts before it. This has always been a high, but not impossible, test, as the case law illustrates. In *Anderson* v *Fife Council*, for instance, there had been an application for an HMO in St Andrews. Objections had been received that there would be noise and problems with parking. The licence was refused on the basis of the location, character and condition of the premises, as well as the nature and extent of the proposed activity. The sheriff upheld the council's decision and accepted that the existing nature of the locality would under threat by the proposed change of use from residential to HMO.[104] The same sheriff, however, did grant a licence subject to conditions some 8 months later, also involving a St Andrews application. In the later case, *Valente* v *Fife Council*,[105] the same issues of social amenity and detrimental character change were involved. The matter, then, will depend very much on the specifics of the exact location. The issue of the compatibility between there being a location designated primarily for families and retired people as a "Home Zone" and the possibility of an HMO came to the fore in the Inner House in 2008. In *Killen* v *Dundee City Council*[106] the reason for rejecting an application for an HMO was the idea of a fundamental conflict between the two zones. The form of "Home Zone" regulation in terms of the Transport (Scotland) Act 2001 has the goals of preserving the amenity of an area in terms of improved safety as well as the environment. The Inner House was of the view that it was perfectly possible for an area to be a "Home Zone" and exist alongside an HMO.[107]

The impact of previous bad experience was the reason in *Hart* v *Aberdeen City Council* for the rejection of an application for an HMO. Here, though the sheriff was satisfied that the problems were historic and

---

[98] HSA 2006, s 159(6)(a).
[99] *Ibid*, s 159(6)(b).
[100] *Ibid*, s 159(6)(c).
[101] *Ibid*, s 159(9).
[102] *Ibid*, s 159(10).
[103] *Associated Provincial Picture Houses Ltd* v *Wednesbury Corporation* [1948] 1 KB 223.
[104] Sheriff G J Evans, 22 March 2006: www.scotcourts.gov.uk/opinions/b92.
[105] Sheriff G J Evans, 21 November 2006: www.scotcourts.gov.uk/opinions/b101_06.
[106] 2008 SLT 739.
[107] *Ibid* at 743, para 18.

had been addressed. In essence, the landlord had replaced five noisy male students with five female students. The real question was whether or not the landlord had acted quickly enough in getting rid of the troublesome tenants. Slowness in doing this had persuaded the Committee that he was not a fit and proper person to hold an HMO licence. The Committee erred, in the view of Sheriff Cusine, by failing to explain why the change of tenants would not make a difference to their assessment of the landlord. The licence was, in this instance, granted on appeal subject to conditions requiring monitoring.[108]

Application for a new HMO licence[109]

Where an application is made for renewal of an HMO licence before the existing licence has expired, the existing licence expires on the date when the new licence takes effect.[110] If the authority refuses to grant a new licence, the old licence expires on the date the appeal process is concluded.[111]

Variation and revocation of HMO licences[112]

The local authority may vary an HMO licence at any time, either on application of the licence holder or of its own accord.[113] The period of the licence, however, may not be shortened,[114] although there is also provision for revocation of an HMO licence at any time.[115] Notice must be given to the licence holder as well as to fire and police authorities inviting oral representations on the proposed variation,[116] along with the reasons for the proposed change.[117] They must consider the representations before making a decision.[118]

A licence may be revoked at any time if the local authority considers:

- that the applicant is no longer a fit and proper person;[119]
- that the living accommodation is no longer suitable for occupation and cannot be made so by varying the conditions in the HMO licence;[120]

---

[108] *Hart* v *Aberdeen City Council*, 23 June 2006 (at http://www.scotcourts.gov.uk/opinions/B907_05.html).
[109] HSA 2006, s 135.
[110] *Ibid*, s 135(1).
[111] *Ibid*, s 135(2).
[112] *Ibid*, ss 138 and 139.
[113] *Ibid*, s 138.
[114] *Ibid*, s 138(3).
[115] *Ibid*, s 139(1).
[116] *Ibid*, s 138(4).
[117] *Ibid*, s 138(5).
[118] *Ibid*, s 138(7).
[119] *Ibid*, s 139(1)(a).
[120] *Ibid*, s 139(1)(b).

- that there has been a breach of any condition of the licence.[121] There is no need for action or criminal proceedings to have been started in respect of the breach.[122]

Notice must be given to the licence holder as well as to fire and police authorities, inviting oral representations on the proposed revocation,[123] along with the ground on which they propose to revoke the licence and with a copy of any relevant written representation.[124] They must give such notice not less than 21 days before the proposed hearing,[125] at which they must consider the representations before making a decision to revoke an HMO licence.[126] A decision to revoke takes effect from the last date on which a decision can be appealed to the sheriff or when such an appeal has been determined or abandoned.[127]

Delivery and cancellation of an HMO licence[128]

A notice granting or varying an HMO licence must be accompanied by such licence.[129] The licence holder is entitled, upon request, to a certified copy of the licence.[130] The licence holder may cancel the HMO at any time by returning it to the local authority along with any certified copy.[131]

Temporary exemption orders[132]

An owner of an HMO which requires to be licensed may apply for a temporary exemption order, specifying the steps to be taken to ensure the property ceases to be an HMO.[133] Such an order means that the property does not have to have an HMO licence during the exemption period, which lasts for 3 months from the date it is granted.[134] The local authority must be satisfied that the steps specified will have the intended effect.[135] There is provision for the temporary exemption period to be extended for a single further period of 3 months,[136] provided that there are exceptional

---

[121] HSA 2006, s 139(1)(c).
[122] Ibid.
[123] Ibid, s 139(2).
[124] Ibid, s 139(3).
[125] Ibid, s 139(3)(c).
[126] Ibid, s 139(4).
[127] Ibid, s 139(5).
[128] Ibid ss 140 and 141.
[129] Ibid, s 140(1).
[130] Ibid, s 140(3).
[131] Ibid, s 141.
[132] Ibid, s 142.
[133] Ibid, s 142(1) and (2).
[134] Ibid, s 142(4) and (5).
[135] Ibid, s 142(3).
[136] Ibid, s 142(6) and (8).

circumstances to justify the extension.[137] The owner under a temporary exemption order may be required to carry out works to improve the safety or security of the occupants during the period the order has effect.[138]

Notice of decisions[139]

Notices must be served within 7 days of the decision.[140] They must give the local authority's reasons for the decision, advise of the right of appeal and, where the HMO licence is granted, indicate the effect in terms of duration. They must be served on any agent who is specified in the application.[141]

Notices must be served on the following individuals:[142]

---

137   HSA 2006, s 142(7).
138   *Ibid*, s 143.
139   *Ibid*, s 158.
140   *Ibid*, s 158(11).
141   *Ibid*, s 165(1).
142   *Ibid*, s 158.

	Applicant or licence holder	Chief officer of the fire and rescue authority	Chief Constable	Representers in writing or in local newspaper	
Grant an HMO licence[a]	Applicant or licence holder	Chief officer of the fire and rescue authority	Chief Constable	Representers in writing or in local newspaper	
Refuse an HMO licence[a]	Applicant or licence holder	Chief officer of the fire and rescue authority	Chief Constable		
Vary or not vary a licence[b]	Applicant or licence holder	Chief officer of the fire and rescue authority	Chief Constable		
Revoke or not revoke a licence[c]					Evidence givers
Grant a temporary exemption order or refuse one[d]					Owners and occupiers
Extend the period for which a temporary exemption order has effect or refuse same[e]					Owners and occupiers
Revoke a temporary exemption order[f]					Owners and occupiers
Make an order of rent suspension[g]					Owners of living accommodation; occupiers of living accommodation; application by any other person on that person

Make an order requiring rectification of a breach or to prevent a breach of a condition[h]	Licence holder	Chief officer of the fire and rescue authority	Chief Constable		Occupiers of living accommodation
Revoke an order relating to rectification of a breach or to prevent a breach of a condition[i]		Chief officer of the fire and rescue authority	Chief Constable		Occupiers of living accommodation
Serve an HMO amenity notice[j]	Owners and occupiers of living accommodation	Chief officer of the fire and rescue authority	Chief Constable		Any creditor holding a standard security over the living accommodation; Any person receiving rent, directly or indirectly in respect of the living accommodation; Any other person appearing to the local authority to have an interest in the living accommodation
Revoke an HMO amenity order[k]	Owners and occupiers of living accommodation	Chief officer of the fire and rescue authority	Chief Constable		Any creditor holding a standard security over the living accommodation Any person receiving rent, directly or indirectly in respect of the living

			accommodation; Any other person appearing to the local authority to have an interest in the living accommodation
Extend period within which HMO amenity order must be completed[(l)]	Owners and occupiers of living accommodation	Chief officer of the fire and rescue authority	Chief Constable
			Any creditor holding a standard security over the living accommodation Any person receiving rent, directly or indirectly in respect of the living accommodation; Any other person appearing to the local authority to have an interest in the living accommodation
Demand recovery of expenses for amenity work carried out under Sch 5[(m)]	Owner of living accommodation concerned		
Refuse to grant a certificate that amenity work has been carried out under Sch 5[(n)]	Owner of living accommodation concerned		

Sanctions and their enforcement by the local authority

It is crucial that, in order for the HMO regime to protect the occupiers of such premises, there be effective sanctions available to the local authority.

SUSPENSION OF RENT[143]

There is provision for the local authority to order that no rent or other sums for occupation is payable under the tenancy or occupancy agreement.[144] It may do this if it is satisfied that an HMO is not licensed or that any condition in an HMO licence has been breached. The power to suspend rent is not affected by whether or not other action, or criminal proceedings are under way in relation to that breach.[145] The terms and validity of the tenancy are not affected by the service of a notice of suspension of rent.[146]

Such a rent suspension notice must specify the name of the owner of the living accommodation concerned and any agent,[147] the address, the effect of the order and the date in which it is to take effect.[148] It must be revoked in the event of the owner of the living accommodation being granted an HMO licence[149] or satisfying the authority that the property is no longer an HMO[150] or that a breach of a condition is no longer being committed.[151]

RECTIFICATION OF BREACH[152]

Where a local authority considers that any condition in an HMO licence has been breached, or is likely to be, it may require the licence holder to rectify the breach or prevent any potential breach.[153]

HMO AMENITY ORDERS[154]

Where there is living accommodation which is, or which the local authority believes to be, an HMO which requires to be licensed and the local authority considers it is not reasonably fit for occupation by the number of people known or believed to be living there, the local authority

---

[143]   HSA 2006, s 144.
[144]   *Ibid*, s 144(1).
[145]   *Ibid*, s 144(1)(b).
[146]   *Ibid*, s 144(6).
[147]   *Ibid*, s 144(3).
[148]   *Ibid*, s 144(2).
[149]   *Ibid*, s 144(4)(a)(i).
[150]   *Ibid*, s 144(4)(a)(ii).
[151]   *Ibid*, s 144(4)(b).
[152]   *Ibid*, s 145.
[153]   *Ibid*, s 145(1) and (2).
[154]   *Ibid*, s 146.

may take action.[155] It may require the owner to carry out work to make it reasonably fit for occupation by the number of persons known or believed to be occupying the premises or such smaller number as the authority considers could reasonably be accommodated there if the work is carried out.[156] This work is effected through service of an HMO amenity notice specifying the work to be carried out and the period within which it must be completed,[157] which may include particular steps to be taken in carrying out the work[158] but does not cover fire safety measures.[159] The issues which are relevant in any decision about an HMO amenity notice are the extent to which the living accommodation falls short of the provisions of building regulations[160] and specified defects – natural and artificial light; ventilation; installations for the supply of water, gas, electricity and for sanitation, space heating and heating water; personal washing facilities and facilities for the storage, preparation and provision of food.[161]

LA POWER TO CARRY OUT OR ARRANGE WORK[162]

The local authority may carry out or arrange for the carrying out of work in relation to HMO amenity notices or to rectify a breach of an HMO licence.[163]

OFFENCES RELATING TO HMOs[164]

It is an offence for an owner of an HMO to not have a licence for a property which requires to be licensed.[165] It is also an offence if there is a breach of a condition included in an HMO licence,[166] if someone is allowed to live in the property when a breach is being rectified[167] or if occupation is allowed via an unauthorised person.[168] Holding out that one has a valid HMO licence when it has ceased to have effect is also an offence.[169]

The defence of "reasonable excuse" is available where an HMO licence is revoked or where the property in question ceases to be an exempt

---

[155]   HSA 2006, s 146(1).
[156]   Ibid, s 146(2).
[157]   Ibid, s 146(4) – minimum period is 21 days from date on which notice takes effect (s 146(5)).
[158]   Ibid, s 146(6).
[159]   Ibid, s 146(7).
[160]   Ibid, s 147(1).
[161]   Ibid, s 147(2).
[162]   Ibid, s 151.
[163]   Ibid.
[164]   Ibid, s 154.
[165]   Ibid, s 154(1).
[166]   Ibid, s 154(2)(a).
[167]   Ibid, s 154(2)(b).
[168]   Ibid, s 154(2)(c).
[169]   Ibid, s 154(3).

property[170] and either where the owner has taken reasonable steps with a view to securing that the accommodation concerned ceases to be an HMO or is unable to stop it being an HMO, as this would breach the terms of any tenancy or occupancy agreement.[171] The defence of "reasonable excuse" applies also to situations where an owner is in breach of a condition of an HMO licence but cannot rectify the matter without in turn breaching the terms of a tenancy or occupancy agreement.[172]

It is also an offence for an agent to allow the occupation of a property which requires to be licensed when it is either unlicensed[173] or the person is not authorised by the HMO licence.[174] Agents are also forbidden from doing anything which will cause a licence condition to be breached[175] or prevents or obstructs an authorised use of the powers of entry.[176]

Penalties for offences range from fines not exceeding £20,000 (no licence by owner or agent), £10,000 (breach of condition) or level 3 on the standard scale (representing property has an HMO licence or obstructing powers of entry).[177] In addition to the penalty fines, the court may, except for the powers of entry offences, not only revoke any existing HMO licence in relation to that property but also disqualify the convicted owner from holding an HMO licence for up to 5 years.[178]

Appeals[179]

Any decision of a local authority can be appealed by way of summary application to the sheriff by the person on whom the notice is served and must follow the procedure laid down in s 159.[180] It must be made within 28 days of the person receiving the notice of the decision,[181] subject to the sheriff allowing out-of-time appeals on cause shown.[182] The sheriff may confirm the decision, remit it to the local authority for reconsideration or quash the decision.[183] When remitting a decision the sheriff must set a date for the local authority to confirm, vary, reverse or revoke the decision after reconsideration.[184] Appeal to the sheriff principal must be within 28

---

[170] HSA 2006, s 155(1)(a).
[171] Ibid, s 155(1)(b).
[172] Ibid, s 155(3).
[173] Ibid, s 154(4)(a).
[174] Ibid, s 154(4)(b).
[175] Ibid, s 154(5).
[176] Ibid, s 154(6).
[177] Ibid, s 156(1).
[178] Ibid, s 157(2).
[179] Ibid, s 159.
[180] Ibid, s 159(1) and (2).
[181] Ibid, s 159(4).
[182] Ibid, s 159(4) and (5).
[183] Ibid, s 159(6).
[184] Ibid, s 159(8).

days of the sheriff's determination[185] and the sheriff principal's decision is final.[186]

PRACTICAL ISSUES

When asked about the operation of the HMO regulatory regime, landlords complained of the lack of consistency of authorities in applying standards both between and within councils. They complained that authorities did not appear to be adopting a risk-based approach to HMO regulation and landlords were critical of what they saw as unnecessarily high standards being set:[187] such conditions as smoke alarms in every room, for instance, as well as other non-safety issues such as beading around sinks were raised.[188]

There is a requirement for guidance to be provided to both local authorities to have regard to any guidance issued by the Scottish Ministers.[189] The guidance, like that in relation to the homeless persons legislation, must be taken into account but is not binding. Guidance is currently available for local authorities,[190] as well there being Guides for tenants[191] and landlords[192] from the Scottish Executive.

THE DEVELOPMENT OF CONTROLS IN SHARED HOUSING

As part of the shift from a rural economy to an industrial one, discussed above,[193] one of the solutions to housing for workers coming to large cities was to provide shared accommodation. Accommodation was shared both with other tenants in overcrowded private lets,[194] or in "farmed" accommodation[195] or private lodging houses.[196] There were also examples of shared accommodation being provided to permit opportunities

---

[185] HSA 2006, s 159(9).
[186] *Ibid*, s 159(10).
[187] Scottish Government (2009d), para 5.47.
[188] *Ibid* at para 5.48.
[189] HSA 2006, s 163.
[190] Mandatory Licensing of Houses in Multiple Occupation: Guidance for Licensing Authorities (July 2004).
[191] *Houses in Multiple Occupation: A Guide for Tenants* (2004).
[192] *Houses in Multiple Occupation: A Guide for Landlords* (2004).
[193] See Chapter 1.
[194] Butt (1973), pp 68–69 (data derived from the Minutes of the Glasgow Municipal Commission on Housing (1902–03)).
[195] The term used for property with rudimentary furniture for the more transient population: *ibid*, p 76.
[196] In addition to seven municipal lodging houses with over 2,000 bed spaces, there were, in Glasgow, at the start of the 20th century, over 100 private lodging houses. Together they were estimated to house just over 1% of the city's population (Butt at 68).

for women to escape the choice of remaining in the family home or marrying.[197] There were no restrictions at common law on what limitations on tenants' rights a landlord might choose to opt for. Prior to 1980 there was no specific legal framework for those sharing accommodation as tenants of social landlords, although municipal authorities could use their powers in relation to overcrowded houses. Overcrowding was first dealt with on a comprehensive basis in the Housing (Scotland) Act 1935. The legislation required each local authority to inspect their areas for overcrowding and prepare and submit proposals for providing additional accommodation. This first inspection took place in 1935–36. No further report or survey was carried in the subsequent 40 years, according to Cochrane.[198] It did not become a major preoccupation over the next 35 years.

In the dominant private rented sector the regulation of lodging houses was obviated to an extent by the fact that a number of these were run by local authorities. Glasgow Corporation had seven of these at the turn of the 20th century.[199] They were partly a response to the inadequacies of private-sector provision. Municipal "Model Lodging Houses" were established in Glasgow in the 1870s to provide superior hostel accommodation for travelling workers and others, whose options were limited to accommodation in overcrowded privately owned common lodging houses with limited facilities and hygiene standards.[200] Other burghs followed Glasgow's lead. In 1894 there were three "models" in Govan – in Napier Street, Helen Street and Craigiehall Street. The Napier Street model was Govan's first, and in 1899 it was rebuilt in Clydebrae Street.[201] The unregulated conditions produced a major catastrophe in 1907 when 39 men died in a fire in a private lodging house in Gordon Street, Glasgow[202] and improved regulation was introduced.

Local authorities such as Glasgow in 1866 and Paisley[203] instituted controls over the numbers of persons who were legally entitled to occupy houses. This was extended to all Scottish burghs by the Burgh Police (Scotland) Act 1903. These properties were "ticketed", with a metal plate fixed above the door indicating the maximum number of people who could occupy at any one time. Between 1866 and 1900 there were

---

[197] *Women in Architecture* (Channel 4, 1984).
[198] Cochrane (1976), Ch VIII.
[199] Laidlaw (1905).
[200] When the author visited the Model Lodging House in Moncur Street in the 1970s the cubicles were constructed with strong wire roofs and were effectively cages to ensure the security of residents' property. They did not look as though they would have met any rudimentary fire precautions..
[201] http://www.theglasgowstory.com/image.php?inum=TGSE00760&remove=99&t=2.
[202] Cross (1905).
[203] Kelso (1922).

75,000 people – one seventh of the total city population – living in 23,288 ticketed houses in Glasgow.[204] Subsequent legislation in relation to overcrowding relied on a mathematical formula dependent on either the number of rooms or their size.[205] There was no regulation of who might be a landlord of shared accommodation.

Sub-letting by tenants was a ground for possession under the Rent Acts unless specifically permitted in the rental agreement.[206] Similarly, in municipal housing, local authorities did not permit their properties to be sub-let. The idea of officially encouraging "lodgers" was first found in the Tenants' Rights etc (Scotland) Act 1980.[207]

Owner-occupied housing was also covered by the restrictions on overcrowding. There is, however, no evidence that this has been regarded as a priority issue for those in charge of regulation of occupancy. They have focused almost entirely on the private rented sector. Recent changes, as in the past, have been driven by tragic events. The issue of HMO safety was raised in a public inquiry into the deaths of two young men in a flat they shared with a third student in Woodlands, Glasgow, in March 1999.[208] The presence of bars on the windows and the fact that the sole smoke alarm was dismantled contributed to the fatalities.

The process of adequately dealing with houses in multiple occupation has been a slow one. The options have, as we have noted, been available for some 75 years. The problem has been one of the lack of adequate housing. Thus, the issue which links the Sanitary Inspectors of the 19th century and housing professionals in the 21st century has always been the question of enforcement of regulation in a situation of chronic undersupply. In addition, the question of incentivising owners to make property available under conditions which are deemed to involve minimal interference with market forces has impacted on housing for those poorer occupiers with fewer market options. Those forced to share kitchens and bathrooms for reasons of their lower cost have had little incentive to seek enforcement of whatever remedies have been available.

Given the limited security of tenure and often transient nature of those living in this sector, it comes as little surprise that the pressure to enforce the regulation has been limited. The Review of the Private Rented Sector noted that avoidance of the modern forms of registration occurred where landlords claimed that property being occupied by migrant workers was

---

[204] Butt, p 68; Glasgow People's Palace has a "single end" on show, with a "ticket" attached.

[205] HSA 1987, Pt VII – this replicates what was found in the Housing (Scotland) Act 1935.

[206] Rent (Scotland) Act 1984, Sch 2, ground 6 (replacing similar provisions in the Rent (Scotland) Act 1971; Rent Act 1965 etc).

[207] HSA 2001, s 32.

[208] *Evening Times*, September 2000.

not the only or main residence of the workers because they have their main homes elsewhere.[209]

As far as the success of licensing is concerned, research projects looked at the early operation of mandatory licensing. One report by Hector Currie looked at the very early days of the operation of the scheme. This review indicated that the scheme was effective for those HMOs which were licensed. Identification of HMOs, however, was generally unsystematic. Regulation had not led to a decline in the number of HMOs nor to rent rises.[210] Following an inquiry by the Social Justice Committee of the Scottish Parliament into the scheme, the changes wrought by the Housing (Scotland) Act 2006 were introduced. Their operation in the future can be expected to herald a new, more proactive approach to this area.

---

[209] Scottish Government (2009d), para 3.43.
[210] Scottish Executive (2002).

10 RELATIONSHIP BREAKDOWN, ABUSE AND HOUSING

The housing rights of women have traditionally been limited in Scotland. When a woman married, her property became that of her husband. With the enactment of the Married Women's Property (Scotland) Act 1881 this ceased to be the case as far as moveable property was concerned.[1] While this did not apply to heritable property, until the Married Woman's Property (Scotland) Act 1920, however, the husband retained a right to the rents or produce under the *jus administrationis*.[2] There was an element of protection for widows in the right called "terce". This provided that a widow was entitled to the income from *one-third* of the late husband's heritable property.[3] Tenancies, in both the private rented and social rented sectors, were granted traditionally to the husband. As was noted above, statutory provisions were enacted to cover the then dominant private sector to allow widows to succeed to the tenancies of their spouses.[4]

On relationship breakdown, the rights to occupy the partnership home[5] depended on whether a person was a tenant or an owner. Until the 1970s it was the traditional practice for the man in a marital relationship to have his name as owner or tenant. By the end of that decade, though, some 78 per cent of property titles were taken in joint names.[6] In the event of relationship breakdown where the couple felt no longer able to live together the spouse who was neither owner nor tenant had no right to remain in the property. There was no Scottish equivalent to the English law notion of "beneficial interest"[7] and cohabitants whose names were not on the

---

[1]   Clive (1997), Ch 14.
[2]   *Ibid.*
[3]   Widowers, where there was a child, had a right called "courtesy" to the income from the wife's heritable property.
[4]   See Chapter 7.
[5]   The term "partnership home" is used as a convenient shorthand to indicate properties occupied by married as well cohabiting couples. The other convenient term traditionally encountered in the legislation, "matrimonial home", fails to cover accommodation occupied by the significant number of people who cohabit – in the most recent statistics amounting to 11% of couples as well as same-sex couples who are either cohabiting or united through a "civil partnership" ceremony as opposed to a marriage ceremony – Baroness Turner of Camden (*Hansard*, HL, 13 Mar 2009, col 1418), 2nd Reading of the Cohabitation Bill.
[6]   Manners and Rauta (1981) at 4.
[7]   Bromley (10th edn, 2007).

title or rent book had no rights to remain against the wishes of the owner or tenant. The weak position of the non-entitled spouse was recognised by the Scottish Law Commission in 1980 and the Matrimonial Homes (Family Protection) (Scotland) Act 1981 introduced significant changes to provide those who had no formal property rights in the matrimonial home with temporary protection by way of statutory rights to remain in the property termed "occupancy rights". These were intended to provide the weaker party with a right not to be summarily evicted by the owner or tenant and not to have to endure intolerable conduct at the hands of her husband as a price of remaining in occupation.[8]

This traditional power imbalance has unfortunately been complemented by a propensity for violence as part of Scottish male behaviour. The National Strategy to Address Domestic Abuse noted that "At least a quarter to a third of all women in Scotland will experience domestic abuse at some point in their lives and the level of 'repeat' victimisation is high."[9]

Prior to 1981, the only protection available against such abuse was the criminal law, with its problems in terms of corroboration of actions with limited witnesses and the unwillingness of the authorities to become involved in "private" matters. Since 1981 legislation sought to provide effective civil protections while the parties determine what is the future, if any, of the relationship which has foundered.[10] This was extended to civil partners by the Civil Partnership Act 2004[11] and same-sex cohabiting couples by the Family Law (Scotland) Act 2006.[12] In the event of the decision being divorce, where there is no agreement between the parties, the issue of who remained in the partnership home has been a matter which the court dealt with as part of the divorce settlement. The Family Law (Scotland) Act 1985 laid down criteria for the courts to determine what should happen in relation to financial provision. The principles of fair sharing of the matrimonial property, recognition of the economic advantage derived from the contributions by the other party, sharing of the economic burden of child care, recognition of the need for support for any party who had been economically dependent and avoidance of hardship were instituted to guide the courts where parties have not been able to agree on a mutually satisfactory division of their assets.[13] As far as living arrangements were concerned, the court has power to make orders

---

[8] Scottish Law Commission Report No 60 (1980), para 2.4.
[9] Scottish Government (2003) at 4.
[10] Both common-law interdicts and the process of "lawburrows" (cautionary bonds) were recorded as being used in scenarios of domestic abuse. Neither involved the perpetrator being found guilty of a criminal offence – Scottish Law Commission Reports No 41, paras 46–47.
[11] Civil Partnership Act 2004, s 101(7).
[12] Family Law (Scotland) Act 1985, s 34.
[13] *Ibid*, s 9(1).

including regulation of the occupation of the matrimonial home, the use of the furniture and plenishings therein which also covers excluding either party from occupying the former matrimonial home. Orders can also cover the financial liability as between the parties for outgoings in respect of the former home, furniture and plenishings.[14]

HOUSING RIGHTS AND ANCILLARY REMEDIES IN THE 21st CENTURY

In the event of relationship breakdown, however, there are various possibilities available to the parties before divorce, ranging from separation to reconciliation. During these post-relationship-breakdown days what housing rights are available to the parties in these difficult times is often crucial for the ultimate resolution of family and emotional relationships. It is also relatively complex. There are different rights available depending on whether the property is in owner occupation or rented. If it is rented, whether or not it is in the private rented sector or rented from a social landlord affects the parties' rights. The formal legal rights which are available do depend on whether there has been abuse. We know that in many instances abused partners often return to the abuser[15] and at one time this led to a less than wholehearted approach to the enforcement of the criminal law aspects of protective legislation.[16] Nonetheless, the rights available operate on the assumption that the relationship termination is final. The rights depend on whether the advisee wishes to stay in the matrimonial home or not. For the purposes of clarity, the different situations are treated separately, although there can be overlap. These, then, are the two possible scenarios which we look at in the undernoted text. First, we assume that the advisee wishes to stay in the property and then we look at the situations where they may wish to leave the home and set up afresh. As indicated, we adopt the term "partnership home" for convenience since this appears best to reflect the range of relationships encompassed by the protective legislation which, as we shall see,[17] has developed well beyond properties occupied by married couples. The crucial concept that exists in all these situations is the notion of "occupancy rights". These stem either from the title[18] or from the tenancy agreement or from the Matrimonial Homes (Family

---

[14] Family Law (Scotland) Act 1985, s 14 – on all matters involving divorce see Clive (1997) and Sutherland (2008).

[15] The recorded Scottish statistics on domestic abuse record incidents up to 11+ (Scottish Government (2009) Domestic Abuse Recorded by the Police in Scotland 2008–09).

[16] Jackson, Robertson and Robson (1989) at 130ff.

[17] See cohabitation rights below at p 323.

[18] Paisley (2008) points out that the rights stemming from ownership are not technically occupancy rights. That, though, is their effect in this context and it is considered more helpful to adopt this terminology.

Protection) (Scotland) Act 1981. We discuss the range of options which are available to those who opt to stay in the partnership home and those available when a woman chooses to leave that place. The framework of rights, then, is based on the notion of a right to occupy the partnership home – occupancy rights. These allow owners, tenants, non-owners and non-tenants to start from a level playing field of entitlement to occupy the home. These rights may be suspended where there is a necessity to protect one partner from abusive behaviour by the other partner with the abuser being evicted pending resolution of the relationship. There are also ancillary rights used as an alternative or supplement to suspending occupancy rights. These rights to interdicts or non-harassment orders or may be supplemented with powers of arrest.[19] These provide the police with the power to arrest anyone breaching the relevant order. They may in turn be charged. There is also provision in terms of the Matrimonial Homes (Family Protection) (Scotland) Act 1981 for the court to transfer the tenancy of the partnership home at the same time extinguishing the rights of the ex-tenant.[20]

HOUSING RIGHTS – STAYING IN THE HOME

Relationship breakdown

OCCUPIER OF OWNED PROPERTY (non-entitled spouse)

Where parties live together in a partnership home, whether married or cohabiting, there is provision for the protection of the spouse/partner who has no rights of ownership to have their right to stay in the property declared and enforced under the provision of the Matrimonial Homes (Family Protection) (Scotland) Act 1981. The Act introduced the concept of occupancy rights for those spouses and partners who were neither owners nor tenants of the partnership home and who are referred to as "non-entitled spouses".[21] As from 1 September 1982 anyone who was married to a property owner or tenant had a statutory right to stay in the property. There was no requirement for a married spouse to register such rights formally. They arose automatically on marriage. The rights were introduced to provide protection in the short term pending the couple settling their differences in either divorce, separation or reconciliation.

As indicated, spouses enjoy occupancy rights in the partnership home automatically. It is, however, standard practice when seeking to have some other order under the Matrimonial Homes Act to seek a declaration of these rights. The legislation provides for declarations also where the

---

[19] MHA 1981, ss 14–17; PHA 1997, ss 8–11; PFAA 2001, s 1.
[20] MHA 1981, s 13 and Family Law (Scotland) Act 2006.
[21] MHA 1981, s 1(1).

couple are able to live in the property at the same time.[22] In determining whether there should be a declaration of occupancy right the sheriff is required to be satisfied as to a number of specific factors. These are broadly the same as apply for transfers of tenancy, discussed below. The court must look at:

(a) The conduct of the spouses in relation to each other and otherwise.

(b) The respective needs and financial resources of the spouses.

(c) The needs of any child of the family.

(d) The extent (if any) to which –
  (i) the matrimonial home; and
  (ii) any item of furniture

  is used in connection with a trade, business or profession of either spouse; and

(e) whether the tenant spouse offers or has offered to make available any suitable alternative accommodation.[23]

The group for whom a declaration of occupancy rights is, however, crucial are those who are living together as partners. Unlike marriage, there is no fixed time period when cohabitation can be said to commence. Accordingly, any cohabitant seeking to remain in the property, relying on occupancy rights, requires to have these rights recognised by the courts. The legislation lays down criteria to assist the court in determining whether or not a couple are cohabiting. The court is to look to "all the circumstances of the case", including:

• the time for which it appears they have been living together; and

• whether there are any children of the relationship.[24]

The interpretation of these criteria does not appear to have been discussed in any reported case to date, although common sense and early research indicated that the judiciary were confident in being able to distinguish between a "fling" and a "proper relationship".[25]

The right to obtain a declaration of occupancy rights is available to married couples as well as cohabiting couples, whether different sex[26] or same sex.[27] There is, however, a limitation to when these rights can

---

[22] *Hansard*, HC, 30 June 1981, col 778, per Bruce Millan.
[23] MHA 1981, s 3(3).
[24] *Ibid*, s 18(2).
[25] Jackson Robertson and Robson at 52ff.
[26] MHA 1981, s 18.
[27] Civil Partnership Act 2004, Sch 1, para 3 (civil partners); and Family Law (Scotland) Act 2006, s 34 (cohabitants).

be exercised where the parties cease to live together.[28] The Family Law (Scotland) Act 2006 provides that if there has been no cohabitation between an entitled spouse and a non-entitled spouse for a continuous period of 2 years and during that period the non-entitled spouse has not occupied the matrimonial home then on the expiry of that 2-year period, the non-entitled spouse shall cease to have occupancy rights,[29] and no longer be able to seek a declaration of occupancy rights.[30] It has been suggested that this means that once the right is lost it does not revive again if the couple become reconciled and the non-entitled spouse returns to the matrimonial home.[31] It is not clear that the wording of the provision really has this effect. It seems perfectly possible to see these two periods of cohabitation as distinct and giving rise to fresh rights, rather like a less elaborate version of the marriages of Liz Taylor and Richard Burton.[32] Be that as it may, it certainly would not affect the rights of the non-entitled spouse reconciling in a new location.

Local authorities are expected to play a role as part of their strategy towards preventing homelessness. Recognising too the phenomenon of "late" relationship breakdown, the Code of Guidance notes that problems may arise in the case of older people, for example where the person has been dependent on their spouse for the house or to handle financial affairs. Such help, for example counselling or basic housing support, may be required urgently.[33]

OCCUPIER OF TENANTED PROPERTY

In contrast to the tenant, the other party relies for their rights to remain in the property on the provision of the Matrimonial Homes (Family Protection) (Scotland Act 1981. This provides occupancy rights for the spouses and partners of tenants the same as we have seen in relation to owner occupied property.

It is possible, though, where there is a lease for this tenancy, for it to be transferred on application of the non-entitled spouse as a separate action[34] as well as in an action for divorce or nullity of marriage.[35] When this was

---

[28] *Armour* v *Anderson* 1990 SLT 490. For a sheriff court interpretation of "living together", see *Verity* v *Fenner* 1993 SCLR 223. Same-sex relationships are covered: *Souter* v *McAuley* 2010 SLT(Sh Ct) 121.

[29] Family Law (Scotland) Act 2006, s 5 – inserting new subs (7) into the Matrimonial Homes (Family Protection) (Scotland) Act 1981, s 1.

[30] Family Law (Scotland) Act 2006, s 5 – inserting new subs (8) into the Matrimonial Homes (Family Protection) (Scotland) Act 1981, s 1.

[31] Thomson 2006 at 8.

[32] Richard Burton and Elizabeth Taylor were married twice, consecutively, between 15 March 1964 and 26 June 1974 and again between 10 October 1975 and 29 July 1976.

[33] COG 2005, para 2.20.

[34] MHA 1981, s 13(1).

[35] *Ibid*, s 13(2).

done on its own it simply transferred the responsibility for the tenancy from one spouse to another, leaving the ex-tenant able to continue in the property by dint of his statutory occupancy rights.[36] For this reason local authorities preferred the option of seeking possession orders and providing alternative accommodation to the displaced tenant. The landlord had had such a right to apply for a transfer of tenancy order where they wished to effect a transfer and the parties no longer live together as partners under the Tenants' Rights etc (Scotland) Act 1980.[37] It disappeared when transfer of tenancy was introduced. This right was restored to them in 1986.

The new tenant takes on all the responsibilities as tenant other than any arrears of rent for the period before the making of the order.[38] The landlord must be given notice of the application and is entitled to be heard by the court.[39] They might, for instance, have comments to make about whether the proposed new tenant will be able to fulfil the tenancy obligations from their past experience with that person or that the property is excessive in size for single occupancy. Certain tenancies are exempted from the operation of the transfer of tenancy provisions. The most common of these is the exemption for service tenancies (ie lets in connection with employment)[40] but also included are agricultural holdings;[41] crofts, cottars or statutory small tenants;[42] long leases;[43] and tenancies at will.[44] The displaced tenant is, under the transfer of tenancy provisions, entitled to "such compensation as seems just and reasonable in all the circumstances".[45] In calculating the compensation where an ex-tenant was a Scottish secure tenant, no account is to be taken of the loss of the right to buy.[46] Where the tenancy is joint or common the same rules apply,[47] except that the liability for rent arrears is not expunged[48] and crofts and tenancies at will are not exempted.[49] Service occupancies are exempt only if both spouses are required to live in the property.[50]

In determining whether to make a transfer of tenancy order the court must have regard to a number of factors. These factors are the same

---

[36] See Chapter 6.
[37] Now covered by HSA 2001, Sch 2, ground 15.
[38] MHA 1981, s 13(5).
[39] *Ibid*, s 13(4).
[40] *Ibid*, s 13(7)(a).
[41] *Ibid*, s 13(7)(b).
[42] *Ibid*, s 13(7)(c).
[43] *Ibid*, s 13(7)(d).
[44] *Ibid*, s 13(7)(e).
[45] *Ibid*, s 13(1).
[46] *Ibid*, s 13(11).
[47] *Ibid*, s 13(9).
[48] *Ibid*, s 13(10)(c).
[49] *Ibid*, s 13(10)(d)(iii).
[50] *Ibid*, s 13(10)(d)(ii).

as those which apply where there is an application for the declaration of occupancy rights. They consider making a transfer of tenancy order having regard to all the circumstances of the cases including:

(a) The conduct of the spouses in relation to each other and otherwise.

(b) The respective needs and financial resources of the spouses.

(c) The needs of any child of the family.

(d) The extent (if any) to which –
   (i) the matrimonial home; and
   (ii) any item of furniture

   is used in connection with a trade, business or profession of either spouse; and

(e) whether the tenant spouse offers or has offered to make available any suitable alternative accommodation.[51]

The court must also consider the suitability of the applicant to become the tenant and the applicant's capacity to perform the obligations under the lease of the matrimonial home.[52]

The case law on transfers of tenancy has been fairly limited and offers only limited indications as to what factors are crucial. These have included determining between parties where one party was "solely responsible for the breakdown of the marriage" and was "of an extremely unreasonable nature". Given the similar financial resources of the parties and the fact that the wife having to lodge with her daughter was causing overcrowding as well as a strain on the daughter's marriage, a transfer was approved.[53] Where the custody of children was an issue the course which was least disruptive for the family as a whole was followed and a transfer refused from the father with custody of one of three children and a business run from the former family house. The mother had nearby local authority accommodation allowing the two children living with her to continue in the same school.[54] Where, however, there have been no "conduct" factors then the availability of alternative accommodation has been regarded as crucial.[55]

OWNER OR JOINT OWNER

The person who is owner or joint owner has a property right to remain in the partnership home by dint of their legal title. There is no requirement

---

[51] MHA 1981, s 13(3), referring to s 3(3) of the Act.
[52] *Ibid*, s 13(3).
[53] *MacGowan* v *MacGowan* 1986 SLT 122.
[54] *Russell* v *Russell* 18 February 1986 OH.
[55] *Wilson* v *Wilson* 10 January 1986 OH.

for them to seek a declaration of these rights. If, however, they are seeking to occupy the partnership home in which their spouse or partner lives, that person is likely to have occupancy rights. There may also be are couples who would like to live separately but who lack the financial resources to run two properties however, uncongenial continued cohabitation is for them. For a range of reasons they may have opted not to pursue the options available through the homeless persons legislation discussed below. "Splitting" the accommodation may be feasible for those with capacious properties capable of being occupied effectively as separate units where it may conceivably be a palatable option.[56]

If, however, the parties cannot thole continuing to live together, and there is no possibility of their exercising their occupancy rights concurrently, one of them will require to leave. In the event that there is no agreement as to who this should be, one party will require to have the other party's occupancy rights suspended. This is the function of the "exclusion order". These can be granted on an interim basis to secure a swift resolution of problems. There are restrictions on when these rights can be suspended, discussed below.[57]

TENANT OR JOINT TENANT

A person who occupies a property as either tenant or joint tenant can rely on their rights as tenant to remain within the home and may not be lawfully evicted by force. In order for the non-tenant to have the other party removed from the property they can apply to have the tenancy transferred into their name. If they wish that the non-entitled spouse – the person whose name is not on the rent book or lease – to vacate the property then they must seek an exclusion order and satisfy the exact same criteria as in owner occupied property, ie the "necessity" test discussed below.[58]

Abuse

OCCUPIER OF OWNED PROPERTY

The victim of abuse who has no formal legal stake in the owned property has traditionally been the more vulnerable. She has in the past been required to rely on her occupancy rights to stay in the property while relying on securing an exclusion order against the perpetrator of the

---

[56] For a sitcom variant on this, see *My Wife Next Door* (BBC, September – December 1972: 13 episodes) with John Alderton and Hannah Gordon as a recently divorced couple, George and Suzie Bassett. Each tries to start afresh after their divorce. They move to the country, only to find that they have moved into adjoining cottages with various shared amenities.

[57] See below at p 328.

[58] *Ibid.*

abuse. The Matrimonial Homes (Family Protection) (Scotland) Act 1981 introduced a new right to address this problem, the exclusion order.

In the first place this cannot be done on an *ex parte* basis. The potentially excluded party must have notice that an order is being sought and have the opportunity to be heard by the court.[59] In making an exclusion order the court must grant an order summarily ejecting the non-applicant from the house, an order prohibiting that person from entering the matrimonial home without express permission and from removing any furniture from the partnership home.[60]

The test is, on the face of it, simple and straightforward. The court must be satisfied that such an order is necessary for the protection of the physical or mental well-being of the non-entitled spouse or any children in the property. Specifically, whether or not the applicant is in occupation of the property at the time of application:[61]

> "the court shall make an exclusion order if it appears to the court that the making of the order is necessary for the protection of the applicant or any child of the family from any conduct or threatened or reasonably apprehended conduct of the non-applicant spouse which is or would be injurious to the physical or mental health of the applicant or child".[62]

In the early days of the operation of the legislation, since the exclusion order involves seeking to interdict one party from entering the property there was a brief flirtation with the notion that the appropriate test for making such an order was that applied to standard interdicts, namely the balance of convenience.[63] In seeking to displace this standard and reiterate the test laid down in the statute, however, the Court of Session in *Bell* v *Bell* [64] appeared to introduce much stricter tests. Two of the judges talked of the need for there to be "serious or irreparable harm" and for the lesser remedy of the matrimonial interdict in relation to conduct to have been tried and failed.[65] After a period of worry and uncertainty this decision was overturned by the Court of Session itself. Denying that these tests had ever been intended to apply beyond the instant case,[66] the court reaffirmed the "necessity" test and laid down a way of deciding whether an order was indeed "necessary".[67]

---

[59] MHA 1981, s 4(6).
[60] *Ibid*, s 4.
[61] *Ibid*, s 4(1), as inserted by the Law Reform (Miscellaneous Provisions) (Scotland) Act 1985, ss 13(5) and 60(6).
[62] MHA 1981, s 4(2).
[63] *Smith* v *Smith* 1983 SLT 275 made it clear that this was not appropriate.
[64] 1983 SLT 224.
[65] Bell at 231 per Lord Robertson and at 233 per Lord Grieve.
[66] *McCafferty* v *McCafferty* 1986 SLT 650 at 655.
[67] *Ibid* at 652.

Ancillary rights

The formal housing rights which can be asserted frequently require something more than the mere suspension of the occupancy rights of the other person in the relationship, although, after a relationship has ended, the evicted spouse/partner, who obviously knows where their ex-partner is residing, may harass the other party. To discourage this it is possible to obtain a special form of court order which:

(a) restrains or prohibits any conduct of one spouse towards the other spouse or a child of the family; or

(a) prohibits a spouse from entering or remaining in a matrimonial home or in a specified area in the vicinity of the matrimonial home.[68]

It is possible to have a power of arrest attached to such matrimonial interdicts. This must be done where an exclusion order is granted[69] as well as where any other interdict is obtained, provided that the non-applicant spouse/partner has had the opportunity of being heard or represented before the court.[70] It is open to the non-applicant spouse to argue that such a power is, in all the circumstances, unnecessary.[71] Thus where an applicant, after being interdicted from returning to the partnership home, suffered a seriously debilitating condition, it might be argued that the need to have the protection of a power of arrest might be sufficiently diminished for this not to be granted.

OCCUPIER OF TENANTED PROPERTY

Only a little less vulnerable has been the non-entitled occupier of rented accommodation. She has, however, in the social rented sector at least, had a chance access to alternative accommodation from her landlord as one of the grounds of possession against a Scottish secure tenant is that the landlord wishes to transfer the tenancy of the property.[72] The conditions which have to be met are that the court must be satisfied that this is reasonable in all the circumstances.[73] In addition, this requires that the tenant's spouse or cohabitant has applied to the landlord for a transfer and the parties no longer wish to live together in the house.[74]

---

[68] MHA 1981, s 14(2).
[69] *Ibid*, s 15(1)(a).
[70] *Ibid*, s 15(1)(b).
[71] *Ibid*.
[72] HSA 2001, Sch 2, ground 15.
[73] See Chapter 6.
[74] HSA 2001, Sch 2, ground 15.

OWNER OR JOINT OWNER

The owner can rely on their title to remain in the property but again will need to seek an exclusion order to have the non-entitled spouse removed. There is, however, one bizarre gap in the provisions of the Matrimonial Homes (Family Protection) (Scotland) Act 1981. The legislation provides for the eviction of people by way of their occupancy rights being suspended. If, however, there are no occupancy rights in existence, then there is nothing to suspend and the court is, on the face of it, powerless to act. This was the conclusion of the sheriff principal in *Clarke* v *Hatten*.[75] In this instance a tenant of a local authority, Margaret Clarke, had fled the violence of her partner, John Hatten, who remained in the matrimonial home. She wanted her daughter to be able to continue in the same school. She sought to have her ex-partner evicted from the home. It was pointed out to the court that the ex-cohabitant had not sought to have his occupancy rights declared and hence was not "entitled or permitted" by the landlord to live there. Until both partners were so entitled the legislation did not come into play. The sheriff principal did note that the tenant might have a remedy in a common law action of ejection and eviction although this would not carry with it the power of arrest.[76] Given the speed with which such orders are available as compared with exclusion orders this was not a particularly satisfactory alternative. Although this case concerned a tenancy, the same logic would apply to a property which was owned by one of the parties who left the partnership home.

TENANT OR JOINT TENANT

The tenant who has his name on the lease can, as we have noted, be displaced as tenant through the transfer of tenancy process. He has the right to remain in terms of his occupancy rights until such time as there is a successful suspension of occupancy rights. As we have noted, this will not take place unless there is some harm, threat of harm or reasonably apprehended likelihood of harm to the physical health of the spouse/partner or a child of the family. In the absence of physical harm it will be necessary for the other party to show that the mental health of the other party has been or is likely to be affected by the presence of the tenant/joint tenant. Unless that test of necessity can be satisfied then the tenant has the right to remain, however unedifying his presence may be. If the spouse/partner is able to satisfy the court that his absence is necessary for the continued wellbeing of her or their children's health then there is no requirement that he be provided with any alternative accommodation. Such a provision was provided for in the Tenants' Rights etc (Scotland) Act

75 1987 SCLR 527.
76 *Ibid* at 528.

1980 pending the introduction of the 1981 Act's reforms. This provided that the local authority could apply to the court for a possession order to transfer the tenancy to the spouse or former spouse in the event of marital breakdown.[77] The major difference here, however, from an application by a tenant was that the local authority required to provide the evicted tenant with another property from their stock. This was briefly removed as an option between 1981 and 1986 but is now one of the options for local authority landlords who have stock from which to make suitable alternative accommodation available.[78]

HOUSING RIGHTS – LEAVING THE HOME

In this section we focus on the rights which are available by contract, common law, statute and otherwise. In addition, of course, there is a range of different options which those who leave the partnership home have available to them and which may well be preferred to seeking to use these rights. The options which are available and which are utilised will sometime depend on the availability of personal financial resources, family and friends as well as the availability and quality of both voluntary and statutory services. These services vary across the country, so that a convenient short-term refuge space at short notice may be much more readily available in some areas than others. Similarly, by their very size and extent the homelessness services of populous urban authorities are likely to be able to offer more choice than sparsely populated rural authorities can.

Relationship breakdown

Where there is relationship breakdown and there is no wish to continue to occupy the partnership home there are two sources of rights for separating couples. The homeless persons legislation discussed elsewhere[79] provides a route for some whose accommodation is affected by relationship breakdown. In very simple terms, local authorities have obligations to those homeless people who are in priority need, who are not homeless intentionally and who have a local connection with the area where they apply. The obligations laid on local authorities not only require them to react to those who apply to them but also to develop policies and procedures which seek to address homelessness before it arises. In order to assist local authorities in carrying out these tasks the Code of Guidance offers advice as to what should be done in a range of situations. One piece

---

[77] Tenants' Rights etc (Scotland) Act 1980, Sch 2, Pt I, para 6; subsequently located in Sch 3, para 16 to the Housing (Scotland) Act 1987 and now in Sch 2, para 15 to the Housing (Scotland) Act 2001.

[78] HSA 2001, s 16(2)(c) and Sch 2, para 15.

[79] See Chapter 2.

of advice which is proffered aims to lessen the impact of relationship breakdown through counselling.[80] The Code goes on to suggest other agencies might be involved:

> "In other cases it may be possible for the authority or another service provide to intervene to prevent family breakdown and resulting homelessness. Local authorities should consider whether it is appropriate for them or another agency to provide relationship counselling or mediation services."[81]

It is careful, though, to point out that the provision of support should never be an alternative to rehousing where there is a risk of abuse.[82]

OCCUPIER OF OWNED PROPERTY

Whether or not a person who has left a relationship and the home where the family lived is entitled to the full range of assistance will depend on whether they are homeless. The test is whether they have any accommodation which is available to them. If there is a matrimonial home which, prior to the relationship, was reasonable to occupy then some courts have regarded this as disqualifying the applicant for assistance at the first hurdle. The Code of Guidance points out that, while advice on rights under the Matrimonial Homes (Family Protection) (Scotland) Act 1981 may be required, exercising these rights should not be made a condition of access to services.[83] This can be seen as a response to a decision in the Scottish courts in the early days of the legislation. When a non-entitled cohabitee did not seek to exercise her rights under the Matrimonial Homes (Family Protection) (Scotland) Act 1981 she was deemed by one Scottish local authority not to qualify for assistance as she could not be said to be homeless.[84] The Court of Session upheld this decision and determined that it was not a decision which no reasonable council could have come to.[85] It can be criticised on the ground that it confuses the right to apply for a declaration of occupancy rights with an actual right to accommodation. The court is not a mere rubber stamp for an application and must apply the criteria about whether or not the couple are indeed cohabiting as well as whether in all the circumstances the criteria of s 3(3) of the 1981 Act are satisfied. Similar sorts of determinations where a couple split up without there being any threat of violence have been made by councils operating the same legislation in England. In one English case a Mrs Cadney quit the matrimonial home for another man – a friend of the family – with whom she lived for 6 months. When that relationship

---

[80] COG 2005, para 2.21.
[81] *Ibid*, para 2.24.
[82] *Ibid*.
[83] *Ibid*, para 2.19.
[84] *McAlinden v Bearsden and Milngavie DC* 1986 SLT 91.
[85] *Ibid*.

went sour she applied to the council as homeless. The council advised that she was not homeless as she could still go back to the matrimonial home. Although there were no suggestions that Mr Cadney had ever been a violent husband, it does seem to place great faith in the nostrum "forgive and forget".[86]

An applicant who has not exercised his or her occupancy rights under the Matrimonial Homes (Family Protection) (Scotland) Act 1981 should not be regarded as intentionally homeless for that reason, regardless of why those rights were not exercised.[87] The question, though, arises as to whether leaving the partnership home where there has been no physical or mental abuse might amount to intentionality. For a local authority to make a lawful finding of intentionality there require to have been the giving up of accommodation which it would have been reasonable to continue to occupy. Where there has been no abuse some of the case law takes a robust and unsympathetic view of the situation. In a case where a husband had been treating his wife badly but which did not involve violence, Mr Justice Woolf delivered some remarks which are less than encouraging to anyone seeking to leave a broken relationship:

"the conclusion that the [housing officer] came to was that there was no fear of any violence and, on that basis, he formed the opinion that it would be reasonable for the applicant to remain in the accommodation provided by the matrimonial home ... that is a conclusion to which the authority were fully entitled to come".[88]

The solution, according to his Lordship, was that:

"there is all sorts of protection that a woman can get if her husband misbehaves ... the local authority could perfectly properly in many cases in this country take the view that it would be reasonable for the wife to continue to occupy accommodation and to say to the wife ... 'If you are having trouble with your husband, go to the appropriate authority ... and get protection against your husband'".[89]

Clearly, provision of alternative accommodation was seen as a last resort after civil remedies had failed.

This contrasts with the kind of advice being put forward more recently in the Scottish Code of Guidance which authorities are obliged to take account of:

Advice may be required by a member of the household on, for example, his or her rights under the Matrimonial Homes (Family Protection) (Scotland) Act 1981. However, exercising these rights should not be made a condition

---

86   *R v Purbeck DC, ex p Cadney* (1985) 17 HLR 534.
87   COG 2005, para 7.23.
88   *R v London Borough of Wandsworth, ex p Nimako-Boateng* (1984) 11 HLR 95 at 102.
89   *Ibid* at 103.

of access to services. It may also be useful to ask a relevant voluntary body, such as a Women's Aid group in the case of domestic abuse, or the social work department, to help in appropriate circumstances, and particularly if there are children in the household."[90]

The Code of Guidance points out that when a local authority is considering a homelessness application:

"staff should interpret abuse widely to include any form or violence, harassment, threatening conduct and any other behaviour giving rise or likely to give rise to physical or mental injury, fear, alarm or distress and not just domestic, racial or sexual abuse".[91]

OCCUPIER OF TENANTED PROPERTY

The tenant in the social rented sector has a number of options deriving from statute. She can request that the landlord make another property available in terms of the Housing (Scotland) Act 2001 or rely on the homelessness provisions in the Housing (Scotland) Act 1987 discussed in Chapter 2. Initially, in terms of the Tenants' Rights etc (Scotland) Act 1980 there was provision for a request to a local authority to make accommodation available on marital breakdown. That power is retained in the Housing (Scotland) Act 2001. It is provided that one of the grounds on which a landlord may recover possession from a tenant in a Scottish secure tenancy is where the landlord wishes to transfer the tenancy to the tenant's current or former spouse, civil partner or cohabiting partner. The proposed tenant must have applied to the landlord where the parties no longer wish to live together in the house.[92] This provision includes same-sex couples. This ground can be used only where the court is satisfied that it is reasonable to evict the tenant and that other accommodation is available for the tenant.[93]

The Code of Guidance suggests that temporary accommodation may be needed for the person receiving the tenancy until the other person leaves and also points out a practical step:

"For the avoidance of doubt, the person leaving should be asked to renounce any occupancy rights under the Matrimonial Homes (Family Protection) (Scotland) Act 1981. Particularly when children or other dependants remain with the applicant, such a transfer can minimise any resulting homelessness."[94]

If that does not occur, then what remains for the occupier of social rented property who chooses to leave a non-abusive relationship where they

---

[90] COG 2005, para 2.19.
[91] *Ibid*, para 4.38.
[92] HSA 2001, Sch 2, Pt 1, para 15.
[93] *Ibid*, s 16(2)(c).
[94] COG 2005, para 2.23.

have no rights *qua* tenant is to rely on the homelessness provisions of the Housing (Scotland) Act 1987 (as amended). This involves as was noted in relation to those leaving owner occupied property, satisfying the "homeless", "priority need", "intentionality' and "local connection" tests.

The position in the private rented sector is rather less promising. There is no provision for a private-sector landlord to make any provision in the event of marital discord affecting his tenants. Any spouse or partner leaving a private rental sector marital home has no recourse to the landlord other than as any other tenant seeking accommodation in the market. The Code of Guidance provides no specific advice as to how best local authorities should deal with these difficult situations but does note that there may be situations where parties can remain in the partnership home: "If it appropriate, and if it requested by both parties, assistance should be directed towards relieving tension within the household so as to enable the household to continue to live together."[95]

OWNER OR JOINT OWNER

While, for the sake of consistency, this distinction between entitled and non-entitled is maintained to clarify the distinct legal rights enjoyed by the parties, this is not a scenario which is encountered extensively in practice. Where the spouse is leaving property which is owned or jointly owned there are likely to be problems if they seek assistance from the local authority. The Code of Guidance notes the possibility of various options, ranging from negotiating with the lender and making use of the mortgage to rent scheme.[96]

As far as delays in providing accommodation are concerned, authorities are urged to avoid disrupting lives if this can be avoided:

"If the local authority is satisfied that the situation warrants making accommodation available, its agreement to secure another house within a definite period of time may be preferable to transferring those involved into some interim short-term accommodation while more lasting arrangements are established."[97]

TENANT OR JOINT TENANT

Similarly, those who have the lease in their name tend not to simply leave the partnership home. Any person who occupies a property as either tenant or joint tenant and leaves in a situation where there is relationship disharmony is also likely to find local authorities having the options of finding him either not homeless or intentionally homeless.[98]

---

[95] COG 2005, para. 2.21.
[96] *Ibid*, para 2.74.
[97] *Ibid*, para 2.22.
[98] See Chapter 2.

Abuse

If an abused spouse/partner wishes to leave both the relationship and the partnership home then the principal source of housing rights is the Housing (Scotland) Act 1987. The housing rights which this provides are buttressed by a range of statutes covering protection from harassment and abuse. The value of interdicts against physical abuse has always been somewhat questionable. As the Code of Guidance points out, taking such action may provoke further abuse.[99] Practitioners routinely advise their clients to ensure that they have effective protection against the abuser around the time when the paperwork is served. The existence of powers of arrest attached to matrimonial since 1982 has provided a more effective remedy for breach than existed for pre-1981 Act interdicts. Breach of common-law interdicts was a matter which required to be brought in the civil courts which did not sit at weekends and in the evenings. While ignoring interdicts allowed the person in breach to be arrested and where appropriate locked up briefly, the sanction was not a criminal offence. That was addressed in the Protection from Harassment Act 1997 which provides for non-harassment orders. Breach of these is punishable as a criminal offence by up to 5 years' imprisonment. Finally, there is the Protection from Abuse (Scotland) Act 2001 which sought to strengthen the previous protections of matrimonial interdicts.

Where homelessness is likely to ensue, the local authority has a significant statutory duty towards those who become homeless and are in priority need. The legislation specifically covers within the priority need category a person who runs the risk of domestic abuse.[100] This 1987 Act definition now adopts that set out in the Protection from Abuse (Scotland) Act 2001 which states that "abuse" includes violence, harassment, threatening conduct, and any other conduct giving rise, or likely to give rise, to physical or mental injury, fear, alarm or distress.

Local authorities are reminded, however, that the assistance of other groups may be vital. The Code of Guidance suggests that it may also be useful to ask a relevant voluntary body, such as a Women's Aid group in the case of domestic abuse, or the Social Work Department, to help in appropriate circumstances, and particularly if there are children in the household.[101] Verifying allegations of abuse is the responsibility of the local authority and this is a task which requires sensitivity. The Code of Guidance notes:

> "If the applicant reports abuse, the local authority should take reasonable steps to obtain information to support the applicant's case and consider

---

[99] COG 2005, para 4.41.
[100] Housing (Scotland) Act 1987, s 33(3), as amended by the Protection from Abuse (Scotland) Act 2001.
[101] COG 2005, para 2.19.

all available evidence and information relating to the circumstances of each case. However, a local authority should never seek proof from an alleged perpetrator and if it proves impossible or inappropriate to obtain confirming evidence the applicant's expressed fears should be considered as sufficient evidence. For example, if the only way to obtain confirming evidence is by asking the alleged perpetrator then this should be deemed to be inappropriate."[102]

As a general rule, a local authority should always rehouse a homeless household within its own area, particularly where temporary accommodation is being provided. In rare cases, however, the local authority may need to consider placing homeless people in another local authority's area, although this should only be done only with the household's consent.[103] Such "outplacements", however, may be appropriate in cases of domestic abuse.[104] While the local authority may look to the question of costs to the household through increased travelling costs and disruption of education,[105] local authorities are urged by the Code to adopt the general rule that the new location should remove them from the range of the perpetrators of the violence.[106] In considering an out of area placement for persons made homeless by domestic abuse "local authorities should give first importance to the expressed fears and wishes of those concerned. The application of this rule should take account of the particular circumstances, for example likely travel routes for the person who has suffered the abuse or violence and for the perpetrator".[107]

The kind of accommodation which might be appropriate will vary and there will be situations where, drawing on the success of Women's Aid refuges, such kinds of accommodation with support might be deemed most helpful to the abuse victim:

> "Local authority hostels, or hostels run by voluntary bodies, can be a useful form of short-term accommodation, as long as these hostels are reasonably small-scale and are an appropriate environment in which to deliver support if required. They may therefore be appropriate for the needs of some individuals. Different models of hostel accommodation may be suitable for different applicants: for example, small high-support units may suit some young people or communal accommodation can enable households at crisis point to have some relief for a short period from coping alone; and the company of other people who have gone through similar problems can be helpful."[108]

---

[102] COG 2005, para 4.39.
[103] *Ibid*, para 9.79.
[104] *Ibid*, para 9.80.
[105] *Ibid*, para 9.81.
[106] *Ibid*, para 9.82.
[107] *Ibid*.
[108] *Ibid*, para 9.47.

OCCUPIER OF OWNED PROPERTY

It may be that a woman does not wish to remain in the partnership home through fear or to make a fresh start away from the site of the abuse. Homelessness may result and while local authorities are urged to intervene to prevent homelessness and keep households together, in cases of relationship breakdown, such intervention by local authorities may be inappropriate in many cases.[109] Specifically, the Code of Guidance states:

> "Where allegations of abuse are involved it would be wholly inappropriate for the authority or another agency to intervene to keep the household together and such an intervention may in fact lead to an exacerbation of the situation. In particular the alleged perpetrator of violence should not be approached for a view."[110]

There may well be a need to weigh up the benefits of having a satisfactory long-term solution where there are delays in effecting this with the need to be safe. While short-term temporary accommodation may be unsettling, it may well be the safer option, as the Code notes:

> "local authorities must not put pressure on people to remain in or return to their previous houses if that would cause distress. In particular, when a person is seeking refuge because of a fear of abuse there will be an immediate need for rehousing".[111]

OCCUPIER OF TENANTED PROPERTY

An abused woman may well not wish to remain in the partnership home through fear or wish to make a fresh start. Where the woman is not the tenant then homelessness may result and while local authorities are urged to intervene to prevent homelessness and keep households together,[112] in cases of relationship breakdown, such intervention by local authorities may be inappropriate in many cases.[113] Again, it should be noted in such circumstances, the Code of Guidance noted above applies in relation to the source of evidence and inappropriateness of intervention to keep such a household together.[114]

OWNER OR JOINT OWNER

An abused spouse or partner who flees the home that she owns or jointly owns will be more concerned with short-term solutions. These may well

---

[109] COG 2005, para 2.18.
[110] *Ibid.*
[111] *Ibid*, para 2.22.
[112] *Ibid.*
[113] *Ibid*, para 2.18.
[114] *Ibid.*

centre around finding safe hostel accommodation. Some local authorities also have responsive abuse units which are able to respond with accommodation appropriate to the circumstances. Insofar as she wishes to access the accommodation available in terms of the homelessness provisions of the Housing (Scotland) Act 1987, there are special statutory rules designed to address the question of safety. In terms of whether or not she is homeless the legislation states that a person is homeless if they have accommodation but it is probable that occupation of it will lead to abuse in terms of the Protection from Abuse Act (Scotland) 2001.[115] This covers violence, harassment, threatening conduct, and any other conduct giving rise, or likely to give rise, to physical or mental injury, fear, alarm or distress. "Conduct" includes speech as well as presence in a specified place or area.[116] In addition, there is deemed to be no accommodation where it is probable that occupation would lead to abuse from some other person who previously resided with that person, whether in that accommodation or elsewhere.[117] Obtaining protection through interdicts against molestation is one remedy. The Code of Guidance points out, however, that even if an applicant has obtained an order under the Matrimonial Homes (Family Protection) (Scotland) Act 1981 guaranteeing his or her occupancy rights, or an interdict against molestation by a former partner, this may not always be sufficient to make it reasonable to expect him or her to continue to occupy the house.[118]

In addition, the normal rules in relation to local connection do not operate. A person may not be referred to another authority if they run the risk of domestic abuse in that other authority's district.[119]

By the same token, the question of intentionality should not arise where a woman leaves the matrimonial home because she is fleeing abuse since it would not be reasonable to continue living in the matrimonial home. The case law on this issue is clear and best exemplified by the decision in *R v Kensington and Chelsea LBC, ex p Hammell*[120] where the Court of Appeal gave a stamp of approval to this notion. It should be noted that the comparable cases in the courts south of the Border still operate a test relating to "violence" rather than "abuse". This has led to questions as to whether a finding of intentionality concerning a woman who suffered emotional, psychological and financial abuse at the hands of her husband could be found to be intentionally homeless when she left the matrimonial home. The Court of Appeal considered that "domestic violence" was no wider than violence from someone with whom the victim

---

[115]   HSA 1987, s 24(3)(b).
[116]   PFA 2001, s 7.
[117]   HSA 1987, s 24(3)(bb).
[118]   COG 2005, para 5.13.
[119]   HSA 1987, s 33(2)(c).
[120]   [1989] QB 518.

was associated.[121] While one would not expect the courts in Scotland to follow this line of decision, it is worth noting the very fragile nature of the progress that appears to have made in rights in relation to abusive behaviour and the process of reasonable interpretation.

TENANT OR JOINT TENANT

In the same vein, the housing solutions for abused women whose tenancies are in their name but where there is fear of continued violence or other abuse may well be seeking a solution away from the area. It may be that a woman does not wish to remain in the matrimonial home through fear or to make a fresh start away from the site of abuse. Homelessness may result and while local authorities are urged to intervene to prevent homelessness and keep households together, in cases of relationship breakdown, such intervention by local authorities may be inappropriate in many cases.[122] Specifically, it is worth reiterating what the Code of Guidance says:

> "Where allegations of abuse are involved it would be wholly inappropriate for the authority or another agency to intervene to keep the household together and such an intervention may in fact lead to an exacerbation of the situation. In particular the alleged perpetrator of violence should not be approached for a view."[123]

PROTECTION OF CHILDREN

One issue which did not emerge as an issue in the early research on implementation of the Matrimonial Homes (Family Protection) (Scotland) Act 1981 nor in the subsequent case law has been the issue of abuse of children. The Code point out that if the applicant alleges assault or sexual abuse of a child, the homelessness officer should advise him or her of the homelessness officer's responsibility to discuss this with the Social Work Department, so that any necessary help and protection for the child and applicant can be arranged. Homelessness officers should, it notes, ensure that they have telephone contact numbers and addresses of local services to which those who have experienced violence or sexual abuse can be referred, for example women's refuges, and other services specialising in violence or sexual abuse.[124]

OVERVIEW

Major changes have occurred in both the rights of women whether as widows, wives, cohabitants or same-sex partners in the post-war era.

---

121 *Yemshaw* v *Hounslow LBC* [2010] 23 HLR 399.
122 COG 2005, para 2.18.
123 *Ibid.*
124 *Ibid*, para 4.43.

Widows – and widowers – in terms of the Succession (Scotland) Act 1964 were given a statutory right to one-third of the moveable property of the deceased spouse as well as having prior rights in the matrimonial home and furniture therein up to a specified limit along with a capital sum from the remaining estate.[125] When the figures were introduced in 1964 the dwelling-house figure was £15,000. The average house price in Scotland at that time was less than £10,000. The figure for succession rights was raised in 1993 to £110,000,[126] by which time the average house price had risen to £75,000.[127] The figure at the time of writing is £300,000[128] and the nominal average house price by 2007 had reached £150,000.[129]

In situations short of divorce, where a couple were experiencing relationship problems and separation was a temporary solution, the legal position of the non-owner/non-tenant was extremely weak. The owner had the right to eject the other party without, it seemed, the need to seek any kind of official sanction. Indeed, examples were given to researchers of police assisting in evicting non-owner/tenant spouses with the threat of arrest for breach of the peace if the evicted spouse did not leave quietly and without a fuss.[130] This issue was examined by the Scottish Law Commission and legislation based on its recommendations was enacted.

Complementing the introduction and use of matrimonial interdicts in terms of the Matrimonial Homes (Family Protection) (Scotland) Act 1981 were orders in terms of the Protection from Harassment Act 1997 and the Protection from Abuse (Scotland) Act 2001. The 1997 Act, which was a piece of British legislation, introduced non-harassment orders. This meant that where there was a course of conduct including speech involving at least two separate occasions of harassment – ie conduct causing alarm and distress – a non-harassment order could be granted.[131] In addition, the procurator fiscal could apply to the court to make a non-harassment order against the harasser which the court could grant if "on the balance of probabilities it is appropriate to do so in order to protect the victim from further harassment".[132] Breach of a non-harassment order is a criminal offence and on conviction renders the affected party liable

---

[125] House £15,000; furniture £5,000; capital sum £5,000.
[126] Prior Rights of Surviving Spouse (Scotland) Order 1993 (SI 1993/2690).
[127] Prior Rights of Surviving Spouse (Scotland) Order 1999 (SI 1999/445).
[128] *Ibid.*
[129] Nominal house prices went from under £10,000 in 1973 to £150,000 in 2007 (based on data from the Bank of England, Deutsche Bundesbank and Nationwide) http://gold.approximity.com/gold_vs_property.pdf).
[130] Jackson, Robertson and Robson (1989) (unpublished field notes not included in Final Report).
[131] PHA 1997 – now see PFA 2001, s 7.
[132] Criminal Procedure (Scotland) Act 1995, s 234A(2) – as inserted by PHA 1997.

on indictment up to 5 years' imprisonment and on summary level up to 6 months' imprisonment.[133]

The Protection from Abuse (Scotland) Act 2001 was introduced to provide further protection by expanding the coverage of interdicts with powers of arrest to cover abuse. "Abuse" is defined as including "violence, harassment, threatening conduct, and any other conduct giving rise, or likely to give rise to, to physical or mental injury, fear, alarm or distress".[134]

Subsequent research suggested that this legislation, introduced to extend protection to those who were previously unable to access interdicts with powers of arrest, was not well known among victims of domestic violence and that success in securing such interdicts was limited.[135] As far as the response to breaches of interdicts under this Act and the Matrimonial Homes (Family Protection) (Scotland) Act 1981 was concerned, this was a cause of concern to the researchers. The civil proceedings remedy was cumbersome, did not attract legal aid, caused delays and, since it took the momentum out of the incident, this impacted on the judges' perceptions of the seriousness of the matter.[136]

A Civil Protection Orders and Access to Justice (Scotland) Bill was proposed in March 2010 by MSP Rhoda Grant. The proposed Bill aimed to increase access to justice for victims of domestic abuse and to improve the ability of civil protection order to deter perpetrators by providing more robust and effective responses to breaches of civil interdicts. There are three major planks in this proposal. First, it would remove the requirement to show a course of conduct before a non-harassment order could be granted, requiring only one incident of harassing behaviour. Second, legal aid would be provided free for any application to a civil court for an interdict with a power of arrest or a non-harassment order where domestic abuse was involved. Finally, breaching an interdict with a power of arrest was to be a criminal offence. The Bill followed a Consultation Document from 1 December 2009 which contained the three main proposals noted above.[137] In the Criminal Justice and Licensing (Scotland) Act 2010 stalking still requires a course of conduct involving such behaviour on at least two occasions.[138] Threatening or abusive behaviour, however, can consist of a single act.[139]

---

[133] PHA 1997, s 9(1) – subsequently Criminal Justice (Scotland) Act 2003, s 49.
[134] PAA 2001, s 7.
[135] Cavanagh, Connelly and Scoular (2003) at para 8.5.
[136] *Ibid* at para 8.10.
[137] Consultation Document on the Proposed Civil Protection Orders and Access to Justice (Scotland) Bill, 1 December 2009: http://www.scottish.parliament.uk/s3/bills/membersbills/documents/RhodaGrantConsultationFINALVERSION.pdf.
[138] Criminal Justice and Licensing (Scotland) Act 2010, s 39.
[139] *Ibid*, s 38.

BIBLIOGRAPHY

Alinsky, S (1971) *Rules for Radicals* (Random House, New York)

Banting, K (1979) *Poverty, Power and Politics* (Routledge & Kegan Paul, London)

Barber, L (2009) *An Education* (Penguin, London)

Barnett, M J (1969) *The Politics of Legislation: The Rent Act 1957* (Weidenfeld & Nicolson, London)

Barrhead Community Council (undated, c 1985) *Housing the Heroes: The Struggles of a Small Town, 1919 –1939* (Barrhead Community Council, Barrhead)

Becker, H (1967) "Whose Side are we on?" 14 *Social Problems* (Winter) 239

Begg, T (1987) *50 Special Years: A Study in Scottish Housing* (Henry Melland, London)

— (1996) *Housing Policy in Scotland* (John Donald, Edinburgh)

Bell, G J (1899) *Principles of the Law of Scotland* (10th edn) (T & T Clark, Edinburgh)

Bell, J (1981) *Policy Arguments in Judicial Decisions* (Clarendon, Oxford)

Berry, F (1974) *Housing: the great British failure* (Charles Knight, London)

Bolderson, H (1991) *Social Security, Disability and Rehabilitation: Conflicts in the Development of Social Policy 1914-1946* (Jessica Kingsley, London)

Bowes, A; McCluskey, J; and Sim, D (1989) *Ethnic minority housing problems in Glasgow* (Department of Sociology & Social Policy, University of Stirling)

Bowley, M (1945) *Housing and the State* (Heinemann, London)

Boyle and Birds (2009): Birds, J; Boyle, A J; Clark, B; MacNeil, I; McCormack, G; Twigg-Flesner, C; and Villiers, C, *Boyle and Birds' Company Law* (7th edn) (Jordans, Bristol)

Bradley, Q (1997) The *Leeds Rent Strike of 1914: a reappraisal of the radical history of the tenants movement* (Housing Studies HNC Research Project)

British Market Research Bureau (1977) *Housing Consumer Survey* (HMSO, London)

Brittain, A; Kennedy, J; Tate, J; and Torrance, A (2007) *Tensions between Allocations Policy and Practice* (Scottish Government, Edinburgh)

Bromley's Family Law (2006) Lowe, N; and Douglas, G (10th edn) (Oxford University Press, Oxford)

Brown, G (1971) *In My Way* (Gollancz, London)

Brown, L N "Comparative Rent Control" (1970) 19 ICLQ 205

Brown, P; and McIntosh, A (1987) *Dampness and Housing* (Shelter, Edinburgh)

Burnett, J (1986) *A Social History of Housing 1815–1985* (Routledge, London)

Burns, J (1938) *Handbook of Conveyancing* (5th edn) (W Green, Edinburgh)

Butt, J (1973) "Working Class Housing in Glasgow" in S D Chapman (ed), *The History of Working Class Housing*

Callaghan, J (1987) *Time and Chance* (Collins, London)

Carr, J L (1954) "Rent Control and Housing Policy" 64 (253) *The Economic Journal* 25

Castells, M (1977) *The Urban Question: A Marxist Approach* (Edward Arnold, London)

— (1978) *City, Class and Power* (St Martin's Press, London)

Castle, B (1993) *Fighting All the Way* (Pan, London)

Cavanagh, K; Connelly, C; and Scoular, J (2003) *An Evaluation of the Protection from Abuse (Scotland) Act 2001* (Scottish Executive, Edinburgh)

Cave, M (2007) *Every Tenant Matters: a review of social housing regulation* (Communities and Local Government Publications, Wetherby)

Chapman, S D (ed) (1971) *The History of Working Class Housing: A Symposium* (David & Charles, Newton Abbot)

Churchill, W (1945) Conservative Party General Election Manifesto: Winston Churchill's Declaration of Policy to the Electors (available at: http://www.conservative-party.net/manifestos/1945/1945-conservative-manifesto.shtml)

Clive, E (1997) *The Law of Husband and Wife in Scotland* (4th edn) (W Green, Edinburgh)

Cochrane, R (1976) *The Law of Housing in Scotland* (W Hodge, Glasgow)

Collins, S; and O'Carroll, D (1997) *Anti-social behaviour and housing: the law* (CIH, Edinburgh)

Communities Scotland (2002) *Thematic Regulations studies: Equalities in practice* (Communities Scotland, Edinburgh) (available at: http://www.scottishhousingregulator.gov.uk/stellent/groups/public/documents/webpages/shr_evictionsinpractice.pdf)

— (2004) *Intervention Strategy* (Communities Scotland, Edinburgh)

— (2005) *Key themes from inspections: Homelessness* (Communities Scotland, Edinburgh and Glasgow) (available at: http://www.scottish housingregulator.gov.uk/stellent/groups/public/documents/webpages/shr_keythemesfrominspection-ho.pdf)

— (2005a) *Thematic Study: Evictions in Practice* (Communities Scotland, Edinburgh and Glasgow) (available at: http://www.scottish housingregulator.gov.uk/stellent/groups/public/documents/webpages/shr_evictionsinpractice.pdf)

Communities Scotland (2006) *Equalities in practice: follow up study* (Communities Scotland, Glasgow) (available at: http://www.scottishhousing regulator.gov.uk/stellent/groups/public/documents/webpages/ shr_equalitiesinp_ia47f1dfa8-1.pdf)

Communities Scotland, COSLA and SFHA (2006) *Performance Standards for social landlords and homelessness functions* (Communities Scotland, Edinburgh) (available at: http://www.communitiesscotland.gov.uk/ stellent/groups/public/documents/webpages/shr_performancestan_ ia47f1df80.pdf)

Constable Committee (1925) Report of the Committee on the Rent Restriction Acts (Cmd 2423) (HMSO, London)

Council for Research on Housing Construction (1934) *Slum Clearance and Rehousing* (King, London)

Cowan, D; and Marsh, A (2001) "There's regulatory crime and then there's landlord crime: from 'Rachmanites' to 'Partners'" 64 *Modern Law Review* 831

Cramond, R D (1966) *Housing Policy in Scotland 1919–1964: A Study in State Assistance* (Oliver & Boyd, Edinburgh)

Creighton (2005) "From Exclusion to political control: radical and working class organisation in Battersea 1803s–1918" (at www.bwtuc.org.uk/pdf/ From%Exclusion.doc%20history%20doc.pdf)

Cross, W (2005) *Death in a Lodging House: the Story of the Watson Street Fire, Glasgow Sunday 19 November 1905* (William P Cross)

Crossman, R (1975) *The Diaries of a Cabinet Minister*, vol 1 (Secker & Warburg, London)

Cullingworth, J B (1968) *A Profile of Glasgow Housing 1965* (Oliver & Boyd, Edinburgh)

Currie, H; and Murie, A (eds) (1996) *Housing in Scotland* (Chartered Institute of Housing, Coventry)

Damer, S (1982) *Rent Strikes! The Clydebank Rent Strike* (Clydebank People's History Pamphlet, Clydebank)

— (1989) *From Moorepark to "Wine Alley": The rise and fall of a Glasgow housing scheme* (Edinburgh University Press, Edinburgh)

— (1994) "Striking out on Red Clyde" in C Grant (ed), *Built to Last? Reflections on British Housing Policy – A Collection of Articles from "Roof" Magazine* (Shelter, London)

Daunton, M J (1983) *House and Home in the Victorian City* (Arnold, London)

Davis, J (2001) "Rent and Race in 1960s London: New Light on Rachmanism" 12(1) *Twentieth Century British History* 69

Denning, A T (1979) *The Discipline of Law* (Butterworths, London)

— (1980) *Due Process of Law* (Butterworths, London)

Department of the Environment (1971) *Fair Deal for Housing* (Cmnd 4728) (HMSO, London)

Donnison, D; Cockburn, C; and Corlett, T (1961) *Housing Since the Rent Act* (Bell, London)

Drudy, P J (ed) (1982) *Ireland: Land, Politics and People* (Cambridge University Press, Cambridge)

Duclaud-Williams, R (1978) *The Politics of Housing in Britain and France* (Heinemann, London)

Dunleavy, P (1981) *The Politics of Mass Housing in Britain 1945–1975: A Study in Corporate Power and Political Influence in the Welfare State* (Clarendon Press, Oxford)

Elliott, B; and McCrone D (1975) "Landlords in Edinburgh: some preliminary findings" *Sociological Review* 539

Encyclopaedia of Scottish Legal Styles (1937) (W Green, Edinburgh)

Encyclopaedia of the Laws of Scotland (1928) (W Green, Edinburgh)

Engels, F (1872) *The Housing Question* (available online)

Englander, D (1977) *The Diary of Fred Knee* (Society for the Study of Labour History, Oxford)

— (1983) *Landlord and Tenant in Urban Britain 1838–1918* (Oxford University Press, Oxford)

Erskine, J (1871) *An Institute of the Law of Scotland* (Bell and Bradfute, Edinburgh)

Field, S (1981) *Rachman* (Hamlyn, London)

Fitzpatrick, S (2004) "Homelessness Policy in Scotland" in D Sim, *Housing and public policy in post-devolution Scotland* (CIH/HAS, Coventry)

Forrest, R; and Murie, A (1988) *Selling the Welfare State: The Privatisation of Public Housing* (Routledge, London)

Forrest, R; and Williams, P (2001) "Housing in the Twentieth Century" in R Paddison (ed), *Handbook of Urban Studies* (Sage, London)

Foucault, M (2001) *Madness and Civilisation* (Routledge, London)

Francis Report (1971) *Report of the Committee on the Rent Acts* (Cmnd 4609) (HMSO, London)

Fyfe, P (1902) Sidelights on the Housing Problem (Municipal Record) 341

Gauldie, E (1974) *Cruel Habitations: A History of Working Class Housing 1780–1918* (George Allen & Unwin, London)

Gentle, C; Dorling, D; and Comford, J (1994) "Negative Equity and British Housing in the 1990s: Cause and Effect" 32(2) *Urban Studies* 181

Gibson, P (1979) "How Scotland Got the Housing (Homeless Persons) Act" in N Drucker and H Drucker (eds), *The Scottish Government Yearbook 1979* (Paul Harris, Edinburgh)

Gilbert, B (1970) *British Social Policy 1919–1939* (Batsford, London)

Goldthorpe, J; Lockwood, D; Bechhofer, F; and Platt, J (1969) *The Affluent Worker in the Class Structure* (Cambridge University Press, Cambridge)

Goodlad, R (2001) "Housing and Local Government" in C Jones and P Robson (eds), *Health of Scottish Housing* (Ashgate, Aldershot)

Gordon, W (1999) *Scottish Land Law* (2nd edn) (Greens, Edinburgh)

Gordon, W; and Wortley, S (2009) *Scottish Land Law* (3rd edn) (Greens, Edinburgh)

Greve, J (1965) *Private Landlords in England* (Bell, London)

Griffith, J (1977) *The Politics of the Judiciary* (Fontana, London)

Gunningham, N (1974) *Pollution, Social Interest and the Law* (Martin Robertson, London)

Guthrie Committee (1907) *Report of the Departmental Committee on House-Letting in Scotland* (Committee to Inquire into Alleged Grievances in Connection with the Letting of Working Men's Dwellings in Scotland) (Chairman: Lord Guthrie) (Cd 3715) (HMSO, London)

Haley, M (1999) "The Statutory Regulation of Business Tenancies" *Legal Studies* 207

Harloe, M (1985) *Private Rented Housing in the United States and Europe* (Croom Helm, London)

— (1995) *The People's Home? Social Rented Housing in Europe and America* (Blackwell, Oxford)

Harloe, M; Isaacheroff, R; and Minns, R (1974) *The Organisation of Housing* (Heinemann, London)

Harvey, D (1973) *Social Justice and the City* (Edward Arnold, London)

— (1985) *Consciousness and the Urban Experience* (Basil Blackwell, Oxford)

— (2000) *Spaces of Hope* (Edinburgh University Press, Edinburgh)

Higgins, M (2002) *Scottish Repossessions: The Mortgage Rights (Scotland) Act 2001* (W Green/Sweet & Maxwell, Edinburgh)

Hill, O (1998) *Octavia Hill and the Social Housing Debate: Essays and Letters by Octavia Hill* (ed R Whelan) (Octavia Hill, Wisbech)

Himsworth, C (1982) *Public Sector Housing Law* (Planning Exchange, Glasgow)

— (1986) — (2nd edn) (Planning Exchange, Glasgow)

— (1989) — (3rd edn) (Planning Exchange, Glasgow)

— (1994) *Housing Law* (4th edn) (Planning Exchange, Glasgow)

Hiram, H (2007) *The Scots Law of Succession* (2nd edn) (Tottel, Edinburgh)

Holmans, A E (1987) *Housing Policy in Britain: A History* (Croom Helm, London)

Hudson, A (ed) (2004) *New Perspectives on Property Law, Human Rights and the Home* (Cavendish, London)

Hunter, J (2010) *The Making of the Crofting Community* (John Donald, Edinburgh)

Hunter Report (1918) *Report of the Committee on the Increase of Rent and Mortgage Interest (War Restrictions) Acts* (Ministry of Reconstruction) (Chairman: Lord Hunter) (Cd 9235) (HMSO, London)

Hunter Scott Report (1915) *Departmental Committee on Increases in Rental of Small Dwelling-houses in Industrial Districts in Scotland. Report of committee appointed by the secretary for Scotland to enquire into circumstances connected with the alleged increases in the rental of small dwelling-houses in industrial districts in Scotland* (Cd 8111)

Ingrams, R (ed) (1971) *The Life and Times of Private Eye* (Penguin, Harmondsworth)

Jackson, A; Robertson, M; and Robson, P (1989) *The Operation of the Matrimonial Homes (Family Protection) (Scotland) Act 1981* (Scottish Home and Health Department, Edinburgh)
Jacobs, S (1976) *The Right to a Decent House* (Routledge & Kegan Paul, London)
Jenkins, R (1991) *Life at the Centre* (Macmillan, London)
Jones, C; and Murie, A (1999) *Reviewing the Right to Buy* (Birmingham University Press, Birmingham)
Jones, C; and Robson P (eds) (2001) *Health of Scottish Housing* (Ashgate, Aldershot)

Kelso, W (1922) *Sanitation in Paisley: a record of progress 1488–1920* (Alexander Gardner, Paisley)
King, A (ed) (1980) *Building and Society: Essays on the Social Development of the Built Environment* (Routledge & Kegan Paul, London)

Laidlaw, S (1955) *Glasgow common lodging-houses and the people living in them* (Health and Welfare Committee, Glasgow Corporation, Glasgow)
Law Commission (2002) *Renting Homes: 1– Status and Security*, Consultative Paper No 162
Lloyd George, D (1886–1936) *Letters to His Brother* (Welsh National Archive) (available at: http://www.llgc.org.uk/index.php?id=lloydgeorgeletters)
Lloyd George, D (1908) *Diaries*

McAllister, A (1989) (1995, 2nd edn) (2002, 3rd edn) *Scottish Law of Leases: an Introduction* (Butterworths, Edinburgh)
McAllister, A; and McMaster, R (1999) *Scottish Planning Law* (2nd edn) (Butterworths, Edinburgh)
MacEwan , M (1991) *Housing, Race and the Law* (Routledge & Kegan Paul, London)
McGarvey, N; and Cairney, P (2008) *Scottish Politics* (Palgrave, Basingstoke)
Mackintosh Report (1951) *Law of Succession in Scotland: Report of the Committee of Inquiry* (Chairman: Lord Mackintosh) (Cmd 8144) (HMSO, London)

McLean, I (1983) *The Legend of Red Clydeside* (Dundee University Press, Dundee)

Manners, A J; and Rauta, I (1981) *Family Property in Scotland* (OPCS, London)

Marley Report (1931) *Report of the Inter-Departmental Committee on the Rent Restrictions Acts* (Ministry of Health) (Chairman: Lord Marley) (Cmd 3911) (HMSO, London)

Melling, J (ed) (1980) *Housing, Social Policy and the State* (Croom Helm, London)

Melling, J (1983) *Rent Strikes: People's Struggle for Housing in West Scotland 1890–1916* (Polygon, Edinburgh)

Merrett, S (1983) *State Housing in Britain* (Routledge & Kegan Paul, London)

Milner Holland Report (1965) *Report on Housing in Greater London* (Chairman: Sir Milner Holland) (Cmnd 2605) (HMSO, London)

Ministry of Housing, Local Government and Minister for Welsh Affairs (1963) *Housing, Land* (Cmnd 1952)

Mitchell, J (2003) *Eviction and rent arrears* (at www.jonathanmitchell.info/uploads/Eviction.pdf)

Mullen, T (2010) *Homelessness and the Law* (4th edn) (Legal Services Agency, Glasgow)

Murie, A (1983) *Housing Inequality and Deprivation* (Heinemann, London)

Nelken, D (1982) *The Limits of the Law: A Study of Landlords, Law and Crime* (Academic Press, London)

Nevitt, A A (1970) *The Nature of Rent Controlling Legislation in the United Kingdom* (Centre for Environmental Studies, London)

Newby, A (2007) *Ireland, Radicalism and the Scottish Highlands c 1870–1912* (Edinburgh University Press, Edinburgh)

Nicoll, R (1985) *Landlords' holdings of property, their letting policies and perception of legislation* (LL.M. thesis, University of Strathclyde)

Norrie, K (2006) *Family Law (Scotland) Act 2006* (Dundee University Press, Dundee)

Norris, M; and Redmond, D (eds) (2007) *Housing Contemporary Ireland: Policy, Society and Shelter* (Springer, Dordrecht)

O'Carroll, A (1996) "Historical Perspectives on Tenure Development in Urban Scotland" in H Currie and A Murie (eds), *Housing in Scotland* (Chartered Institute of Housing, Coventry)

Onslow Report (1923) *Final Reports of the Departmental Committee on the Increase of Rent and Mortgage Interest (Restrictions) Act 1920* (Chairman, Lord Onslow) (Cmd 1803) (HMSO, London)

Paddison, R (ed) (2001) *Handbook of Urban Studies* (Sage, London)

Paice, L (2008) "Overspill Policy and the Glasgow Slum Clearance Project in the Twentieth Century: From One Nightmare to Another?" 1(1) *Reinvention: a Journal of Undergraduate Research* (available at: http://www2. warwick.ac.uk/go/reinventionjournal/volume1issue1/paice (last accessed July 30 2010))

Paish, F W (1952) "The Economics of Rent Control", *Lloyds Bank Review*

Paisley, R (2000) *Land Law* (W Green, Edinburgh)

Paley, B (1978) *Attitudes to Letting in 1976* (HMSO, London)

Paterson, A (1974) "The Judges: A Political Elite?" 1(2) *British Journal of Law and Society* 118

Pennance, F G (ed) (1972) *Verdict on Rent Control* (Institute of Economic Affairs, London)

Petrie, A (2008) *The 1915 Rent Strikes: An East Coast Perspective* (Abertay Historical Society, Dundee)

Philippopoulos-Mihalopoulos, A (2007) *Law and the City* (Routledge, London)

Piven, F; and Cloward, R (1971) *Regulating the Poor: the Functions of Public Welfare* (Vintage, New York)

— (1972) — (Tavistock, London)

Rankine, J (1916) *The Law of Leases in Scotland* (3rd edn) (W Green, Edinburgh)

Reed, R; and Murdoch, J (2008) *A Guide to Human Rights Law in Scotland* (Tottel, Edinburgh)

Reid, K; and Gretton, G (2009) *Conveyancing 2008* (Avizandum Publishing Ltd, Edinburgh)

Rent Act 1957 (1960) *Report of Inquiry* (Cmnd 1246) (HMSO, London)

Ridley Report (1937) *Report of the Inter-Departmental Committee on the Rent Restrictions Acts* (Ministry of Health) (Chairman: Lord Ridley) (Cmd 5621) (HMSO, London)

— (1945) *Report of the Inter-Departmental Committee on Rent Control* (Chairman: Lord Ridley) (Cmd 6621) (HMSO, London)

Robertson, D (1992) *Choices for Tenants: A Guide to the Housing (Scotland) Act 1988* (SCVS, Edinburgh)

— (2001) "Scottish Homes: A Legacy" in C Jones and P Robson (eds), *Health of Scottish Housing* (Ashgate, Aldershot)

Robertson, D; and Bailey, N (1994) *Business Planning for Housing Associations* (Scottish Homes, Edinburgh)

Robson, P (1979) *Housing and the Judiciary* (Ph.D. thesis, University of Strathclyde)

— (1981) "Problems of Judicial Study" in P Robson and P Watchman (eds), *Justice, Lord Denning and the Constitution* (Gower, Farnborough)

— (1994) *Residential Tenancies* (W Green, Edinburgh)

— (2000) "The House of Lords and homeless people's rights" 22(4) *Journal of Social Welfare and Family Law* 415

Robson, P; and Halliday, S (1998) *Residential Tenancies* (2nd edn) (W Green, Edinburgh)

Robson, P; Halliday, S; and Vennard, A (2012) *Residential Tenancies* (3rd edn) (W Green, Edinburgh)

Robson, P; and Poustie, M (1996) *Homeless People and the Law* (3rd edn) (Butterworths, London)

Robson, P; and Watchman, P (eds) (1981) *Justice, Lord Denning and the Constitution* (Gower, Farnborough)

Rodger, R (1989) "Crisis and Confrontation in Scottish Housing 1880–1914" in R Rodger (ed), *Scottish Housing in the Twentieth Century* (Leicester University Press, Leicester)

— (ed) (1989) *Scottish Housing in the Twentieth Century* (Leicester University Press, Leicester)

Roughead, W (1929) *The Oscar Slater Trial* (J M Dent, London)

Royal Commission on Housing in Scotland (1917) *Housing of the Industrial Population in Scotland, rural and urban* (Cd 8731) (HMSO, London)

Sabatino, R A (1954) "Rent Control Policy in Great Britain" 30(1) *Land Economics* 61

Salisbury Report (1920) *Report of the Committee on the Increase of Rent and Mortgage (Restrictions) Acts* (Chairman, Lord Salisbury) (Cmd 658) (HMSO, London)

Scottish Development Department Scottish Housing Statistics (1980) (HMSO, Edinburgh)

Scottish Executive (2000) *Helping Homeless People: Legislative Proposals on Homelessness – The Homelessness Task Force Initial Rep*ort (TSO, Edinburgh)

— (2001) *Housing (Scotland) Act 2001 – Homelessness Strategies* (TSO, Edinburgh)

— (2002) *A review of the first year of the mandatory licensing of houses in multiple occupation in Scotland* (TSO, Edinburgh)

— (2002a) *Helping homeless people: an action plan for prevention and effective responses. HTF Final Report* (Scottish Executive, Edinburgh)

— (2002b) *Housing (Scotland) Act 2001 Homelessness Section 5: Guidance on Good Reasons* (TSO, Edinburgh)

— (2005) *Code of Guidance on Homelessness* (Scottish Executive, Edinburgh)

— (2005a) *Helping Homeless People Homelessness Statement Ministerial Statement on Abolition of Priority Need by 2012* (TSO, Edinburgh)

— (2006) *Helping Homeless People – Delivering the Action Plan for Prevention and Effective Response: Homelessness Monitoring Group Third Report* (TSO, Edinburgh)

Scottish Government (2003) *A national strategy for the prevention of domestic abuse* (available at: http://www.scotland.gov.uk/Publications/ 2003/09/18185/26437)

— (2003a) *Stewardship and Responsibility: A Policy Framework for Private Housing in Scotland – Final Report and Recommendations of the Housing Improvement Task Force* (available at: http://www.scotland.gov.uk/Resource/Doc/47034/0028741.pdf)

Scottish Government (2005) *Final Evaluation of the Rough Sleepers Initiative* (March 2005) (available at: http://www.scotland.gov.uk/Publications/2005/03/20886/54982)

— (2007) *Firm Foundations: The future of housing in Scotland* (Scottish Government, Edinburgh) (available at: http://www.scotland.gov.uk/Publications/2007/10/30153156/0)

— (2007a) *Scottish Social Attitudes Survey 2006: Public Attitudes to Homelessness* (available at: http://www.scotland.gov.uk/Publications/2007/11/13153139/0)

— (2007b) *Statistical Bulletin Operation of the Homeless Persons Legislation in Scotland: national and local authority analyses 2006–07* (Edinburgh)

— (2007c) *Tensions between Allocations Policy and Practice* (Research Findings No 3) (available at: http://www.scotland.gov.uk/Publications/Recent) (web-only document)

— (2008) *A guide to how we regulate*

— (2008a) *Guidance on post-inspection improvement plans* (available at: http://www.scottishhousingregulator.gov.uk/stellent/groups/public/documents/webpages/shr_postinspectionimprovementp.pdf)

— (2008b) *Ministerial Code of Practice for The Scottish Housing Regulator* (available at: http://www.scottishhousingregulator.gov.uk/stellent/groups/public/documents/webpages/shr_codeofpractice.pdf)

— (2008c) *Review of Scottish Registered Social Landlords 2006/2007* (Communities Scotland, Glasgow)

— (2008d) *Scottish Housing Regulator Framework Document* (available at: http://www.scottishhousingregulator.gov.uk/stellent/groups/public/documents/webpages/shr_executiveagencyframeworkdo.pdf)

— (2008e) *Scottish Housing Regulator: Guide to Inspection* (available at: http://www.scottishhousingregulator.gov.uk/stellent/groups/public/documents/webpages/shr_guidetoinspection.pdf)

— (2009) *A draft Housing Bill and consultation paper* (available at: http://www.scotland.gov.uk/Publications/2009/04/27095102/12)

— (2009a) *Domestic Abuse Recorded by the Police in Scotland 2008–09* (available at: http://www.scotland.gov.uk/Publications/2009/11/23112407/0)

— (2009b) *Operation of the Homeless Persons Legislation in Scotland* (Scottish Government, Edinburgh)

— (2009c) *Research to evaluate the operation and impact of the National Mortgage to Rent Scheme* (Scottish Government, Edinburgh)

— (2009d) *Review of the Private Rented Sector* (Scottish Government,

Edinburgh) (available at: http://www.scotland.gov.uk/Publications/2009/03/23153136/11)

Scottish Government (2010) *Housing: Fresh Thinking, New Ideas* (Scottish Government, Edinburgh)

Scottish Home Affairs Committee (1984) *Report on Dampness in Housing*

Scottish Homes (1995) *Annual Performance Return* (SHGN 95/08) (Scottish Homes, Edinburgh)

Scottish Housing Advisory Committee (1957) *Choosing Council Tenants* (HMSO, Edinburgh)

— (1967) *Allocating Council Houses* (HMSO, Edinburgh)

— (1977) *Scottish Housing* (Cmnd 6852) (HMSO, Edinburgh)

— (1980) *Allocation and Transfer of Council Houses* (HMSO, Edinburgh)

Scottish Housing Regulator (2009) *Annual Report and Accounts 2008/09*

— (2009a) *Executive Agency Framework Document* (available at: http://www.scottishhousingregulator.gov.uk/stellent/groups/public/documents/webpages/shr_executiveagencyframeworkdo.pdf)

— (2009b) *Registered Social Landlords in Scotland: Summary Facts and Figures 2007/2008* (available at http://www.scottishhousingregulator.gov.uk/stellent/groups/public/documents/webpages/shr_scottishregiste_ia49903758.pdf)

— (2009c) *Social Landlords in Scotland: Shaping Up for Improvement* (available at: http://www.communitiesscotland.gov.uk/stellent/groups/public/documents/webpages/shr_shapingupforimprovement.pdf)

Scottish Law Commission (1980) *Report on Occupancy Rights in the Matrimonial Home and Domestic Violence* (Scot Law Com No 60) (Edinburgh)

Scull, A (1980) "A convenient place to get rid of inconvenient people: the Victorian lunatic asylum" in A King (ed), *Building and Society: Essays on the Social Development of the Built Environment* (Routledge & Kegan Paul, London)

Sharp, E (1969) *The Ministry of Housing and Local Government* (Allen & Unwin, London)

Smith, S; Knill-Jones, R; and McGuckin, A (eds) (1991) *Housing for Health* (Longman, Harlow)

Sim, D (1995) *The Scottish House Factor: a study in housing management* (Housing Policy and Practice Unit, Stirling)

— (2004) *Housing and public policy in post-devolution Scotland* (CIH/HAS, Coventry)

Simmonds, A (2002) "Raising Rachman: The Origins of the Rent Act 1957" 45 *The Historical Journal* 843

Simon, E D (1933) *The Anti-Slum Campaign* (Longmans Green & Co, London)

Stalker, A (2007) *Eviction in Scotland* (Avizandum, Edinburgh)

Sutherland, E (2008) *Child and Family Law* (2nd edn) (W Green, Edinburgh)

Swenarton, M (1981) *Homes Fit for Heroes: The Politics and Architecture of*

Early State Housing in Britain (Heinemann, London)

Tenant Services Authority (2010) *The regulatory framework for social housing in England from April 2010* (available at: http://www.tenantservicesauthority.org/upload/pdf/Regulatory_framework_for_social_housing_in_England_from_2010.pdf)

Thane, P (1984) "The Working Class and State 'Welfare' in Britain, 1880–1914" 27(4) *The Historical Journal* 877

Thomson, J (2006) *Family Law (Scotland) Act 2006* (W Green, Edinburgh)

Watchman, P (1991) *The Housing (Scotland) Act 1987* (W Green, Edinburgh)

Watchman, P; and Robson, P (1983) *Homelessness and the Law* (Planning Exchange, Glasgow)

Whelan, R (1998) *Octavia Hill and the social housing debate: essays and letters* (IEA, London)

Whyte, W; and Gordon, W (1938) *The Law of Housing in Scotland* (W Hodge, Glasgow)

Willis, J W (1950) "Rent Control: The Maximum Rent Date Method" 98(5) *University of Pennsylvania Law Review* 654

Wilson, J H (1971) *The Labour Government 1964–1970* (Weidenfeld & Nicolson)

Wolmar, C; and Wates, N (eds) (1980) *Squatting: the real story* (Bay Leaf Books, London)

Workmen's National Housing Council (1902) *The Housing of the People* (WHNC, London)

Xu, L (2008) "Problems in the Law of the Tenement" *Juridical Review* 131
— (2010) "Managing and Maintaining Flatted Buildings: Some Anglo-Scottish Comparisons" *Edinburgh Law Review* 236

Yanetta, A; and Edwards, L (1996) "Homelessness and Access to Housing" in H Currie and A Murie (eds), *Housing in Scotland* (Chartered Institute of Housing, Coventry)

Yevov, L (1983) "Unfit for Heroes? The Housing Question and the State in Britain, 1890 to the present" 26 *The Historical Journal* 499

Young, E; Rowan Robinson, J; and Himsworth, C (1985) *Scottish Planning Law and Procedure* (W Hodge, Glasgow)

INDEX

Location references are to page numbers. Any footnotes indexed are shown by page number followed by "n". Authors are indexed if they are discussed in the text.

abandonment procedure, 222
abuse
  definition, 336, 342
  domestic *see* **domestic abuse**
  proposed Bill 2010, 342
  protection from, 339, 342
access to social housing
  admission to housing list, 31
  allocation, 31, 32–34
  "back door" residence requirement, 33
  background, 29–30
  Below Tolerable Standard, 34, 36
  discrimination, 30, 32
  homelessness *see* homelessness
  legislation prior to 1987, 37–38
  modern developments, 30–38
  publication of rules, 37–38
  reasonable preference, 34–37
  residence rules, 32
  restrictions on allocation, 31, 32–34
  rules and policies, 37–38
  social housing, 31–32
  tenant selection, 32–37
accommodation
  see also **repair issues**
  duty to secure permanent, 57–58
  interim, 56–58, 64
  interpretation, 57–58
  temporary, 56–58, 64
  tenantable and habitable, 96, 107, 108
  unreasonable accommodation test, 43
aemulatio vicini, 267
agricultural holdings, 74, 116, 325
agricultural land, 74, 97
agricultural premises, 89

Allocation and Transfer of Council Housing
  1980 SHAC Report, 31, 38
Allocation Policy Advisory Group, 36
amenity order, 312–313
ancillary rights, 322, 329
  see also **housing rights; occupancy rights; property**
anti-social behaviour, 68, 92
anti-social behaviour management control order, 302
anti-social behaviour notice (ASBN), 278–279
anti-social behaviour order (ASBO), 92, 227, 231, 278
armed service accommodation, 301
ASBO, 92, 227, 231, 278
assured tenancy
  agricultural holdings, 74
  agricultural land, 74
  excluded tenancies, 74–76
  generally, 72–73
  holiday lettings, 74–75
  repossession, 204–214, 232–239
  requirements, 73
  resident landlord, 75
  shop tenancy, 74
  succession, 248–250
  tenancy which cannot be assured, 74–76
  transitional cases, 76
assured tenancy market rents
  adjustments from existing market rents, 156–157
  comparables, 155–156

355

assured tenancy market rents (*cont*)
  deductions, 156–157
  factors relevant for increases, 157
  fluctuations in market, 157–158
  increase mechanisms, 154–155
  inspecting the property, 155
  matters to be ignored, 155
  private rented housing committee,
    154–155
  sitting tenant, 155
assured tenancy – repossession
  absence from house, 239
  annoyance, 211–213
  anti-social behaviour, 211–213, 234
  breach of obligations of tenancy,
    209–210, 233
  common stair, 211
  condition of furniture deteriorated,
    213, 236
  condition of house deteriorated,
    210–211, 235
  discretionary grounds of possession
    alternatives available, 205
    annoyance, 211–213
    anti-social behaviour, 211–213,
      234
    breach of obligations of tenancy,
      209–210, 233
    condition of furniture deteriorated,
      213, 236
    condition of house deteriorated,
      210–211, 235
    ex-employee tenant, 213–214
    illegal/immoral purposes, 211–213,
      233
    nuisance, 211–213
    persistent delay in rent payment,
      208–209
    postponing execution of possession
      order, 205
    reasonableness, 205
    rent due, 209, 232
    sheriff's discretion, 204–205
    specific, 206–214
    suitable alternative
      accommodation, 206–207
    tenant withdraws notice to quit,
      207–208
  dispensing with notice, 200

assured tenancy – repossession (*cont*)
  demolition or substantial work,
    202–203, 238
  educational body non-student
    tenancies, 201–202
  ex-employee tenant, 213–214
  grounds for possession to be
    established, 195–196, 232–240
  grounds specified in tenancy
    agreement, 196–197
  illegal/immoral use of premises,
    211–213, 233
  landlord formerly occupied house as
    principal home, 198–199
  landlord requires property for own
    occupation, 199–200, 236
  lay missionary, property for, 202
  mandatory grounds of possession
    demolition work, 202–203, 238
    educational body non-student
      tenancies, 201–202
    landlord formerly occupied house
      as principal home, 198–199
    landlord requires property for own
      home, 199–200
    lay missionary, property for, 202
    minister, property for, 202
    mortgage default, 200–201
    notice of proceedings, 196
    off-season holiday property, 201
    prior notice, 197
    reasonable to dispense with prior
      notice, 197–198
    reasonableness test, 198
    reconstruction work, 202–203
    rent arrears, 203–204, 232–234
    specific, 198–204
    tenancy inherited under will or on
      intestacy, 203
    3 months' rent arrears, 203–204
  minister, property for, 202
  mortgage default, 200–201
  notice of proceedings for possession,
    196
  nuisance, 211–213
  off-season holiday property, 201
  only or principal home, 239
  persistent delay in rent payment,
    208–209

assured tenancy – repossession (*cont*)
  possession order, 195, 205–206
  reconstruction work, 202–203,
    238
  rent arrears, 203–204, 232–234
  rent due, 209, 232–233
  suitable alternative accommodation,
    206–207
  table of grounds for possession,
    232–240
  tenancy inherited under will or on
    intestacy, 203
  tenant withdraws notice to quit,
    207–208
  3 months' rent arrears, 203–204

"back door" residence requirement,
    33
Barrhead, 8
Battersea, 7n
bedsit, 85
Below Tolerable Standard, 34, 36
beneficial interest, 319
British Market Research Bureau
    Housing Consumer Survey 1976,
    187
British Property Federation, 183,
    184
Building Regulations, 68
business premises, 88–89
Butt, John, 136

capital gains tax exemptions, 151–152
capital return method, 160, 177–178
care home, 301
Cathy Come Home, 59, 62, 101
cautionary bonds, 320n
Cave Review, 291
Civil Protection Orders and Access to
    Justice (Scotland) Bill, 342
closing order, 132
Clydebank, 8
Cochrane, 10
Codes of Guidance
  abuse, 336, 340
  homelessness, 39, 40, 51
  relationship breakdown, 331, 332,
    333, 334, 335
common stair, 211

Communities Scotland
  see also **Scottish Housing Regulator**
  housing regulation, 134, 189,
    282–283, 289
community charge, 69, 149
Community Relations Council, 15
community-owned housing provision,
    1
comparables method, 155–156, 178
Constable, A H B, 169
contractual tenancy, 83
Co-operative Housing Association,
    302
cottars, 325
council tax, 69, 149
Country Landowners Association,
    184–185
crofts, 97, 116, 325
Crossman, Richard, 79, 80, 169, 170,
    171, 173, 175, 184, 185, 186
Cullingworth, J B, 133
Currie, Hector, 318

dampness
  cause of established, 113
  establishing existence, 112
  quantifying the loss, 114–115
  tenant's obligation to heat, 114
Decency Standard (England), 133
declaration of occupancy rights,
    322–324, 330, 334
delectus personae **doctrine,** 246, 247
demolition order, 132
disability
  see also **discrimination**
  accommodation for those with,
    19–22
  impairment, 20–21
  progressive conditions, 21
  provider of services, 21–22
  quota approach, 20
disability audit, 19
disability discrimination, 18, 20–21,
    22
Disability Rights Commission, 20
discrimination
  disability, 18, 22
  housing, 14–19
  indirect, 15

discrimination (*cont*)
 race, 18
 sex, 18–19
 unlawful, 275–276
domestic abuse
 see also **abuse**
 housing rights, 327–340
 occupancy rights and, 320, 321
 protection prior to 1981, 320
 protection since 1981, 320–321
 rights on leaving the home, 335–340
 rights on staying in the home,
  327–331
 statistics, 321n
domestic violence
 Court of Appeal meaning, 339–340
Donaldson's School, Edinburgh, 20n
Dorward House, Montrose, 7
Duclaud-Williams (1978), 168, 169
Dunleavy (1981), 171

ECHR *see* **European Convention on
 Human Rights**
EHRC *see* **Equality and Human
 Rights Commission**
Elliott and McCrone (1975), 230
endowment mortgage, 151
entailing of land, 267
Equal Opportunities Commission, 15
**Equal Opportunities Committee,
 Scottish Parliament**, 19
**Equality and Human Rights
 Commission (EHRC)**
 availability of remedies, 16
 Codes of Practice, 17
 compliance powers, 18
 duties, 16–17
 functions, 15–16
 powers, 17–18
 public equality duties, 18
Erskine, 96
Erskine Homes, 20
Erskine Hospital, 20
Estates Gazette, 173
**European Convention on Human
 Rights (ECHR)**
 Article 2, 24
 Article 6, 24
 Article 8, 23, 24, 26

ECHR (*cont*)
 generally, 23–27
 "respect for the home", 23–24
eviction *see* **rented property and
 eviction**
exclusion order, 328, 329

"factors' lines", 29
fair rent
 approach by Scottish courts, 176–179
 avoidance of intervention by courts,
  175–176
 capital return method, 177–178
 comparable method, 178
 courts, 175–179
 criteria, 158–159
 Housing Act 1988 impact, 187–188
 housing regulation, 269–271
 impact, 170
 interpretation by rent officers,
  173–175
 introduction, 169
 judicial interpretation, 175–182
 landlords: role, practice, perspective,
  182–186
 meaning, 3, 171
 objective strategy, 172
 opinions on, 172
 optional, 169–173
 practice, in, 173–190
 private rented housing committees,
  171
 process, 159–160
 reason for, 169–170
 reconciling conflicting approaches,
  179–181
 Register of Rents, 171
 satisfaction levels, 187
 Scottish approach by courts, 176–179
 subjective strategy, 171
 tenants' role, 186–187
Fair Rents Association, 183
family
 hallmarks of new, 262–263
 "living together as man and wife",
  264–265
 meaning of term, 256–258, 259–265
 "member of the family", 3, 254,
  256–258, 272

family *(cont)*
  significance of sex, 263–264
  social rationale, 263
fire service accommodation, 86–87
Firm Foundations
  Scottish Government consultation
    document, 291–292
First Tier Tribunal, 125
fitness for human habitation, 132,
  138–140
Foucault, 5
Francis Report (1971), 178–179, 230

Gauldie, 136
gender audit, 19
Germany, 2
Glasgow
  human rights, 24–27
  Model Lodging Houses, 316
  municipal housing 1908 to 1915, 7–8
  population expansion, 29
Glasgow Improvement Trust, 137n
good repair, 107–108
Gramsci, 189
Gunningham, 4
Guppys Property Group, 185

harassment, 227–228, 341–342
Hill, Octavia, ix, 7, 29
Himsworth, C, 10
HMO *see* **houses in multiple
    occupation**
holiday lets
  generally, 74, 80
  off-season, 197, 198, 201
  working holiday, 74–75
homelessness
  applicant numbers, 59–61
  asylum seekers, 49
  background, 39–40
  categories, 41–44
  Code of Guidance, 39, 40, 51
  definition, 41–42
  deliberate actions, 47
  development of post–war policies,
    61–63
  educational needs, 50
  employment, 50
  failure to act, 47

homelessness *(cont)*
  family, definition, 42
  family associations, 50
  health treatment, 50
  intentionality, 47–48, 64, 332–333,
    334, 339
  interim accommodation, 56–58
  judicial review of decision, 52–54
  legislation, 39–40, 41, 59–61, 63–64
  local authority duty, 40, 55–56, 331
  local authority enquiries, 51–52
  local connection, 48–50, 64, 335, 337,
    339
  modern legal rights, 41–50
  normal past voluntary residence, 49
  outplacements, 337
  postponing decision, 52
  priority need, 45–47, 64, 335, 336
  protection from abuse, 336, 339, 340
  protection of children, 340
  public attitudes, 2006 survey, 60–61
  reasonable for a person to reside, 42
  reasonable to continue to occupy, 43,
    44, 47
  referrals to other local authorities, 58
  referrals to RSLs, 58–59
  refugees, 49
  re-housed within own area, 337
  right of review, 55
  right to buy legislation and, 40
  RSL obligation, 40
  Scottish Public Services
    Ombudsman, 55
  Scottish secure tenancy, 87–88
  short Scottish secure tenancy, 93
  special circumstances, 50
  suitable temporary accommodation,
    56–57
  temporary accommodation, 56–58
  unreasonable accommodation test, 43
  unreasonable to occupy test, 44
  vulnerability, 46
homelessness strategy, 64–65
Homelessness Task Force, 45, 63, 64
Homes and Communities Agency,
  291
Hoogstraten, Nicolas van, 227, 274,
  297n
hostel, 85, 337, 339

house within curtilage of other non-housing buildings, 89–90

houses in multiple occupation (HMO)
additional categories, 299
amenity order, 312–313
anti-social behaviour management control order, subject to, 302
appeals against licence decisions, 304–306
appeals against local authority notice, 314
armed service accommodation, 301
breach of condition, 313
cancellation of licence, 307
care home, 301
consistency in standards, 315
Co-operative Housing Association, 302
delivery of licence, 307
duration of licence, 304
exempt from licence requirement, 301–302
fees, 299
guidance, 315
Housing (Scotland) Act 2006, 298–299
independent health care, 301
individuals requiring notice, 309–311
legal framework, 296–308
licence application process, 302
licensed by local authority, 299
licensing, 297–308
local authority duties, 298
local authority power to carry out or arrange work, 313
meaning, 299–300
"members of same family", 300–301
notices of decision, 308–311
number of unrelated sharers, 268
numbers, 295
offences relating to HMOs, 313–314
penalties for offences, 314
planning permission, 295–296
prison accommodation, 301
private rented sector, 296
property occupied by owners, 301
"reasonable excuse" defence, 313–314
rectification of breach, 312
refusal of application, 299

HMO (*cont*)
registration, 297–298
regulatory powers, 271
relative, meaning, 300–301
religious order, 302
renewal of licence, 306
restriction on applications, 303–304
revocation of licence, 306–307
sanctions, 312–314
school care accommodation, 301
secure accommodation, 301
students, 295
suitability of licence holders, 302–303
suitability of living accommodation, 303
suspension of rent, 312
temporary exemption order, 307–308
terms of licence, 304
variation of licence, 306–307

housing action area, 133

housing association properties
average rents, 189
right to buy, 98

Housing Associations, 281

housing benefit, 188–190

housing costs
assured tenancy market rents, 154–158
average dwelling-house prices 1964 and 2007, 341
development of policies on meeting costs, 165–173
owner occupation, 150–152
private renting generally, 152–153
regulated tenancy rents, 158–165
short assured tenancies, 153–154
social renting, 165
tied housing, 165

Housing Improvement Task Force, 117, 132, 134

Housing Information Packs, 13

housing list admission, 31

housing quality criteria, 135

housing regulation
anti-social behaviour notice, 278–279
background to housing law, 9–11
common law, 268
Communities Scotland, 282–283, 289
conflicting policies, 269

housing regulations (*cont*)
development, 1–14
disability, 19–22
discrimination, 14–19, 275–276
future changes, 291–292
generally, 267–268, 292–294
human rights, 22–27
impact of landlord registration, 277
inspection, 287–289
interpretation of statutes, 3–4
leases prior to 1989, 270–271
limitations on disposal of property, 267
management control order, 279–280
nuisance, 267
performance assessment of social landlords, 284
protection for tenants, 13
registration of private landlords, 271–277
regulatory intervention, 289–290
Rent Act 1965, 12
rent assessment committee, 271
rent freeze, 269
rent income suspension, 279
rent level controls from 1965, 12
Rent (Scotland) Act 1984 s 2, 12
Scottish Homes, 281–282
Scottish Housing Regulator, 283–284, 287–290
Scottish Social Housing Charter, 284–286, 289
sitting tenants, 270
social rented sector, 280–292
social renting, 280–292
statutory interventions, 268–271
summary, 292–294
housing renewal area, 133
Housing Revenue Grant, 165
housing rights – leaving the home
abuse, 335–340
child protection, 340
Code of Guidance, 336–337, 338, 339, 340
definition, 336
hostels, 337, 339
interdicts, 336, 339
legal protection, 336
occupier of owned property, 338

housing rights – leaving the home
abuse (*cont*)
occupier of tenanted property, 338
outplacements, 337
owner or joint owner, 338–340
priority need homelessness, 336
social work department, 336
tenant or joint tenant, 340
Women's Aid, 336, 337
relationship breakdown, 331–335
Code of Guidance, 331–332, 333, 334, 335
counselling, 332
intentionally homeless, 332, 333, 335
local authority obligations to homeless persons, 331
occupier of owned property, 332–334
occupier of tenanted property, 334–335
owner or joint owner, 335
social work department, 334
tenant or joint tenant, 335
Women's Aid, 334
housing rights – staying in the home
abuse, 327–331
ancillary rights, 329
declaration of occupancy rights, 330
exclusion order, 328, 329, 330
matrimonial interdict, 329
occupier of owned property, 327–329
occupier of tenanted property, 329
owner or joint owner, 330
tenant or joint tenant, 330–331
relationship breakdown, 322–327
Code of Guidance, 324
declaration of occupancy rights, 322–324
non-entitled spouse, 322–324
occupier of owned property (non-entitled spouse), 322–324
occupier of tenanted property, 324–326
owner or joint owner, 326–327
tenant or joint tenant, 327
transfer of tenancy provisions, 325–326

housing standards – development
common law background, 136–138
fitness for human habitation, 138–140
housing quality criteria, 135
implied repairs provision, 140
political context, 140
public health legislation, 138
Scottish Housing Quality Standard,
133–136
social and historical context, 136–140
*Housing: The Government's Proposals
for Scotland*
White Paper (1987), 281
human rights
breach of the right to life, 24–27
eviction proceedings, 24–27
Glasgow City Council v *Al-Abassi*,
24–27
legislation, 23–27
violation, 24
Hunter Committee, 166, 167

implied repairs provision, 140
improvement notice, 131
improvement order, 132–133
independent health care, 301
indirect discrimination, 15
indirectly accessible quality standards,
133–136
interdict, 320, 322, 329, 339, 341, 342
Irish Tenant League, 5
irritation of lease, 101
ish, 215, 225
Islands Council
educational staff property, 224

**judicial review of homelessness
decision**
see also **homelessness**
case law, 52
cost, 52
delegation, 53
duty to act fairly, 54
duty to give adequate reasons, 54
guidelines, 53
real exercise of discretion, 53
relevant matters only considered,
53–54
unreasonable decision, 54

Kelso, William, 5, 136, 138
Knee, Fred, 7
Kyrle Society, ix, 7

landlord
disabled tenants, 99
duties, 96–99
fair rents, 182–186, 187
fire safety, 97
gas appliances, 97
habitable and tenantable, 96
loans and grants provision, 99
performance assessment of social,
284
possession of the subjects, 96
rent book, 97
repair and maintain private rented
housing, 117–119
role, 182–186
satisfaction levels, 187
social rented sector, 268
tenant's right to buy, 97–99
written lease, 96–97
landlord registration
anti-social behaviour, 275
appeal against non-registration or
removal, 276
criminal offences, 276–277
disability awareness, 276
dishonesty or violence, 275
exemptions, 272–274
"family member" definition, 272
fee, 273
fees and income, 277
"fit and proper person" criteria,
274–276
funding, 277
impact of legislation, 277–280
local authority duty, 272
notification, 276
occupancy agreements, 272
period, 271
process, 274
religious use of premises, 274
removal from register, 276
rent penalty notice, 277
repairs, 275
tenant awareness, 278
transitory ownership, 273

landlord registration (*cont*)
  types, 271–272
  "unconnected person", 277
  unlawful discrimination, 275–276
Law Commission, 4
lawburrows, 320n
Lehman Brothers, viii
licensed premises, 74, 89
LIFT initiative, viii
local authority certificate, 241
long lease, 325
Long, Walter, 166

McAllister (2002), 10, 204
Mackintosh Committee, 246
MacPherson Report, 18
mainstreaming, 19
maintenance order, 68, 133
maintenance plans, 68
Man About the House, 296n
management control order (MCO),
  279–280
Marley Committee, 167n
Marley Report, 230n
matrimonial home, 319n
matrimonial interdict, 227, 329, 341,
  342
MCO (management control order),
  279–280
Milner Holland Report on Housing,
  15, 30
Mitchell, Jonathan, 140, 208
mobile home
  assignment to family member, 104
  generally, 101–102
  immobile, 102
  rent control, 105
  residential occupiers, 105
  security of tenure, 102–104
  unlawful eviction, 105
Model Lodging Houses, 29, 316
Modernising Scotland's Social Housing,
  134
mortgage, 69, 191–193
mortgage interest relief, 151, 293–294
mortgage to rent scheme, 192–193,
  335
municipal housing, 13
My Wife Next Door, 327n

National Association of Estate Agents,
  185
**National Land League of Great
  Britain**, 5
**National Strategy to Address
  Domestic Abuse**, 320
**National Voluntary Landlord
  Accreditation Scheme**, 291
negative equity, 150
Nicoll (1985), 186
non-harassment order, 227, 322,
  341–342
nuisance provisions, 130

occupancy agreements, 272
occupancy rights, 320, 321–322
offenders
  accommodation for, 88
off-season holiday property, 197, 198,
  201
only or principal home, 84–85
Onslow Committee, 167n
Onslow Report, 230n
**Open Market Shared Equity pilot
  scheme**, 152
overcrowding, 237, 315, 316, 317
owner occupancy
  anti-social behaviour, 68
  capital gains tax exemption, 151–152
  council tax, 69
  development control, 67–68
  growth of sector, 2, 149, 150–152
  housing costs, 150–152, 341
  mortgage interest relief, 151
  mortgages, 69
  rates, 69
  repossession, 69–70, 230
  standard security, 69
  tenements, 68

Parris, Matthew, 152, 188
Part VII tenancy, 81
partnership home, 319, 321
Patten, John, 152
Peabody, Joseph, 6, 29
Peabody Buildings, 6n
Pilcher, Denis, 174
police accommodation, 86–87

possession
　assured tenancy repossession
　　discretionary grounds, 204–214,
　　　232–239
　　mandatory grounds, 197–204
　　notice of proceedings, 196
　　Scottish secure tenancy repossession,
　　　217–224, 237–240
　　short assured tenancy repossession,
　　　214–216
　　short Scottish secure tenancy
　　　repossession, 224–225
possession order
　alternatives, 205
　cancellation, 206
　imposing conditions, 206
　postponing execution, 205–206
　reasonableness, 205
　requirements, 195
　rights to sist and postpone, 206
Powell, Enoch, 170
pressured area status, 98–99
PRHP *see* **Private Rented Housing
　Panel**
PRHPR *see* **Private Rented Housing
　Panel Regulations**
prison accommodation, 301
Private Eye, 170
private landlord registration *see*
　**landlord registration; registered
　social landlord**
private rented housing *see* **private
　rented sector**
private rented housing committee,
　154–155, 171
**Private Rented Housing Panel
　(PRHP)**
　content of notice, 121
　decisions, recording and notification,
　　123–124, 125–128, 275
　determinations, 125–136
　enquiries, 121–122
　evidence, oral and written, 122–123
　expenses, 123
　fair rent, 158
　fire safety, 123
　notification of referral, 121
　obligatory matters, 122
　operation, 120–121

PRHP (*cont*)
　Part VII tenancies, 81
　RSEO link, 128
　standard form
　　background, 125–126
　　decision, 128
　　findings of fact, 127
　　hearing, 126
　　inspection, 126
　　reasons for decision, 127
　　summary of issues, 126–127
　timeous, 122
　work of, 124
　writing up decisions, 125–128
**Private Rented Housing Panel
　Regulations (PRHPR)**
　acknowledgement, 142
　additional application, 142
　additional work, 142–143
　adjournment, 145
　amendments, 145–146
　application to panel, 141–142
　attachments, 141
　conjoined applications, 143
　decision, 146
　directions, 143
　enquiries, 143
　evidence, 143–144
　expenses, 147
　hearing, 144–145
　inspection, 144
　list of applications, 147
　processing the application, 142–147
　representation, 141
　resolution, 142
　withdrawal of application, 142
　written applications, 141
private rented sector
　assessment, 291
　comparison with England and Wales,
　　291
　controlling market charges, 165–173
　decline, 149
　demise of rent control, 189
　fair rents, 169–173
　freezing of rent, 166–169
　funding and regulation functions split
　　in England and Wales, 291
　houses in multiple occupation, 296

private rented sector (*cont*)
   personal subsidy approach, 188–190
   Rent Assessment Committee, 153
   rent control abolition, 168–169
   rent control policy on or after 2 Jan
     1989, 152–153
   repair issues *see* **repair issues –**
     private rented housing
   Scottish Government Report (2009),
     278, 315, 317, 318
   shared housing, 295–296
Profumo scandal, 170
property
   ancillary rights, 322
   declaration of occupancy rights,
     322–324
   divorce and financial provision,
     320–321
   occupancy rights, 320, 321–324
   partnership home, 321
   relationship breakdown, 319–320
property ownership
   arrears, 192
   borrowers' rights, 192
   default, 192
   effect of marriage on women's
     property, 319
   homelessness provisions in Housing
     (Scotland) Act 1987, 193
   joint title, 319
   loss of accommodation, 192
   mortgage, 191–192
   mortgage to rent scheme, 192–193
   non-entitled spouse, 320, 322–324
   restraints on owner, 9
protected tenancy
   absence from house, 239
   anti-social behaviour, 234
   breach of terms of tenancy, 233
   condition of furniture deteriorated,
     236
   condition of house deteriorated, 235
   death of original tenant, 251
   death of original tenant's first
     successor, 251
   excluded coverage, 80
   house required by landlord for own
     occupation, 236
   immoral or illegal purposes, 233

protected tenancy (*cont*)
   overcrowded, 237
   protection from exploitation, 79–81
   rent arrears, 232
   special needs adaptation, 238
   succession, 250–251
   table of grounds of possession,
     232–240
   under Rent (Scotland Act 1984, 80
Protection from Abuse (proposed) Bill
   2010, 342
public health legislation, 138
public sector rented housing *see* **social**
   rented sector

qualifying repairs, 111–112

race discrimination, 18
Rachman, Peter, 79, 152, 170, 227,
   274, 292, 297n
Rankine, John, 10, 96, 107, 139
Rating and Valuation Association, 184
reasonable preference
   explanation of term, 35–36
   interpretation of phrase, 36
   large families, 35, 36
   performance standards, 37
   social housing allocation, 34–37
   stock transfer, 36
   unsatisfactory housing conditions, 35,
     36
registered social landlord (RSL)
   see also **landlord; landlord**
     registration
   obligation to homeless applicants, 40
   referral from local authority, 58–59
   request to house homeless applicant,
     58–59
Registrar of Friendly Societies, 281
regulated tenancy rents
   capital return less scarcity, 160
   comparables, 160
   "fair rent", 158–160
   generally, 158–160
   locality, 164–165
   market rent less scarcity, 161–162
   personal circumstances, 164
   scarcity, 163–164
   state of repair, 162–163

relationship breakdown
  housing rights, 322–327, 331–335
  leaving the home, 331–335
  staying in the home, 322–327
religious order, 274, 302
remand centres, 301
Rent Acts
  temporary nature, 166–168
rent allowances, 188–190
Rent Assessment Committee, 123,
  125, 153, 154, 155, 175
rent deposits, 100
rent income suspension, 279
rent penalty notice, 277
rent rebates, 188–190
Rent Registration Service, 183
rent relief order, 129
rented property and eviction
  accommodation deemed suitable by
    sheriff, 241–242
  assured tenancy *see* **assured tenancy –**
    repossession
  background, 229–231
  generally, 193–194
  human rights violation, 24–27
  interests of tenants and landlords
    contrasted, 193–194
  local authority certificate, 241
  notice of proceedings for possession,
    196
  overcrowding, 223, 237, 243
  proximity to place of work,
    242
  Scottish secure tenancy *see* **Scottish**
    secure tenancy – repossession
  security of tenure, 194–195
  short assured tenancy, 214–216
  short Scottish secure tenancy *see*
    Short Scottish secure tenancy –
    repossession
  similar as regards rental and
    accommodation, 242
  suitable alternative accommodation,
    241
  suitable to means of tenant,
    242–243
  table of grounds of possession,
    232–240
  unlawful eviction, 226–228

repair issues – private rented housing
  see also **private rented house panel;**
    private rented housing panel
    regulations
  access, 119
  avoiding repair obligation, 118–119
  closing order, 132
  community regulation, 131–133
  contracting out, 120
  demolition order, 132
  determinations, 125–128
  enforcement, 120–124
  enforcement of RSEOs, 129–130
  fire or flood, 119
  improvement notice, 131
  improvement order, 132–133
  inevitable accident, 119
  lack of rights, 119
  landlord's duty to repair and
    maintain, 117–118
  landlord's duty does not apply,
    118–119
  maintenance order, 133
  nuisance provisions, 130
  private rented housing panel, 120–124
  repair notice, 131, 132
  repairing standard, 116–119
  repairing standard enforcement order,
    128–130
  statutory notices, 131
  tenant accepts responsibility, 118–119
  tenant's fault, 119
  tenement management scheme, 133
  tolerable standard, 131–132
repair issues – Scottish secure tenancy
  access by landlord, 111
  cause of established dampness, 113
  chronic problem, 112
  damage caused during work, 111
  dampness, 112–113
  enforcement, 112
  establishing existence of dampness,
    112
  legislation, 109–110
  pre-tenancy inspection, 110
  qualifying repairs, 111–112
  quantifying loss, 114–115
  reasonable time, 111
  sanitary defects, 110

repair issues – Scottish secure tenancy (*cont*)
    standard to be maintained, 110
    tenant's obligation to heat, 114
repair notice, 131, 132
repairing standard
    private rented housing, 116–118
repairing standard enforcement order (RSEO)
    contentious issues, 129
    demolish rather than repair, 129
    enforcement, 129–130
    failure to repair, 129–130
    failure to repair timeously, 130
    landlord not in control of repair, 129
    link with PHRP decision, 128
    refusal to repair, 130
    tenant no longer in occupation, 129
    tenant's complaints are excessive, 129
repossession, 69–70
residential hotel, 85
residential tenancies
    assured tenancies, 72–76
    contractual tenancies, 83
    generally, 70–72
    Part VII tenancies, 81
    post-1915, 12–14
    private–sector tenancies, 72–83
    protected tenancies, 79–81
    protection against rent exploitation, 71–72
    Scottish secure tenancies, *see* **Scottish secure tenancies**
    "Scottish tenancy", 70, 71
    short assured tenancies, 76–79
    social rented tenancies, 83–95
    tied tenancies, 81–83
"respect for the home", 23–24
Ridley Committee, 167n, 168, 195
Ridley Report, 230n
right to buy, 40, 97–99, 149, 325
Rising Damp, 296n
Robson & Watchman, 183, 184
Rough Sleepers Initiative, 62–63
Royal Blind School, 20n
Royal Commission on the Housing of the Industrial Population of Scotland, Urban and Rural (1917), 1, 7, 273, 292

Royal Institution of Chartered Surveyors, 185
RSEO *see* repairing standard enforcement order
RSL *see* registered social landlord
Rumsfeld, Donald, vii

St Andrews, 8
Salisbury Committee, 211n
Salisbury Report, 208, 230n
Sandys, Duncan, 168, 169
sanitary officers, 138
SAT possession order
    short assured tenancies, 214–216
Schedule A property tax abolition, 150–151
school care accommodation, 301
school premises, house within, 89–90
Scott, Hunter, 166
Scottish Government Private Rented Sector Report (2009), 278, 315, 317, 318
Scottish Homes, 158, 189
    housing regulation, 281–282
Scottish Housing Quality Standard (SHQS), 133–136
Scottish Housing Regulator, 134, 189
    good practice, 290
    housing regulation, 283–284
    inspection, 287–289
    Intervention Strategy, 288
    performance standards, ix, 37, 287, 289, 290
    regulatory intervention, 289–290
    report, 288
Scottish Public Services Ombudsman, 55
Scottish Rent Assessment Committee, 177
Scottish Sanitary Inspectors, 5, 6
Scottish secure tenancy
    see also **short Scottish secure tenancy**
    accommodation in property not owned by landlord, 90
    agricultural premises, 88–89
    bedsit, 85
    business premises, 88–89
    conversion to and from short Scottish secure tenancy, 94–95

Scottish secure tenancy (*cont*)
　exclusions, 86–90
　fire service accommodation, 86–87
　homeless persons, 87–88
　house is only or principal home, 84–85
　house within curtilage of other
　　non-housing buildings, 89–90
　individual, 84
　landlord in recognised category of
　　secure landlords, 85–86
　offenders, 88
　police accommodation, 86–87
　premises occupied under a contract of
　　employment, 86
　repair obligations of landlord,
　　109–113
　repair obligations of tenant, 114–115
　repossession, 217–224, 233–240
　requirements, 84–86
　separate dwelling, 85
　shared ownership agreement, 88
　short, 90–94, 224–225
　student lets, 87
　temporary during carrying out of
　　work, 87
Scottish secure tenancy – repossession
　anti-social behaviour, 234
　assessing reasonableness, 219–220
　breach of terms, 233
　condition of furniture deteriorated,
　　222, 236
　condition of house deteriorated,
　　221–222, 235
　criminal behaviour, 221
　demolition or substantial work on
　　home, 238
　disputing the facts, 218–219
　factors, 216, 219
　false statement, 222–223, 237
　grounds of possession, 217–224
　　criminal behaviour, 221
　　condition of furniture deteriorated,
　　　222, 236
　　condition of house deteriorated,
　　　221–222, 235
　　illegal use of premises, 218, 233
　　Islands Council exemption, 224
　　immoral use of premises, 217–218,
　　　233

Scottish secure tenancy – repossession
　grounds of possession (*cont*)
　　inter-spousal/partner transfer, 224,
　　　240
　　landlord's leasehold interest
　　　terminated, 223–224
　　mitigating factors, 219
　　offence committed in house, 218
　　offence committed in locality, 218
　　overcrowded, 223, 237
　　special needs adaptation, 223,
　　　238–239
　　tenancy obtained fraudulently,
　　　222–223, 237
　　tenancy transfer, 224, 240
　　tenant absent for at least 6 months,
　　　222, 239–240
　Islands Council exemption, 224
　illegal use of premises, 218, 233
　immoral use of premises, 217–218,
　　233
　inter-spousal/partner transfer, 224,
　　240
　landlord's leasehold interest
　　terminated, 223–224
　mitigating factors, 219
　offence committed in house or
　　locality, 218
　overcrowded, 223, 237
　reasonableness, 216, 219–220
　rent arrears, 232
　special needs adaptation, 223,
　　238–239
　table of grounds of possession,
　　232–240
　tenancy obtained fraudulently,
　　222–223, 237
　tenancy transfer, 224, 240
　tenant absent for at least 6 months,
　　222, 239–240
Scottish Social Attitudes Survey 2006:
　　Public Attitudes to Homelessness,
　　60–61
Scottish Social Housing Charter
　activity standards, 285, 286
　guiding standards, 285–286
　outcomes, 284–285, 289
　services for owners, 286
　social inclusion, 285–286

Scottish Special Housing Association, 8, 158

secure accommodation, 301

security of tenure, 1, 12

service occupancies, 325

sex discrimination, 18–19
see also **discrimination**

shared housing
development of controls, 315–318
generally, 295–296
houses in multiple occupation *see*
houses in multiple occupation
lodging houses, 316
Model Lodging Houses, 29, 316
students, 87, 197, 198, 295
sub-letting, 317
ticketed properties, 295, 316–317

shared ownership agreement, 88

shared ownership schemes, 76

Sharp, Evelyn, 171

Shelter, 64
Landlord Registration report, 277
succession rights, 250

shop tenancy, 74

short assured tenancy
AT5 notice, 78–79
free trial period, 79
housing regulation, 271
introduction, 76–77
pool of comparables, 153
rents, 153–154
repossession, 214–216
service of warning notice, 78–79
"significantly higher" test, 154
6 months' minimum term, 77

short assured tenancy – repossession
ish, 215
no further contractual tenancy, 215
notice by landlord on tenant, 215–216
right to evict, 214
SAT possession grounds, use of, 214–216
SAT possession order, requirements, 215–216
tacit relocation, 215

short Scottish secure tenancy
see also **Scottish secure tenancy**
anti-social behaviour, 92

short Scottish secure tenancy (*cont*)
conversion to and from Scottish secure tenancy, 94–95
criteria, 90
decants, 93
grounds for tenancy, 91–94
homeless persons, 93
housing support services requirement, 93–94
information for prospective tenant, 91–94
previous anti–social behaviour, 92
property not owned by landlord, 94
repossession, 224–225
temporary letting pending development, 93
temporary letting to person seeking accommodation, 93
term, 90–91

short Scottish secure tenancy – repossession
conversion to Scottish secure tenancy, 224
generally, 224–225
ish, 225
no further contractual tenancy, 225
notice that landlord requires possession, 225
tacit relocation, 225

shorthold assured tenancy, 77, 153n

SHQS (Scottish Housing Quality Standard), 133–136

Sim, 29

Simon, Sir E D, 167

Sitting Targets, 297n

Slater, Oscar, 137n

slum clearance, 140

Small Landlords Association, 184, 231

social rented sector
assessing regulation in, 290–291
background, 280–281
Communities Scotland, 282–283, 289
constraints of support, 189
Firm Foundations Scottish Government consultation document, 291–292
housing benefit, 188–189
housing costs, 165

social rented sector (*cont*)
    housing regulation, 268–271,
      280–292
    local authority discretion, 280
    personal subsidy approach, 188–190
    rent allowances and rebates, 188–190
    rent levels, 189
    repair issues, 109–115
    right to buy, 149
    rise, 149
    Scottish Homes, 281–282
    Scottish Housing Regulator,
      283–284, 287–290
    Scottish secure tenancy, 268
    Scottish Social Housing Charter,
      284–286, 289
    short Scottish secure tenancy, 268
    succession, 251–253
Social Science Research Council
    study of private rental market, 185
special needs housing, 98
squatting, 39
Stalker (2007), 227
Standard Delivery Plans, 134
standard security, 69
statutory small tenants, 325
students, 87, 197, 198, 295
succession
    assured tenancies, 248–250
    background, 245–248
    cohabitation, 255, 258–261
    concept of "home", 254
    dead's part, 246
    development of property rights,
      254–265
    expanded family, 254–256
    family, meaning of term, 256–258,
      259–261
    Fitzpatrick decision, 261–262, 264
    joint tenancy, 247
    "member of the family", 254, 256–258
    prior rights, 245
    protected tenancy, 250–251, 255
    qualified person, 252–253
    same-sex relationships, 255, 261–262,
      264–265
    social rented tenancy, 251–253
    tenancies, 246–248
    widows and widowers, 256

"suitable alternative accommodation",
    3, 206–207, 241
Sweden, 2
Switzerland, 2

tacit relocation, 215, 225
tenancies at will, 97, 325
tenant
    access for repairs, 101
    care of the subjects, 100
    Charter, 186
    fair rents, 186–187
    false or fraudulent representations,
      100
    heat property, 114
    inversion of the subjects, 101
    obligations, 99–101, 114
    payment of rent, 101
    rent deposits, 100
    satisfaction level, 187
    take and maintain possession of the
      subjects, 100
    views of the Rent Acts, 186–187
tenantable and habitable, 96, 107–109
Tenants Services Authority, 291
tenants' Charter, 186
Tenement Management Scheme, 68,
    133
tenements
    common repairs, 68
    good repair, 108
    mutual obligations, 68
    urban, 11
terce, 245, 319
"Three Fs", 5
tied housing, 149, 165
tied tenancy, 81–83
To Kill a Mockingbird, 267
tolerable standard, 131–132
transfer of tenancy order, 325, 326
transfer of tenancy provisions,
    325–326
treatment area, 133
Trump, Donald, 227

**United Nations Declaration of Human
    Rights**, 22
unlawful eviction, 226–227
    damages, 228

unreasonable accommodation test, 43
unsatisfactory housing conditions, 35, 36

Welsh Housing Standard, 134
Weslo, 193
Wheatley, John, 30
Whyte and Gordon, 10
Wilson, Harold, 13, 172

winkling, 227
winter lets, 197, 198
Women's Aid, 57, 334, 336, 337
Workmen's National Housing Council, 7

Yorkshire Ripper, 210
Young, Sir Hilton, 167–168
young offenders institution, 301